Practical Leadership

Practical Leadership

The 9 Management Skills Needed for Health Professionals to Thrive in the 21st Century

Harry van Bommel, M.Ad.Ed., C.T.D.P.
with
Beverley Powell-Vinden, R.N., B.N.Sc., M.Ed.
Michèle Chaban, M.S.W., DPhil.
Elizabeth Latimer, M.D., C.C.F.P., F.C.F.P.
Larry Lewis, M.A.

Legacies: Family and Community Resources

Canadian Cataloguing in Publication Data
van Bommel, Harry
Practical leadership: the 9 management skills needed for health professionals to thrive in the 21st century
Includes bibliographic references and index.
ISBN 978-1-55307-033-7
1. Health services administration. 2. Medical personnel–
Professional relationships. 3. Communication in medicine.
4. Leadership. I. Powell-Vinden, Beverley, 1963- II. Title.
RA971.V35 2000 362.1'068'4 C00-901514-0

To contact the authors, write or call:

Legacies: Family and Community Resources Inc.
11 Miniot Circle, Scarborough, Ontario CANADA M1K 2K1
(416) 264-4665
info@legacies.ca
www.legacies.ca

Dedicated to those health care providers who demonstrate daily the PRACTICAL knowledge and skills required to work together with their colleagues to meet the physical, emotional, spiritual and information needs of their patients and their patients' families.

Table of Contents

Read this First

The chapters in this book are divided by the acronym: PRACTICAL as a memory aid for the materials covered. The acronym stands for the 9 practical skills needed to lead and manage and includes the following sub-chapters:

Principled Leadership
- The 7 Principles of Leadership
- Humor and Memories at Work

Resolving Conflicts
- Conflict Resolution
- Negotiation Skills

Awareness
- Career Planning
- Diversity in the Workplace

Communication
- Listening and Speaking
- Assertiveness
- Telephone Skills
- Presentations & Public Speaking
- Writing Letters, Memos and Reports

Team Skills
- Group/Team Skills
- Effective Meetings
- Creative Problem Solving

Impassioned Supervision
- Supervision 101
- Interviewing Skills

Change Management
- Managing Change in the New Millennium

Action Oriented Planning
- Action Oriented Planning
- Customer Service

Life-Long Skills
- Stress Management
- Time Management

Introduction

There is a general body of leadership knowledge that is the same for everyone. This book is based on a series of management and staff development self-study modules called *Learn for yourself.* This generic information has been used over the past decade by tens of thousands of managers and front-line staff in various sectors including health care.

This book is unique because it takes the generic information written by Harry van Bommel, an adult educator and management consultant, and adapts it specifically to the health care sector. The co-authors all have extensive, ongoing, practical experience modeling the knowledge and techniques in this book. They are not ivory tower theorists. They are passionate and practiced leaders in their field – your field. They know that advanced leadership skills are really just practicing the fundamentals of leadership predictably, fairly and firmly with a good dose of humor.

Introduction for Administrators

In the real estate industry, the answer to every question seems to be location, location, location. I think for health care administrators the correct answer is usually communication, communication, communication. And as much as we communicate–we always feel like we are over doing it–it is still not enough.

The complexities of health care and the large number of people involved in most facilities and programs make communication all the more important. Effective communication is time consuming and costly but the consequences of doing it poorly lead to even larger financial and employee morale costs and potential legal liability costs.

The themes in this book and the topics addressed are basic building blocks that are absolutely required for individuals in any kind of organization, whether it be the health care industry or not. The pieces that cannot be covered in a national book on leadership, of course, include any legislation that affects (1) hospital administration (in Ontario, the Public Hospital Act), (2) professional disciplines and their own body of legislation and regulations, and (3) legislation such as human rights, waste management and occupational safety. This detailed information must be learned elsewhere. Such information is up-dated often and each province and territory is different. You may obtain some of that through your workplace and your professional associations and some of it will be part of your professional recertification or licensing.

I think much of our time as administrators is spent receiving data, converting it into information and making decisions about what that can be used for–what we call identifying opportunities and closing the gap between where we are now and where we need to be. That is, forever identifying where things can be improved. So you have some basic information, perhaps you have done something with it, changed something and now see an increase in performance. You actually make something happen, empower individuals, or see that a group is working on a task to raise a performance level. I think a lot of skills sets for administrators revolve around decision making, interpreting information and problem-solving activities.

Leadership skills are generally learned through one's own professional discipline; in my case psychology. We learn it partly, I think, in taking workshops and courses and in the line of fire. I think you find yourself in the company of some great minds and you see how they work. That's the model for learning. This book will provide you with some shortcuts to new information and reinforcement of knowledge and skills you already possess.

My work as a hospital administrator is energizing. It might have to do with control, perhaps. Everything is resting on my shoulders if something happens. I have some degree of freedom. I close the door for 2 hours and people know to leave me alone. I have some control. I am the director of decisions rather than the receiver of decisions. I am an old guy, and I can tell you that I have been elsewhere doing other activities but I have never had more excitement than here. If you talk to other hospital administrative folks who have been around a while, they have pretty powerful mandates they are carrying around. They work hard and long hours and so on, but I think they are generally on a high. You see it when you meet with them. The president sometimes doesn't sit down. He walks around to express his ideas. He's excited. That is not nervous energy. He is genuinely happy to be doing what he is doing.

There are certainly people who have more control than I do. But I have to make decisions. I have to institute change. I have to turn the corner quickly. Life never seems to unfold here as I planned. I make a presentation about the upcoming priorities. This is how we are going to proceed with a plan. After two months, things have changed. You don't throw your work out, you adapt it. Making change and decision making affects not only you but you have an impact on much of the organization. That is pretty exciting. You have been given a gift. That gift is going to have impact on a wide variety of areas.

It's not unusual to meet with a vice-president who asks me, "Are you still having fun?" It's a check-in thing. Are things reasonably under control? If you are having fun, stress is different. Sometimes I think, "If you mean by having fun, have I had to completely change how I am about to do something, and introduce new methodology, or alter the plan dramatically, and I don't know if I have the time to present it in the style I would like–if that's what you mean by having fun, then I am up to my ears in fun!"

I also like encountering our clients and their family members. To actually get involved in a direct client event is for me a 'wow', it's exciting.

The opportunity to be involved in this book is fun, too. I hope you have as much fun as I have in developing and implementing your leadership skills.

Larry Lewis, M.A.
Former Program Director, Community Living, West Park Hospital, Toronto, Ontario
Current Educator, North York Community Care Access Centre,North York, Ontario

Introduction for Nurses

Change is the one constant as we look forward to a new millennium, not only in society as a whole, but in our professional and personal lives as well. Over the last decade, the profession of nursing has undergone tremendous change. Some of the key issues nurses have had to deal with include: increasing patient acuity; constant change; new roles; better informed and more demanding clients and families; cost effectiveness driving decision making, rather than health needs, and last but not least; coping with job loss and the 3 "Rs"–reorganization, restructuring, reengineering.

Staff nurses, in particular, often lament their lack of autonomy and ability to control their work environment. Staff nurses and nurses in other positions, can in fact, have a tremendous impact on clients and families by taking leadership positions in their work settings and organizations.

Nurse leaders are not only in formally recognized leadership roles like nurse manager, clinical nurse specialist or educator but also in the day-to-day practice of providing care to clients. Here are some examples of things you might do on a regular basis but don't tend to think of as leadership in action: ensuring that your client has enough information to safely care for themselves at home; mentoring a new graduate or student nurse; easing the fears of a patient about to undergo surgery; consistently treating your clients with care and compassion; and providing a staff nurse perspective on a hospital committee or workgroup.

Leadership in action is really caring in action.

Prescription Leadership has been written as a guide for today's nurse struggling to be a caring leader amidst constant change and workplace turmoil. I encourage every nurse in a leadership role, formal or informal, recognized or not, to spend some time reviewing the information in this book.

All of the skills necessary for leadership in a health care setting have been addressed. You may want to use this book to help you meet some of the quality assurance requirements of your regulatory body. Ask yourself what skills are lacking or need improvement and then review the appropriate section in the book to help you meet this goal. At the same time, congratulate yourself on the leadership skills you already have and those that have improved.

Remember that leadership and care are not exclusive of one another; a successful nurse leader provides compassionate care to clients, regardless of job description.

Beverley Powell-Vinden, R.N., B.N.Sc., M.Ed.
Health Education Consultant, PowerPhrase Communications, Mississauga, Ontario

Introduction for Physicians

Physicians are going to enjoy this book! They have been and continue to be leaders in health care. In these pages they will find new information and ways of developing skills as well as an affirmation of their current skills and ways of functioning in the leadership role.

Physicians, like many health professionals, have been educated to provide patient and family care. While being very skillful in this important area, they have not likely had any education or training in the areas of leadership, management, team work, supervision, communication, life-long learning skills and other subjects that are necessary to manage and lead in the current and future health care climate. The content and exercises will provide physicians with the opportunity of looking at aspects of their leadership and management roles in new and enlightened ways. There are few places where such a scope of subjects relevant to leadership are all brought together between the covers of one book which can be read and utilized in sections that are of use in a problem-based way.

Leadership roles come to physicians in a variety of ways. The setting up of a practice, negotiating for space and services, hiring and managing office staff represent one area where knowledge and skills in communication, negotiation, preparing a budget, dealing with difficult people, working with teams and resolving conflicts can make the whole process not only more understandable and manageable, but also more satisfying all around. Physicians will also find themselves working with interdisciplinary teams in hospitals and, increasingly, in the provision of patient care in the community. Some familiarity with the theory of teams and ways of developing and working in teams will help the physician to feel at home, and to be a more effective and responsive team member.

To paraphrase the song, "the times they are a-changing". Physicians will be involved in change in patterns of health care delivery that will impact their practice in the office and in hospital. The sections on managing change and supervision will provide physicians with some of the tools and knowledge to understand what is happening around them. Such knowledge can enhance a sense of confidence to deal with the attendant stresses of change oneself and also to assist staff and groups to do so. The section on presentation skills will assist physicians who find themselves in new roles of leadership, as well as assisting them to present educational rounds in more dynamic and effective ways. The section titled "Awareness" gives some perspectives on career path planning which can assist the physician in reviewing and affirming or changing one's career path.

Some of the language and perspective of the book will be new to physicians. For example, the word "client" will be used to represent those who are users of service. We, of course, will be more comfortable calling these people our "patients", as has been our tradition and because the word patient is a better word to encompass the fiduciary relationship and covenant that we hold with them. However, the perspective of "client" can be of help if it more fully allows us and our staff to see that we want to provide them with a respectful, timely and effective "service". The physician will, I hope, find that new language provides a new perspective on issues of care delivery for them and for their clinic, hospital and office staff.

Many of the concepts and approaches outlined in the book will also be applicable to effective and mutually satisfying patient and family-care relationships. Skills in communication, negotiation, humor and resolving conflicts have a universal application to our dealings with people in many aspects of our lives. The book encourages self-reflection, which can very helpful in one's personal life and relationships as well as leading to more career satisfaction.

Most physicians have not had the opportunity to gain skills in leadership and management in their medical training. Here is that opportunity. Enjoy!

Dr. Elizabeth Latimer, M.D., C.C.F.P., F.C.F.P.
Professor, Family Medicine, McMaster University
Consultant Physician, Hamilton Health Sciences Cooperation, Hamilton Regional Cancer Centre, Hamilton, Ontario

Introduction for Social Workers

This book is a mosaic of possibilities. Enter it with the imagination of perspective.

Social Work is a profession that has its origins in social reform and social change. Clearly the last decade in health care has seen an ample amount of both these dynamics as we endured human and fiscal cuts. The intent of these strategies was to enhance care and allow for a more equitable distribution of goods and services to other sectors. For those of us in social work, we watched as programs, services and other resources crumbled. For a time we tried to invent new ways to conduct our work. Eventually, we had no choice but to surrender to the inevitable changes. While we may have found fewer of us serving more in a cost effective way, we could not help but ask if we were serving our clients as well as we had in the past.

Social Work's commitment to equity, process and consensus building has often kept us from taking an overt leadership stance. We can no longer afford to do this. *Prescription Leadership* can help social workers marshal the best of their skills so that they can contribute to a more stable health care system from which to care for others.

On a personal note–I was 23 years old when a drunk driver ran his car into my body. Over the course of the next 8 years, I began to lose functioning in my arms, hands and legs. Various other systems in my body became progressively compromised. Those years taught me a great deal about attitude, humor, disabilities, public speaking, and coping with stress and time management. Many of those skills are in this book. The material was written for your professional development but, as my experiences have taught me, it can also help you personally.

Dr. Michèle Chaban, M.S.W, DPhil.
Social Worker, Mount Sinai Hospital
Clinical Thanatologist, Educator and Consultant, Private Practice, Toronto, Ontario

Don't Panic!

There is a lot of information in this book. However, this may be *the only book you ever need to learn how: to be a principled leader, to be an effective supervisor, to manage change, to provide excellent client service, to run effective meetings, to build a team of dedicated people, to negotiate your needs, to interview others to join your health care facility/team in its successes, to plan strategically, to resolve conflicts, to solve problems creatively, to manage your stress and time, to increase your use of humor, and to plan your career.* This book was written to help different people:

- Administrators, nurses, physicians, social workers, other healthcare professionals and volunteers.
- Managers and staff in different types of health care organizations.
- Students in high school, college, university and other schools.
- Other adult learners who want to learn on their own.

The book is divided into separate sections for each major skill area. Some material is repeated or explained further in different chapters. We assume you will not read the book cover to cover but will read those chapters most helpful to you now, which is why it is necessary to be repetitive..

Self-Evaluation

When you finish reviewing a new section, it is helpful to take some time to evaluate what you have found most useful and what you would like to do with that information. This process can be very useful whether you write out the answers or just think about them.

1. What general concepts, ideas or techniques have you learned?
2. List at least three techniques from this section that you could use immediately.
3. What other concepts, ideas or techniques do you want to learn?
4. Is there anything you have learned that you could pass on to your colleagues, family members or friends?
5. Do you have any further comments or ideas you want to record based on what you have learned?

1.

Principled Leadership

The 7 Principles

Humor and Memories at Work

Introduction

This will be the shortest section in this book because it is **the most important**. It should be read, re-read and practiced daily within your leadership role. It is important to note that leadership and management is not necessarily synonymous. It is possible to be a leader even when not in a management role. Without the basis of a principled leadership style, your organization, the people you work with, and your clients will suffer. It may not be immediately evident in your financial statements, but principled leadership is clearly reflected in the morale of the people in your organization and the degree of loyalty of your clients.

Clients are loyal for several reasons. Either you are the best in your field at providing excellent products and/or services or your organization is perceived as just as good, or bad, as your competition. Clearly, the second reason someone may be loyal to you is not good enough. The fact that people may see no tangible difference in how they are treated by different health care facility/team (e.g., gasoline service stations, financial institutions or hospitals) means that your organization has the opportunity to make a real difference in the lives of your clients and your own staff.

Principled leadership means ***the right people are doing the right things, for the right people, in the right way, at the right time, in the right place, at the right cost, and for the right reasons.*** Whenever you compromise on any of these elements in your mission, you must record and explain that compromise to everyone involved so that it is always seen as a compromise. Too often organizations begin with a compromise to their mission, but since it is not recorded as a compromise and explained as a compromise, the situation is soon seen as the ideal. One only has to look at how clients were once seen as vital to a health care facility/team' success. Fairly quickly after World War II, clients were treated more like a nuisance. Only in the later 1980s and during the 1990s have clients (baby boomers with more disposable income) demanded high quality products and quick, efficient service.

After World War II, patients/clients were taught that dying in the hospital was better than dying at home. There was more money and patient beds available that had to be used, whether the patient benefited or not. Today, we have an opportunity to provide the leadership based on the simple principle, "Whatever we do must benefit the patient." Baby boomers, as only one group, will expect nothing less.

Leadership – A Simple Perspective

The principles of leadership are **simple**, although not always easy, to implement. Whenever you have difficult leadership or management decisions to make, think about the "simple" solutions before making the situation more complex than is necessary.

You will have your own basic principles under which you make your decisions. Below are the ones we try to use whenever making decisions that affect our work, the people we work with and our clients.

1. **Have a personal and predictable vision and style.** People and organizations need to plan where they are going in the short and long-term. The people you work with and your clients need to know where you plan to go with your organization. They also need to know that when they approach you, they can successfully predict what your response will be to most situations. One of the most important aspects of this predictable vision is that it requires a predictable leadership style on your part as well. People need to know, predictably, how you will deal with them personally. Are you the type whose mood changes are so abrupt that people are afraid to approach you? Or do you have a style that includes periods of joy, anger, determination and sorrow but in more predictable ways?
2. Have **clear expectations** of what your staff and colleagues should be doing and well understood methods of **praising** and **criticizing** their performance. People often expect to be told when they are doing something wrong. Few of us have learned to expect to be told when we do something right. Too often in the past few decades people have had to wait for a yearly performance review to know how well they were doing at work. People need regular, consistent praise and constructive criticism of what they are doing. You must also make sure that how you evaluate their work is based on your own clear expectations. People cannot do well if you are not clear about what is expected. It is 100% your responsibility to make sure people understand what you expect.
3. Provide people with real **choices** (3 or more) whenever possible to give them a sense of control. Even when situations seem uncontrollable (e.g., layoffs, economic downturns, client dissatisfaction), people can still look at the situation and come up with 3 real choices. For example, if there must be layoffs in your organization, what choices can you offer? You can offer people an option to retire early or leave the organization voluntarily with a financial settlement. You can offer people, in advance, career planning training to help them understand further career options. You can help people find skills training that might help them begin a different career. **Most important, you offer these choices with an attitude of concern and**

compassion. You do not tell them on a Friday night that they are laid off. You do not let the media tell them about potential layoffs – you tell your people first. You do not have security escort people to their office in full view of the other staff. You do not ignore the staff that remains behind who wonder if they are next and how the layoffs will demand more work from them. **Choice** gives a sense of control to people in an atmosphere that says we care about you. Otherwise, choice is just another technique to imply control when control was never possible.

4. Incorporate and encourage the use of **humor** and **fun** at work to help create positive work **memories**. You take your work very seriously but not solemnly. The happier you are, the more productive you are. The happier you are, the happier other people are. The more effort you put into using appropriate humor, fun and creating memories, the more other people will do the same in return for you. This is not about having clowns and balloons at work; nor is it about everyone being a stand-up comedian. It is about creating an atmosphere and environment that says we are here working together and we might as well enjoy the work and the excellent results. People need to go home at the end of most working days and tell their families that they had a good day at work. That feeling of enjoyment, encouragement and support will carry on at home just as people who have miserable days tend to have miserable evenings with their families. Which would you choose? Humor, fun and creating positive memories of work is about an energizing, safe and enjoyable work environment. The second section of this chapter discusses ways to enhance this positive approach to the workplace.
5. Understand that people only hear/read **20%** of what anyone, including you, say. They forget **80%** of that within 24 hours. Therefore **repeat** important instructions, and use verbal and written backups. Most conflicts between people stem from the fact that they think you did, or did not, say something. You mistake people's intentions or forget what they have said as often as they do. These misunderstandings lead to us make assumptions about people that are not true. These assumptions lead to feelings and actions that are often hurtful. You must take 100% responsibility for making sure that you understand what people say or write to you and 100% responsibility for making sure that people understand you. You cannot do this all the time, but when a communication or personality problem arises, you must try to resolve the conflict. If you do not, you cannot blame the other person for their ongoing behavior.
6. Understand that everyone, including you, is doing **what they think is best for them and best for others** with the information and skills they have right now. Few people wake up in the morning with the sole purpose of making your day at work

miserable. Yet many times we feel that is exactly what someone has done. They are habitually late. They yell at you in front of other people. They take pleasure in assigning you meaningless work. They turn their back to you, when you enter the room.

Let us look at this principle a little more carefully. How many of us eat unhealthy food? How many of us smoke knowing the effects it has on our health and the health of others? How many of us over use alcohol or drugs on occasion? How many of us drive at unsafe speeds or in unsafe ways? How many of us get too little sleep?

Regardless of how much we know about what is **good for us** we still do things that are "wrong". We do that because we would rather face the consequences of doing something wrong because the behavior still feels better to us than the alternatives.

In the examples described above, the person who arrives late all the time may have all sorts of good reasons but they may also just like to start work later. Since there appear to be no consequences of their lateness, other than some people being upset, they will continue that behavior. They need choices to help them make better decisions. They may even have accepted the job because the ad asked for a creative person and mentioned nothing about punctuality. Many creative people do not arrive on time, but many stay very late to get their work done.

The person who yells at you in front of other people has probably learned over time that yelling gets results. Until they learn another way of getting similar results, they will continue to yell. They know yelling isn't nice, but they are driven by results not good feelings. Show them other ways of accomplishing the same results but in a way that makes you feel more comfortable.

Someone who takes pleasure in assigning you meaningless work or who turns their back to you when you enter a room has probably made some assumptions about who you are and what you are like. These assumptions are probably based on mistaken communications (remember the 20%-80% rule here) where they thought you said something that you really did not say. Or they have heard rumors that are not correct or should not affect your working relationship. Or you remind them of someone else they do not like. Whatever the reason, principled leadership requires you to try and resolve the problem/conflict or stop complaining about the situation. It is not fair that you have to make the initiative, but the alternative means the situation will not change. Confront people in a respectful and assertive way and with the understanding that you believe they are doing the best they can for themselves and for others with the knowledge and skills they have right now. You may be surprised at how easily the conflict can be solved. **Remember, you cannot change someone's personality but you can help them change their behavior**. You must also remember that it may be your behavior that needs changing as well.

7. Understand that people learn up to 7 new things at a time, therefore, don't overwhelm them with information. People learn best through experience (50%), through role models and relationships (30%) and through formal education (20%). As a leader you can provide a **learning environment** where success and mistakes are used as a learning experiences. Sending people to formal education or training programs may help them a little, but most of their learning will still come from you and others at work and at home.

When I need to make major decisions (while I am doing planning or in a crisis situation) I try to base those decisions on these 7 principles. All the other details and techniques described in this book stem from these 7 principles. When I have even less time to think, I return to the single most important ethical question: Are the right people doing the right things for the right people in the right ways at the right time in the right place at the right cost and for the right reasons?
Harry van Bommel

Exercise #1
Your Beliefs and Principles

Everyone has different principles upon which they base their decisions. Often we do not take the time to understand what our principles are and how they affect our decisions. If you hold certain political, religious, psychological, and/or philosophic beliefs, they will affect the kind of principles you use to make decisions. For example, if you believe strongly in equality as a justice principle, then your organization will probably have ways for staff to share in the rewards of their work (beyond wages) and try to encourage the recruitment and development of all types of people who live in your community. If you believe strongly that success in health care comes from meeting the needs of your clients, then you probably have strong client service principles within your organization's mission statement and use those principles to evaluate the success of your staff in meeting clients' needs.

It is always helpful to spend a little time reviewing your beliefs and understanding, consciously, the principles you work with in making your organization successful. Not surprisingly, many of these principles also affect how we deal with family, friends and strangers outside of our work.

Describe the major beliefs you hold about your work, the people you work with, your clients, and your overall philosophy of life.

Your Beliefs and Assumptions

Describe the major beliefs you hold about your work, the people you work with, your clients, and your overall philosophy of life. Consider how your principles have help others and how, if at all, they may hinder others. For example, a person who openly shares their strong religious beliefs can be immensely comforting to clients of similar beliefs but quite disquieting to others who do not share them.

Question	Answer	How May Your Belief Help Or Hinder Others
What fundamental personal beliefs (e.g. spiritual, political, medical, cultural) do you strongly adhere to?		
Which of your basic assumptions are in conflict with those of your service? with your clients? How can you address these?		

Other questions to ask yourself: Which elements of the health care philosophy do you practice most comfortably and why (physical, emotional, spiritual, informational)? Where do you most comfortably practice the care and why? Do you see your relationship with a patient or client as caregiving or mutual care? What do you fear most about dying and death? What gives you the most comfort about dying and death? How do you deal with your fears? What can you do for others? What can you not do for others? What can others do for you? What can others not do for you? Are the right people giving the right care to the right people in the right way in the right place at the right time for the right reasons? ***Why would a patient, client or colleague want you in the same room with them?***

Exercise #2
What Kind of Leader Are You?

It is important to review, regularly, how you are doing as a leader. This may happen during a performance review where you tell others how they are doing and they tell you how you are doing. The following exercise may be a little different than a typical performance review, however. Before you do the exercise, make a few copies. After you have done the exercise yourself, you may want to ask some of your colleagues to fill it out for you as well. Comparing what people honestly think are your strengths and learning needs will help you become an even better leader. People may find it difficult to be honest with you if they believe that you will become defensive about their comments or they may think their evaluation of your skills may lead to bad feelings between you. It will be up to you, if you choose to get other people's opinions, to make sure only positive feelings will come from them helping you.

Put a check mark beside those skills and characteristics that you have now (both positive and negative). Put a circle beside those skills and characteristics you would like to improve or change.

Note: the skills are not listed in any particular order.

Positive Skills/Characteristics

___I admit my mistakes (accountable)
___I give positive feedback
___I allow autonomy
___I give sincere praise
___I understand job & people
___I include staff in planning process
___I am a team leader
___I give recognition where due
___I am responsible
___I am knowledgeable
___I am trusting
___I am approachable
___I encourage fun at work
___I try to resolves conflicts
___I am fair
___I am interested in staff as people
___I am supportive
___I am calm
___I am funny
___I have clear expectations
___I am friendly
___I have good organizational skills

Negative Skills/Characteristics

___I am close minded (bull headed)
___I yell privately-publicly
___I am inconsistent
___I am too nice or too friendly
___I can be condescending
___I can be bigoted sometimes
___I can be verbally abusive
___I can be incompetent
___I single people out
___I have a superiority complex
___I make unreasonable demands
___I use selective listening
___I play favorites
___I have prejudices: personal/racial
___I take credit for others
___I can shift blame
___I can be unfair
___I can be frustratingly indirect
___I can be mean and vindictive
___I can be sarcastic
___I do not give enough direction
___I cannot delegate

___I am confident
___I am predictable
___I listen and observe body language
___I trust judgment of staff
___I am flexible toward staff needs
___I hold regular staff meetings
___I share information
___I am efficient
___I delegate clearly
___I am understanding
___I respect all staff (up & downwards)
___I have a good sense of humor
___I am supportive of staff to others
___I mentor/teach
___I empathize with others
___I understand employees have an outside life

___I am insecure
___I plagiarize
___I am unpredictable
___I cannot keep confidences
___I have abrasive people skills
___I do not know staff's job
___I am unorganized
___I criticize in front of others
___I am always late
___I have extreme mood swings
___I don't give positive reinforcement
___I use people for personal gain
___I am a workaholic & expect the same from others
___I am a procrastinator
___I am selfish
___I am insincere in attempts to boost morale

What Can You Do to Improve Your Skills?

Choose one or two skills to work on at a time. You will not become a better leader in all situations without concentrating on **specific skills** in situations that are normally uncomfortable for you. Begin with situations that hold little risk for you (e.g., practice giving clear expectations about relatively simple tasks at first). Ask your peers or colleagues for feedback on your skills.

Pick another one or two new skills to practice once you are comfortable with the first ones. Over a matter of months and years you will continually develop your leadership skills.

Remember:

The best way to learn leadership is to role model yourself after someone you consider an excellent, principled leader. Once you have become more comfortable, be a role model yourself to colleagues, your family and friends.

To reward yourself (!) whenever you succeed at enhancing a leadership skill in situations that are normally uncomfortable for you.

Summary

Leadership-A Simple Perspective

The principles of leadership are **simple**, although not always easy, to implement. Whenever you have difficult management decisions to make, think about the "simple" solutions before making the situation more complex than is necessary.

1. Have a personal and **predictable** vision and style.
2. Have clear **expectations** of what your staff should be doing and well understood methods of praising and criticizing their performance.
3. Provide people with real **choices** (3 or more) whenever possible to give them a sense of control.
4. Incorporate and encourage the use of humor and fun at work to help create positive work **memories** for your staff.
5. Understand that everyone, including you, is doing **what they think is best for them and best for others** with the information and skills they have right now.
6. Understand that people only hear/read **20%** of what anyone, including you, say. They forget **80%** of that within 24 hours. Therefore **repeat** important instructions, and use verbal and written backups.
7. Understand that people learn up to 7 new things at a time (therefore don't overwhelm them with information). People learn best through experience (50%), through role models and relationships (30%) and through formal education (20%). As a manager you can provide a **learning environment** where success and mistakes are used as a learning experiences.

Are the right people doing the right things for the right people in the right ways at the right time in the right place at the right cost and for the right reasons?

Resources

The following resources are only a few of the many useful resources that you can find in your local libraries, within your own organization, and in your local bookstores. Look for other books but also for journal articles, magazine reports, films, videos and audiocassettes. Also keep in mind how much you can learn from experts in the field, including people within your own organization!

Beck, J., Yeager, D. W., & Yeager, N.M., (1994). *The leader's window: Mastering the four styles of leadership to build high performing teams.* Toronto: Wiley & Sons.

Bennis, W. (1994). *On becoming a leader.* New York: Addison-Wesley.

Blanchard, K., Hybels, B., & Hodges, P. (1999). *Leadership by the book: Tools to transform your workplace.* New York: William Morrow.

Bolman, L. G., & Deal, T. E. (1995). *Leading with soul: An uncommon journey of spirit.* San Francisco: Jossey-Bass.

Dosick, W. D. (1994). *The health care facility bible: Ten commandments for creating an ethical workplace.* New York: Harperperennial.

Dreher, D. (1996). *The Tao of personal leadership.* New York: Harper Health care facility/team.

Drucker, P. (1995). *Managing in a time of great change.* New York: Truman Talley.

Gilkey, R. W. (ed.). (1999). *The 21st century health care leader.* San Francisco: Jossey-Bass.

Helgesen, S. (1995). *The female advantage: Women's way of leadership.* New York: Currency/Doubleday.

James, J. (1996). *Thinking in the future tense: Leadership skills for a new age.* New York: Simon & Schuster.

Klebe T, L, & Nelson, K A. (1995). *Managing health care facility ethics: Straight talk about how to do it right.* Toronto, ON: Wiley & Sons.

Kouzes, J. M., & Posner, B. Z. (1996). *The leadership challenge: How to keep getting extraordinary things done in organizations.* San Francisco: Jossey-Bass.

Kriegel, R., & Brandt, D. (1997). *Sacred cows make the best burgers: Developing change-ready people and organizations.* New York: Warner Books.

Maxwell, J. C. (1999). *The 21 indispensable qualities of a leader: Becoming the person others will want to follow.* Cheltenham: UK.

Pearson, G. J. (1995). *Integrity in organizations: An alternative health care facility ethic.* New York: McGraw-Hill.

Sonnenberg, F. K. (1996). *Managing with a conscience: How to improve performance through integrity, trust, and commitment.* New York: McGraw-Hill.

Humor and Memories at Work

Much of this section deals with humor, laughter and play at work. We seem to have less difficulty enjoying ourselves with our family and friends. However, many of the ideas presented in this section can be easily used regardless of where you are. If humor is an attitude then it should not be limited to only one environment!

Humor is, above all, an attitude. People who can see humor in everyday situations give off a contagious positive attitude towards life that helps everyone around them. Humor often comes easiest from delight rather than comedy; the delight of a baby's smile, or the delight in sharing a story with someone who will enjoy it.

Laughter is one expression of this humorous attitude. It is one of the most recognizable and easiest communicated expressions of humor. Laughter can also be an expression of other attitudes such as fear or anger. Regardless of its source, laughter can help us feel better and less stressed.

Play is the act of amusing ourselves and, perhaps, other people. Play is a way to search for humor and laughter. It is a way to release some of our self-imposed limits of how we should behave professionally. Most of all, play is the act of searching out wonder, just as some children search for wonder in any and all situations.

Telling jokes or laughing at jokes is not the same thing as having a sense of humor. Jokes are one way of causing us to laugh and the types of jokes we like often reflect our personality or our mood at the time. However, you do not need to be a good joke teller or need to laugh at other people's jokes to enjoy humor, laughter and play!

One of the great lessons of history is to understand that every individual can change the world. A second great lesson is that people who do change their world usually use their sense of humor to go from one day to the next. They use laughter as a mechanism to reduce their anxiety, their fear and their stress.

The third lesson from history is learned by reading biographies. Regardless of the difficulties and joys of one's life there is room for humor, laughter and play to help them. Whether someone is a political hero, a famous singer or actor, or our family and friends, humor, laughter and play are used by most people as a stepping stone to that time in their lives when they become "wise". Wisdom is that body of knowledge gleaned from life's experience that helps us understand what is, and what is not, important enough to worry about. Wisdom is also the knowledge of what is, and is not, important enough to understand, to laugh about and to learn.

The use of laughter workshops in the work place has become a popular fad. Laughter at work is not a new phenomenon, however. In the history of the world, laughter has been used to express great happiness but also used as a way to deal with horrifying situations, embarrassing situations and to help relieve the tensions of everyday life.

I think in Palliative Care that it is often not the work itself but the colleagues we work with that make things stressful. Each of us comes to work with a strong value and belief system associated with dying. If we can respect each other's differences and still do the work that is great. Often, however, in the abbreviated timeframe we find ourselves, this degree of collegiality does not persist. To be able to reflect with humor on the tension that passes between us can dissipate some of the stress. One of my favorite physicians is often very strong willed and determining of his and others' time. If he is not listening to me, I say, "I'm getting my 2x4 out any minute so we can have a talk." If that doesn't work, I say, "...time for my 4x4." He's come to know this as me drawing a line in terms of his need to listen yet it is a humorous, non-threatening way to get his attention.
Michèle Chaban

Women, men, and children have used laughter in seemingly contradictory places: at weddings and funerals, in concentration camps and at parties, at murder trials and religious services, at work and at play. Laughter, and seeing the humor of the moment, is one of our best techniques for choosing to enjoy life to the fullest. Laughter and humor can also provide us with necessary relief at times of mourning and anxiety.

Used well and often, humor, laughter and play can improve our health, our attitude, and perhaps most importantly, can encourage other people to do the same. Appropriate humor is also one technique that provides support and a way to express understanding to people who are fearful in new or strange settings.

In this section we will not spend a lot of time looking at the historical and theoretical reasons why we should use humor, laughter and play to improve our physical and mental health. Rather, we will concentrate on some of the practical things we can all do to increase the use of humor, laughter and play in our work lives. One only has to look at our friends and colleagues who use appropriate humor, laughter and play to understand that it makes them and us feel better!

When we are teaching others about Palliative Care, we try to use cartoons to capture the essence of our point. I think laughter and humor capture the sacred meaning of

things sometimes better if not equal to a philosophical or theological concept.
Michèle Chaban

For laughter and humor to be used regularly at work, people need the permission and encouragement of their peers and supervisors. Without that encouragement, humor, laughter and play will be relegated to cafeterias, storerooms and after work hours when it will be less effective and often used to ridicule individuals dealt with during the day.

Types of Humor

Humor is basically an attitude or perspective we have about life. What one person finds humorous, another will not. Humor that ridicules other people is often destructive of social relations and we should discourage it. Humor can also ridicule yourself and to varying degrees that can be very funny.

Humor is not the same as telling jokes. There are some people who can tell wonderful jokes and make people laugh. Humor, on the other hand, is something from everyday life that makes us laugh, smile and enjoy in the delight. It may be a cartoon. It may be a story that someone has told about what their child did at school yesterday. It may be a secret shared between two people (e.g., one of the persons is pregnant and only one other person in the department knows). It may be the smile that comes from a co-worker or the love from a pet.

People do not usually laugh because they are happy. We often laugh because we want to feel happy and laughing helps us do that. Laughter can create a sense of happiness, then. We use laughter to help us when we are frightened and we use it when we are embarrassed. We use humor to try and get closer to people and we use humor to tell someone we care.

People assume incorrectly that we must have a reason to laugh. Humor and laughter are different things. What we might find humorous may not cause us to laugh. Sometimes we laugh for no apparent reason, and that is okay. We may laugh out of fear, anger, boredom or because our perspective of life sees humor in situations when other people do not.

There are different types of humor that make us smile or laugh. Nonsense or situations that are unbelievable can be very humorous. There are books, cartoons and stories based on:

- Political and social satire.

- Observing how different people react to life.
- Embarrassing moments.
- Children's expressions.
- Actions of animals.

There is also the humor that many of us laugh at but that may be inappropriate. Sexist, sexual, ethnic, religious, and sarcastic humor can be enjoyable sometimes and inappropriate at others. For example, "Newfy" jokes are often appropriate because they are an industry in Newfoundland where people make money poking fun at themselves. They are inappropriate when we use them to demean people from Newfoundland in a malicious way just as jokes about people from Holland, Poland, Ireland, or the Caribbean, can be funny or inappropriate.

The gauge of appropriateness of any activity depends on who is telling a joke or describing a situation or doing a playful activity and who is receiving them. Healthy humor, laughter and play depend on everyone enjoying the activity. What may be acceptable in one group of people may not be acceptable in another group. Common courtesy and common sense are usually good judges.

An example of what some people would call inappropriate humor, while others would think is very helpful, is the kind used in television programs like M*A*S*H or in many of our hospitals, police forces, and the military. "Sick" or black humor is often used to reduce the stress experienced in life and death situations. "Outside" people might find the humor used in emergency and operating rooms, in funeral homes or in times of war inappropriate. "Inside" people find this particular type of humor helpful to cope with feelings of sadness and stress.

> *It is not until we have a visiting scholar or student and I see the look of either horror or delight on their faces that I realize that we are using "sick" humor to deal with some of the situations we find ourselves in. Underneath the sick humor is an understanding for us of the sacredness of that which we speak or else we could not play with it so irreverently. It takes a level of trust between people to do this. It also takes an understanding that life is precious and we would never demean its essence.*
> *Michèle Chaban*

The Benefits of Laughter

Appropriate laughter is contagious and brings people together.[1] To learn to laugh more often, it is helpful to watch people who laugh. Four-year old children, for example, laugh on average 500 times a day. (They also know that tears are therapeutic so they cry more often than we do too!) Adults laugh on average 15 times a day but that figure really depends a great deal on the individual, their work and whether they have permission to laugh from their peers and supervisors.

Buddhist monks have equated 15 minutes of good belly laughing to 6-8 hours of meditation. Both forms of stress release have physiological, sociological and psychological benefits; both are appropriate and useful.

Physiological Benefits

- Dilates cardiovascular system benefits.
- Exercises respiratory system (air leaving the mouth has been clocked at 115 kph); laughing can often lead to coughing which helps stimulate someone who is ill clean out their lungs while reducing the chance of their getting pneumonia.
- Muscles relax to the point when people cannot stand up or sit up straight.
- Brain and nervous system responses include chemical releases that make us feel good.
- Laughter is used as a natural pain relief technique.
- Diaphragm contracts to massage internal organs ("internal jogging") similar to sobbing or vomiting, but much more pleasant.
- Produces the "healing tears" we find useful at times of real stress, sadness or loss.
- Reduces blood pressures to levels below the pressure measured before the laughter.

Sociological Benefits

- Helps establish rapport and relationships.
- Creates greater group cohesion even in times of group stress.
- Reduces social conflict.
- Corrects unacceptable behavior by acting as a change agent (e.g., to de-escalate a violent situation, or reduce tensions at a staff meeting).
- Improves communication.
- Improves co-operation.

Psychological Benefits

- Helps in coping with internal stress.
- Benefits.
- Helps relieve anxiety, stress, tension and embarrassment.
- Socially acceptable outlet for anger and frustration.

- Helps balance reality for a short time to give people an opportunity to get new energy and gives them time to think.
- Lightens heaviness of tragedy, disability, crisis and death.

Final note: When all is said and done about the physiological, sociological and psychological benefits of laughter think of people who laugh a lot. They don't do it because of all the benefits listed above. They don't necessarily do it because they took a workshop in humor or read a book about laughing. They do it as part of their "way of being" because it makes them feel good and it helps other people feel good. You don't really need any more reason than that to increase the amount of laughing you do every day.

Self Examination

Once you know more clearly what it is you enjoy you will be able to find it more often. Asking yourself questions can help you identify what you find humorous.

You can exchange the lists on the next page with your friends and colleagues to see what they like and whether or not you can help provide them with their kind of humor. For example if you know someone enjoys a good Bob Newhart cassette or if you know someone who really gets a chuckle out of Herman cartoons, you might bring some of these along for them to enjoy. People who exchange humorous items and situations find it more enjoyable to come to work!

Exercise #1

1. What do you most enjoy laughing about? Why?
2. When do you laugh most often? Why?
3. What types of cartoons, jokes and situations do you find most humorous?
4. What types of humor do you dislike and how do you discourage it?
5. How do you use humor to feel better, to deal with stress or to cope with an embarrassing situation, grief or loss?
6. How is humor used in your work area now?

Ways to Start

The following is a list of ideas you can use that may increase the humor, team spirit and laughter found in your work areas. In many work areas where humor, laughter and play are often present there is already a team spirit amongst the staff. These ideas are to reinforce this attitude and encourage other ways of enhancing the work atmosphere.

This is not an exhaustive list and there is room at the end for you to write down your own ideas. The ideas are not intended to make everyone in your area fall down laughing but many of them are just little things you can do to bring a smile to someone's face.

As mentioned before, humor, laughter and play only work in a nourishing environment. Your supervisor and peers may be hesitant at first to try certain things because it may appear inappropriate in a professional or work setting. You need people's permission to change their environment and the prevailing attitude of a work area. You may be able to try new things with lots of encouragement from the people around you or you may have to start slowly and build up the trust that is necessary in order for people to laugh openly. There is a lot of history in any work setting and you must be sensitive to it.

From a supervisor's perspective, you must know your staff and get their permission (formal or informal) to try new things. People may suspect a "hidden agenda", such as improving productivity, rather than your good intentions. Again you will need the permission of your own supervisor so that the atmosphere of your work area does not change when your supervisor is present.

Remember that the best starting place is your list of what genuinely makes you smile. Your genuine laughter is what is most contagious.

Smiles

Increase the amount of times you smile. Smiles are contagious and are the quickest expression of your own mood and disposition.

Body Language

Your body language tells people if you are genuinely enjoying yourself or whether you have read something about humor and are trying to follow someone else's suggestions. Humor, laughter and play work best if you are truly enjoying yourself or if you use humor, laughter and play as a technique to help yourself feel better. Anything else is just acting and may lead people to mistrust your motives.

"Hello"

Give a friendly "hello" to anyone who looks directly at you as you walk down a hallway, especially if you don't know them. I did this one day to someone while waiting for an elevator and their whole face lit up and they looked just a little less frightened than before.

Funny Items

Bring in the odd cartoon, greeting card, poster, mug or quote and share it with those people you think will enjoy it.

Surprises

Put little surprises on someone/everyone's desk for no apparent reason, e.g., a home baked cookie, a small flower, a humorous card, anything you have made, or an inexpensive gift you thought that person would enjoy. In other words, don't wait for Christmas or a birthday to do something special for someone.

Music

For people who enjoy whistling or singing you might share a song or two while you are working or walking down a hall.

Be Silly"

If you don't mind doing "silly" things, you might wear mix-matched socks or another clothing faux pas to get people's reactions.

Toys

Have a favorite toy or stuffed animal by your desk that you can play with or hug when you want to do something totally different. You can even pass along your stuffed animal to a colleague who is having a particularly hard day. Scan a picture of your children or pet into your computer and make it into a screensaver.

Collection Box

Have a special box where people can put in their favorite cartoon, quote, baby picture, or their most outrageous story from a tabloid newspaper. After a set period (e.g., one month) the best can be collected in a department or area book for distribution with a lottery to determine a winner of a special prize.

Magazines/Books

Consider putting adult comic books (e.g., Herman, Garfield) in your lobby and waiting areas.

Secret Pal

Have people put their names, birthday, workplace anniversary date and a short list of things they like (e.g., sports, chocolate, special post cards) in a draw. Over a period of 3 - 6 months your secret pal may send you a gift at home, leave it on your desk or send a birthday/Valentine's card months early as a surprise.

Get Others Involved

Offer the people you work with something special that they do not have to "earn" and that they get for just being themselves (e.g., a quick private walk with just the two of you during a break or slow period, or a gift of their favorite food).

Special Pre-Arranged Events

Lottery

Have a lottery every month amongst the staff and whoever wins gets a part of the day or the whole day off with the other staff members covering for that person. The winner's name is removed from the lottery next time so that everyone gets a fair chance at winning.

Dress-Up

Have a casual Friday when people can dress as they like as long as it meets standards of cleanliness and good fun. Include others in this event if you choose a well-advertised theme day to enhance your public relations while boosting internal morale.

Choir

Rather than wait for Christmas and other holidays, have a choir go around work singing a few tunes every few months.

Special Skills

Encourage staff who have special skills (e.g., juggling, singing, playing an instrument, arts and crafts, drama, magic tricks) to use them more often for the benefit of others. Teach each other these skills.

Videos

Bring in a humorous video or cassette once a month during a staff lunch break. People bring their own lunch and get a chuckle at the same time.

Roasts

Rather than waiting for someone to retire or leave, hold a special party or roast for someone on their birthday, their anniversary in your department, or after a particularly difficult assignment.

Welcoming Party

Again, rather than wait until someone leaves, have a special welcoming party for new staff members and use the occasion to pass along some praise to present staff as well.

Compliment Box

Display a compliment box where anyone can put in an extra compliment for something that someone did for them. Have a draw at the end of the week/month to give the winning staff member a "Dinner-for-Two" coupon or other prize.

5th Tuesday

Any time there is a fifth Tuesday (or any other day you choose) in a month have a special activity, e.g., longer lunches, potluck lunch in your area, or something else special to your group.

Change of Season Party

Celebrate a change of season with a potluck lunch with foods representative of the new season.

Joint Self-Help Project

Have a special joint project to encourage even more teamwork, e.g., everyone agree to lose whatever amount of weight they would like to and provide support to each other.

Skills Exchange

Everyone lists skills they have that they are willing to share in exchange for learning a new skill from someone else, e.g., one person teaches others to cook special dinners, someone else teaches people to play guitar, and someone else teaches home renovations.

Health Care Facility/Team Cards

Have someone design a special health care facility/team card for your area and get them printed. People could design funny cards to give to family and friends or a more serious card to use at conferences or while traveling.

Special Notes

Stress

When situations get tense examine the way the situation is versus the way it appears. Is there any element that lends itself to humor? There are many situations at work and in our personal lives that are not funny. However, there may be elements in those situations that can be humorous and that we can use to help relieve some of the stress. Is there a way you will describe this situation in a day/week/year that may be humorous?

Earlier in my career as a management consultant I was working part-time with an education and organizational developmental department in a teaching hospital. While on vacation, my office was moved away from the rest of the team as a necessary, cost-cutting exercise. My colleagues knew that I would not be pleased to return from vacation to find I was separated from the best working team that I had ever worked with. To ease the adjustment, they bought a corner store Elvis bust and placed it on my new desk. They put small, flashing Christmas tree lights around him. When I opened my new office door for the first time, the room was dark except for Elvis appearing to rise above my desk. It was wonderful! It was very thoughtful and led to a 10-year running joke within the hospital. As word spread of Elvis' visitation to my office, people I had never met before came to my new office to introduce themselves and wish me well. Long after I left that job (leaving Elvis behind), he was spotted in various parts of the hospital. A short-run Elvis newsletter was circulated telling people where he might be found and his favorite peanut butter and banana sandwich recipes. Going back recently for a going away party for a past colleague, people I hadn't seen in 10 years came up to tell me of Elvis' recent sightings.

When you incorporate humor into your working attitude it has immediate benefits but also encourages the development of long-term memories that are comforting and bring a smile to your face years later.

Harry van Bommel

When my wisdom teeth were removed, post-op went badly. I needed to make an emergency visit to my dentist. Making a dash through the crowded waiting room with most of my face covered by ugly purple bruising was not funny at the time but somehow seems funnier now.

Beverley Powell-Vinden

Sense of Humor

People have different senses of humor. Before trying anything too extravagant, find out what people enjoy and what people find very uncomfortable. A surprise party for someone's birthday may be a wonderful joy to one person and extremely embarrassing to someone else.

Discouraging Inappropriate Humor

Sometimes, people who you like or people in a position of authority over you will use inappropriate humor, e.g., sexist, racist, or humor that ridicules people. Discouraging this kind of humor is difficult. Depending on whom the person is you can decide:

Not to laugh at all.

To talk to the person later on about how their humor makes you feel.

To talk to the person right away to tell them their humor is upsetting and that you would prefer they not use it when you are around.

To use appropriate humor yourself to "instruct" the person in how good humor is just as funny as inappropriate humor.

Exercise #2
How to Help Others

You can use this exercise to help you remember what you have learned and to identify ways that you can help others through humor, laughter and play.

1. List three new ways you can use laughter and play in your work to reduce stress.
2. How can you use laughter and play to improve relationships with your colleagues or clients?
3. List some of the physiological, sociological and psychological benefits of laughter that are meaningful to you.
4. When are humor, laughter and play inappropriate and how can you discourage it or change it?
5. What will you do today and tomorrow to use some of the information you have learned so far?
6. Many people use humor, laughter and play to cope with stress. Having this knowledge, how can we help them?

Summary

The kind of humor we have been talking about goes beyond jokes and even beyond laughter. We are talking about looking at life in a humorous and playful way. Humor, laughter and play are natural ways of showing that we are happy or have fear, anxiety and embarrassment. It is our own method of coping with life's ups and downs.

An integral part of humor, laughter and play is to look for, and enjoy, the wonder of life. There are so many instances where we can find something wonderful to be in awe of. Children do this every day but many of us are too busy to take the time to look. One of the greatest tools for stress management is to always search for wonderment. If you have trouble finding wonder, take an expert with you who thrives on this kind of adventure; perhaps a child, an older person who has experienced much but still searches for more, or perhaps the adventuresome childlike person inside you!

Humor, laughter and play are not always our top priorities. They are, however, skills that can improve with practice and by encouraging others to do the same. With the permission of those around us we can try many of the practical ideas listed in this section to enhance the playfulness of the people we work with, live with and spend time with.

One of the best philosophic summaries about living life fully and joyfully comes from Robert Fulghum, an American who has been a bartender, folk singer, cowboy, sale representative and now a minister. He wrote a short book titled *All I Really Need to Know I Learned in Kindergarten*. His perspective learned in Kindergarten is:

> *Share everything. Play fair. Don't hit people. Put things back where you found them. Clean up your own mess. Don't take things that aren't yours. Say you're sorry when you hurt somebody. Wash your hands before you eat. Flush. Warm cookies and cold milk are good for you. Live a balanced life – learn some and think some and draw and paint and sing and dance and play and work everyday some. Take a nap every afternoon. When you go out into the world, watch out for traffic, hold hands, and stick together. Be aware of wonder.*

Resources

The following resources are only a few of the many useful resources that you can find in your local libraries, within your own organization, and in your local bookstores. Look for other books but also for journal articles, magazine reports, films, videos and audiocassettes. Also keep in mind how much you can learn from experts in the field, including people within your own organization!

Chapman, A. J., Foot, H. C., & Derks, P. (Eds.) (1996). *Humor and laughter: Theory, research, and applications.* New Brunswick, NJ: Transaction Publishing.

Cousins, N. (1981). *Anatomy of an illness as perceived by the patient.* New York: Bantam.

Gruner, C R. (1997). *The game of humor: A comprehensive theory of why we laugh.* New Brunswick, NJ: Transaction Publishing.

Klein, A. (1989). *The healing power of humor: Techniques for getting through loss, setbacks, upsets, disappointments, difficulties, trials, tribulations, and all that.* Los Angeles: J.P.Tarcher.

McGhee, P.E. (1979). *Humor: Its origin and development.* San Francisco: W.H. Freeman.

Metcalfe, C.W., & Felible, R. (1993). *Lighten up: Survival skills for people under pressure.* New York: Addison-Wesley.

Wickberg, D. (1998). *The senses of humor: Self and laughter in modern America.* Hartford, CT: Cornell University Press.

Wooten, P. (1996). *Compassionate laughter: Jest for your health!* Mount Shasta, CA: Commune-A-Key.

2.

Resolving Conflicts

Resolving Conflict

Negotiation Skills

Introduction

Mary Vachon's work reminds us that communication difficulty and conflict with colleagues is the number one source of stress within health care professionals. It is not what patients and their families' demand of us or the government's inability to understand what providing excellent care is all about. Our principal source of stress is within our own disciplines and between disciplines.

How do you resolve conflicts? There are several questions that must be asked first:

- Does everyone involved recognize that a conflict exists or is it just you who wants someone else to change their ways to make your life easier or more enjoyable?
- If everyone involved does recognize that a conflict exists are they as committed as you to resolving that conflict? If not, you have to find something that the others will see as a benefit to them to help you resolve the conflict.
- Is someone else causing the conflict or are you also a reason for that conflict? (Conflict is usually not a one-sided problem.)
- Do you recognize that you resolve problems for yourself first and for other people second?
- Do you recognize that you always have control over how you respond to a conflict and that sometimes your response includes making small changes versus big ones or making the decision to leave the work situation yourself?

Whether conflicts are large or small you must understand that other people are not likely to change their personalities or behaviors just to please you. There must be clear benefits for people to change themselves in the same way that you have to believe that changes you make will benefit or improve yourself. Anyone who changes their personality or behavior just to please someone else will usually become resentful about those changes.

As a social worker, I spend my life trying to bring about change in the way people think, feel and behave. Palliative Care is ripe with conflict because of this ongoing change. I always say to my students who encounter conflict and are discouraged by it that they should embrace it, for with every conflict you build a team, a program and get that much closer to changing public opinion and perhaps policy. If I see conflict as a personal attack on me alone, which it often feels like, I would have given up long ago. I see conflict as an opportunity to get to the root of the issues. To do this with compassion and conviction is a skill that must develop over time. To do this with dignity and a gentle voice is for me to reside in the eye of the storm I find myself in.
Michèle Chaban

There will always be personality differences between people that can cause difficulties. **People will not (and often, cannot) change their basic personalities.** (Ask newly married couples who thought their spouse would change their habits for them out of love.) Since personality conflicts will always exist we must concentrate on looking at specific behaviors people use versus evaluating their personalities.

Behaviors can be changed or modified if the other person knows how they affect you. When all is said and done, you will not like everyone you work with; nor do you have to. You should be able to respect or at least tolerate most people and still achieve job satisfaction.

In this section we will present some general background information on what can cause conflicts, what types of conflict there are and specific methods to help resolve conflicts.

The comment I get most often when I present conflict resolution workshops is: "All this information is wonderful but it just won't work in my case. I've tried everything but they just won't change. I'm powerless." No one is powerless. We cannot resolve all conflicts but we can solve many more than we think. When someone says, "I've tried everything!", I ask some questions (like the ones at the beginning of this chapter) to see if they really have tried everything. If they haven't, I try to give them suggestions like the ones in this chapter. If a conflict cannot be resolved, I help people choose a different way to respond to the conflict that is more comfortable for them. Read on to see what I mean.
Harry van Bommel

We don't believe that people are powerless. We always have the power to choose how we respond. Other people cannot make us happy or unhappy, angry or sad. If we have a conflict with someone and we have tried everything we can to resolve that conflict in good faith (a key element!) then we have several choices:

- Evaluate whether the conflict is a mutual problem between you and the other person(s) **or** is it really a problem that only you can deal with.
- If the other person is not willing to make any effort to resolve the problem can you:
- Ignore them and continue on with your work/life.
- Arrange for either you or the other person to leave the environment where this conflict is taking place (e.g., can you transfer/fire them or will you quit and accept the challenge of changing your work environment).

Viktor Frankl, a survivor of the Nazi concentration camps lost his family during the Holocaust. He said that regardless of what horrors were inflicted on him during those years no one was ever able to dictate to him how he must respond. How he responded to these most difficult of situations was always under his control. He has used that practical philosophy to help people make real changes in their lives.

Viktor Frankl understood that sometimes you cannot change the circumstances you face because of major systemic problems. In these situations you control how you respond to those circumstances and makes those small changes that are possible to make such severe situations more tolerable. People can often still laugh, cry, join together, use their memories of the past, make their plans for future, and use their inner strength, to help themselves in these situations.

In the less severe situations that we often face we can certainly do many of the same things: laugh, cry, join together with others, use our memories of the past, make plans for the future, use our inner strengths, develop the love of our families and friends, and use a clear-headed analysis of what is really happening to us to make the changes we need to maintain control over our lives and our feelings.

In the day-to-day conflicts that we face and with the foresight to imagine how we will evaluate these situations 10 years from now, we can put our conflicts into perspective and decide how hard and for how long we will try to resolve the conflicts before moving onto greater challenges.

The principle of using your conflict resolution skills effectively is to **participate actively** in the process of using these skills, **organize** your skills, **persist** during difficult times, and **be creative**. The more effectively we use our skills, the more time we have to enjoy other parts of our lives.

Definitions

The *New Lexicon Webster's Dictionary* defines conflict as: "a struggle between opposing principles or aims, a clash of feelings or interests". Conflict can also be defined as an opportunity to make changes. All conflicts have opportunities built into them that allow people with vision to make small changes in their lives or historical changes for the benefit of the world.

The thought that conflict and opportunity can be seen as the same thing is enlightening and the basic premise of this section. Whenever people disagree with each other's opinions, methods, beliefs or perceptions there is an opportunity to learn, to teach, to enhance your professional and personal lives. Of course, some conflicts are just a pain you must suffer through and forget but many of the conflicts (small and large) you face daily are opportunities. This is not a pie-in-the-sky belief but one proven by practical people. Gandhi used racial conflict as an opportunity to seek independence for India. Churchill, Roosevelt, Mackenzie King and others used World War II as an opportunity to change social structures within their countries. Children constantly use conflicts at home and at school to discover new lessons about living and playing.

> *Our Department of Social Work has trained in Brief Solution Focused Therapy. However, we have taken this clinical paradigm and used it as an organizational theory so we are often heard to ask, "What can I do to make this situation a little bit better?" or "What is it that needs to happen for this to be different or a little better?" It emphasizes a timeframe in the future. It assumes an understanding of the problems and concerns but engages the thinker at a level of solution.*
> *Michèle Chaban*

Conflict is ever present at work, at home, at places where you worship and socialize. Conflict can be present in yourself, between people, between groups and between organizations.

Conflict can be useful if it::

- Results in solutions to problems.
- Helps you to understand yourself and others better.
- Helps you discover new and important issues and priorities.
- Helps you to communicate more honestly and openly with others.
- Helps you to get rid of anger, anxiety and fear resulting in a more adaptable and flexible personality.
- Helps people to work better together.
- Helps you to develop your personality and skills to every increasing heights of personal satisfaction.

Conflict is destructive if it:

- Drains you of your physical and mental energies.
- Forces you to concentrate on complaining and ridiculing people.
- Reduces cooperation between people.
- Causes you to diminish yourself and others and encourages further deterioration of your own self image.
- Detracts you from working on your primary goals.
- Taints your environment and reduces your quality of life.

People's Working Styles

There has been a great deal written about people's different working styles or personality styles. The basis of most of this research and writing is the belief that all of us have a basic personality that does not change. Within your personality you have different "roles" you play with your boss, colleagues, spouse, friends, children, acquaintances, and people you have just met.

These different roles may cause some people to think you are the most loving and generous friends they have while other people think you are the most arrogant, authoritarian person they know. Many of our political leaders are examples of people fulfilling a number of roles (private/public). They are also people that we view differently depending on our knowledge of them and our values and beliefs.

In your organization, the staff may see someone as a shining light while others may think she is aloof and argumentative. This same person probably has friends who understand the deep convictions of her faith while others assume that her belief against swearing is pure snobbery. Others may see her cultural heritage as a great benefit in this multicultural society while others wished she would lose her strong "foreign" accent.

The differences other people have can be seen as a rich resource for learning or an invasion of those who don't agree with you. A useful insight is that most people have similar views about us!

What are the different basic personalities? Depending on what you read you will find varying viewpoints. Many of us have heard of Type A personalities; people who are ambitious, highly energetic, workaholics who suffer more heart attacks than others. Other personality types are people who enjoy family-centered activities and see work as less important. Regardless of what research you read the key point is that some people are generally more extroverted while others are more introverted. Some people enjoy making plans while others enjoy doing what is necessary to make a plan work. Some people enjoy working on detailed financial accounts while others enjoy supervising a large group of people. Some people explode with anger while others keep their feelings hidden inside.

There are no right or wrong personalities; just different ones. We all have characteristics similar to other people but to differing degrees. We all get angry, we all like some kinds of work, we all enjoy relationships with people and we all have our own dreams and hopes. Our differences actually make it possible for things to happen. We need people who like to plan, we need people who like to teach, we need people who like to do detailed work and we need people who are family-centered.

When people are asked which work style or personality style they believe is best they often choose their own style. People who hire staff often try to hire people with similar styles as their own. This belief that one's own style is best is what often leads to difficulty in getting work done well and on time. It leads to people judging other people's personalities rather than their behaviors. Imagine a team of four that are required to complete a project within 30 days. The same person has hired all four and they all want to be leaders. A common result is that all four can generate wonderful ideas of how the project should be done and all resent having to do the actual work required. The result: a disorganized project with each member believing his or her methods and ideas are best. Another likely result is that the project will be delayed as the four team members procrastinate in completing any tasks they disagree with. See Chapter 5 on Team Skills for more information.

Conflict Resolution Styles

There are many parts to a conflict. We can use questions to isolate some of those parts and therefore think of ways to affect positive changes within those conflicts.

What do people have conflicts about?

- Differing on what the facts are
- Differing on how to do something
- Different expectations
- Different belief systems

Who do you disagree with?

- Conflicts within yourself
- Conflicts between two people
- Conflicts within a specific group of people (e.g., within a profession)
- Conflicts between two or more groups (e.g., between professions)

What has caused the conflict?

- Differences in thoughts, feelings, ideas, and perceptions about the same situation.
- Job roles are not clear and therefore, people are not sure who is responsible for what.
- Systemic problems: scarce resources, little time, or internal political difficulties. Many conflicts begin with systemic problems and many people throw up their hands in frustration as systemic problems are often the most difficult to resolve. Although this is true, there are many opportunities to make smaller changes that can affect the system!

The way work is organized, structured and divided may appear unfair or wasteful.

Where are you in the present conflict? Does knowing at what point you are help to generate ways to resolve this particular conflict?

- **Just before the conflict begins**: a general uneasiness that a problem exists and will probably get worse.
- **People know there is a conflict but no one acknowledges it**: conflicting parties have signs and symptoms of a problem but do not acknowledge its existence.
- **Discussion**: people talk about their differences of opinion in appropriate or inappropriate ways.
- **Open dispute**: the conflict is openly recognized and other people start to take sides.
- **Open conflict**: rigid positions are taken by the people originally involved as well as other people who have joined in formally or informally. Conflict resolution is limited to a "win/lose" option unless facilitated by an experienced person.

Once you identify at what point the conflict exists you can begin to look at various strategies for dealing with that specific conflict.

Conflict Resolution Strategies

There are various strategies for resolving conflicts. Depending on the specific situation and who you have the conflict with (e.g., your boss, spouse, child, friend, colleague, or stranger), you will use some strategies more often with some people than with others. In fact we often are less likely to resolve conflicts with family members than with colleagues because we assume family is forever and doesn't require as much effort as our work relationships.

Avoiding Conflict

We use this strategy when we think the issue is not worth fighting about or if we deny there is a problem. We may avoid important issues because we are afraid of hurting someone's feelings or because we just "can't be bothered".

Giving In

We may use this strategy when it is easier to give in than to spend time resolving the conflict. We may be more passive than others or bored with trying to smooth things out. We may also be afraid of conflict or disharmony and, therefore, always give in to "keep everyone happy". We may decide that the issue is one we can "let go".

Win/Lose

Children often think their parents follow this strategy which is "I'm the parent so you have to do what I say." It is similar to people of different levels of authority in an organization or people who are more aggressive who say "Just do it!" This survival-of-the-fittest strategy may be very appropriate during an emergency (e.g., a fire); it is destructive in maintaining long-term working and personal relationships.

Compromising

Compromise does not mean that everyone is happy. Usually it is used when two people have extreme positions and agree to meet in the middle. Compromising is often used in political, economic, arms control, and management-labor negotiations. If the end result is just a compromise then the parties will leave dissatisfied and this dissatisfaction will make the next negotiations even more difficult.

Problem Solving

This is the most time-consuming but most rewarding strategy for resolving major and minor conflicts. In this strategy people are committed to making the effort to resolve the conflict. People listen to each other and use good communication skills to speak openly and honestly. People may not end the conflict liking each other, but they will respect the other person's commitment to their honestly held beliefs and their willingness to discuss behavioral changes. This type of conflict resolution ends in a mutually agreed upon and beneficial solution without the people having to make major concessions. It is often called a win/win strategy.

Exercise #1

Examine a specific conflict you are having now or have had recently. Answer some of the following questions to help you decide on a specific resolution strategy.

1. Who is involved in this conflict?
2. What is the source of this conflict?
3. At what point is this conflict (e.g., just beginning or has it been escalating for several months)?
4. Do the others involved recognize there is a conflict?
5. Are the others committed to resolving the conflict? If yes, for what personal reasons?
6. What are several alternatives for resolving this conflict?
7. What can I do immediately to begin resolving this conflict?
8. What can I do to avoid or minimize similar conflicts in the future?

9. Are there any personal behaviors I might change to encourage more productive and enjoyable relationships with the people I work with?

Preventing and Dealing with Conflict

The potential for conflict within any organization is great because of: the constant need to communicate complex issues to people with different skills in expressing and comprehending language; the need for many people to work together as a team despite considerable differences in attitude, training, commitment, socio-economic background and personal competencies; and the personality differences between staff, clients and colleagues.

> *Perhaps because of my ethics background, I like to think of us as disciplines who have different practice ethics that we are bound to in such a way that we don't often reflect on how they determine practice. For instance, social work comes from a history of social reform movements. We, as a profession, work with those marginalized in society such as the poor, the single parent the elderly, etc. We work to bring about social reform, looking at the tension between environments and individuals. Over the course of time, social work became integrated into the systems that were designed to help others. Now social work walks a fine line between being system changers and system maintainers. For those of us strongly committed to ongoing social reform, we are often the thorn in the side of those trying to maintain the status quo. Conflict can reside within the profession simply by the ethics driving our practice.*
> *Michèle Chaban*

For example, a staff member who has dedicated her life to her work clashes with a colleague who plans to quit as soon as a better paying job comes along. Their lack of mutual loyalty and respect may be the real source of the conflict; not the issue they are talking about.

Most conflicts, however, usually grow out of personality differences or petty disagreements. An ugly scene is more likely to occur because someone was slow to follow a colleague's instructions or because someone overheard a sarcastic remark, rather than a life-and-death situation which has put everyone on edge.

Preventing Conflict

The following are some techniques for preventing conflict:

Assume that everyone is doing the best they can with the knowledge they have at that time. Few people get up in the morning with the sole purpose of making your life miserable. If something they do upsets you, assume that it was not intentional and try to talk to the person about it. Tell them how you feel when they do something specific. Talk about their behavior. Do not accuse them. Try to understand why they did something.

Use humor, laughter and play at work. Humor, laughter and play bring people closer together. It is hard to dislike people with whom you spend time laughing. Laughter and smiling are contagious and encourage an environment where people can talk out problems with a sense of humor.

Communication skills. Communication skills are critical for us to avoid and deal with conflicts. You must accept 100% responsibility for understanding someone else and making sure they understand you. You don't do this for someone else; you do it for yourself because it gives you control. Don't be afraid to ask questions.

Courtesy. Courtesy is still the key to unlocking people's positive feelings. Saying "thank you", "please", and "would you please" encourages people to respect you and others. You can act as a role model to others who have forgotten the power of courtesy.

Participate. People need to see you involved in various aspects of the work at hand. Helping other people with their work in the organization is the best way to tell them that you respect their work. When helping someone with their work be careful not to "show them up" by doing it better or very differently. Helping them in this case means being an assistant in times of difficult work stresses or when you have a few free moments and can see that someone might appreciate your assistance.

Acknowledge people's success and your mistakes. A sincere compliment and acceptance of your own mistakes shows your honesty and your willingness to recognize excellence in other people. Be specific about whatever someone has done well so that your compliments do not appear superficial or just a public relations ploy. Also, avoid complimenting routine work as the other person may assume you are being rude. For example, "The way you typed those letters was very professional and punctual." may be interpreted by the person in this way: "I have been typing letters in the same way for 10 years and now he thinks they are professional. What did he think my letters used to be like? Does he think because he took a course in management that now he has to be nice to me?"

Often people who sue a hospital may do so because they are looking for recognition. They seek lawyers because the organization has failed to respond to a very basic human need. I think it is very healthy to say: "We are absolutely wrong." Every lawyer would say that you cannot say that because it is admitting liability. But if it was said early on, what a difference it could make. But we are really afraid to say those things out loud. I am sure that is a prime motivator for some of the ugly legal incidents that occur. They want to be recognized and receive a sincere apology
Larry Lewis

Do not argue with or criticize someone in front of colleagues. Few things upset people more than being embarrassed in front of colleagues or the public. Always provide constructive criticism in the privacy of an office.

Gossip can hurt. Rumors hurt people. As fascinating as gossip may be to listen to, you must recognize that the information is probably inaccurate. Do not repeat gossip. If you respect other people's privacy they may do the same in return.

I think of gossip as storytelling but if it is mean spirited or sensational it is hurtful. Social work values a person's story and tries to get to the concern underneath. Social work also uses information to look at the impact on people and systems. If one of my colleagues is ill but unable to let me know and someone did not tell me this, I may never know about their illness nor would I be allowed to respond at a human, personal or caring level while at the same time respecting their need for distance or privacy. Hopefully, the principles of caring and health are a part of how the "gossip" is shared. I believe it is the underlying intent that is the issue.
Michèle Chaban

Dealing with Conflict

Talk it out. If someone does something that hurts you, physically remove yourself from the situation to think clearly about what happened. Use this time to identify and deal with your emotions, identify the issues in the conflict, determine what you want to change, and develop an approach to deal with the conflict. Then use "I statements" to tell the person clearly how you feel when they do something. For example, "I feel like you don't respect my work when you assign choice assignments to Bill all the time". This is more effective than "You are a bum for not giving me that assignment!" When you have resolved the problem do not bring it up again in the future.

> *The Social Work Department has a history of a practice ethic that says if you have a problem with someone, deal with it. We think that we can't ask our clients to communicate clearly, directly and openly if we don't do it ourselves. Particularly in health care, I think we should try to practice what we preach. If we do not support the principles of health in all that we do, if we do not try to treat each other well, I believe that we become dispirited and the health care system becomes diminished. Particularly now, with so much reform going on within the system, it takes little or no extra cost to treat each other well even when we are in conflict.*
> *Michèle Chaban*

Get help. Sometimes a conflict cannot be resolved by some of the strategies suggested in this section. Perhaps a mutual friend, a supervisor or another facilitator can help people communicate more clearly and specifically without some of the emotion that clouds issues.

Ultimately someone may have to leave. When all the suggestions and strategies in this section have been tried, and have failed, you may have to recognize that your only alternative is for one of you to leave. If your difficulties are with a supervisor you may need to transfer or leave the organization (it is unlikely that they will leave). If your dispute is with a colleague, one of you may have to transfer or leave. If the dispute is with someone who reports to you, it is your responsibility either to transfer the person where they can be more effective, ask them to leave and help them find more suitable employment, or recommend that they seek outside counseling if the situation warrants it.

Hot Buttons

Hot buttons are personal triggers in us that cause us to react to other people's behaviors without thinking about what to do first. We may respond irrationally and powerfully. For example, someone has pushed your hot button if you react with instant anger when they call you a name you really dislike. Our brothers and sisters were very good at finding our hot buttons when we were children!

The assumption that many people have about hot buttons is that other people can control our behaviors. This is a belief that you can choose not to have any more. You always have control over how you react to other people's words and behaviors. First you must be aware of what causes immediate responses from you.

> *I find that it is important to know oneself, one's feelings and likely reactions in situations of conflict. This takes some time for self-reflection–"what caused me to feel that way", "why did I react that way today", "what is the source of my discomfort with that situation"?" My best reflection time is often while waiting in traffic. It is a peaceful time that I can put to good use by reflecting over the day's events.*
> *Elizabeth Latimer*

Exercise #2

List those words, behaviors and body language that cause you to react immediately and without thinking first. It could be something as simple as identifying nicknames that really anger you, situations where are you accused of bad work or blamed for things you did not do, or when someone points their finger at you or ignores you.

Once you have identified your hot buttons you can plan what to do the next time someone presses them. For example, if someone calls you a name you really dislike, use the situation to find out what purpose it serves that person to upset you. Rather than being aggressive or defensive, you can turn the tables and help teach the person a better way to get what they want from you.

Ask some close friends or colleagues what they think your buttons may be and how they might suggest you learn to reduce your instant response into something more productive. For example, ask them to give you a "sign" when you begin to react.

Helping Others to Resolve Their Conflicts

Sometimes in the course of your work you will be asked to help other people resolve problems amongst themselves. If there is some commitment between the people to resolve their conflict then you can play an important role.

> *Resolving conflict requires large doses of trust and willingness, mingled with mutual respect. Confidentiality of the nature of discussions is also important. These values should*

be clearly articulated and agreed upon before the team process of conflict resolution begins.
Elizabeth Latimer

If the others choose not to participate or cooperate then it will be very difficult to resolve the conflict to anyone's satisfaction. If this happens, more dramatic and autocratic methods may be used in the most just and fair way possible.

Some steps to try if the people with the conflict are willing to try to resolve the conflict are:

1. As the mediator, ask each person separately and privately to describe what the conflict is. You can use open and closed-ended questions and listening techniques to bring out the most important points. Do not permit people to complain about someone else's personality by using words like lazy, stupid, or ignorant. Limit them to describing what specific behaviors the other person uses and how that affects them, e.g., "They arrive 5 minutes late everyday.", "They do not follow the standard procedure we all agreed upon.", "They always call me by my last name as if I were in the army.", "They never give me credit for work that I do but only complain when I make a small mistake."
2. Get the people together for a meeting and summarize, as best you can, what you think the others have told you. Concentrate only on specific behaviors, not personality differences. Ask them if you have summarized their viewpoints accurately or if they have any corrections or additions to make.
3. Get the two to agree to what the specific conflict is.
4. Ask them whether or not they are willing to work out a win-win solution to the conflict so that everyone feels satisfied with the results.
5. Together or individually ask them to brainstorm all possible alternative solutions without judging if they will work.
6. If possible, wait a few hours or a day before reviewing all the alternative solutions. Perhaps the people have come up with further possibilities when they were away from the others.
7. Select the best alternatives that the people involved will agree to.
8. Either verbally or in writing, decide on an action plan which will define clearly what things will happen, who will do what, by when and how you can evaluate the success of the agreed-upon solution.
9. Make sure that there is a follow-up of some sort soon after you have made this agreement to see if unexpected problems arise. Also acknowledge any small suc-

cesses in this process to encourage the continuing efforts of everyone involved.

10. If there was no acceptable solution for the people involved:
    - Make sure they still agree on what the conflict actually is,
    - Go through steps 4 - 9 again,

Acknowledge that for now you have reached a roadblock and that they may need some time apart before you can start the process again,

If the conflict is so great that there really is no real commitment to resolve it by the participants, other people will need to get involved such as supervisors or senior managers.

As a manager, conflicts are brought to my attention. There are discussions on how best to handle the conflict and what, in fact, are the client's rights, the family's rights and the staff's rights and guidelines governing their behavior and, of course, the feelings about the situation. The first knee-jerk reaction is to point the finger of blame. The smart manager gets past that as quickly as possible and tries to collect the information–what really is the situation? Feelings are so entangled up that it often becomes a quagmire to try and resolve it. How do we deal with it? Has there been a transgression of the rules and regulations? If so, it has to be documented and disciplinary steps may occur. The public relations piece of it must look at whether the family's nose is out of joint because of the high emotions involved, how do you reduce that and create communication that resolves the whole thing.
Larry Lewis

If You Have Conflicts with Your Supervisor

Whenever you have conflicts with people who have authority over you there are some extra techniques you might use. However, most conflict resolution techniques are similar to others presented in this section. Combine any of the techniques that you think will fit the circumstances of the specific conflict.

- You resolve conflicts for yourself; not for others. You are responsible for resolving conflicts. You do not need to like the people you work with but you are responsible for ensuring a productive working relationship.
- Use your supervisor's name in the way they prefer, e.g., first name versus Mrs. Smith, Dr. Brown, or Ms. Jones.
- Set a time limit to discuss a conflict if you have no appointment, e.g., "I'd like to talk to you about 'x' for 12 minutes." Stick to the 12 minutes to show your respect

for their time. If it takes longer, make an appointment to block out sufficient time. You may want to choose a neutral place to meet.

- Pick a good time to discuss serious conflicts but do not avoid the discussion for weeks. Unresolved conflicts lead to more conflicts.
- Write down some specific facts and points you want to mention. Usually we get so emotionally involved during serious conflicts that the key points are never mentioned.
- Use specific examples of what is wrong. Rather than statements like "Jill isn't doing her work.", you might say "When I arrive in the morning I find that Jill has not filled in the name labels from the night before and that isn't fair. What can you do or what can we do to change this?"
- If your conflict is specifically with the behavior of your supervisor, use "I" statements. For example, "When you criticize me in front of the other staff I feel very embarrassed and angry. You certainly have the right to criticize my work but could we agree to do that in the privacy of your office?"
- Once you have agreed upon a solution, follow through with your part of the agreement. Set aside some time in the next few days or weeks to evaluate the success of the solution.
- If the difficulties you have with your supervisor are irreconcilable you have several options:
- Ask to speak to your supervisor's boss to get assistance in resolving the problem.
- Ask to be transferred to another area, if possible.
- Recognize that it is unlikely that your supervisor will quit first. Therefore, you may choose to leave the organization and accept the challenge of change in your career. As difficult as this choice is, it has proven as a valuable "push" to many people to re-evaluate their work, their career choices and the way in which they want to work. If you choose this option, plan for it. Get some career counseling and make some necessary and exciting choices, for your future.

If You Have Conflicts with Your Staff

Not surprisingly, the techniques for resolving conflicts with your staff are similar to resolving conflicts with your supervisor. The only difference is that you have a greater responsibility (as part of your job description) to ensure a proper working relationship within your area of control.

The tips recommended on the previous pages reflect a respect for the other person (the supervisor) involved in the conflict. As a supervisor you need to reflect that same degree of respect for your staff. Again, you do not have to like the people you work with but you do have to respect them as contributing individuals.

Some further tips (staff might try some of these tips as well!):

- As the supervisor you have the ever present responsibility to acknowledge people's good work with specific comments of what they do well. Catch people doing things right and tell them that you will continue to do so.

If someone is very anxious and that anxiety impacts on the team, I think it is important to identify it at first but then continue to reinforce the quality of their interaction when they are less anxious. If I find them being anxious, I often say, "Slow down, take a deep breath and pretend you are someone else. Try to tell me in a calm manner what it is that you need to say about this patient." Having done this with some degree of success, I then use humor to say, "...see what you are able to do when you center yourself!

Michèle Chaban

- If you need to reprimand or criticize a staff member, begin with the criticism or a reprimand and end with a specific praise of their work. **Never** begin a reprimand or criticism with a compliment or praise. That will undermine all your future compliments; people will expect a "but" at the end of all your future compliments.
- Actively search out possible conflicts between staff members. Find out what is happening and follow the techniques in the section *Helping Others to Resolve Their Conflicts*.
- If you know you have a personality conflict with a staff member, actively work out strategies with them to minimize conflicts. Honestly discuss some of your feelings and what specific behaviors bother you and get that same kind of information from them.
- Understand people's work styles, cultural diversities and personal interests. Understanding how people are similar and different can improve the overall understanding of why your team is working very well or not working well together.

When You Cannot Avoid Conflict

As conflict is inevitable and not necessarily negative, try the following steps to put the conflict in perspective.

- Remember that most conflicts are only a small part of your life and not worth the emotional energy you give to them.

- Do something to try and resolve the conflict even if it doesn't work. We use most of our emotional energy during conflicts on anger and frustration. Instead, use your creative energies to understand the other person's point of view and how resolving the conflict can be mutually beneficial.
- If your work is being criticized remember that only one aspect of your work is probably being criticized. Use this opportunity to see if your work can be improved or if the criticism is really based on other issues.
- Get away from the conflict to cool off. Try and place the conflict in perspective to the rest of your life and also in perspective to time; will you remember this conflict next year, will this conflict change your life in the next 10 years?
- Learn from the conflict. Whether the conflict is a win/lose situation or resolved to your mutual benefit see if there are things you can learn from it to prevent or resolve similar conflicts more quickly in the future.
- In extreme situations, evaluate whether or not you may leave the situation. If your conflict is with a supervisor, you may be the one who has to decide to transfer or leave. If your dispute is with a colleague, one of you may have to transfer or leave. If the dispute is with someone who reports to you, it is your responsibility: to transfer the person where they can be more effective; ask them to leave and help them find more suitable employment; or recommend that they seek outside counseling if the situation warrants it.

Summary

People always do the best they can with what they know at the time. Few, if any, people wake up in the morning with the sole purpose of making your life miserable.

The more we understand people the more we respect them even if we don't agree with them.

The opposite of love is not hate but fear. So much behavior that we dislike is because of our own fear or the fear of others.

If you choose not to resolve conflicts, accept the responsibility of your decision. This may include leaving the circumstances where the conflict occurs.

When you resolve conflicts you do it for yourself and not for others.

Why do I always have to make the first move? It isn't fair! Resolving conflicts has little to do with fairness. It has to do with seeing the opportunity and satisfaction of resolving conflicts and with accepting responsibility for your share of working with people.

Resources

The following resources are only a few of the many useful resources that you can find in your local libraries, within your own organization, and in your local bookstores. Look for other books but also for journal articles, magazine reports, films, videos and audiocassettes. Also keep in mind how much you can learn from experts in the field, including people within your own organization!

Axelrod, R. (1984). *The evolution of cooperation.* New York: Basic.

de Bono, E. (1985). *Conflicts: A better way to resolve them.* Middlesex, England: Penguin.

Frankl, V. E. (1963). *Man's search for meaning.* New York: Pocket Books.

Jampolsky, G. G. (1985). *Goodbye to guilt: Releasing fear through forgiveness.* New York: Bantam.

Kaufman, B. N. (1979). *Giant steps.* New York: Fawcett Crest.

Kottler, J.A., (1994). *Beyond blame: A new way of resolving conflicts in relationships.* San Francisco: Jossey-Bass.

Levine, S. (1998). *Getting to resolution: Turning conflict into collaboration.* San Francisco: Jossey-Bass.

Pascale, R. T. (1990). *Managing on the edge: How the smartest companies use conflict to stay ahead.* New York: Simon and Schuster.

Tjosvold, D. (1993). *Learning to manage conflict, getting people to work together productively.* Toronto: MacMillian.

Vachon, M. (1987). *Occupational stresses in the care of the critically ill, the dying and the bereaved.* New York: Hemisphere.

Negotiation Skills

Negotiation is about two or more people, or organizations, achieving their own objectives through a change in their relationship. It is about getting the best possible deal for yourself while trying to ensure that the other people get as much of what they need and want as well. Effective negotiations ensure a long-lasting working relationship.

Negotiation at its simplest is an easily understood process but one that takes continuous practice to perfect. Negotiation at higher levels and in matters of life and death should not be done lightly. People's beliefs run deep and negotiators are apt to run into distrust and strong emotions. In addition, when the stakes are high, such as in labor, legal or governmental negotiations, members may use negotiation strategies that are meant to trick the other party. Negotiators need to be highly skilled to work within these environments.

This section is based on the assumption that your negotiations will be with people you probably know and that your intent is to get results that will benefit everyone involved. If you are interested in more political or complex negotiations, we recommend reading some of the materials listed in the Resources section at the end of this section.

Definition

We negotiate whenever we try to influence other people's decisions through an exchange of ideas, money, material goods or power. We negotiate with others primarily for our own benefit and, in enlightened negotiations, for our mutual benefit.

Attitude

Successful negotiators view conflict as normal and as an opportunity to improve a working relationship using the positive attitude of mutual benefit. In the long view of negotiations, these people try to do only things that will benefit a working or personal relationship while also benefiting themselves **whether or not their actions are returned in the same spirit by the other people involved**.

Negotiating for the Long-Term

Everyone who negotiates wants to get something from someone else. Short-term victories for one side (win-lose) lead to long-term mistrust. Grudging compromises (lose-lose) lead to anger or only short-term commitment to the agreement. Negotiating for consensus (win-win) produces results that are both ethically better, and good for long-term relationship building.

Assumptions

We begin all negotiations from our own set of unique beliefs and assumptions. For example, if we have limited education we may assume that someone with a Ph.D. is either much smarter than us or we may assume that they have no practical experience. Depending on our assumptions, we will negotiate either from a position of perceived weakness or strength.

Let us examine some specific assumptions that different people might have when they negotiate:

- We must share values in order to get agreement.
- To have a good working or personal relationship with someone we must always have their approval and nonjudgmental support.
- The fastest way to get agreement is for me to know more than the other person.
- We must avoid disagreement at all costs or else we risk losing a valuable working or personal relationship with the other person.
- The most successful negotiation strategy to date has been the adversarial one used by lawyers and politicians. After all, we live in the best country in the world under this system so it must work.
- I am who I am and no one is going to change that. I got to where am I today by how I do things, so it would be stupid for me to change now.
- I don't get paid to make big decisions, so I leave negotiating up to other people.
- For me to have a good working or personal relationship, I need to have my basic needs met while also being able to sleep at night.
- If I just had the negotiating tools I needed, I could get what I want (or what I need)!

This list of common assumptions about negotiating often lead to frustration, confusion and unclear roles and responsibilities. Many of these assumptions may give someone the impression that they cannot negotiate or learn to negotiate. They are self-defeating.

The basic assumptions necessary for successful negotiations are:

- You can learn to be an effective negotiator.
- You can help people get some of their needs (must have) and wants (would like to have) met while also meeting your own needs and wants.
- You can negotiate in an ethical way regardless of how other people negotiate with you.

The Basic Skills You Need

The successful negotiator has the following in their bag of skills.

Basic Communication Skills

Verbal and written communications can make the difference in making your points clear and acceptable. Basic communication is the ability to speak or write in short, clear sentences and to get ideas across to others.

Balance

Balance in your life (your physical, emotional, career, family, education, spiritual and economic needs). This balance means you can deal with stress effectively. It also means you can manage a negotiating situation better because you can put it into perspective with all the other important parts of your life. A sense of balance will help you avoid personalizing the process or the results of a negotiation and help you concentrate on being the most effective negotiator you can be under the circumstances.

Understanding

Understanding someone's viewpoints and needs is not the same as approving of them. Countries constantly negotiate treaties even though their basic philosophies are different. The purpose of understanding someone else is not just to gain a negotiation tool, but also to take on an attitude of negotiating **with** someone rather than **against** someone.

Constant and Trustworthy

If you are constant in your behavior, fair with your colleagues, families and friends and firm in keeping your commitments to others, then people will be able to trust you even when they strongly disagree with you.

Acceptance

You may strongly disagree with a person's behavior or ideas without having to strongly dislike their personality, culture or beliefs. Such an acceptance may allow you to persuade people (over time) that your viewpoints are equally valid and worth their time to listen to and understand. Persuasion has longer lasting results than forcing someone to do things your way.

Some physicians may not see that it is necessary for them to develop these skills, given their historical role as "the doctor who knows best". However, they will find that successful negotiation will help them when working in interdisciplinary teams and when outlining a treatment plan with patients and families. Successful negotiation can result in a "win/win" situation with colleagues and patients and increase compliance with the plan that is developed.
Elizabeth Latimer

Everyday Negotiations

Not all negotiations involve complex research, or back-and-forth debating over difficult points. Everyday we are involved in routine negotiations. What is important to remember is that some of the things we negotiate routinely can be done to the benefit of all parties. The benefits of the resulting cooperative relationship will continue over the long term.

For example, most stores will negotiate the price, delivery or services they provide if you ask. This is especially true with those stores that you do regular health care business with and whose staff you get to know by name. For example, you might benefit from asking for next-day delivery (when deliveries usually take three days) while the store may benefit from a quick sale on a slow day. In addition, you may consider the store for future purchases, and they may continue to offer you better service.

When you go to your doctor, dentist, lawyer, accountant and other professionals you can negotiate the amount of time they spend with you, the amount of information they help you learn, and the kind of service they provide.

When you ask for service from the telephone company, the electrical utility, cable TV company and others, you can negotiate the type and level of service you want. When you go to a teacher in your continuing education programs you can negotiate the kind of studying you want to do, the kind of evaluation you find most useful and the content you want to concentrate on.

Negotiation is an every day thing if you live with others in your home. Who uses the bathroom and when, who does which chores, what happens during emergencies, etc.

All of these negotiations are underestimated and often done poorly. In fact, many of us do not negotiate very much at all in stores, with professionals or even with our family members. Negotiation is often seen as too time consuming. Many people have also experienced failures or embarrassments when they have tried to negotiate in everyday situations and find it easier to accept service, products or relationships that are less than fulfilling.

A few tips:

- Be clear about what you want to see happen. Decide if it is worth your efforts to negotiate for the results that you want. Some negotiations do take up time, but many will result in better services, products and relationships for you. If you are unwilling to try to improve things for yourself, carefully examine why. It may be easier for you to give in to the needs or wants of someone else. You may want to compromise and you understand that this negotiation result will probably not satisfy anyone. It may help you to study assertiveness skills so that you better understand your rights and responsibilities. Assertiveness skills also help you understand what the benefits and risks are of being more assertive in different situations.
- Spend time actively listening and understanding (and we mean really understanding) what the other person wants.
- Look at some alternatives beyond the normal answers you come up with.
- Agree on something that is fair to everyone.
- Make sure that your agreement also helps the long-term relationship you may have with the other person.

Beyond these basics there are many strategies that we will look at later in this material. The important point in everyday negotiations is not to harm the other person or yourself or to let anyone else harm you either. Mutual respect and mutual benefits are what lead to long-term negotiating successes.

The Negotiation Process

There are two basic models of negotiation: (1) negotiating from your well thought out position (based on what you need), and (2) negotiating a common agreement based on mutual interest and needs (what everyone needs). The first model begins with each side stating what their position is and negotiating over time some give and take in those positions. A legal battle, political debate or labor negotiations are good examples of this model.

The second model begins with people looking deeper into their arguments for the underlying need upon which they want action. For example, someone may start by saying they want a raise but what they really want is recognition for their work and more responsibility so they can continue to develop their career. They would not mind getting a raise, but that is secondary to their career needs.

Let's look at how the models are different. Both are used and the one you choose may depend on the circumstances, the knowledge of the other negotiators and what you feel most comfortable with yourself.

Negotiating a Position

In this process, you prepare by answering some of the following questions:

Issues

What are you negotiating? For example, do you want a raise, increased authority, a better sale price, home delivery, etc.? Write down the major and minor issues you are negotiating.

Who

Who is involved? Write down what you know about the person, their organization or department, background, past negotiating history, their style, preferred tactics, etc.

Results

What outcome do you want? The results are more specific than the issues listed above. For example, you may want a 5% raise, permission to authorize petty cash purchases, a reduction in the sales price by 10%, and home delivery by next Monday. What are the best and worst results you can expect and accept? What outcome do they want? What are the best and worst results you think they can expect and accept?

Research

What specific items will be discussed and what are the differing views? You can research similar information that you have and that the other negotiators have that might be helpful. For example, consumer reports, budgets and financial plans, promotional material (e.g., brochures, flyers, media coverage), and minutes of previous negotiation meetings. If you are negotiating with people from different cultural backgrounds, find out what their preferred negotiation styles might be. Use your public library, people who have negotiated with them before and your colleagues to get help.

Needs

What does each side need (must have) versus want (would like to have)?

Environment

What is the negotiating environment like? Where are the negotiations taking place? When? Are there climate concerns (extremes in temperature that may affect people's comfort)? What kinds of time pressures are there?

Strategies

What strategies can help you? What strategies can hurt you?

Factors

Have you considered the following factors: economic and legal consequences, supply and demand, time lines, long or short term advantages and disadvantages?

Once you have answered these questions alone or with the help of others to get their perspectives, you can begin the actual negotiations. These usually follow a fairly standard process.

The Phases

1. Getting to know each other. People may be quite genuine or try to play all sorts of "mind games" to make you feel at ease or uncomfortable. Good preparation on your part and skills in keeping your emotions under control will minimize any unwanted effects of such strategies.
2. Each person says what his or her goals and objectives are for this negotiation.
3. Understanding each other's positions. During this phase people try to clarify what they understand the other people are saying, if there is any give-and-take in the positions and try to identify major areas of agreement and disagreement.
4. People may outline, clarify, or summarize any possible points of conflict. Disagreements and conflicting views are not present in every negotiation. This depends a great deal on the working relationship between the negotiators and their long-term goals.

   However, negotiations often do have this phase and it involves using some of the strategies outlined later in this material. There are games played, efforts made to change people's positions, tempers flared and a sense that everyone is wasting each other's times. This phase can come up time and again from the beginning of negotiations to months after an agreement has been reached.
5. Reviewing your own position and areas of agreement and disagreement.
6. Agreement or settlement. This is often a discussion with the aim of ensuring you get what you need (must have) while getting as many of your wants met as possible.

Returning to the next negotiation hoping to get even more for your side.

These steps are not always sequential and assume a great deal of preparation work in advance so you know what your limits are, who the other people involved in the process are and your understanding the difference between what you **want** versus what you **need**.

Negotiating Common Interests and Needs

The second model of negotiating begins with people looking deeper into their arguments for the underlying need upon which they want action. This model is most often associated with the work of the Harvard Negotiation Project and its founder Roger Fisher. They call this model "Principled Negotiation".

Their approach is not to use a soft or hard position that you add to or take away from during a negotiation. They concentrate on identifying common interests and needs and asking that people do not concentrate on their own positions until later in the negotiations.

Their criteria for measuring a successful negotiation:

1. The negotiation should produce a wise agreement, if agreement is possible. By wise agreement, they mean the agreement can be defined as one that meets the legitimate interests of each side to the extent possible, resolves conflicting interests fairly, is durable, and takes community interests into account.
2. The agreement should be efficient and workable.
3. The negotiation process should improve or at least not damage the relationship between parties.

This method is hard on merits (very specific and objective standards) and soft on people (encouraging mutual respect whenever possible). Rather than a mix-match of various elements of each party's positions they try to end with a single document that addresses the specific needs of all negotiators. They do this through four principles: people, interests, options and criteria.

People Separate people from the problem. At some point the negotiators should begin working together on the problem rather than arguing with each other personally. You do not have to like the people you negotiate with but it helps to concentrate on the problem rather than the people if you want a successful negotiation. This strategy does not require that you trust the other negotiators.

Interest Focus on interests not positions. Look for mutual gains whenever possible. When interests conflict, go to point 4. Avoid bottom lines during this examination of mutual interests as this prevents people from identifying unspoken needs that really are at the root of the negotiations. You need to understand that getting what you want does not usually mean that the other person or organization does not get what they want.

Options Generate a variety of possibilities before deciding what to do. Using creative problem solving techniques can free people from their biased positions and allow solutions that go beyond the norm. Do not allow decisions or comments about which alternative is best. Use this time to concentrate on generating more alternatives than you normally would.

Criteria Insist that the result be based on some objective standard. (Later in this material we examine how to define specific objectives and standards.) Using fair standards such as market value, expert opinion, custom or law to determine the outcome can allow people of different beliefs to agree on criteria without having to give up their strongly held beliefs.

In this model, consensus is built on avoiding fixed positions and concentrating on the specific interests and needs of the combined group of negotiators. It has been used successfully, as has the model of negotiating positions, from everyday negotiations to international arms negotiations between super powers.

The model you choose will depend on the circumstances, the comfort levels and knowledge of the other negotiators and the previous history of negotiations between the various people and organizations involved. Understanding both models is important to use either model successfully.

Strategies

Strategies are tools you can use to change a situation including the important elements of timing, location of negotiations and the specific techniques of negotiation.

Different strategies are helpful in different situations. Consider both the short-term objectives and the long-term effects of any strategy. If you plan to work with the people for any length of time you must understand the long-term consequences of the negotiation to your working relationship. Mend bridges whenever possible rather than destroy relationships for short-term gains.

I think mending bridges means building bridges. A bridge built out of straw may look functional but in a strong wind it may not hold. Building bridges that will support the weight of our work is important and in this I believe there must be an element of sincerity, integrity and intent. Surrendering and submitting for the sake of avoiding larger issues is not helpful as they will only show up again.
Michèle Chaban

Expect Disagreement, Conflict and Tension

Many negotiations reach a point where people begin to think that they have wasted their time and there is no hope of reaching an agreement, for example, negotiations between unions and management. This is usually the most important time to review and take stock of what points you have already agreed to, what criteria for success have been identified, what interests you have in common and what areas you can choose to disagree on without losing the opportunity to get some kind of written, effective and amiable agreement.

Asking Questions

Good communication tools, such as asking genuine, open-ended questions, open people up to negotiating in good faith. Used as a technique to get your way, this strategy will fail. Used as a genuine means of understanding the other person's needs and interests, this strategy will encourage a negotiating environment of mutual gain.

Avoidance

You can either delay or avoid negotiating or taking any action. You can use this strategy to provide you (and perhaps others) time to develop a clearer plan. You can use this to allow time for people to express their anger, re-evaluate differing positions, allow the problem to remain until it changes by itself or accept the situation as it is.

The Unexpected

Sometimes doing the unexpected will help others see your point of view differently while you maintain your negotiating objectives. You can either do something that brings you closer to others' ways of thinking or take an opposite approach to highlight areas of differences. For example, you are sharing an office with someone else and you have been quite angry that they do not respect your privacy. The other person feels the same way about their privacy. In your negotiation to improve your working relationship with this person you have been discussing ways to respect each other's private space more effectively but with little success. One day you arrive with a beautiful, inexpensive floor plant that divides your private spaces elegantly and professionally. Your unexpected, kind gesture leads to further discussions of how you can both respect each other's privacy more fully and professionally.

I Win

You can (if you have the power) direct people what to do without accepting any room for negotiation. This strategy works in emergencies or in smaller disagreements where people do not have the energy to reach a negotiated settlement. This strategy is not effective for any long-term changes you may want to make.

Leave

Sometimes it is necessary to leave a negotiation for either a short time or a longer time. The timing depends on your power or influence and the type of negotiation you are involved in. Leaving may also signal that you accept a portion, or all, of a settlement but that you continue to disagree with the decision making process. Unless you follow-up with some changes to improve the situation and clarify your concerns, the end result will not satisfy anyone.

One Person Leaves, Another Remains

Sometimes it is necessary for one or several team members to leave a negotiation but leave one person behind to indicate commitment to resolving the negotiating issues. When some people leave, it implies you have some negotiating strength and the timing can permit people to re-examine their perspectives.

Do the Opposite

If you negotiate in a predictable way and it is not working, you may try doing the opposite to produce some changes in others' reactions to you.

One Thing at a Time

Try to limit your negotiations around specific issues of time, space, resources, interpersonal communication, supervision, etc. Trying to accomplish too much at once reduces the chances of effectiveness and getting results that are mutually agreeable.

Get Support

Find peers, staff or supervisors who agree with your general points and be flexible enough to adapt your negotiating style with theirs to add strength to your position. Understand people's styles, hidden agendas and consider the long-term consequences of such alliances.

Compare to Similar Situations

Sometimes research up front will find situations similar to the one you are presently negotiating. These other situations may provide you with statistics about possible successes or difficulties. The situations can be either internal or external and if possible both. Your research also gives you useful information and, therefore, credibility as a professional willing to go the extra bit to resolve a situation to everyone's benefit.

Mix and Match

Sometimes it is useful to use several strategies at once to increase the possibility of success and to allow others to pick strategies they are more comfortable with.

Role of Dimes

A role of 50 dimes equals $5.00. Sometimes it is easier to ask for several dimes at a time rather than the whole $5.00. Even within one negotiation you can get commitment to smaller portions of your wants and needs and increase your requests a bit at a time to get to the point you really want. It may be a little more time consuming but it can get you the results and commitment you want.

Asking For Too Much

A standard negotiating strategy is to ask for more than you expect to get. This is a common sales approach where one side asks for a large amount of something and the other side purposefully offers much less. Over time the negotiation results in a settlement somewhere between these two extremes.

Bottom Line Limits

Some aspects of your negotiation may involve issues or items that are non-negotiable for ethical, economical or organizational reasons. Be clear about these points to indicate your level of commitment and power over these points.

Caucus

Often when reading about politics you will hear the term "caucus", e.g., "The Prime Minister met with his caucus to prepare them for the upcoming election." Caucus is another word for team and means a time for you to discuss elements of the negotiations with other members of your team privately to identify what is going well and what should be done differently.

Giving Up Some Control

Sometimes it is very useful to allow others to take some control over the negotiation to symbolize your trust in them or your willingness to meet them half way. You can also use this strategy to offer others a range of choices and give them the responsibility of choosing the next move.

Changes After Agreement

A common strategy by sales people is to imply that a sale has been made and all the costs incorporated. When everyone is ready to sign the papers, a few extra items are casually brought up. For example, in purchasing a car it is common, while filling in the final paper work, to be told that you probably want extended warranties, rust proofing, extra insurance, etc. Because it is implied that everyone purchases these extras the client often agrees and finds out that the sale price just went up by several hundreds (if not thousands) of dollars.

Identifying a Strategy

Sometimes it is helpful to tell the others that you believe they are using such-and-such a strategy and that you do not approve. Catching someone's strategy, especially if it is based on secrecy and negative manipulation, gives you extra strength and credibility.

Keeping a Secret

Sometimes you will know something about a situation or person which could cause others in the negotiation humiliation or dishonor. If the others know you have this information but you keep it out of the negotiation it will strengthen your position personally, professionally and ethically.

Dirty Tricks

When someone uses intimidation, lies, psychological abuse and other pressure tactics there are several things you can do. Often people react by ignoring this illegal, unethical or uncomfortable tactic in hopes that ignoring it will go away or that it will help the negotiation end in success. Other people fight back in similar ways and the negotiation turns out to be a battle of wills and ill-conceived strategies

It is more effective to recognize the tactic as unfair, tell the other negotiators that you have recognized the inappropriate tactic and ask them why they feel the tactic is legitimate or helpful. Again concentrate on the procedures used rather than who used them. Often just speaking about what you think is happening, in a non-threatening way, takes the power out of the tactic and allows the negotiators to get back to the real problems being negotiated.

Goals, Objectives and Standards

Often in negotiations it is necessary to write down specific goals, objectives and standards that the negotiators agree to. Without such written specifics it will not be possible to objectively evaluate the success or failure of the agreement in the future.

A **goal** is a generalized result one aspires to, such as the goals of improved client satisfaction, better health and safety at work, job satisfaction, or a more loving family.

> "One of our departmental goals this year is to increase the level of client satisfaction with our services."

An **objective** is a statement of the specific results one wants to achieve. Objectives describe what the specific result will look like, when it will happen and what is needed to make the objective happen. In establishing objectives one also looks at what can cause the objective to not happen. Objectives must be realistic yet challenging and based upon the consensus and commitment of the people involved in reaching the objective.

> "To increase client satisfaction with our services this year we will, by July 1: decrease the time to fill prescriptions to within 10 minutes of the request. Susan, Jim and Tyler will receive training on our new computer software in May to assist them in increasing response time by the July 1st deadline."

A **standard** refers to specific minimum criteria that must be met in order to accomplish a specific task over and over again. Standards are usually written out quantitatively and refer to such things as technical specifications of products, safety standards, rate of complaints, minimum requirements (e.g., procedure for medication administration, documentation requirements).

Use standards to write out what a specific job or action requires routinely or repetitively. This standard becomes the minimum acceptable performance expected of a person, process or equipment. For example, in job performance negotiations:

Staff requires minimum expectations for successful completion of their work such as:

> "Unit clerks must answer the telephone within three rings."

To reinforce expectations regarding safety, communications processes and technical specifications such as the standard: "All equipment used in this organization must be serviced every 6 - 12 months to meet the safety standards set by the government."

Use objectives to assist someone to reach the minimum standards for their work. For

> shorter-term projects specifically related to unit or organizational standards. For example, if a nurse needs to learn a new nursing skill: Susan will attend a workshop, complete the learning package and do a demonstration with the clinical educator within a month's time."

Objective Writing

To write objectives that are practical and useful to all negotiators it is important that they meet what some people call the S.M.A.R.T. test:

Specific
Measurable
Achievable
Realistic
Time-lines to complete objective.

Other experts use the R.U.M.B.A. test: relevant, understandable to clients and staff, measurable (quantifiable), behavioral and achievable over time and under predictable circumstances. Which ever test you use, be consistent in its application.

Objectives must be written so that it is absolutely clear to anyone (all negotiators, their respective departments or organizations, management and staff, and physicians) whether the objective has been met or not met.

Types of Objectives

Problem solving To develop criteria and action plans to meet needs presented by a problem or opportunity or to improve substandard performance to an acceptable level.

Maintenance To clearly state minimally acceptable levels of work performance within specific time frames and allow for changes to meet differing demands.

Innovative To bring about long term changes or improvements within a unit or department based on general goals.

The following chart shows examples of unacceptable objectives rewritten to meet the SMART test.

Unacceptable Objectives	Acceptable Objectives
To expand services to meet clients' needs by January.	To expand evening hours in the pre-op clinic to two evenings a week by hiring a part-time RN.
To reduce time lost because of injury appreciably by the end of the year.	To reduce time lost by injuries by 90% by next March 31 using a part-time staff person for 6 months to coordinate new safety measures.
To make sure that all hospital staff knows fire safety procedures.	To provide staff with time to attend a 15-minute fire safety inservice each September, where correct use of a fire extinguisher is reviewed.

Exercise #1
Writing Objectives

- For each objective below, decide whether it meets the SMART criteria and if it does not meet the criteria, why not?
- Rewrite the statements so that it meets the SMART criteria. NOTE: You can also improve the objectives that meet the criteria.
  For example, "To centralize Health Records filing and issue departmental filing guidelines for unit clerks and secretaries."
  Meets criteria? No
  If not, why not? No time frame given for accomplishment.
  Improved objective statement: "To centralize Health Records filing and issue department filing guidelines for unit clerks and secretaries by July 1st."
- To improve our storage of hazardous materials.
- To reduce unnecessary petty cash purchases significantly by year end.
- Maintain current response time to physician requests for consults.
- For Jim to improve his interpersonal communication skills by next August 30th.
- To maintain the current servicing rate on clinical equipment of twice annually while decreasing the overall servicing costs throughout the fiscal year ending March 31st by 3.4%.
- To be more professional.
- To reduce absenteeism of staff.
- To improve patient care on our unit.

Exercise #2
A Successful Negotiator

What makes a successful negotiator? Like all skills, negotiation skills are learned over time with practice and understanding. You are not born with them.

You can use this exercise in two ways. First, review the following list of characteristics of a successful negotiator. This will help you develop your general negotiating skills. Secondly, use this chart before every major negotiation to see which skills areas you may need help with during this particular negotiation. Each negotiation is different and, therefore, you will need some different levels of skills depending on the people, situation, issues and environment.

Regardless of which way you use this chart, write down whether you do the skill very well, average or not very well (either generally or for a specific negotiation).

Very well You do it very well, therefore, there is no need to spend time improving this skill right now.

Average You have an average amount of this skill but you need to keep up-to-date and/or develop this skill to higher levels.

Not very well You need to develop this skill within the next few months to reach an average level of competency expected for your job.

Skill	Description	Very Well, Average, Not Very Well
Self-awareness	For negotiations to be successful people must understand their own strengths and weaknesses as well as their own wants (would like to have) and needs (must have). You understand how you react under stress, what negotiation skills you do very well, and how to adapt your own working style to the situation. You understand your role in the negotiations involving a team from your organization. You understand what the bottom line is that you, or your organization, will accept in a final agreement.	
Understanding other people	You are sensitive to the needs and wants of the other participants to the negotiation. Those you are unclear about you confirm through genuine questions of interest and mutual respect.	
Mutual gains approach	Whenever possible you concentrate on negotiating in the spirit of mutual benefit that can be objectively verified and that improves your long-term relationship with the other negotiators. When this is not possible you do what you can to minimize any short and long-term negative effects of the agreement and look for opportunities to improve long-term gains and relationships for everyone.	
Researching	You have the skills to understand past agreements between the parties, research their present wants and needs, find out, as best you can, the best and worst results that could happen, and know how to research quickly during the actual negotiations any areas of factual dispute.	

Skill	Description	Very Well, Average, Not Very Well
Dealing with conflict	You have the personal stamina and skills to tolerate professional and personal conflicts during the negotiation. This allows you to concentrate on the desired end agreement rather than concentrate on personality conflicts with other negotiators.	
Understanding negotiation strategies	You are aware of both legitimate and illegitimate negotiation strategies so that you will act ethically yourself and inform others if their tactics are inappropriate for the negotiation. Knowledge in strategies helps you avoid or minimize how others may try to manipulate you unfairly (while also adding to your own professional image).	
Communicating	You know basic communication skills that allow you to speak and write clearly while also having the skills to actively listen and draw out other people's interest and concerns.	
Speaking for your group	You can communicate your position and the position of the other parties fairly and concisely to people outside the negotiations.	
Negotiating in a team	You can work with a team of negotiators using your knowledge and expertise to add to the total effectiveness of the team.	
Principled	You understand what principles you use in negotiations and what principles (personal and organizational) that are not negotiable.	
Asking for help	You know when to ask for help from other members of your negotiation team or from your own managers or executive before committing to decisions you are unsure of.	
Third party negotiating	You can negotiate between people who have different points of view, different cultural and historical backgrounds than your own in a way that everyone benefits.	
Problem solving	You can identify specific problems and use techniques to help the other negotiators generate alternative solutions creatively and effectively.	

Skill	Description	Very Well, Average, Not Very Well
Resolving conflict	You can help others and yourself resolve conflicts as they arise in a mature and respectful manner that brings people closer together, even if they dislike each other personally.	

You have identified some of the negotiation skills that you do very well, average and not very well. Now you must design a plan of action to reinforce what you do well and learn new knowledge and skills to improve other skills. All of the skills listed above are learned. You do not get them when you are born. All negotiators need to identify what they are good at and what they need to work on.

How Do You Identify What Skills You Need?

Review the chart above with special attention to the second column describing specific skills. Which of those skills do you need to strengthen to help you become more effective under the different categories listed in column 1? For example: to resolve conflicts well you must know specific creative problem solving techniques, how to communicate your ideas effectively, how to lead a group in a meeting through a problem-solving process, and how to work with your own team in designing alternatives to the negotiating problem. You also need some practice in dealing with stress and incorporating appropriate humor. Once you have identified the skills you need to learn, you must think of how you can go about learning them. To help you, you may use other sections in this book as well as other literature, your colleagues, and your family and friends.

Use the sample chart to help you plan out what skills you want to improve on and by when. It is also important for you to write down how you know you have learned the skills and how you can prove it to a colleague or friend who is supportive of you improving your leadership skills. Writing these points out will help ensure you actually improve your skills. Just thinking about improving your skills usually does not lead to changing your behaviors or skills.

Action Plan

Skill	How	By When	Successful? (Check)

Negotiation Ethics

We often hear about ethics and whether or not negotiators have made agreements that are ethical. We read in newspapers and magazines everyday about people in politics, medicine, law, retail industries, education and others who have done unethical things in the name of doing "good" for themselves, for their organizations or for the good of all people.

How do you know if what you are doing is ethical or not? How will you negotiate if the other negotiators are doing things or agreeing to things that are unethical?

Most of us know when something is right or wrong. Asking yourself a few of the following questions will help you instinctively know if what you are negotiating is right or wrong and if the process you are using is right or wrong.

1. Is the agreement and negotiation process legal?
2. Would you want your family and friends to know what you are doing or agreeing to do?
3. Would you want your actions publicized in your organization's newsletter or in the local media?
4. Do you sleep well at night after the action or decisions have been made?
5. Was the final negotiated agreement fair to all to the best of your ability?
   Would you like your negotiation to be used as a case study for how to negotiate well?

If you answer any of these questions with discomfort or uncertainty, then you may wish to review your negotiation methods and results.

It is also helpful to read books about work ethics. Specific examples from your own type of work may help clarify questions of doubt about what is right or wrong.

A Negotiator's Checklist

Use the following checklist to make sure you are prepared for a specific negotiation.

___ 1. Know what you want (goals and objectives).
   What do I want and need?
   What am I willing to give in return?
   What are the financial, legal, time and working relationship requirements?

___ 2. Be specific.
   What is/are the important issue(s) as I see them? As others see them?

What information and power supports us?
How will I present my viewpoints?
What may be the areas of greatest differences, conflicts or perceptions?
What options already exist?

___ 3. Do your research.
Who will I negotiate with? How do they negotiate? What are their personal needs in negotiations?
Where and when will we negotiate? What advantages or disadvantages are there for both of us?
What are the implications of the negotiating process to us?
What individual powers do we bring to the negotiations?

___ 4. Be personable.
How can I best make the others feel comfortable and safe?
How can I establish a win/win attitude towards the negotiations?

___ 5. Deal with conflict.
What are our major points of differences (see point 2 above)?
How will I know what the others really need versus what they want?
How can I adequately respond to their needs?

___ 6. Win/win.
What strategies will help me meet my needs and wants while providing the others with the benefits they need and want?
What am I prepared to give up (bottom line)? Under what circumstances?
What do I expect in return?

___ 7. Agreement in principle. Make sure the agreement is written in standards and objectives that can be evaluated for success or failure after a pre-determined time.
How formal must the agreement be, (in written letter/memo, contract, using lawyers)?
Who else must approve? How long will this take?
What follow-up steps are necessary to implement the agreement?

Summary

Negotiation is about changing a relationship between two or more people or organizations. It is about getting the best possible deal for yourself while trying to ensure that the other people get as much of what they need and want as well to ensure a long-lasting working relationship.

Negotiation for some people is a game and you win when you get most or everything that you want regardless of what the other people get. For others, negotiation is a process of finding out what everyone needs and coming up with the best alternative to help them fulfill those needs.

Regardless of which view you take, negotiations involve preparation, working closely with other people, agreeing to a specific course of action, and understanding what your own strengths and learning needs are.

Negotiations are done through two models: (1) negotiating from a specific position and (2) negotiating common interests and needs. Both models are effective and have been used extensively in various forms.

Too often negotiations get muddled into uncertainty and frustration because the negotiators have not written out and understood clear goals, objectives and standards. Specific objectives help people achieve general goals such as improved working relationships between organizations. Standards are the minimum acceptable guidelines for specific actions or services and are quite different from objectives.

Ethics are an extremely important part of negotiations. Often people are tempted to avoid ethical issues in hopes that they will accomplish short-term gains for themselves or their organizations. Effective negotiators concentrate on the long-term and make sure that all parties to an agreement understand the ethical and legal consequences of their agreements.

Negotiation is an everyday thing and many of us enjoy the give and take of negotiating with family and friends and colleagues. Formal negotiations do not have to be any less enjoyable if you have built a reputation as a honest, fair and professional negotiator. Over time, that reputation will save you a great deal of time and effort and will allow people to work more openly and enjoyably with you during negotiations.

Resources

The following resources are only a few of the many useful resources that you can find in your local libraries, within your own organization, and in your local bookstores. Look for other books but also for journal articles, magazine reports, films, videos and audiocassettes. Also keep in mind how much you can learn from experts in the field, including people within your own organization!

Block, P. (1990). *The empowered manager: Positive political skills at work.* San Francisco: Jossey-Bass.

Cohen, H. (1980). *You can negotiate anything: How to get what you want.* Secaucus, NJ: Lyle Stuart.

Donaldson, M.C., & Donaldson, M. (1996). *Negotiating for dummies.* Foster City, CA: IDG Books.

Fisher, R., & Brown, S. (1988). *Getting together: Building relationships as we negotiate.* New York: Penguin.

Fisher, R., & Ury, W. (1991). *Getting to yes: Negotiating agreement without giving in.* New York: Penguin.

Illich, J., & Heady, R.K. (1996). *The complete idiot's guide to winning through negotiation.* New York: MacMillan.

Karrass, C.L., (1993). *Give and take: A complete guide to negotiating strategies and tactics.* New York: Harper.

McCormack, M.H. (1995). *On negotiating.* Marietta, GA: Dove.

Shell, G. R. (1999). *Bargaining for advantage: Negotiation strategies for reasonable people.* Minneapolis, MN: Viking Press.

Ury, W. (1993). *Getting past no: Negotiating your way from confrontation to cooperation.* New York: Bantam Doubleday Dell.

3. Awareness

Career Planning

Diversity

Career Planning

The following information represents a bare bones approach to career planning. Check the references at the end of this section for more detailed information on various career planning alternatives.

This section is designed to help you review your career options. You will discover at least nine career alternatives. You will need to do a lot of writing to help you evaluate your goals. As an alternative you can use the format of this section as a basis to discuss your options with a friend or colleague. Also keep in mind the books and services available within your organization, in your public library and through various community programs.

You should review your career options regularly to make sure your choices fit in with your immediate and future personal, professional, family and social needs and wants. You may decide to stay in the position you presently have or you may choose to change your job or your career. On average we change our position every 3-5 years and our careers 2-3 times in our lifetime. Change is not always easy and requires real thought, research and planning. Enjoy the process and the opportunity!

Physicians need to choose their future career path much earlier now and some medical schools are hiring career counselors to assist them to look at all aspects of their lives while making these decisions. They encourage a balance of work, self, family and life interests in young trainee physicians. Physicians reaching mid-life or those seeking a new direction as a result of restructuring are also engaged in career review and planning for their future.
Elizabeth Latimer

Understanding Your Interests and Skills

Exercise #1

By completing the following exercise you will have a better understanding of your own interests and the skills you have developed over the years.

Write an autobiography of your life. Concentrate on the points listed below but **do not edit** yourself as you write, just continue to write until you have finished. Quickly read the whole list before you begin to write to get an idea of what you may want to write about.

The final biography should be about 20-200 pages long depending on how much time you are willing to spend. The results can be quite enlightening and exciting so have fun! Your family and friends may enjoy reading your biography too!

1. What have you done personally that you enjoyed doing? (This is so broad a question that it allows you to decide what is important for you to write about.)
2. Where have you travelled, lived, and studied?
3. How did your family, friends and personal needs fit in?
4. Where have you worked (paid and volunteer work):
   What have you achieved personally and professionally (we have all achieved at least 20 major things so don't stop writing until you have found 20 major items)?
   - What skills have you developed?
   - Which parts of your work did you enjoy/dislike?
5. Brag about yourself – no one will see your biography, unless you show it to them, so be proud.
6. What do you do in your spare time (honestly now!)?
7. What do you enjoy doing:
   Hobbies
   In what kind of environment do you enjoy being in (eg. out in the country, on a beach, in your favorite room at home, working in a small/large office)?
8. What do you dream about?
   What skills do you want to develop?

Once you have finished your biography (it can well take a few days or more) go through your written work and circle, in a different colored pen, those points that can help you decide what you would like to have or to use in your work. Also circle points you do not want to have or use in your work. Use the sample chart to organize your points.

What I want to have or use in my present and future career(s)	**What I want to avoid in my present and future career(s)**

Once you have finished filling in the chart go back through each point:

Underline the most important points you have made about what you want to have or use (based on your priorities) in your future career.

Use a highlight pen to highlight your top 5-10 skills that you enjoy the most and do best.

Write a number beside the highlighted points in order of priority, i.e., #1 for the most enjoyable skill, #10 for the least favorite of the top ten.

Next take those last highlighted points and put them into a chart like the following sample. This chart can help you summarize your accomplishments as well as your professional goals.

Things I Have Already Accomplished	Things to be Accomplished (in order of priority)	Steps Needed to Accomplish the Things in Column 2

Career Options

There are 9 options available to anyone reviewing their career alternatives:

Researching

While continuing with your present career you use some free time to research, interview and test out other career ideas.

Staying Put

After reflection, you decide your present career situation is actually the right opportunity for your professional growth or personal life style.

If you cannot change positions or careers you might decide to look for further fulfillment through continuing education programs, volunteer work, or self-directed learning. These other activities can help you evaluate your skills and interests before making major changes in your professional life.

Moving Across

You use transferable skills and knowledge in your own field but in another area (e.g., a different job within your professional field), and you maintain the professional status and responsibilities you are presently comfortable with.

Returning to Previous Level

You return to a position you had previously to move back to more rewarding work, and to enjoy your work with less stress and professional tension.

Moving Up

You decide to move up in your present organization to increase the money you earn, to improve your professional status, and to increase your responsibilities.

Same Career Different Organization

After reflection you decide that you want to stay in the same career but in a different organization.

Different Career

You decide to change careers completely, either within your present organization or in another organization (including self-employment).

Stopping Work Temporarily

If circumstances permit, you may decide to stop work temporarily to further your education, raise a family, or take an extended trip.

Retiring

After reviewing your working life and economic status you may decide to retire earlier.

Take a look at the list you developed in the previous exercise under "Things to be accomplished". Which of the nine career option(s) allows you to accomplish some of your priority goals?

The Job/Career I Want

You have described the skills you enjoy and are most competent in doing. You have also chosen a specific option or two from the previous pages. Now you need to make some decisions about what job situation you actually want.

- In what city, town or area of the country would you like to work?
- What type of organization would you like to work in (e.g., large organization, smaller department, self-employment, etc.)?
- What type of people do you want to work with (e.g., those who enjoy a very social atmosphere or people who enjoy working more alone and quietly)?
- What goals, purposes, or values must the organization have that you want to work with?
- What specific working conditions are important to you?
- What level of pay and responsibility do you want to have?
- What skills have you previously described that are transferable to this job?

- How will this job affect your personal, family and social life?
- What are the next 3 steps you need to take towards getting that job, e.g., call and ask for an information interview, research the organization, speak with your spouse and family, evaluate staying or leaving your present position, etc. Once you have listed these steps, give yourself some time lines for completing each one. Review after you have finished each step to follow or change your process until you have the job you want!

I have encountered the process of career planning several times in my life, the most significant step being in my change of career from nurse to doctor in 1976. This change involved a major examination of goals and wishes for life and work from a personal and professional viewpoint. It was a valuable and formative life review time.
Elizabeth Latimer

Researching Your Career Options

Once you have reviewed your autobiography and filled out the charts you will have a pretty good idea about what career options you are interested in. Now may be the time for you to use that information to do further research.

- Go to your public library and begin to research your career options.
- What do you need to learn to accomplish your option?
- Where can you find organizations that will meet your needs if your present organization can no longer do that for you? If you have chosen another town, city or area of the country to live in, are there organizations there that meet your needs?
- What qualifications is that type of organization interested in? Is there a way around some of the qualifications so that you do not need to return to school?
- What is the salary range for this career option?
- Check with professional associations to find out as much as you can about your career option and which organizations they might recommend. Your public library has a Directory of Associations to help you find the right one to contact.
- Talk with experts in the field to get their impressions and advice. Ask them what kind of questions you should be asking other people. Asking the right questions will give you the most valuable information you need so ask the experts what kind of questions they recommend you should use.
- Talk with people who have the kind of job or career you would like. People love to give free advice and to help others further their career as long as they do not think you want them to help you get the job through references or hiring you themselves.

- Take careful notes of what you are learning and write down new questions as they come to you.
- Take as much time as you need to research, think, evaluate and plan. Spend time with your family and friends to get some of their ideas and their support.

The Information Interview

Sometimes during your research you may find it helpful to interview people who have the kind of job or career you would like or experts in the field you are researching. How do you handle a telephone or personal interview with them?

- Make it very clear to them that you are not asking their help in getting a job. You want to talk with them only to get information to help you make some career decisions. Appeal to their interest in giving "free advice".
- Write your questions in advance and leave enough room on the page for you to write in the answers. Prepare a master copy of these questions and use a photocopier to copy these pages so that you have a different set of questions and answers for each person you talk to.
- The types of questions you want answered will depend on the person you are talking to. The questions will be similar to what you have been using for your research at the library. Questions about: the person's organization, what kind of education the person has, how did they get to the position they are in now, and what advice they could offer you based on your past experiences and education. Also ask them what questions they think are important for you to ask other people. Ask them if they could recommend anyone else to talk to, to get more information.
- Before you actually visit someone for an interview, do a little research about them and their organization (through the library health care section or through contacts you have in that organization). If possible, arrive for a personal interview a little early and collect any information the organization has about themselves in their waiting room, e.g., an annual report, brochures, etc.
- Always present yourself as a professional doing practical research. Your image is very important so dress professionally.
- Remember that you are "in charge" of the interview. You are not there to get a job. You control the questions and, therefore, the interview. Tell the person in advance that you will take only 20 minutes of their time. Your question sheet should be specific enough to get the important information you want within 20 minutes.
- Often the person you are interviewing will appreciate your respect for their time.

They may also extend the interview time if they think they have more useful information to give you. Be flexible.

Note: There will be times when you will not get the kind of information or support you want from people. Do not get discouraged (at least not for too long!). You often have to go through some frustrating times to get what you want so consider each difficulty as one more step to get through the process of learning what you need to know.

One of the things that I found helpful when changing careers (moving from a hospital to being self-employed) was to make a list of people that I respected who were also self-employed in the health care field. I then spent some time interviewing these people and found that not only were they willing to share their experiences with me but I was able to apply what I learned from them to my own business.
Beverley Powell-Vinden

Summary

Where do you go from here? As I said at the beginning, this section is a start to understanding your present skills and career options. If you have enjoyed the journey in learning more about yourself then I strongly recommend you look at other resources in your library and bookstores that can give you a more in-depth process for career planning.

There are many organizations that provide career counseling, many of which are free through public programs. To find out more about these programs call or write your government employment center, your local community college or request assistance through your local library.

Without wanting to sound too melodramatic, dreams do come true. It requires you to understand yourself better than you have ever understood yourself before; to research the options that appeal most to you; to interview people who are presently in the kind of career you want to have; to make real changes and accept the positive (and possibly, negative) consequences of those changes.

The last question you must always answer is, "Am I happy with what I am doing now and, if not, what can I do to change that?" More often than not, there are changes you can make for yourself in the organization where you are working. Sometimes, however, you may need to move within that organization or move to a different job or career. There are **always** things that you can do if you take the time to do the required research to understand what options are available.

Dreams do come true, but it takes the dreamer working with the dream to make it so. Step by step, inch by inch, knowing that trying is more than half the battle. I failed every grade in high school because I was busy dating. My brothers were much more successful than I was. One teacher told me if I wasn't so stupid, I might try learning something in school. I always thought that I was stupid. After high school I went to work for a large cosmetic company. They saw something in me and so taught me to model and teach about their products. I came to dislike the world of cameras and modeling. I announced one night at the dinner table that I was thinking of going to university. There was dead silence and everyone's head ducked into their plate except my father who said I could not go. When my brother challenged this on my behalf, my father said, "I do not want Michèle to be hurt anymore by what school does to her." I said just let me try. After my first year of university I had a C+ average. I wasn't proud of it but at least I had a chance to return the following year.
Michèle Chaban

Resources

The following resources are only a few of the many useful resources that you can find in your local libraries, within your own organization, and in your local bookstores. Look for other books but also for journal articles, magazine reports, films, videos and audiocassettes. Also keep in mind how much you can learn from experts in the field, including people within your own organization!

Bette, C. (Ed.). (1997). *Career planning for nurses.* Albany, NY: Delmar.

Bolles, R.N. (1992). *How to find your mission in life.* Berkeley, CA: Ten Speed Press.

Bolles, R.N.& Nelson, R. (2000). *What color is your parachute.* Berkeley, CA: Ten Speed Press.

Charland, W.J., & Charland, W.A. (1993). *Career shifting: Starting over in a changing economy.* Holbrook, MA: Adams.

Danek, J., & Danek M. (1997). *Becoming a physician: A practical and creative guide to planning a career in medicine.* Toronto: Wiley & Sons.

Farr, J.M. (1997). *The right job for you: An interactive career planning guide.* Indianapolis, IN: JIST.

Gaither, R, & Baker, J. (1995). *The wizard of work: 88 pages to your next job: A simple, straightforward job-search book for people who'd rather be working than reading a book.* Berkeley, CA: Ten Speed Press.

Kanchier, C. (2000). *Dare to change your job and your life.* (2nd ed.). Indianapolis, IN: Jist Works.

Sheldon, B., & Hadley, J. (1995). *The smart woman's guide to networking*. Franklin Lakes, NJ: Career Press.

Tieger, P.D., & Barron-Tieger, B. (1995). *Do what you are: Discover the perfect career for you through the secrets of personality type*. Boston, MA: Little Brown and Company.

Diversity

What must we know to provide compassionate care to our patients and to better understand our colleagues from outside our own cultural, racial and religious traditions? What must we understand about our own gender and the opposite gender to work more effectively? What must we know about a person's sexual orientation so that we are inclusive in our work rather than exclusionary in our behavior?

We begin with a basic assumption: people are all equal. If we treat all people exactly the same, we are not treating them equally because we are not recognizing their unique physical, emotional, spiritual and informational needs. Therefore, treating people equally means not treating them the same.

This is not a study in cultures, races, religions, gender biases or sexual orientation. The following material is designed to be as practical as possible on a day-to-day basis. It concentrates on the one-to-one working relationship between care providers and those who receive services. It does not examine broad policy development or population studies.

In identifying how people from various cultures, races, religions and backgrounds are different, it is important to also identify how we are all fundamentally the same. Everyone is born and everyone dies. Everyone laughs and everyone cries. Smiles are universal just as love, compassion, empathy, prejudice, cruelty and violence are universal.

On a train trip home from university, I stopped into the station bookstore and picked up a little book, Mister God, This is Anna. I read about a girl who grows from five to eight years old through the book. A teenager named Fynn found her on the docks of London. He wrote years later about the genius and wonder of this young girl, Anna. At one point in the book, Anna, 6 or 7, tries to identify a scientific way to see the commonality of all humanity. She didn't know about cellular biology or quantum physics. After much thought and experimentation she came up with this method. It is an excellent analogy for a discussion on the diversity and similarity of the people we care for.

1.Stand any person in front of a light and draw their outline on a piece of paper.

2.Cut out their silhouette and place it perpendicular to the light and draw its shadow (a straight line).

3.Cut out the straight line and put it perpendicular to the light and draw its shadow (a dot). [This step is easier to do in one's head than on paper!]

Conclusion: Any person, regardless of their size, age, origin or background, will produce a dot by taking their shadow three times. Just as wonderfully, any dot on a piece of paper can be any person, past or present, in the whole world. For that matter it could also be an elephant, a house, the planet, a tree or any object made of matter. Anna was most impressed with her logic!
This analogy is to highlight the key point of this material – while identifying an individual's differences from us, we must always begin with how fundamentally alike we are as members of the human family.
Harry van Bommel

The Universal Golden Rule

The following are specific sources for the golden rule found in ancient world religions. They strengthen our belief that at fundamental levels, we share many of the same beliefs.

Buddhism
Hurt not others in ways that you yourself would find hurtful. (Undana-varqu: 518)

Christianity
As you would that men should do to you, do you also to them likewise. (Luke 6:31)

Hinduism
This is the sum of all true righteousness: deal with others as though wouldst thyself be dealt by. Do nothing to thy neighbor which thou wouldst not have him do to thee after. (The Mahabharata)

Islam
No one of you is a believer until he desires for his brother that which he desires for himself. (Sunnah)

Judaism
What is hateful to you, do not to your fellow men. That is the entire Law, all the rest is commentary. (The Talmus, Shabbat 31a)

Georges P. Vanier, Canada's Governor General in the 1960s wrote: "The more you know people, the better you will understand them and the more you will like them." Caring for others at the end of their lives is a time where this may be easier to practice than at other times. People tend to concentrate more on issues of fundamental value to them at these times than on who won the baseball game last night or who should win the next election.

Language

Words are immensely powerful. They can be comforting or disquieting, healing or hateful. The working assumption of this material is that everything is presented in the hopes of being helpful and educational. Anything that inadvertently offends a reader should be brought to our attention.

Definitions

These change over time as we struggle to find more accurate terms.

Community
One's own family, friends, neighbors, spiritual community, colleagues and acquaintances.

Culture
Social behavior patterns characteristic of a people.

Ethnic Group
A group of people with common characteristics that may, or may not, constitute a separate race. Country of origin is a common characteristic in identifying ethnicity.

Family
One's biological family and, perhaps, closest friends.

Race[2]
A local geographic or global people distinguished by genetically transmitted physical characteristics such as skin color (e.g., Caucasian, black) or facial features (e.g., Chinese, Japanese).

For example, the Race Relations Directorate of the Ontario Government has divided populations in the following groups for statistical records since 1986:

Black includes African Black, Canadian Black, American Black, West Indian Black and other Blacks.

East Asian includes Chinese, Japanese, Korean, Fijian and Polynesian.

Native includes Canadian Native People (e.g., Inuit, Metis, Status and Non-status Indians); American Native People, and Central and South American Native People.

South Asian includes Indians (India), Pakistani, Sri Lankan and Bangladeshi.

South-East Asian includes Burmese, Cambodean (Kamuchean), Laotian, Vietnamese, Thai, Malaysian, Indonesian, Filipino, Singaporean.

West Asian/Arab includes Egyptian, Israeli, Iranian, Lebanese, Palestinian, Syrian, Turks and other Arabs.

White includes European Whites, North American Whites and other people of Caucasian background.

Other includes people with mixed racial heritage not listed above.

Sexual Orientation

One's preference for either, or both genders. A preference for someone's own gender is often referred to as "gay" or "lesbian". Preferring either gender is "bisexual". A person's sexual preference should not interfere with their ability to provide compassionate health care to others.

Choosing the 'Right Words'

In writing and speaking about various cultures, races and religions, as well as about age, gender, sexual orientation and other sensitive subjects it is easy to get caught up in finding the right words. The 'right' words are constantly changing. Within a few short decades we have moved from describing people in the U.S. with black skin as Negroes, to blacks to the more common term of African-American. At differing times, each word was common place and acceptable. Changing views required new words to describe the same population.

People with disabilities have also seen dramatic changes in how they are described. For example, people with developmental disabilities used to be called mentally retarded or mentally disabled. A self-advocacy group for people with developmentally disabilities calls itself "People First" to remind people that "labels are for jars."

However, we must use words, no matter how imperfect or how often we change them, to identify specific groups of people apart from other groups of people so that we can discuss ways of caring for them in all of our communities.

If we begin with the assumption that no one in health care is purposefully trying to say things in ways to upset patients and families, then we can begin to concentrate on the message as well as how the message is delivered in an open and honest communication.

To help us understand some of the 'how the message is delivered', I suggest we need some common ground. There is a mixed consensus on what words are correct. The source that I use as a writer is the *Canadian Press Stylebook*. There are many different style books (e.g., *The Chicago Manual of Style, The New York Times Stylebook, The Globe and Mail Stylebook*). These are constantly updated to stay as current as possible as not to offend their readers. Regardless if one agrees with the ever-changing language used in these sensitive areas, these style books represent what can be best considered a general agreement on public language.

In the *Canadian Press Stylebook*, for example, there are sections on the common ways to write about native peoples in Canada. "Canada's Indians are not a homogeneous group with a standard set of interests and grievances. An effort should be made to reflect their diversity in stories specifically dealing with Indians and native groups; there are status (or reserve) Indians, non-status Indians (living outside reserves), Metis (people of mixed native and white origin) and Inuit. Collectively, they are known variously as Aboriginal Peoples, original peoples, aboriginals, indigenous peoples, the First Nations and other variations."

Some further tips:

- *Canadian Press* uses uppercase for **Aboriginal Peoples**, which includes all Indian, Métis and Inuit people in Canada. **First Nations** is also uppercase. Other variations are lowercase.
- In all references, be guided by the preference of those concerned.
- Use **Indian** with discretion. Some people object to it because it originated with Columbus' misconception that they had landed in India. Others, especially status Indians, prefer it to be used.
- Use **native** advisedly. **Aboriginal** is more specific and is preferred by many.
- **Tribe** originally was reserved for primitive peoples. Some natives use it casually and it need not be entirely avoided. However, community, people, nation, band, language group are alternatives.

Disabilities

Disabilities are only one part of a person's humanity. Avoid such unqualified terms as disabled, crippled or people 'afflicted with' or 'suffering from'. Be specific. Afflicted with or suffering from imply that people's conditions are always painful, permanent, unavoidable. For example, many people in wheelchairs are not 'confined' to the chair. Their condition may, or may not, be permanent. People with life-threatening illness should not be 'suffering' physical pain if they are getting good palliative care. For example, 40% of people with cancer do not have physical pain associated with their condition at all.

Victim connotes helplessness. A child who is has a **developmental disability** (slow learner) is not necessarily **mentally disturbed** (ill). People with **epilepsy** have **seizures**, not **fits**. Avoid defining people by their disabilities: **the disabled, the blind, the dying**. Writing or saying **people with disabilities** emphasizes the people first and not their disabilities.

Names of Races

Capitalize the proper names of nationalities, peoples, races and tribes. For example, **Aboriginal Peoples, Arab, Jamaican, Jew, Polish, Latin American**.

Remember that **black, mulatto, red, white** and **yellow** do not name races and are lowercase.

The term **black** is acceptable in all references in Canada and the United States. In the U.S., **African-American** is increasingly in use. In Bermuda, **colored** is correct usage for both black and mulatto. In South Africa, the **Cape Colored** are regarded as an ethnic group of mixed blood, and the term is capitalized. In the U.S. there is a National Association for the Advancement of Colored People, usually identified as the NAACP.

Body Language

Verbal and written language, as we have described, are very powerful. Body language begins to speak to people before you begin to talk. Your body language is either comforting, intimidating or uncertain. People's cultures and personal backgrounds will 'screen' your body language and make conclusions that may, or may not, be correct. This is just as true for you as for the people you care for.

Some examples:

- In Europe, men most often cross their legs at the knee. In North America, men tend to put the ankle of one leg over the knee of the other. This is often misinterpreted by Europeans as aggressive body language.
- In many parts of Europe, people use a knife and fork throughout their meal. In North America, the trend is often to cut one's meal, put the knife down (usually held in right hand) and switch their fork over to their right hand to eat. American and Canadian spies during World War II were often spotted because of their table manners rather than their accents.
- Distance between people is often very cultural. For example, Spanish-speaking people are often quite comfortable with close physical contact between themselves and others. People of British backgrounds tend to prefer people at more than arm's length away. Japanese people would be very uncomfortable with the

physical touch so common in daily North American business contacts.

- As a general rule: keep slightly more than arm's length away from others until you get to know their preferences. This is a safe distance both culturally and between men and women generally (the fear of violence against women is real in North America and must be understood as well).
- Ask permission to touch someone in a gesture of comfort and understanding. One can do this verbally or one can place a hand near the person as an invitation to them to reach out and touch you.
- When someone is sitting or lying down, it is best to be at eye level with them. Therefore, try to sit down next to them. Women tend to be comfortable with another woman directly opposite to them, while men often prefer to sit side-by-side. Kitty corner may be the best compromise so that people have some open space between you and them to avoid direct eye contact when they need to look away.
- Many people carry pens, notes books and other objects in their hands. They are necessary some of the time, but for the rest, put them down. Keep your hands free from fidgeting so that your attention can remain with the person.

Demographic Information

The following statistics are a national snapshot. They may not reflect the reality of people in your program, service and community.

Faiths

The predominant faith in Canada continues to be Christian (1991 statistics). Since 1971 there have been more Catholics than Protestants. Between 1981-1991 there has been a 144% increase in Eastern non-Christian religions. Before 1971, less than 1% of Canadians reported having no religious affiliation. This went up to 12.5% in 1991. Almost one-third of British Columbians reported no religion while less than 2% of Newfoundlanders reported no religion.

Religion	Canadian #	Percentage
Roman Catholic	12,335,255	45.7%
Protestant	9,780,710	36.2%
Eastern Orthodox	387,395	1.4%
Jewish	318,070	1.2%
Eastern non-Christian:	747,455	2.8%

Buddhist	163,415	
Hindu	157,015	
Islam	253,260	
Sikh	147,440	
No reported religion	3,386,365	12.5%

Language (1991 most recent statistics):

Language	Canadian #
English alone	16,516,180
French alone	6,505,565
Aboriginal alone	169,615
Languages other than English, French or Aboriginal	3,384,255

Culture (1991 most recent statistics):

Heritage	Canadian #	Percentage
Reporting Aboriginal Origin	1,002,670	3.7%
Reporting British alone or with some other origin	12,047,920	44.6%
Reporting French alone or with some other origin	8,389,180	31.1%
Reporting neither English or French Origin	8,336,160	30.9%
Reporting single Asian origin	1,607,230	6%
Reporting single African origin	26,430 .	1%
Reporting single Latin, Central or South American origin	85,535 .	3%
Reporting single Caribbean origin	94,395	.4%
Reporting other single origin	1,011,870	3.7%

Urban versus Rural Living (1991): There has been a consistent number of urban Canadians over the past 25 years. Provinces east of Ontario have become more rural while west of Ontario, there has been an increased urban population. Ontario has remained constant at over 80% urban.

Where Canadians Live	Canadian #	Percentage
Urban	20,907,957	76.6%
Rural	6,388,902	23.4%

Designing a Cultural, Racial and Religious Self-Study Guide: A Practical Tool

The underlying assumption of this work is that trends within societies and peoples do exist but that individuals should not be forced to fit within those trends. We must examine a person's unique story within the context of common and distinct personal experiences, ask questions and enhance our own knowledge and skills to meet the physical, emotional, spiritual and information needs of people receiving care. We must be aware of time constraints in our practice and who else might better meet the specific needs of the individual and their family.

We often hear, "Do not stereotype people" as if this were possible. It is not possible. In order to deal with the magnitude of information we hear/see/feel everyday, we automatically categorize information and 'stereotype' others to make sense of this information overload. The suggestion would be more usefully put as, "Find out if your stereotype is correct." Stereotypes, which constantly change in us as we learn more about others and more about ourselves, are excellent starting points to discover which parts of our assumptions about people are correct.

> *For example, in Europe, Dutch people have a reputation for being very careful with their money and not spending it quickly. Although this is a trend within the Dutch culture it is often not apparent to Canadian visitors who continue to be treated royally as liberators of Holland during World War II. A Canadian may not understand this trend to 'stinginess' while other Europeans make regular jokes about it. Which view is correct? It depends on the individual Dutch person, how long they have lived in Canada, when they immigrated, etc.*
> *Harry van Bommel*

It is necessary for professional and volunteer caregivers to try and understand the racial, cultural and religious needs of their clients. The more one works with a specific population (regardless of race, religion or culture) the more one must understand that population. Included in this understanding are the typical kinds of illnesses people of specific populations get. For example, Francophones in Canada are more likely to suffer from smoking-related illnesses, therefore, caregivers must learn as much as possible about those illnesses and trends by Francophones in coping with such illnesses.

Some of the questions we will try to answer include:

- What specific behaviors demonstrate cultural, racial and religious respect for the people receiving service?

- What specific behaviors must be avoided so as not to show disrespect?
- How is illness, aging, dying, death and grieving generally seen within this person's community?
- Is illness, aging, dying, death and grieving easily discussed within this person's community?
- What areas of conversation are supportive to the person?
- What areas of conversation would feel threatening or uncomfortable for the person (for example, truth telling about a prognosis)?
- How are decisions made by this person and within their family? Who in the family is the person's 'spokesperson', both for when the person is able to speak for themselves and for when the person cannot speak for themselves?
- Are children included in the day-to-day events happening to the person and how are they included in discussions about dying, death and grieving (if at all)?
- Is Western medicine seen as helpful or harmful to the person? What alternative healing practices are seen as helpful? In their experience, are there negative side effects to mixing Western medicine with treatments of personal choice? Are hospitals or other health care facilities seen as helpful or harmful?
- Is pain and suffering viewed as something one should experience fully, partially or not at all?
- What dietary practices should we know about to help the person be as comfortable as possible?
- How are the person's cultural, racial and/or religious beliefs uniquely practiced? How can we be supportive of those beliefs within the confines of our own fundamental beliefs?
- What does the person 'expect' will happen? Is that accurate to the best of your knowledge?
- Who can help us understand this person's life story better? (So often a person or their family is asked to explain the most basic elements of their beliefs to well meaning strangers. How can you minimize intruding into their time together? How can you help other caregivers learn more about the person and family indirectly so as not to bother them even more?)
- How long has this person lived in Canada (e.g., born here, 2nd generation, recent immigrant)?
- Does the person live in a identifiable community (little Italy, Chinatown, Rosedale) which may contribute to how they are dealing with their illness?
- Aside from multicultural issues, we must not forget how other factors influence their decision-making, their communication style, their behavior and their needs.

For example, how does their gender, age, career, education, and economic standing affect them? How does their family dynamics (size, grief history, geographic location) affect them?

Exercise #1

Look at your own background first and answer the questions above as clearly as you can. Show your answers to others you work with to see if they understand your background better through your replies.

Exercise #2

Identify someone from a different race, culture or religion and ask them to answer the questions above. Do their answers help you understand them better? Compare your answers from Exercise #1 with their answers and ask each other questions about areas that are unclear. It is through specific conversations with people of diverse backgrounds that we learn both the specifics of the individual and some generalities about people with similar backgrounds. For example, all Christians have certain beliefs in common while each individual Christian has beliefs specific to them which may, or may not, be part of the religion's theology.

Collect similar information for any major group that is different from your own background. Write out specific information that will help you work with members of that group or clients from that group. Constantly update your information so that you are being as accurate as possible. **Remember, there are trends within identifiable groups of people but each individual is different. Find out as much as you can in any given situation and help others to do the same with you so they better understand your background. This is a mutual endeavor.**

Some Cases

A Chicago Children's Aid worker removes a Vietnamese 4-year old child with scratches, bruises and angry red inflammation of the skin. The boy's father commits suicide out of shame and confusion before a caseworker, familiar with Vietnamese culture, could explain the traditional home treatment of 'scratching out the wind'. In this treatment, Vietnamese people believe that painting alcohol or oil on the skin brings the illness to the surface where it is scraped off, often with a porcelain spoon.

A common practice amongst many European and Asian families is to crowd into a patient's room during visiting hours even though this is against hospital rules. Culturally, the family is very important to the well being of the patient and the greater the number, the greater the respect shown the patient. They may also believe that a patient should remain immobile (e.g., a mother after birth in Mexico is not to get out of bed or must be carried for days after the birth).

In Chinese families where a baby has been born, they may refuse to bathe the child in 'raw' water but come to a hospital with many thermoses of boiled or 'cooked' water. In general, many Chinese people also believe in a balancing of hot and cold (ying and yang) so they may accept only hot water when other patients are routinely given only ice water.

Hindu women can often be seen with a dot on their foreheads. Often assumed to have religious significance, this dot ('Bindi') is actually an ornamentation; a fashion thing. Originally married women in villages were the only ones who wore them, but in Canada women will wear different colored Bindi just as other women wear different coloured lip stick. Non-Hindu people have been making assumptions about these 'dots' and their significance for years without realizing their ornamental use.

Kosher meat in the Jewish tradition is called "halal" meat in the Muslim faith. Their dietary rules are quite similar. Meat (excluding pork for Jews and cow for Hindu and Sikh) must be drained slowly of all blood and blessed by a spiritual leader before it can be eaten. Jains eat no meat at all. How does a lack of this information affect one's care of Jewish, Muslim, Hindu, Sikh and Jain clients?

A Quiz

The following modified quiz is based on the complete quiz in Pamela Brink's book *Transcultural nursing: A book of readings* (p. xi-xvi). The purpose is to help you become aware of any misconceptions involved in multicultural health care issues. Place a check mark beside the answer you think is most correct.

1. Cardiovascular diseases and malignant neoplasms are the two leading causes of death for:
   (a) everyone (b) whites
   (c) Asians (d) Hispanics
2. Pallor in the dark-skinned individuals is observable by the absence of the underlying ___________ tones that normally give the brown or black skin its 'glow' or 'living color'.
   (a) blue (b) white
   (c) red (d) gray
3. Faith healing is practiced in which church?
   (a) Church of Christ Scientist
   (b) Seventh Day Adventist

(c) Eastern Orthodox
(d) Church of Jesus Christ of Latter-Day Saints
(e) None of the above
(f) All of the above (depending on specific groups).

6. Which statement is true?
   (a) Yang represents the female, negative force.
   (b) Yang represents the female, positive force.
   (c) Ying represents the female, negative force.
   (d) Ying represents the female, positive force.
7. Western-based culture, as opposed to most other cultures,
   (e) does not distinguish between physical and mental illness.
   (f) treats the whole person rather than concentrating only on the system involved.
   (g) places the client's difficulties in the light of spiritual and religious values.
   (h) distinguishes rather sharply between physical and mental illness.
8. Friendly inquisitiveness is considered ____ by traditional Native North Americans.
   (a) necessary
   (b) nosiness
   (c) helpful
   (d) good manners.

Answers 1 (a) 2 (c) 3 (f) 4(c) 5(d) 6(b)

Cultures

The underlying assumption of this work is that trends within societies and peoples do exist but that individuals should not be forced to fit within those trends. We must examine a person's unique story within the context of common and distinct personal experiences and ask questions and enhance our own knowledge and skills to meet the physical, emotional, spiritual and information needs of people receiving care.

Some general points for discussion first:

Cultural Differences

People the world over have a different sense of the proper use of space and time. People of some cultures like to be physically close to others while others prefer a more comfortable distance apart. People of some cultures or geographic locations (e.g., southern U.S. versus New York State) have a different sense of time and the urgency of punctuality. They also choose to eat supper at different times (e.g., New Yorkers and Mexicans eat later in the evenings while Southerners often eat earlier to have more evening time with family and friends.)

People have a different sense of priorities. People of some cultures or within some families, put family values ahead of work values, income values or accumulation of assets.

People have gender differences. These relate specifically to what is labeled one's feminine and masculine sides. Men may have more feminine characteristics just as women may have more masculine characteristics but typical trends divide along gender lines.

People from around the world have different traditional dress, food and beverage preferences. Certainly multicultural events tend to highlight the uniqueness of each culture in these areas.

We have different expectations of behavior.

> *In Costa Rica in the mid 1970s, I found that people, out of respect, would give me directions to a place I was trying to find, even if they did not know the correct directions. They could not say, "I'm sorry. I don't know where that is." So they made up elaborate directions. This was frustrating at first until I realized they were trying to be helpful and to save face.*
> *Harry van Bommel*

Barriers to Cross-Cultural Communication

Language and non-verbal communication barriers are common. For example, many European men cross their legs at the knees while many North American men cross their legs with one ankle resting on the opposite knee. This North American body language is consciously or unconsciously seen as aggressive in Europe while North Americans often misinterpret the European preference as weak.

Stereotyping is a barrier when no effort has been made to identify the accuracy of your stereotype. Some people from a particular culture do fit the stereotype while many others have a part of that stereotype in their character.

> *Dutch people have a stereotype of being 'cheap' (*Dutch treat*). The stereotype, in fact, does fit many Dutch people in some circumstances while in others, Dutch people are seen as highly sociable and generous hosts. It depends on the situation but the stereotype has legitimacy and can be used as a starting point to find out about a particular person.*
> *Harry van Bommel*

Different value systems arise from one's cultural background, education level, family and environment. Some values are mutually exclusive (e.g., one believes war is justifiable while another believes it is never justifiable). One must determine if the difference in values will prevent one from helping someone who is ill or dying.

Overcoming Barriers

One must identify those perceptions that are correct from those that are incorrect. Then one must determine if one's differences with someone else make it impossible to work together (rare) or not. The way someone eats or what they eat should not usually prevent one from helping that person.

Language Barriers

If people speak completely different languages, it is hard to communicate. There are hand gestures and facial expressions to help understand where someone is experiencing pain but it becomes much harder to help with their other physical, emotional, spiritual and information needs without adequate translation. Translation, even in diverse cultural communities is difficult because the vocabulary of medicine and health are often not well understood by translators. Finding a suitable translator can be difficult. Family members may translate only that thing that they agree with and will not translate what you think is important. For example, in cases where one is trying to explain a terminal illness, if the family member does not want their loved one to hear the news, they will not translate the information correctly.

In situations where there is no one to translate, it is perhaps, only possible to attend to the physical needs and use one's body language of empathy, love and spirituality to convey the best support one can. It may not be enough but it is more than would otherwise occur.

Practical help: if you are working with people from a particular culture quite often, it is important to learn a few key phrases to offer support and ask the right questions. Have a pad with a few important phrases written out in the different languages you encounter so that a person can point to those phrases they want to communicate to you.

If you do not know what language a person is speaking, create another pad of paper with the sentence "Hello, my name is ________, and I speak __________." If the person is literate they can point to the sentence of their language. Underneath will be the name of that language in English.

Speak slowly at a normal volume. Ask the person to repeat their name as often as necessary until you can say it properly. Write it out phonetically so you can remember it the next time.

> *I find that mindset and way of thinking are most crucial. One must celebrate diversity of all kinds and seek uniqueness of people and cultures, rather than emphasizing difference. For example, "what makes this person unique", rather than, "how are they different". Where significant language barriers exist, I find that kindness and respect, as conveyed by demeanor, tone and facial expression are universally understood as caring.*
> *Elizabeth Latimer*

Phonetics

In writing down foreign words phonetically, the biggest challenge is getting the vowel sounds correctly. Consonants can be spelled out fairly clearly. For example, **clear** would be written as **kl-ear**. Here are a few tips to help from the *Oxford paperback dictionary*:

a *as in* hat
ah *as in* palm
air *as in* chair
ay *as in* hay

e *as in* bed
ee *as in* beet
ear *as in* beer
er *as in* her
ew *as in* dew

i *as in* tin

I *as in* cry
I *as in* eye
o *as in* stop
on *as in* lemon
oh *as in* most
oi *as in* join
oo *as in* spoon

oor *as in* poor
or *as in* horn
ow *as in* wow

u *as in* cup
us *as in* circus
uu *as in* look
y *as in* yes

Religious Beliefs & Rituals

The Similarities We Share

In 1993 the World Parliament of Religions held its second Parliament to look at the similarities and differences between world religions and faiths. This parliament is held every 100 years. At the 1993 Parliament, a global world ethic was presented in draft form and signed by 141 leading figures from all the world's ancient religions.

This document was based on the common elements within all world religions, namely, that all people be treated humanely and equally. It further described all humans committing to: (a) a culture of non-violence and respect for life, (b) a culture of solidarity and just economic order and (c) a culture of tolerance and a life of truthfulness with equal rights and partnership between men and women. It noted that what was taught in all ancient religions was often not practiced and, therefore, there is often global confusion about what someone of another faith is directed to believe and practice.

Religious Beliefs

Another way to learn more about each other's religious beliefs is to begin with some basics. The following gives a brief sketch of some of the major faiths represented in Canada. They are a starting point for discussion. Ask someone of a particular faith to tell you how accurate the summary is.

Buddhism

The word Buddha means 'one who has woken up'. The purpose of one's faith is to take advantage of being born as a human being, by developing energetically the qualities of kindness and awareness in order to achieve freedom from suffering, and to help others to do the same.

Christianity

The Crucifix is a symbol used to represent life, death and resurrection. There are many denominations within the Catholic and Protestant faiths but a belief in Jesus Christ as the Son of God is common to all. One's purpose is to live according to the loving nature of God as revealed through Christ's life and death helped by the Holy Spirit and through prayer. Christianity is the second Abrahamic faith.

Hinduism

OM expresses the complete nature of God. "Hindu" is originally a Persian word for Indian. It has no founder nor is there a specific prophet but is a complex religious tradition. Buddhism, Jainism and Sikhism arose within the Hindu tradition. One's faith helps them to learn how to be reunited with God and to learn this through study, devotion, prayer and service to others.

Islam

Islam is an Arabic word meaning 'submission' (to God). It prescribes patterns of right and wrong ways of behaving in business, dress, etiquette, family life, and food. It is over 1400 years old. There are 72 sects including major ones of Sunnis and Shi'ites. The Ismaelis sect began in the 9th century and is led by the Aga Khan. The Islamic crescent symbolizes the new moon that determines the Islamic calendar. One's purpose is to submit life to the will of Allah as revealed by the prophet Muhammad through the Qur'an and to do so through a declaration of faith, regular prayer, almsgiving, fasting and pilgrimage. Islam is the third Abrahamic faith.

Judaism

With roots back some 4,000 years, Jews are generally affiliated to an Orthodox, Conservative, Reconstructionist, Reform or Liberal synagogue. Their faith is based on the Torah to help Jews live according to God's laws as revealed by Moses. The most important law is to believe in one God and to learn to love God through study, through prayer and by celebrating the yearly cycle of holy days. Judaism is the first Abrahamic faith.

Religious Holidays

The following holy days will mean very little to you unless you ask people in your community, your colleagues and your clients about what they mean. It is most logical to begin to talk to those people you have the most contact with to understand their religious holy days. You may want to get a calendar with the following holy days specific to this year's dates.

The dates are in general order from January to December. Most change dates every year. Look for multicultural or multi-religious calendars each year for accuracy. See the Resource list for examples. Capitalized days are the holiest and work may be abstained.

Bahá'í
(All holy days begin at previous sundown before the indicated date)
Intercalary Days
Ala
Na Ruz - New Year
RIDVAN
Declaration of the Bab
ASCENSION OF BAHA'U'LLAH
Martyrdom of the Bab
Birth of the Bab
Birth of the Baha'u'llah
Day of the Covenant
Ascension of Abdu'l-Baha

Buddhism
CHINESE/VIETNAMESE NEW YEAR (1997 = 4692)
SONGRAN (NEW YEAR) - Asia
WESAK
Wassa
Dhamma Day
Pavarana
Kathina

Christian (Georgian=Western)
Epiphany
Ash Wednesday
Palm Sunday
Holy Thursday
GOOD FRIDAY
EASTER
Ascension
Pentecost
Assumption
Advent begins
CHRISTMAS

Christian (Julian = Eastern)
ARMENIAN CHRISTMAS
CHRISTMAS
Theophany
Lent
Palm Sunday
Holy Thursday
HOLY FRIDAY
EASTER
Ascension
Pentecost
Assumption - Armenian
Assumption

Hinduism
Lohri
Basant Panchami
Shivratri
Holi
BAISAIKHI
Ram Navami
Raksha Bandhan
JANMASHTAMI
Ganesh Chaturthi
Navratri
Durga Puja

Dussehra
DIWALI

Islam
(Holy days are subject to sighting of the moon)
First of Ramadan
EID-UL-FITR
Day of Hajj
EID-UL-ADHA
First of Muharram
Ashura
Eid-Maulad-un-Nabi
First of Ramadan

Jainism
MAHAVIRA JAYANTI
Akshaya-tritiya
PARYUSHANA-PARVA
Dashalakshani-parva
Samvatsari
Ananta-chaturdasi
Ksamavani
Mahavira Nirvana
Lokashah Jayanti

Judaism
(All holy days begin at previous sundown before the indicated date)
(*Some Jews may abstain from work)
Purim
Pesach*
Shavuoth*
ROSH HASHANAH*
YOM KIPPUR*
Sukkot*
Shemini Atzeret*
Simchat Torah*
Hanukkah

Sikhism
Birthday of Guru Gobind Singh
Hola Mohalla
BAISAIKHI
Martyrdom of Guru Arjan Dev
Parkash
DIWALI
BIRTHDAY OF GURU NANAK
Martyrdom of Guru Tegh Bahadur

Zorastrianism
Fravardeghan Days
Gahambar Hamaspathmaedem
NAW RUZ - NEW YEAR (Fasli)
Birthday of Prophet Zarathustra
Gahambar Maidyozarem
Gahambar Maidyoshem
NAW RUZ - NEW YEAR (Shenshai)
Gahambar Paitishem
Gahambar Ayathrem]
DEATH OF PROPHET ZARATHUSTRA
Gahambar Maidyarem

Ethical Questions

1. When should health care providers insist on Western treatments (if ever) over

someone's alternative treatments?

2. What are the ethical issues inherent in imposing North American medical values and practices on people who have different beliefs?
3. How does one deal with a patient/family's fundamental beliefs when they conflict with one's own beliefs? For example, if one believes strongly that euthanasia is wrong and immoral, what does one do when asked to help a patient to commit suicide?

Summary

The more you work within a specific community, the greater the importance that you understand their customs, language, beliefs and common experiences.

As long as you work with others, it is important to follow the advice of Georges Vanier: The more you know people, the better you will understand them and the more you will like them.

Help people to relax by being relaxed yourself. A few moments of informal conversation or a body language that projects respect and understanding of the person's dying process can often reduce stress and build rapport.

Determine what language a person speaks using the "Hello, my name is .." form described earlier.

Do not criticize people for speaking their own language amongst themselves. They need to be comfortable in their communications whenever possible.

Prescribe meals containing foods common to the person's diet whenever possible. Encourage family and friends to bring food which may help the patient feel more in control of their environment and their health.

Allow family members to visit as often as possible with a specific cultural norm. Encourage one or two family members to act as a spokesperson so that you can provide consistent and necessary information to the family.

Avoid commenting on a person's culture, religion or beliefs with colleagues in hallways, elevators, etc. These comments are often overheard and reflect badly on you and your colleagues.

Take advantage of opportunities to learn about people from other cultures, especially those cultures that have a high ratio in your catchment area. Accept invitations to social events that highlight the important rituals of a culture. Attend alternative theatre and films to see how a culture is represented by members of that culture.

Learn a few key phrases of different groups with whom you work. Often the effort is more important than the actual phrase or pronunciation.

Ask permission before you do things. Explain anything that may be new to the person or their family before you do it so they can tell you if it will be perceived as helpful and respectful.

Follow the customs of the home. If people do not wear their shoes in the house, bring slippers to wear. If people do not smoke, follow that lead. Never use profanity or criticize a person's home or their belongings (especially with your body language).

Recap important information in different ways to try and ensure that people have understood you. Write out specific information for them, or someone else, to read.

Resources

The following resources are only a few of the many useful resources that you can find in your local libraries, within your own organization, and in your local bookstores. Look for other books but also for journal articles, magazine reports, films, videos and audiocassettes. Also keep in mind how much you can learn from experts in the field, including people within your own organization!

Brink, P. J. (1976). *Transcultural nursing: A book of readings.* Englewood, NJ: Prentice-Hall.

Buckley, P. (Ed). (1995). *Canadian Press stylebook: A guide for writers and editors.* Toronto: The Canadian Press.

Fynn. (1974). *Mister God, this is Anna.* London: William Collins.

Lind Infeld, D.; Gordon, A. K., & Harper, B. C. (Eds). (1995). *Hospice care and cultural diversity.* New York: Haworth Press.

The Oxford paperback dictionary (1994). Oxford, England: Oxford University Press.

Saint Elizabeth Visiting Nurses' Association of Ontario. (1988). *Caring across cultures: Multicultural considerations in palliative care.* Toronto: Self-Published.

The Vanier Institute of the Family. (1996). *Canada's families: They count.* Nepean, Ontario: Self-Published.

For a yearly Multicultural Calendar of holy days within 10 religious groups in Canada, contact Sheena Singh at Creative Cultural Communications, (416) 203-3595. For a catalogue of wall posters of religious and folk festival days, contact The Festival Shop in England at 0121 444 0444.

4. Communication

Listening and Speaking

Assertiveness

Telephone Skills

Presentation and Public Speaking

Letters and Memos and Reports

Listening and Speaking

The word communication comes from the root word "common". Communication, then, means using a common language that is easily understood by your audience.

We spend about 70% of our wakening hours communicating through speaking, listening, watching and reading. Yet many people still say that they are too busy to learn to be an effective communicator. They say they are too busy keeping up with their work, family and social life to take courses in speaking, writing and other forms of communication.

If we spend about 70% of our time communicating should not we learn how to do it effectively so that our communication time is not wasted?

It has been said that we typically hear or read only about 20% of the information communicated to us and that we forget about 80% of that within 24 hours. That means that we must communicate clearly, briefly and repeat important information often or else most people will only get about 4% of the information we want them to have. Surely we must learn to help people remember and use more than that 4%.

Definition: For the purpose of this material we will concentrate on **speaking and listening**, mostly in one-to-one conversations. Written communication and public speaking are covered in other sections.

Speaking clearly is critical to the effectiveness of all of us. For example, if someone else needs to follow your spoken instructions but they do not clearly understand what you have asked them to do, you have wasted your time. Speaking clearly also helps you develop a rapport with other people. What you SAY is as important as what you DO NOT SAY. Imagine all the costly errors made because verbal communications were unclear.

People like to know where they stand with you. Therefore, a clear communication style is the foundation for good working relationships whether with your boss, co-workers, your family and your friends and in healthcare, with patients and families.

To give you an example of not using a common language read the following paragraph. This paragraph is a "modern" version of another text. See if you can interpret what is said. Does this look like any memo or letter you have read lately?

It is imperative in the post-modern, multi-cultural society of the late twentieth century to comprehend fully, and in great detail, the nature of the human species in varying multi-level situations. It is through an interdisciplinary approach to the psychosocial aspirations, ambitions and resultant behaviors that we develop a clear understanding of their individualistic psyche, and thereby, fully integrate with them in a harmonious, resonant lifestyle.

Would you believe that it actually means:

The better you know people, the more you will understand them, and the more you will like them.
Georges P. Vanier

Using common language is not speaking down to people. Winston Churchill told us to use short, old words to speak best. If communication is all about understanding each other then we should not have to have a dictionary with us when we talk to people. The foundation of effective, speaking and listening includes:

- Meeting the needs of the other people.
- Understanding the similarities and differences between you.
- Interpreting their body language and finding out if your interpretation is right.
- Speaking in a clear, common language.

Remember: you have been speaking for all but a few early years in your life. This material is designed to help improve your communication skills and build on your strengths. This material is not designed to force you to completely change how you speak with others. The techniques are presented to you so that you can choose those techniques or ideas that work best for you.

Exercise #1
How Do You Communicate Now?

Each speaking situation includes several factors. We are all more comfortable speaking in some situations than in others. This will depend on how these factors present themselves in a given situation. Each situation includes some of these factors:

People How many there are, who has informal or formal power, do you like them, do you need to talk to them or do they need to talk to you?

Content What are you talking about? Is it personal, professional, instructional, anxiety provoking, discipline, complimentary, serious, light-hearted, formal or informal?

Setting Where are you speaking? Are you alone with the person or in a crowd? Is it in your home, at work or during a recreational activity?

Role Do you play the role of listener, advisor, parent, child, leader, follower, boss, staff, friend or interested stranger?

Now that you understand some of the factors involved when you speak with someone, answer the following questions to help you decide what your communication strengths are right now, and how you might like to communicate differently in the future?

1. Under which circumstances are you most comfortable speaking now? Why? For example, speaking with friends about personal issues, talking about sports or weather, speaking with colleagues about your work, discussing politics with your family, counseling patients, giving information, etc.
2. Under which circumstances are you least comfortable? Why?
3. Based on your first two answers, what are your strengths as a communicator? For example, are you best at giving instructions, talking about your family, listening to people's problems, giving people advice, talking to clients, discussing work with your boss?
4. What areas of communication would you like to improve most as you go through this section: speaking, the tone in your voice, listening skills, summarizing what other people say, presenting information, etc.?

Basic Communication

The central principle of good communication is to act in the best interest of the person with whom you are talking. That is, try to put yourself in the other person's shoes. Imagine how they are feeling, what information they most need from you, and what is the best way to communicate with that particular person.

When you do communicate, keep some of the following goals in mind. The relationship you have with a person will determine how many of these rules apply in each situation. Try:

- To reduce uncertainty
- To help the person speak for themselves
- To improve relationships
- To be truthful
- To limit your answers to questions rather than giving people too much information

When you achieve your communication goals you can expect some of the following results for **both** you and the person you are communicating with:

- Less time spent communicating because you are a more effective communicator
- Better comprehension of both the content and the other person's point of view
- Less stress
- Mutual support
- Less fear and anxiety
- Greater productivity
- More control

Remember that communication means speaking in a common language This will help you to choose your words carefully, to try and meet the needs of the person you are talking with, and to make your own points clearly, concisely and effectively. In clinical situations, health professionals must meet the additional challenge of choosing words that are readily understood by patients and families.

Basic Rules

We are always communicating. We **cannot** not communicate. Our body language, facial expressions, and tone of voice all communicate without a word being said. When we enter a room, people begin to make assumptions about who we are, what we think, how we will behave and what we will say. Body language is a powerful communication tool. People will believe what you say only if your body language says the same thing. For example, people will not believe you if you tell them how much you enjoy their company but your eyes are staring at the ceiling, your tone of voice is neutral and you have a bored expression on your face. Physicians who look busy and rushed will dissuade patients from sharing fears and asking questions, even though they do not intend to do so.

You may exchange words with someone without exchanging meaning. What you intend to say may not be what someone else hears. Therefore, it is **your** responsibility to make sure that the other person understood your intended meaning. If it is a very important point, ask them to repeat what you said in their own words. You can do the same to make sure you understand what someone has said to you. This is very important when communicating with patients and families.

With Whom Are You Communicating?

The most important part of communicating is knowing with whom you are talking. This does not mean that you should change what you say for every different person. It does mean that you must understand the similarities and differences of the various people with whom you talk. For example, people with different cultural backgrounds, education histories, or communication abilities than yours will require different communication techniques.

> *Doctors and all team members must learn to use "regular language" that the patient can understand. Obvious medical words like "hepatosplenomegaly" must be reduced to "large liver and spleen". However, we must also be aware of less obvious language issues. For example, we say, " your test results are negative" to report a good thing–the absence of pathology. However, negative means not good in our general language and can be misunderstood by lay people. I find it helpful to sometimes "step outside of myself" to see how my general language might sound to other people, particularly those who are stressed and ill.*
> *Elizabeth Latimer*

You cannot always find out about the similarities and differences of all the people with whom you talk. Therefore, you must recognize signs that your message is not getting across as you would like. (See *"Body Language"* section for tips.) Once you know there is a communication problem you can ask yourself some of the following questions to help you identify what the specific problem may be.

- Do they already know something about the topic you are discussing? If people already know, or think they know, a lot about what you are saying they may get bored by the repetition and not listen to what you are saying.
- Are they familiar with the jargon (words used in a specific profession) you are using?
- Does their education help or hurt them in understanding what you are saying. For example, if you are speaking to someone who has many years of university education are they comfortable understanding non-academic speech? The reverse is also important. If you have had many years of education, can you speak a common language without sounding like you are talking down to people?
- Is the age difference between you causing a communication problem? People of different ages sometimes have different assumptions about what is, and is not, important and appropriate to talk about.
- Are cultural differences causing miscommunication? Again, people with different backgrounds may have different assumptions about what is, and is not, important and appropriate to discuss. They may also have different ways of saying the same things but may not understand each other's methods. What sounds like

a joke to one person may sound like an insult to another. One person's tone of voice may sound normal to people of the same background but sound passive, condescending, arrogant or argumentative to someone of another background.

- Are there socioeconomic differences between the communicators? People from different economic backgrounds may have assumptions about each other that may, or may not, be right. You must find out if these assumptions are helping or hurting your communication together.
- Does the other person have different values? For example, do they believe that a particular political party or religion is better than someone else's? Do their views on capital punishment, gender differences, nationalism, etc., help or hurt communication with other people?

Body Language: Is Your Body Saying the Same Thing as Your Words?

Body language is simply how other people interpret your posture, hand movements, head tilt, and other body movements. For example, if you tell people that you are enjoying your conversation with them very much, but you are slouching, staring into space and playing with a pen in your hand, they may interpret that your body language is not saying the same thing as your words. They may doubt your sincerity.

Body language is not a science. You cannot read a book and assume that you can understand everyone's body language. There are personal and cultural differences that must be understood. For example, a person standing with their arms crossed in front of them may appear authoritarian or arrogant when they really are only cold and crossing their arms to help keep themselves warm. In North America we often show our children's height by raising our flat hand to about the same height as our child. In some Latin American countries showing a child's height this way is offensive and rude. They raise their hands to the same height but the palm is not flat (as North Americans do) but pointing forward.

Although no single book can teach you all about body language, you can work at learning some of the basics. Watch people in shopping malls, on television shows, in foreign films and watch the similarities they have in expressing joy, anger, anxiety, happiness. Their facial features will be quite similar. Then look for differences in how men and women move their bodies, their hand gestures, and how they sit. Watch how people from different cultural, economic and educational backgrounds move, stand or sit. Watch the similarities and differences between children; children with adults;

and adult children with their senior parents. Go to your local library and pick up a few books on body language (also called nonverbal communication) to look at pictures and diagrams of similarities and differences in body language.

The key to understanding body language is to watch other people, decide what you think their body language is telling you and find out if you are right. You may often be right but you will also be wrong sometimes. Do not make assumptions about people until you know if your assumptions are right.

Body Language

According to Ray L. Birdwhistell, when we communicate with another person 35% of the communication comes from the words and 65% comes from how we speak (e.g., pitch, tone, voice quality), movements, gestures and how we handle space between us.

Mixed Messages

If we only watched people's body language to understand what they were trying to tell us (no talking) we might get some very mixed messages. For example, they may slouch in a chair while showing lots of dynamic hand movements. We might interpret the first position (slouching) as showing little interest in the conversation. The hand movements might show great interest. What in fact might be happening is that this person likes to slouch for comfort and their dynamic hand movements are how they almost always speak. Again, the key here is to find out if what you think their body language is saying to you is right.

> *If I had a nickel for every time someone has interpreted my body language incorrectly, I would be a rich woman. Consider this. My spinal injuries make sitting and moving my head difficult. In lectures and at conferences I usually try to sit at the back of the room so I can see everyone and keep my spine straight at the same time. This is often interpreted as my lack of willingness to participate. Some presenters ask me to sit near the front and when I say "no thank you", this is seen as my resistance rather than my not wanting to explain my disability to everyone. I have had to explain my circumstances to the teacher at the break if they are struggling with my body language. I have even had teachers think that I am disagreeing with them when I am having a bad pain day and my face is showing the strain. Body language is a language but we do not speak with the same tongue.*
> *Michèle Chaban*

We have looked at the importance of understanding people's body language, finding out if our assumptions are correct and understanding that people may give unintentional mixed messages through their body language.

Now, let us look at some general body language positions and gestures from which we can suggest some possible messages being given. The more you understand different types of body language the more you will rely on more than one position or gesture to understand the person. **To truly use body language effectively you must be able to combine many parts of body language to help you confirm your assumptions.**

Note: We are not saying which body language is preferable. We are giving some general guidelines as to what is considered appropriate or inappropriate body language as seen by a majority of people. The first two sections look at the emotions of nervousness and paying attention while the following ones look at some specific gestures.

Nervousness

- Little or no eye contact
- Tugging at their clothes
- Sweaty palms, forehead and around lips
- Repetitive gestures such as: tapping their foot, hands in pocket jingling coins noisily, playing with their hair, drumming their fingers in rhythm on a table, their lap or on a book, playing with a pen, paper clip, scrap paper in their hands.

Caution: Some of the body language listed above can mean other things as well. Tugging at clothes, tapping one's foot, playing with their hair can also mean they are bored. Little or no eye contact can also be a cultural preference of the person who may consider it rude to look directly at a person of authority or consider it a gesture of great respect not to look directly at the person.

Paying Attention

- Looking directly at the person (eye contact)
- Leaning toward them
- Nodding their head in agreement
- Smiling or laughing at appropriate moments
- Taking notes
- Tipping one's head to the side
- Scratching one's chin.

Caution: Some of this body language can also mean other things. Scratching one's chin can mean you are thinking about the person's comments or that you have an itch. Leaning toward them can show interest or that your lower back hurts. Smiling can mean agreement or that you are daydreaming about something else.

Hand Gestures

- Open hand usually implies an openness or acceptance of the other person's views.
- Closed hand often implies lack of acceptance, anger, or frustration.
- Forming fingers of both hands into a "steeple" implies leadership, knowledge or agreeing with someone else.
- A hand formed in a fist is seen as aggressive or defensive.

Arm Positions

Crossed arms are often seen as aggressive, defensive or angry. Open arms are seen as more accepting, even welcoming of other people. Keep in mind that people often cross their arms for warmth or when they are anxious as well.

Leg Positions

In Europe crossing your leg with the ankle resting just above your other leg's knee is considered aggressive. In North America this leg position is seen as "manly" and assertive. Both cultures tend to see crossing legs at the knee as the more acceptable position for women.

Body Positions

Standing straight and comfortably shows leadership, assertiveness and confidence. Standing too straight implies a military stance that may be seen as aggressive. Slouching is more often seen as passive, uncomfortable or disrespectful.

Placing a chair, desk or other object between you and the other person can be seen as being defensive, authoritarian (as in a health care meeting or job interview) or patronizing. In the doctor-patient relationship, the placement of the desk between the two may limit necessary communication.

Turning your body away from someone can be seen as dismissing them, disagreeing with them or not bothering to show any respect. This is often used in movies to show total disrespect while also showing no fear that the person will attack you.

Facing a person directly, as opposed to standing slightly to their side, may be seen as aggressive body language. This is especially true if the situation is already stressful or tense.

A space between people is often a cultural difference. In Latin American cultures it is often very common to see people standing close together and even touching each other's shoulders, back or arm. In British cultures it is more common to see people standing farther apart and not touching each other very often (or at all). These differences often lead to conflict as people see the physical distance between them as too aggressive or too defensive.

Note: a safe distance is usually an arm's length apart. As you get to know the other person better that distance may become larger or smaller depending on each other's comfort zones.

Your Voice

The third element to communication (after what you say and your body language) is how you use your voice. How loud you speak, the tone of voice, your accent, and how fast you speak are all things that people use to infer meaning from your words. Some people believe they can tell if someone is lying by the tone in their voice. Unfortunately, they are often wrong. Cultural and educational differences often explain why we misunderstand people. For example, people who speak English as their first language, include a broad range of accents – some slower, some faster, some with different syllable emphasis, some often seen as needing "correction" by others.

We tend to see our voice as a very personal part of ourselves. However, with knowledge and insight, we may identify some aspects of our voice that can be changed to help us communicate more effectively.

Tips

Tape yourself. Evaluate strengths and weaknesses and decide which you can, or want to, improve.

Pick one thing at a time that you would like to change about your voice. Do not try to become another person. Just build on your strengths and reduce your voice weaknesses.

Remember that your weaknesses will return when you are tired or stressed. If you know this about yourself then you can minimize the effects when you are tired or stressed.

Some areas for possible change include:

Pitch

Women and men tend to trust a lower pitched voice. This sexist perception that high-pitched voices are less serious crosses many cultural lines. It is unfair but common.

Part of the reason for this perception is due to the modern media age of the 20th century. When radio and television were first introduced the frequencies that transmitted voices worked best for low frequency voices (mostly men). High-pitched voices could not be transmitted through the airwaves. Therefore, for most people born before the 1960s, their news and other radio/television came from men. Add to that the fact that men were often the political leaders (remember Roosevelt's fireside chats) and we can understand some of the reasons why women and men have learned to prefer low pitched voices.

> *A technique to help lower your pitch includes breathing deeply so that your vocal cords use air from your stomach rather than just from your throat area. Also, I find that singing songs at a lower key than normal before I give a talk or speech helps to lower my pitch over all. Remember that fear raises your pitch so concentrate on some relaxation exercises before speaking in stressful situations.*
> *Harry van Bommel*

Tone

The tone of your voice also shows whether you are angry or happy, sad or excited. It is different from pitch in that it indicates mood. To have your emotions clearly understood, aim your voice at the person you are speaking to rather than to the floor, to your notes or up in the air.

Volume

Changing the volume of your voice every so often makes listening easier. If you are excited about a point, speak a little louder. If you want to dramatize a point or make people listen more carefully, speak softly.

Speed

People tend to breathe at the same speed that you talk to them. If you speed up or slow down your rate of speech you will affect the rate at which the person breathes. Change your rate of speech to get different reactions from the people with whom you are talking.

Speak Clearly

Let people hear the end of your words. Watch their body language to see if they understand what you are saying. If you are not sure, ask them.

Rhythm

Often when people are nervous they end their sentences as if they were questions. They voice goes up at the end of the sentence and gives the impression that they are not confident in what they are saying. Tape your voice to see if you do this with your sentences.

"Uhms, You Know, Eh, Cool"

Most of us use fill-in words or sounds when we are trying to say something. You will probably never stop using them completely. Therefore, concentrate on reducing the number of times you use them. Think before you speak and your sentences will come out clearly with less fill-in words. Some people swear repeatedly when they talk.

Many people have other aspects of their voice that are not amenable to change. These may include regional or national accents, physical aspects of speech, stuttering or lisps. Remember that speech is only one way in which we communicate. You may wish to concentrate on other components of communication.

> *Because of my disabilities, I have trouble with my voice. It is very soft and often is simply not there. This is not great for someone who is invited around the world to give lectures on death and dying. People expect that the speaker should have a strong booming voice. I think that they have a right to expect this, yet I cannot deliver it. My strength is in what I say, not in the voice I say it in. What I find is that when I identify my limits to my audience they tend to listen more attentively and thereby compensate for my inability.*
> *Michèle Chaban*

Your goal is to become a more effective communicator, not a perfect one.

Where You Communicate

Where you speak with people is sometimes as important as the body language you use. When people come to your home or workplace they make assumptions about you by looking at your environment. You do the same thing when you go to their homes or workplace. You need to understand your environment and the type of assumptions people may make about you. This is especially true if you are negotiating something important with someone or if you are someone's supervisor. If you meet in your area they will make assumptions about you that may, or may not, be true. If you meet in their area you will do the same.

In practical terms this means that when you visit someone in their area you naturally look to see what kind of pictures, paintings, posters hang on their walls. You look at nearby trophies, certificates. You check to see if the place is neat or not, what types of books or objects they keep and more. All these things say something about the person. Just like body language, the environment you live, work and play in says something about you as well.

What does your environment say about you? What did you wish it said versus what you think other people may actually conclude? What can you do differently?

A messy desk conveys a strong message. I can recall two professionals that I needed to see several years ago, both of whom had large and shifting piles of paper on their desks and the floors of their offices. This made me feel very uncomfortable as I wondered how my issues and the work they were doing for me could possibly be kept separate from the mess. I also wondered how far behind they were and whether they could complete the task. All in all, I lost confidence in them and went to someone else.
Elizabeth Latimer

Exercise #2
Your Environment

Take a look around you at your work, in your home and the places where you often speak to people. Describe your environment in some detail. Look at your environment from the perspective of other people coming to visit you there. What assumptions are they making about you? Which assumptions are right? Which may be wrong? Check your descriptions with people you trust to see how accurate you are.

Active Listening

Listening is a magnetic and strange thing, a creative force. The friends that listen to us are the ones we move towards, and we want to sit in their radius, as though it did us good, like ultraviolet rays. When we are listened to, it creates us, makes us unfold and expand. Ideas actually begin to grow in us and come to life. it makes people happy and free when they are listened to. When we listen to people there is an alternating current, and this recharges us so we never get tired of each other. We are constantly being recreated. I just listen with affection to anyone who talks to me, to be in their shoes when they talk.
Charles Moustakas

There is one quick way to know if you or someone else is listening well. If there is silence after someone has talked, then the other person(s) was probably listening. It is when there is no silence in a conversation that you know people are thinking and rehearsing their reply while the other person is still talking. We do this all the time. Active listeners listen, reflect in silence and then respond.
Harry van Bommel

The ability to listen brings power to communicators. Good listening skills give you control over the communication process. Active listening is not a natural process. It requires practice. Hearing and listening are not the same. You can hear a person's words without listening to their message or understanding their meaning.

Physicians need to learn and develop a lot more in the area of listening skills. This is difficult for them, because the emphasis throughout medical training is on showing how much you know, usually by talking. Some physicians actually believe that patients will gain reassurance from hearing their doctor talk. Certainly this is true, but only after patients feel their doctor has attentively heard them. It makes patients and other team members very anxious if they feel that the doctor did not effectively listen to what they had to say.
Elizabeth Latimer

Some facts about listening:

People can hear at a speed three times faster than what is normally spoken. This means they often become bored or restless when listening for long periods of time. 70% of our time of our waking time is spent communicating. Of that time we spend about:

- 10% writing
- 15% reading
- 30% speaking
- 45 % listening

We only hear 20% of what is said. The rest is screened out or changed by our interests, needs, memory skills and perceptions.

It is not what you say that is important, but rather what people hear. It is our responsibility as communicators to ensure that other people understand what we have said and that we understand what other people say to us. We do that by asking people to repeat, using their own words, what we have said. For example, "How will you go about organizing the work for the project?" We do the same for them by repeating what they have said so they know when we understand them. For example, "You think that our meetings could be more productive if we meet weekly?"

Listening Skills

To be a good listener you must also act like a good listener. You can:

- Maintain good eye contact but do not stare at the person. If you are uncomfortable looking at the person's eyes, look at the bridge of the person's nose. The person will not be able to tell the difference.
- Be attentive. Lean forward at times if you are sitting or move forward if you are standing. Sit more beside a person rather than directly opposite them. This will respect the space between you and will appear less confrontational or intimidating.
- Show empathy. Use facial expressions, nod and tilt your head slightly, laugh, and touch (when appropriate). Acknowledge what is said by summarizing and repeating to make sure you have understood. (This last point is often over used. Sometimes a person needs to talk without interruption, therefore, use only nonverbal cues.)
- Ask open ended questions to encourage conversation i.e. Who, What, Where, When, Why, How versus Is, Will, Do, Would (which can be answered by Yes/No).
- Use silence to permit people to think about their answer to you. Sometimes you may need to be quiet for up to 60 - 90 seconds after a question. This gives the other person time to decide if they trust you and how much they want to tell you. Resist the temptation of filling the silence with what you think they may want to say.
- With patients, sit down whenever possible. Patients will read this as a sign that you are ready to listen. They will also perceive the time you spend with them as longer and more directed to their needs.
- Be patient, relaxed: eyes, posture and attitude should show interest -- focus all your attention on the person speaking. Do not use this conversation to work out some of your own concerns. Be there for the other person. Use a friend to talk to about your own ideas, worries and fears.

I listen a lot, I must say. I find I do better if I don't talk. I listen and I make time. I have stayed here late into the night listening to people who have a lot to say. Whether they just want some assurance or whether they have an idea they want to work through. I get excited by what they say even though I would like to go home when it's late.
Larry Lewis

Communication Skills Improvement

We have examined some basic communication skills. The following techniques will help you enhance your basic skills and help you to become an effective communicator.

Common Courtesies

Know the other person's name and help them remember yours.

Use words like "please, thank you and I'm sorry" often to show respect and consideration.

Understand mutual stresses.

Pay attention to words and body language.

Ask the other person what name you should call them (e.g., elderly patients should not become Mary, dear or honey unless you have first established that they prefer the use of their first name). Maintain the social distance you have kept in the past unless the person wants a change.

Getting the Message

Repeat what a person has said in your own words to make sure you have understood an important point.

Ask the person to repeat what they have said in different words if you were unable to understand their point.

When you do understand, nod your head in agreement or acknowledgement. Say "Uh-huh" to show your understanding and lean forward to indicate interest. Ask specific questions that require a yes, no or a few-word answer to make sure you have understood key points.

Acknowledge the person's feelings and story instead of "topping" their story with one of your own experiences. We cannot concentrate on someone else if we are thinking about ourselves.

Helping People to Talk

The most powerful communication tool we know of to help people who have a major problem or concern is to ask the person a broad question. Broad, or open, questions cannot be answered by yes or no or in a few words. These questions start with words like why and how instead of closed questions that use words like do, did, will. An example of a broad, open-ended question is: "What do you understand about your illness?"

The broad question is followed by complete silence on your part. The other person may need up to two minutes to come up with an answer if your question was about a major point or feeling the person has. During this silence the person will decide how much to trust you and they will begin to form their answer in their head. If you interrupt with more questions or with your own ideas they will stop thinking of their answer and will probably not trust you with their answer later on. When they do start talking you must actively listen to their words and watch their body language.

If the person gets stuck in making their points, ask further questions. Questions are much more powerful than statements in helping people to figure out their own solutions to their own problems. It worked for Socrates thousands of years ago!

You must not judge people when they are talking. If you tell them you disagree with them or that they are talking nonsense they will stop talking to you. Many family arguments happen when people do not listen to each other without judgment.

If it becomes appropriate later on in the conversation you can provide the person with practical information that may help them with whatever problem they have.

Resolving Problems

If a person complains to you about a communication problem, discover what communication process was actually used and offer recommendations to improve situation. (Often a few practical tips can help resolve communication problems.)

People's Lament

"I don't have enough time." We spend 70% of our waking hours communicating, therefore we have to use our communicating time effectively. We spend only a fraction of our formal education learning to do something we do 70% of our time. We could avoid many of the simple misunderstandings that can lead to unnecessary meetings, memos, letters, redoing work, or simply bad feelings between people if we continually improve our communication skills. Good communicators can say "ten minutes with me is like 50 minutes with someone else". And it's true!

As we have discussed, there are other forms of communication besides talking. Using body language, a touch, a smile, a look of concern and empathy to show genuine interest can shorten many conversations by getting right to the important issues.

Difficulties

People have a personal story. They may have experienced family problems, possible abusive relationships and problems with work or pain. You cannot change people. You cannot force family or work reconciliation. You can offer help and understanding.

You can provide an opportunity to meet a person's needs without personal judgments about what they "should" do. This can be a valuable gift as solutions may emerge as you listen.

Exercise #3
Successful Communication

The following are several exercises you can try to see whether or not you are communicating well. Try these with family, friends or work colleagues to see how all of you communicate. Have some fun with the Exercises and exaggerate some of the situations to see what happens in the extreme.

Many people tried this exercise as children but it is worth repeating. Get 8 - 10 people together.

Have the first person tell only one other person a short story. Then have the second person tell only a third, etc., until the 10th person hears the final (10th) version of the story. See how closely the 10th version is to the first version. What facts were the same? What facts were changed? How does this apply to your verbal communications at work or in your family?

In groups of three give each person one of the following roles:

One person talks about a belief they hold strongly.

Second person sits on their hands and listens carefully to the first person. The second person can only speak to clarify a point. They cannot give a personal opinion themselves. Once they think they understand what the other person believes, they summarize their points and get the first person to agree or disagree with the summary.

Third person takes notes about how the first person tried to make their points clearly and concisely and how the second person tried to understand what was said. They then take notes on how well the second person was able to summarize the first person's beliefs.

Have the participants change roles so each has an opportunity to speak, listen and record or evaluate the communication process. Ask each other which role was easier for them to do, and why.

In groups of three have two people sit back-to-back. First person describes a geometric shape to the second person who must draw it as exactly to scale as possible.

The first person cannot use names like triangle, square or rectangle. They can only describe lines and angles to help the second person draw the shape. The second person cannot ask any questions except to ask the person to repeat their description or to slow down. The third person makes sure the other two follow the rules and observes how clearly the first person speaks and how accurately the second person draws.

Switch people's roles and repeat the exercise. This time the second person may ask questions to clarify what they are drawing.

Compare the two exercises to see whether the second person asking questions is helpful or not. Your results will depend on the individuals participating.

Watch a television program or video tape of people in a crowded area and identify their body language. Make assumptions about what you are interpreting and see if there is other body language that supports or rejects your assumptions. Also look carefully at the clothes people are wearing. Is there a wedding ring to tell you the person is married (or pretending to be married)? Are there children nearby and do they belong to the person you are watching?

Use this exercise as a regular game to help you begin to look at people more carefully. Discover if people are happy, sad, angry, or worried. Do not stare at people in public places or make them uncomfortable but do look more carefully around you to see what information you can discover about people.

Videotape yourself talking for a few minutes. Watch your own body language. Is your body saying the same things as your words? What nervous energy can you see? Are your words clear? Is your voice interesting to listen to? What changes can you make before you videotape yourself again?

Whenever possible, have yourself videotaped. Only by seeing yourself and listening to yourself as others do can you begin to understand why people react to you in the different ways that they do.

Summary

The word communication comes from the root word "common". Communication, then, means using a common language that is easily understood by whomever you are speaking or writing to. Successful communication is based on a broader concept of what is important in life and how communication can help you achieve success in those important areas. Ralph Waldo Emerson gave this summary of success:

- To laugh often and much;

- To win the respect of intelligent people and the affection of children;
- To earn the appreciation of honest critics and endure the betrayal of false friends;
- To appreciate beauty;
- To find the best in others;
- To leave the world a bit better, whether by a healthy child, a garden patch or a redeemed social condition;
- To know even one life has breathed easier because you have lived;

This is to have succeeded.

Basic and effective communication skills can help people achieve success in the areas they define as important for themselves. The foundations of communication are: concentrating on meeting the needs of the person you are taking to, understanding their similarities and differences to you, interpreting their body language and fording out if your interpretations are correct, and speaking in clear, common language. Follow these simple principles and you cannot lose -- in fact you will almost always guarantee yourself success.

Resources

The following resources are only a few of the many useful resources that you can find in your local libraries, within your own organization, and in your local bookstores. Look for other books but also for journal articles, magazine reports, films, videos and audiocassettes. Also keep in mind how much you can learn from experts in the field, including people within your own organization.

Aubuchon, N. (1997). *The anatomy of persuasion: How to persuade others to act on your ideas, accept your proposals, buy your products or services, hire you, promote you.* New York: AMACOM.

Birdwhistell, R.L. (1970). *Kinesics and context: Essays on body motion communication.* Philadelphia: University of Pennsylvania Press.

Booher, D. (1994). *Communicate with confidence: How to say it right the first time and every time.* New York: McGraw-Hill.

Fast, J. (1970). *Body language.* New York: Pocket Books.

Gschwandter, G., & Garnett, P. (1985). *Nonverbal selling power.* Englewood Cliffs, NJ: Prentice Hall.

Heyman, R. (1997). *Why didn't you say that in the first place? How to be understood at work.* San Francisco: Jossey-Bass.

Kim, Y.Y. (1988). *Communication and cross-cultural adaptation.* Philadelphia: Multilingual Matters.

Krisco, K.H. (1997). *Leadership and the art of conversation: Conversation as a management tool.* Rocklin, CA: Prima Publishing.

Larkin, S., & Larkin, T. J. (1994). *Communicating change: How to win employee support for new health care directions.* New York: McGraw-Hill.

Nierenberg, GI, & Calero, H.H. (1973). *Meta-talk: How to uncover the hidden meanings in what people say.* New York: Simon and Schuster.

Stone, D., Patton, B., Heen, S. & Fisher, R. (2000). *Difficult conversations: How to discuss what matters most.* New York: Penguin.

Assertiveness

Assertiveness is a popular approach to help people improve their relationships with others. It is based on the ageless wisdom that we all work best with those people who are honest and fair in their communications and their behavior.

Assertiveness allows you to get what you want more often. At the very least it tells people what you believe and what you consider to be fair in a given situation. Assertiveness skills are meant to give you the confidence to deal with those situations that have made you uncomfortable in the past. You may still be somewhat uncomfortable in those situations but you will not let someone else deny you your rights as a person, a co-worker or as a family member.

First of all, what is assertiveness?

Assertiveness Being assertive means that you stand up for your personal rights and express your feelings, beliefs, requests and thoughts in direct, honest and appropriate ways without violating the rights of others. Some of the most assertive people you know are probably also some of the most quiet, peaceful, persistent, and truthful people you know.

Aggressiveness Being aggressive means that you stand up for your rights in a punishing, threatening, assaultive, demanding or hostile way. Loud, rude people may get results but they do not get respect or voluntary cooperation.

Passiveness Being passive means that you often do not express your feelings, thoughts, requests or beliefs. People tend to take advantage of you but you keep your anger bottled up.

Passive Aggressiveness Being passively aggressive means that you often do not express your feelings, thoughts, requests or beliefs directly, honestly or in a timely way to someone else but do whatever you can behind their back to punish or threaten them

All of us are assertive, aggressive and passive in different ways and in different situations. We change the way we act and speak depending on the situation and who we are with. We act differently with our friends, with our boss, with different family members, and with our spouses.

Becoming More Assertive

Before you become more assertive you need to ask yourself a few questions:

1. Why do I want to become more assertive?

2. How will being more assertive help me?
3. What can stop me from becoming more assertive?
4. What is my present general style: assertive, aggressive, passive, or passive aggressive?
5. How does my general style change in different situations and with different people (at work, at home, socializing, or shopping)?
6. Who can I use as role models for becoming more assertive?
   Who can I ask to help me become more assertive? Who can give me suggestions and comments as I try more assertive behavior?

Before we get too deeply into a discussion of assertiveness techniques, lets look at some basics. You can use these suggestions to build up your confidence in situations and with people you feel most comfortable with. When you have practiced enough, to your own satisfaction, try being assertive in more difficult situations.

The Process

Observe Your Own Behavior to see what kind of situations you are most and least assertive in and why?

Record Your Assertiveness with a diary or log to note down situations when you are assertive, aggressive, passive and passive aggressive.

Focus on Specific Situations and imagine how you will deal with people in that situation. Imagine yourself being assertive and fair with the people and try to "feel" what you will feel.

Review Your Assertiveness after each situation to see if you are comfortable with: your knowledge of assertiveness, your ability to be assertive in similar situations, and thinking of changes you might make in similar situations.

Pick a Role Model who is assertive in the way you would like to be assertive. Ask them how they would handle different situations. Pick someone who is similar to you in personality so that you can feel most comfortable using similar assertiveness techniques.

What are Some Alternatives to the approaches you have selected for specific situations.

Role Play different situations with someone you trust to find out what you are most comfortable in doing. Have your friend respond in different ways to the same situation so that you can practice different assertive techniques.

Ask People for Constructive Suggestions to how you have handled situations in the past and how they see you handling situations now. Is there a difference? Do they think your new approaches are working? What constructive suggestions can they offer to make you more comfortable with being assertive.

Reinforce Your Success by having friends give you specific compliments when your assertiveness is successful. Treat yourself whenever you try to be more assertive, even if it didn't work out perfectly. Assertiveness is a skill that takes time so you need to reward any and all of your efforts!

> *While working as a very nervous and very new graduate on a busy neurosurgical unit, I had to very quickly learn how to speak up for my patients and their families. The first time I discussed a patient with a neurosurgeon was very intimidating but with time and practice, I was able to do this with confidence and at times, even state why I didn't think a particular approach was best for the patient! We can all learn to be assertive in various situations; it starts with making a decision to step over our "comfort line".*
> *Beverley Powell-Vinden*

Limiting Beliefs

Many of us have underlying beliefs that prevent us from saying what we feel and think, even when we know we are right.

Some common beliefs are:

"If I let go of my aggressive feelings, I might lose control of myself."

"It's inappropriate behavior to say what I feel and think. It might upset someone."

"If I'm open about these feelings and thoughts they will reject me."

"If I tell them how I really feel and think, they won't be able to take it. They may fall apart."

"I'm afraid of what they'll do in return."

"If I'm really their friend, I don't have any right to be annoyed. Real friends understand each other and don't get annoyed at each other."

"When I told them about why I was upset, they told me that if I loved them I wouldn't get angry."

"If I can't say something nice to someone, then I shouldn't say anything at all."

Our beliefs can prevent us from being comfortable with who we are. Just as importantly, these beliefs prevent us from truly understanding our family, our friends and our colleagues because we are constantly assuming how they feel, think or will act. If we don't talk openly and assertively with people we prevent relationships from improving and getting stronger.

If we let small situations continue to bother us without telling people how we feel about them, we build up a resistance and anger that one day will surface in a more negative way. People who purposely avoid subject after subject because it may upset someone will end up only talking about weather, television or sports. This is not very fulfilling for anyone involved in long-term relationships of any kind.

Changing a Negative Self-Image

We often use negative statements to put ourselves down. Let us look at some typical negative statements we might use in the common situation of having to meet a deadline. Here are some suggestions of how we could change them into more positive assertions.

Negative Statements

"I'll never get finished."
"If I miss this I've really blown it."
"Why am I so anxious? I hate feeling like this."
"I must get going. I must hurry."
"I know people think I can't do this."
"I hate myself."
"I just don't have enough time, so why bother?"

Positive Statements

"Just take it one step at a time."
"Some tension is inevitable but I don't have to worry about it."
"I really do have confidence in my basic ability. What else matters?"
"Mistakes happen and the work will still get done."
"Don't anticipate problems, just get started."
"What's reasonable for today -just do it."
"I've done good work before and I will do this project well too."
"I love to learn and try new things. I learn from my successes and from my mistakes."
"If I break this project into smaller units, it will get done."

I have a few tricks that I employ if I am in a situation that requires a particularly assertive stance. I focus on a very positive image of myself as an effective person, some of my successes and strengths, and sort of imagine myself having the conversation I need to have. I will stand up during the actual exchange, even if it is over the phone. This gives me a feeling of more mastery. I also employ a pleasant and energetic voice, even if I

don't feel that way inside. It's rather like rehearsing a stage performance and well worth it, I find.
Elizabeth Latimer

Communication Behaviors

Our beliefs and self-image determine how we act in certain situations and with certain people. If our beliefs and self-image limit our openness and honesty we have a tendency to be passive. If our beliefs and self-image limit other people's openness and honesty we have a tendency to be aggressive. If our beliefs and self-image encourage us and other people's openness and honesty we have a tendency to be assertive.

Passive	**Assertive**	**Aggressive**
Tendency to:	Tendency to:	Tendency to:
Allow self to be interrupted, subordinated and stereotyped	State feelings, needs and wants	Interrupt, subordinate and stereotype others
Have poor eye contact	Have good eye contact	Have intense and glaring eye contact
Have poor posture and defeated air	Have straight posture and self confidence	Have invading posture and arrogant air
Withhold information, opinions and feelings	Able to disclose information, opinions ad feelings	Conceal information, opinions and feelings
Ineffective listener	Active listener	Ineffective listener
Indecisive	Make positions and decisions clear	Dominate decisions
Apologize, avoid and leave.	Confront people assertively.	Be loud, abusive, blaming and sarcastic.

What Are Our Personal Rights and Responsibilities?

Rights

Personal rights are not all listed in law. However, there are many moral rights that we can legitimately ask other people to respect.

People intellectually agree that these rights are fair and should be true for all people, regardless of race, color, creed, gender or, sexual orientation. However, we often do not believe that these rights always apply to us. Look at your own assertive style. Ask yourself, "How would I be different if I believed this right applied to me in most/all situations and with most/all people?"

Exercise #1

I have:

- The right to act in ways that promotes my dignity and self-respect as long as others' rights are not violated in the process.
- The right to judge my own behavior, thoughts and actions.
- The right to be treated with respect.
- The right to say no and not feel guilty.
- The right to experience and express my positive and negative feelings.
- The right to take time, slow down and think.
- The right to change my mind.
- The right to ask for what I want.
- The right to do less than I am humanly capable of doing.
- The right to ask for information.
- The right to make mistakes.
- The right to feel good about myself.
- The right to a reasonable workload.
- The right to an equitable wage.
- The right to say "I don't know", "I don't understand".
- The right to give and receive information as a professional.
- The right to choose not to assert myself.

Which rights would you add?

Responsibilities

Whenever we have rights we also have responsibilities. As assertive people, we have certain responsibilities if we expect others to respect our rights.

If you want others to accept your more assertive style you must also ask yourself, "Will I accept the responsibility for my own actions and their consequences?" If you answer yes, then you have the right to be more assertive.

Exercise #2

I have:

- The responsibility to respect and encourage other people to be assertive.
- The responsibility to tell others how I feel if their behavior affects me negatively.

- The responsibility to help other people be more effective communicators.
- The responsibility to understand and fulfill my moral obligations to others.

List some other responsibilities you will have as a more assertive person:

Assertiveness Skills

Assertiveness, like all skills, is an evolving process. Reading a section on assertiveness helps you understand the concepts and skills you may want to learn but it cannot make you more assertive. Only practice leads to more assertiveness.

From the following list, note those techniques you are already comfortable with. Then pick one or two suggestions that you can add to your assertive skills and begin to apply these new skills immediately. When you are comfortable with your new skills, pick a few more suggestions and repeat the process until you have become the assertive person you want to be.

Self-Awareness

Take time to look at yourself. Take time to identify how you feel in different situations and with different people. Use that knowledge to discover your strengths and identify things you would like to change in yourself. Over time, start to let others know about your efforts to change.

Attitude

Take a moment to look at a different attitude. Assertiveness is easier to learn and apply when you begin with an attitude that recognizes that everyone is doing the best they can with what they know at that time. This attitude recognizes that people may be rude, arrogant or without communication skills, but these people have learned these skills over the years and do not understand what the alternatives are This attitude may help you to be more patient with a person, while using assertive language to have your needs met at the same time.

An assertive person may recognize that people are not always capable of behaving appropriately but that does not mean they have to stand there and take abuse. You can tell the person you will discuss the matter later. At a later point you can use assertive and conflict resolution strategies and techniques to help the other person find more appropriate ways to communicate and behave.

Interest

Assume an attitude of interest. An assertive attitude is also an attitude of interest; interest in what people do, what they say, and how they feel. This attitude of interest can be disarming and leads to mutually satisfying communication.

Recognize People

Catch people doing things well. Compliment a family member, colleague, supervisor, cafeteria employee, bus driver, and anyone else you meet whenever they have done something well. Assertive people recognize the worth and talents of people around them and are not afraid to let them know. What a wonderful gift.

Questions

Ask open-ended questions. Few assertiveness and communication tools are as powerful as an open-ended question followed by silence. An open-ended question begins with a why, how, if, or what. Close-ended questions can be answered with a yes or no. Closed-ended questions often begin with do, will, can, or would.

The secret to open-ended questions followed by silence is that they permit people to say things they might otherwise not say. The silence (up to 60- 90 seconds!) gives them permission to decide how much they trust you and how much they want to tell you. The tone of your voice should reflect interest and curiosity versus judgment.

Examples of open-ended questions might be: "What is it about my behavior that gets you angry so often?" or "What have I been doing differently lately that has caused you to avoid me?" or "Why do you need to interrupt me whenever I am talking to Sue?"

Listen

Listen actively. The second most powerful assertiveness and communication tool is active listening. Listen to what the person is saying. Look at their body language to see if what they are saying is similar to how they look. For example someone who tells you that the problem you had together is over but who does not look at you and is standing with their hands tightly clenched together may not be telling the truth.

When you listen, listen for the actual words but also for hidden meanings. When you listen actively you should not have time to be thinking up responses in your head. Your total concentration is on that person. When it is your turn to reply, take a few seconds to think about what you want to say. They will give you, or you should ask, for that time to think.

Expectations

Outline your expectations at the start. When you are working with someone else on any kind of project, tell them what they can expect from you and what you expect them to do. If necessary, put these expectations in writing so that each of you can refresh your memories.

If you have not decided on what work needs to get done, ask them what they want from you and tell them what you want from them.

Information

Build in your support. When you meet people or are working together, offer to give useful information to help them and ask for similar kinds of information in return. This can help build a supportive relationship.

Body Language

Use assertive postures. Assertive body language is critical to assertiveness. Most of our communication is non-verbal. The way we stand or sit, the way we use our hands, whether we are looking at people when we talk, our facial expressions; are all key to being properly assertive and supportive of other people.

Watch various people at work, in your family or on television to see how their body language encourages or discourages people to listen and participate.

You may wish to videotape yourself as a way of assessing your posture, movements and image of assertiveness.

Develop an attitude of interest using your body to indicate that interest, for example, look at people, lean towards them when they speak, give them enough physical space to talk and move so they do not feel intimidated.

Speak slowly and clearly but with enough energy to encourage other people to pay attention.

"I" Messages

In frustrating situations or when you are angry, use "I" statements to show your own feelings and send messages that say you still respect the other person but their behavior is harmful to you in some way. Talk about the person's behaviors instead of calling them names or talking behind their backs.

"I feel embarrassed and angry when you yell at me in front of the others at work. Next time you disagree with something I have done could we please discuss it in your office.", instead of, "You're a stupid jerk! How do you think I feel when you yell at me like that?" The second sentence doesn't present an alternative and insults a person rather than identifies a specific behavior you would like them to change.

Mistakes

Admit your mistakes. If someone confronts you with an error you have made, admit the mistake but not necessarily their judgment of you. If someone tells you that you are incompetent or stupid because of an error, you might say, "Geez, I'm sorry that I forgot to mail that report yesterday. I will certainly do that right away. However, my mistake does not instantly make me incompetent or stupid, wouldn't you agree?"

Cooling Off

Leave the situation if you are being abused. When someone is very upset or is demeaning to you because this is their normal reaction to stress or frustration, let the person know you will be available later to discuss the matter. You do not need to let someone abuse you, nor do you have to "fight back" with the same style.

Praise and Criticism

Accept both praise and criticism. People often find it just as difficult to accept praise as they do to accept constructive criticism. If the person's opinion or comment is accurate, a polite "Thank you" is all you need to say. If you are being praised or criticized for something you didn't do, give specific and concise information to correct the misunderstanding.

Criticize

Criticize a person's behavior only. Whenever you criticize someone else make sure to criticize their behavior and not the person themselves. See criticism as an opportunity for learning rather than an occasion to attack their personality. For example, "What has to happen in order for. . . ?"

Rudeness

Sometimes we are confronted by rude service people in stores or repair shops. Assertiveness requires you to:

- Give specific, detailed and concise information of what you want them to do.

Politely, but firmly, demand the kind of service or information that the store or service advertises.

- Politely, but firmly, demand to see a supervisor if the person you are talking with is unable or unwilling to serve you properly.

Sometimes your humor and your attitude that these people are doing the best they can with the skills they have used for years can be very helpful. They may have a personal or professional "crisis" that does not excuse their behavior but may explain it. Beginning from that assumption you can respond assertively and get farther than if you responded aggressively or too passively.

Uncertain Behavior

Question people with curiosity. When someone is putting other people down, being rude, insensitive to others you might try to find out why. If your tone of voice tells the person you are curious rather than judgmental or angry, they may actually answer your question. For example, "Why do you find it necessary to put people down?" or "How does it help you to ignore other people when they try to explain their opinions?"

Risks

Sometimes you have to risk that someone will respond angrily or withdraw from you. You cannot cause these feelings in other people. Your honest, assertive style cannot cause people to respond in certain ways. Other people, consciously or unconsciously, choose how to respond. It is their choice.

If You Loved Me You Would...

Refuse to accept responsibility that is not yours. People often use the phrase "If you loved me you would..." to get you to do things you do not want to do. Your love or friendship does not mean doing specific things for people. Your love or friendship does not decrease if you do not visit someone, if you forget a birthday, if you wear that ugly yellow silk shirt, or if you clean too much/too little. Whenever someone says, "If you loved/really liked me, you would... ", you can respond quite simply, "Do you really believe that?" If they do, sit them down for a chat to discover what they are really saying. Perhaps they think your behavior reflects a change in your feelings for them.

Your Boss

Judge the situation. It is difficult sometimes to be assertive with a supervisor. That person's personality may not take kindly to someone who honestly expresses their thoughts and feelings. You will have to judge how far you can go and whether or not you can become more assertive over time rather than overnight. If the person dislikes your assertiveness you may have to choose between returning to your previous behavior or transferring/leaving your position.

The good news is that most supervisors like staff who are assertive (not aggressive or passive aggressive). Assertive staff members decrease communication errors, are more productive and consistent, work better with their colleagues and resolve conflicts more effectively.

If you are having a particularly difficult time with a supervisor, write down your thoughts and feelings and rephrase them in assertive and acceptable words. Set an appointment with your supervisor and use your notes to prepare concise statements and questions to help resolve the situation. You may want to rehearse with a trusted friend or family member first.

One at a Time

Limit yourself to one issue at a time. You cannot deal assertively with many issues at once. Do not permit others to bring in old or new concerns until you have examined and resolved the present one.

Once an issue has been resolved, do not bring it up in future arguments, disagreements or discussions.

Reading Minds

Ask questions when you do not know something. Unless you have exceptional powers you cannot read other people's mind nor should they assume that you can. Ask specific questions until you understand what someone has said or is what they are trying to say.

Some More Tips

Be specific when you are being assertive. If someone is being "disagreeable" with you, you must concentrate on specific behaviors rather than the person's personality.

Work towards change rather than complaining. If someone is doing something you dislike, concentrate on their behavior and suggest alternative behaviors that the person is likely to accept.

Ask for and give feedback so that you are both clear about what is said and heard. Poor and misunderstood communication is the root of many disagreements.

Stick to the subject without bringing in past problems or potential future difficulties. Staying to one subject at a time will help you concentrate on specific behaviors and alternatives rather than stretching out your discussion into a debate of each other's personalities and personal histories.

Listening actively and asking questions are wonderful assertiveness tools because listening and asking are powerful means to help you understand people and to force yourself to be fair and open.

Discourage counter-demands from the other person until you have resolved the present concerns. You cannot deal with many situations at once so concentrate on one at a time.

You cannot read someone's mind or expect them to be able to read your mind so be clear and concise in your messages and ask the other person to paraphrase important things you say so that you both understand each other. It takes more time this way but it can slow the discussion down to a more manageable, and less emotional, pace.

Avoid labeling and stereotyping people except as a tool to get to know them better. Use your beliefs about someone and ask enough questions to find out if you are right. We naturally label and stereotype people but if we do not find out if we are correct we will miss important information they can give us. Stereotyping or labeling people focuses only on their personalities, culture and visual appearance. Assertiveness concentrates on people's behaviors and how you can help them understand how their behavior affects you and others.

Concentrate on the present and avoid bringing in the past. You can change what people do now but you cannot change the past. Do not wait to discuss someone's behavior with them till next week, next month or next year. For change to be effective, people need to know what their behavior causes now.

Take time to think about your concerns, your needs, how you will approach a situation, and what benefit there is for the other person to change their behavior for you.

Humor is a wonderful assertiveness tool because it helps people to see that change does not have to be painful. Humor gives us perspective and reinforcements to change if change will make our life and other people's lives more rewarding.

Manipulation

Exercise #3

Manipulation is an ability to handle or control people and situations skillfully, either in a positive or negative way. Manipulation also means influencing or managing people and situations shrewdly or deviously. When people manipulate us in a devious way, it requires us to be assertive.

People often try to manipulate others in a negative way. Examine the following situations and decide what you would do in similar situations based on what you have learned about assertiveness.

1. Making excessive demands of you to convince you that it is not worth the effort or to make you feel defensive.
   "I think we need a detailed report on your idea by Monday or we'll just end up doing it my way, okay?"
2. Considering you irresponsible and untrustworthy when you change your mind.
   "Yesterday you said you would give me some help ...and now you say you can't."
3. Insisting that you mean something other than what you have said.
   "I know you didn't really mean that..."
4. Putting you down by assuming you are less intelligent.
   "You mean to tell me that you don't know how this procedure works? Didn't you learn anything in school?"

Becoming More Assertive

The following questions may be helpful when you choose to be more assertive in a specific situation or with a particular person.

1. What is the situation? What do you want to accomplish?
2. How will being assertive help you in this situation or with this person?
3. How could being assertive harm you in this situation or with this person?
4. What would you normally do in this situation or with this person?
5. What usually stops you from being assertive in this situation or with this person? How can you overcome these barriers?
6. What are your rights and responsibilities in this situation or with this person?
7. What specifically will you do in this situation or with this person to be more assertive and to accomplish your goal?
   How will you deal with the anxiety that becoming more assertive may cause? How will you reward yourself after trying to be more assertive, regardless of the outcome?

Summary

Assertiveness, like other social behaviors, is learned. You have the ability to change yourself You have to work at change but you have the control to do it.

Change is hard work. Plan to take small steps. Pick one behavior you would like to change and begin there. For example, when you are more comfortable being direct with a colleague with whom you have had some difficulty, you can pick another behavior to work on.

Assertiveness is not the only answer. Assertiveness works in most, not all, situations. The alternatives of being passive or aggressive usually fail and cause greater problems. Be persistent in trying to be more assertive before giving up.

When you are satisfied you have been more assertive in a particular situation or with a specific person, reward yourself! Go to a movie, take a long walk, or have a treat of some sort.

The best way to learn assertiveness is to watch an assertive person in different situations. Once you have become more comfortable, be a role model to your family, friends, and colleagues. It helps you remain consistently assertive while providing people near you an opportunity to change as well.

Resources

The following resources are only a few of the many useful resources that you can find in your local libraries, within your own organization, and in your local bookstores. Look for other books but also for journal articles, magazine reports, films, videos and audiocassettes. Also keep in mind how much you can learn from experts in the field, including people within your own organization!

Alberti, R.E. & Emmons, M. (1995). *Your perfect right: A guide to assertive living.* Greenwich, CT: Impact Publishing.

Axelrod, A., Holtje, J., & Holtje, J. (1997). *201 ways to say no effectively and gracefully.* New York: McGraw-Hill.

Burley-Allen, M. (1995). *Managing assertively: How to improve your people skills-A self teaching guide.* Toronto: Wiley & Sons.

Crisp, SR., & Lloyd, M. (Eds.) (1995). *Developing positive assertiveness.* Menlo Park, CA: Crisp Publications.

Michelli, D. (1997). *Successful assertiveness.* Monroe, WA: Barrons.

O'Brien, P. (1997). *Positive management: Assertiveness for managers.* Nicolas Brealey.

Peiffer, V. (1997). *The duty trap: How to say 'no' when you feel you ought to say 'yes'.* Rockport, MA: Element.

Phelps, S., & Austin, N. (1997). *The assertive woman.* Greenwich, CT: Impact Publications.

Stubbs, DR. (1997). *Assertiveness at work: The ultimate management skill.* Philadelphia, PA: Pan Books.

Telephone Skills

How much of your time do you spend using the telephone? How much of your time do you spend using the telephone effectively?

Effective use of the telephone means that:

- You are able to get the information and services from other people you want.
- Other people can get the information and services they want from you.

You will know you are more effective when this process increases the rapport you have with people and when you can do it in less time.

It is important to remember that the suggestions in this section need to be adapted for your own working situation. Obviously someone who uses the phone a few times a day is different from someone who is answering 5-10 telephone requests at one time. You can modify some of the recommendations listed in this section to meet your specific needs. Use the recommendations as a starting point and have fun putting a "smile in your voice!"

Telephone skills are particularly important for the receptionist in the physician's office, the hospital or health clinic. Patients may feel frightened when they call. A courteous, friendly and personal response to their concerns makes a world of difference to them.
Elizabeth Latimer

Communications Within Your Organization

Exercise #1

When I talk to people in Communications Departments and to secretaries and receptionists they often say that they would like people within their organization to become more aware of what responsibilities there are for communication clerks, secretaries and receptionists. Try and answer their telephone for an hour or so to understand how much information they must know to help your clients and colleagues!
Harry van Bommel

Try to find out some of the following information. Spread the information around to other people within your area. You may be surprised at how many calls are handled by your communications clerks, secretaries and receptionists.

1. How many requests are made per year through the main console of your organization, department and area?

2. How many messages per week are taken for you by the people within your Communications Department and by your secretary or receptionist?
3. If you have a locating or pager ("beeper") system, how many requests are made per year to locate staff?
4. How many telephones are there within your organization, department and area that the Communications Department and your secretary or receptionist are responsible for?
5. How many pagers are there within your organization, department and area?
6. Is the Communications Department responsible for the alarm system within your organization (e.g., to inform fire departments of fires)? If so, how many different alarm systems are involved?

Some Tips

Communications clerks, secretaries and receptionists have passed along some of the following tips to me over the past few years. Keep in mind that these suggestions need to be modified to meet the specifics of your own organization's structure, size and systems.

Finding an Internal Phone Number

If you cannot find a number in your organization's Directory you can call the Communication Clerk for assistance with a friendly: "May I have the number for ..? Thank you."

Using the Directory

A lot of calls asking for the internal extension number of another person in the organization can be avoided if people use their internal Directory more often. If you use your Directory more and keep them up-to-date you could give the clerks, secretaries and receptionists more time to answer external requests. If you cannot find the number and need assistance, make sure to write the new number into your directory for future reference.

Identify Yourself

People cannot always recognize someone who says: "It's me." Always say who you are so that the other person doesn't feel incompetent if they cannot guess your identity.

Being Patient

A single communication clerk, secretary or receptionist may handle 5-10 requests at the same time. Your patience will help them a great deal and will also enhance your working relationship.

Courtesy

Using "please" and "thank you" has a powerful effect on people. It also encourages other people to use the same words with us.

Put a Smile in Your Voice

It has been scientifically proven that your voice changes when you smile. The tone of your voice is friendlier, your rate of speech is easier to understand and the person listening to you enjoys speaking with you. Fifteen seconds of speaking with someone with "a smile in their voice" is worth a great deal and the gift of a friendly voice may be returned to you by the person you are talking to.

A Mirror

Telemarketing organizations often have their staff look at a small mirror when they use the phone. The mirror shows them if they are smiling and if their body language is appropriate for building rapport with the caller.

Various Perspectives

Yourself: Attitude is Critical

Attitude is the way we view things and is shown most clearly through our body language.

When we talk on the telephone our attitude toward the caller, toward our work, and toward ourselves is reflected in the tone, rate of speech, and presentation skills we use.

We have a choice whenever we use the telephone; we can choose to be the kind of speaker we enjoy talking with or we can talk like the stereotypical, bored, overworked person we often get when we call other organizations.

Some points to remember:

The words you use when speaking cannot hide how you feel about your work, your life, and the callers.

Your attitude is reflected in your voice by:

- Whether or not you are smiling.

- How you sit or stand.
- Whether or not your facial expressions are relaxed or tense.
- The tone in your voice and your rate of speech.

Have you ever talked to your spouse, children or a friend on the telephone when you were a bit down and they asked you what was wrong? Have you ever talked to them when you were very happy and they asked why? People can tell your mood just as you can tell their mood.

It is common to feel that people expect too much from you. You may feel that people should take the time to understand some of your problems dealing with callers. You may want callers to have more patience and be more courteous. You may want them to solve their own problems rather than depending on you to solve the problems for them. Your assumption may be that you treat people the way they treat you.

Here is an alternative perspective: all communication depends on you taking responsibility for clear communications. You accept this responsibility to make your life easier; not just because it is good public relations. Your attitude recognizes that callers may be impatient or less than courteous because of problems that have nothing to do with you. Your positive attitude (not always easy to have when someone is yelling at you!) needs to acknowledge that you are a capable communicator and a professional.

Can you remember any times when you were upset about something and called an organization to complain? Have you experienced the calming effect of a professional versus the frustration of talking to someone who accepted no responsibility for themselves or their organization?

The challenge of dealing with callers professionally is that you can take an upset or discourteous caller and present them with a positive alternative for getting results. You act as a role model who treats all people with respect and courtesy. This attitude and tone of care and competence is key in the health care setting.

On the other hand, the caller may not respond at all to your courteous manner. Then, at the very least, you are able to finish the conversation with a smile and continue with your day. The caller's attitude does not have to affect your attitude or ruin your day

I found when working as a staff nurse that my attitude on the phone with another department greatly influenced whether I got what I needed or not. If I let my stress or impatience show in my voice, the person on the other end wasn't so willing to help me. If I made an effort to be pleasant and polite, often they couldn't do enough for me. I soon learned that making the effort to be civil on the phone not only made my job

easier but made the next encounter with that department easier as well.
Beverley Powell-Vinden

Yourself: The Quality of Your Voice

All of us speak differently; have voices that are deep or meek, a voice that is pleasant, annoying, clear, or muffled. You control the voice you have!

Energy

The energy in your voice reflects your attitude and enthusiasm. If you feel particularly low in energy: answer the phone standing up, close your eyes and think of some happy times you have had recently, try meditation, do chair exercises, some deep breathing or go for a quick walk. Whatever works!

Rate of Speech

A normal rate of speech is about 125 words a minute. People can listen to up to 450 words per minute and still comprehend what you say. What this means is that people often get bored if you use long sentences, if your rate is too slow or too fast, and if you are not talking about what they want to hear. Speak at the rate that is comfortable for you and involve the other person through questions to keep their interest.

Pitch

Your pitch can be monotone, low or high. Ideally you should vary your tone and inflection so that it doesn't sound like you are reading from a boring book.

Physical Concerns

A correct, upright posture increases the effectiveness of your breathing and, therefore, the effectiveness of your voice. As well, any objects in your mouth can ruin all the other things you do to improve your voice, therefore, do not have a pen, gum, paper clips, or cigarette in your mouth.

When I teach proper telephone skills in healthcare I get the participants to call three or four people at other healthcare facilities in the same department and ask for some help. They ask specific questions or fumble around a bit to see how much help they get. In doing this they have found excellent examples of what works as well as examples of inappropriate use of tone, voice, words or attitude.
Once they are comfortable with their own voice, they ask a number of people to call them anonymously and have them note their attitude, tone, voice, words and helpful-

ness. Getting honest feedback to improve one's telephone skills is one way to become a role model of telephone excellence.

Harry van Bommel

Exercise #2

Try some of the following tips for a while and see if your callers treat you differently or if you feel differently about your callers.

- Warm up by humming or singing a song. This will help deepen the sound of your voice, help relax tense muscles and put a smile in your voice.
- Practice your pitch and control by calling an answering machine and deliver several messages. Then listen to the playback and critique yourself or ask a friend to help.
- Put a smile in your voice. It's easy to do. Simply remember to smile as you answer a call or have a small mirror on your desk. Believe it or not, your voice will sound friendlier and people's anxiety will decrease.

Exercise #3

Evaluate your desirable and undesirable traits to help you learn what you want to continue to do well and what you want to improve.

Desirable traits	Undesirable traits
My voice:	**My voice:**
is pleasant sounding	is nasal
has pitch variations	monotone pitch
has a normal rate	is too fast/slow
varies in volume	squeaks, is too loud
says I'm smiling	says I'm tense, bored

Other People: What Callers Want

Whenever we talk about callers it almost sounds like it is them against us. We are all callers. We all respond to other callers. What is it we all want? Callers to our organizations may be professionals, patients, families or suppliers. How can we understand what they want?

If a caller says:	They may mean:
Listen to me.	Pay attention. Understand me. Please listen to what I have to say. I'm afraid, please help.

I want dependable service.	I need to know you will meet your commitments.
Give me correct information.	Don't guess at the right answer. If you don't know or have to check, okay, but don't give me the wrong information.
Do you know your job?	I depend on your knowledge. Please offer suggestions or practical advice.
I need consistent service.	Be dependable. Treat me like the important caller I am.
I expect action.	Don't make me wait unnecessarily as I'm frightened, in pain etc. I know you can't always meet my demands but be as responsive as possible.
I can't hold.	I am calling long distance; or don't put me on hold again (I'm frightened, in pain). Please ask to put me on hold and wait for my answer.

Other People: Caller's Reactions to What We Say

We often use the following statements when we use the telephone. How do callers react to what we say? How might we change what we say to make our jobs more satisfying?

Good morning, [The name of your organization]. May I help you?

Caller's Reaction: Good. The telephone was answered using the three courtesy points: 1) a greeting, 2) giving the department or area name, and 3) an offer of help.

If you feel it is appropriate, you may wish to give them your name as this adds a personal touch. This overall approach will not be completely realistic in situations when you are answering many phone lines at once. In this situation a simple [The name of your organization] with your voice inflection going up at the end to indicate the question "May I help you?"

Ms. Jones is out. Any message?

Caller's Reaction: Poor. The receptionist may sound abrupt and impersonal.

If you change the phrase to: "May I take a message?" The sentence will be more acceptable.

Who were you holding for?

Caller's Reaction: Poor. The caller may think that they have been forgotten or are not important enough to your organization.

Not knowing whom the caller is holding for is a common problem. When this happens, get on the line and say: "I'm sorry, I have forgotten who you were holding for." Then write the person's name so you will remember. Whenever possible provide the caller with a status report, e.g., "Ms. Brown is still on another call. Would you like to continue to hold or may I take your number and have her call you?" If possible give them a choice.

Thank you for calling.

Caller's Reaction: Good.

This simple statement, when said sincerely, gives the caller a feeling of importance.

Complications: Managing Objections

There are basic techniques to help manage people's objections. Good techniques will only work if you have an attitude that says: "This person has a real objection and I can help."

Listen to the specifics of the caller's objections. When you are not clear about what the objection is ask open-ended questions that cannot be answered with a yes or no; questions that begin with who, what, where, when, why, how, **versus** close-ended questions – did, do, is, will.

Who is the person you were talking with?
What is it that I can do to help?
Where were you when this incident happened?
When could you come in to help resolve this problem?

Always provide an immediate response. This is how you can show the person you understand their situation and can empathize with their difficulty. **Many lawsuits against organizations involve the person saying "No one listened to me or cared about my problem."**

State your response in clear and positive terms. Tell them what you can do to help, e.g.:

- Transfer their call to Ms. Jones who can best help her.
- Do some research into the matter and call back at 11:15 with some kind of response (always call back even to tell them you need more time).
- Do not provide unnecessary information and conversation. Be positive and service oriented by sticking to the details except to make them feel comfortable with you.
- Ask them for their approval for any action you have suggested.

Sample Conversation

Mr. White has asked you to interrupt your supervisor because he has a complaint. Your loyalty is to your supervisor yet you want to help Mr. White.

You	Would you like to continue to hold for Ms. Jones or would you like to leave your name and number so that Ms. Jones can call you as soon as she is available.
Caller	No, I can't wait and I don't want to leave my number. Interrupt her and let her know that I must speak with her now.
You	Mr. White, I'm sure Ms. Jones wants to talk to you but since she is not available, please explain what you need and I will either take care of it personally or find someone who can help you. Will that be all right?
Caller	Well, maybe you can help but I doubt it. Ms. Jones promised to tell me why our meeting was postponed.
You	When was the meeting scheduled for? Who was supposed to attend?
Caller	It was scheduled for yesterday at 2:30 p.m. Ms. Jones was supposed to attend with one of her staff to explain some new procedures.
You	I will speak with the departmental secretary and find out what happened. I will call you back in 10 minutes to let you know what I have found out. Will that all right?
Caller	I don't want another run around. How will I know you'll call me back?
You	Regardless of what I find out in the next 10 minutes I will call you to let you know. If I need more time to get details I will let you know then. Will that be all right?
Caller	I guess I don't have much choice.
You	Thank you for your patience Mr. White. I will call you in 10 minutes.
Caller	Okay, thanks for your help.

You call back in 10 minutes to tell Mr. White that Ms. Jones had postponed the meeting until next Wednesday or Thursday, whichever is convenient for him. The other staff person was delayed overseas and Ms. Jones wanted to verify his return before telling Mr. White when the meeting could be rescheduled. You give Mr. White further information about the place and time of the meeting and thank him for his understanding.

Complications: Managing Caller Behavior

Every caller is different. When you recognize these differences you can provide people with excellent service while also enjoying your work more.

Let's look at three behavior styles callers often demonstrate on the telephone: assertive aggressive and/or irate and passive.

The Assertive Caller

An assertive person knows what they want and how to get it. When you have a telephone contact with an assertive caller, it is important to initially be passive and listen closely to what is said. Once you understand what is needed you should become specific and direct. Normally you do not need to ask an assertive caller many questions because they make it clear what they want. Closed questions will allow you to manage the conversation. Assertive callers are interested in quick and efficient results.

Assertive callers are easy to work with if you can meet their immediate needs. Sometimes, however, when dealing with an assertive caller you may need to raise your assertiveness level to simply manage the conversation. Sometimes it is difficult to build rapport with an assertive caller because they may not be interested in exchanging pleasantries. It is important not to take this lack of rapport personally.

Summary: How to Respond to Assertive Callers

Be passive and listen until you understand the problem or request.

Be friendly, but specific and direct in your statements.

Use closed questions to manage the conversation. "Did, do, will, is" are the words that start closed questions which result in yes/no answers and speed the conversation along.

If your voice is soft, raise it slightly.

Stand up if you need to add a more assertive tone to your voice.

Don't get upset if you have difficulty establishing rapport.

Responsive service will satisfy the assertive caller.

The Aggressive/Irate Caller

Managing an aggressive/irate caller is a great opportunity to show off your skills. If done properly, it can be very rewarding. Your body language can help you handle the caller in a professional way.

Diffuse their complaint or request by offering your understanding and sympathy (not by arguing), offering specific help and provide choices.

"I don't blame you for being upset.."

"You are right. You were promised and it hasn't happened. Let's get this problem solved now."

"We've made an error. This time we will do it right."

"I'm sorry you are not satisfied. What can I do now to help the situation?"

If you cannot meet the demands of an aggressive or irate caller because they are unwilling or unable to listen to you, you may have to advise your supervisor and ask them to deal with the caller. Sometimes a caller will only respond to someone in a higher position of authority. Don't take their attitude personally! People have learned through previous experience that dealing with someone in management or senior management is the fastest way to get results.

Summary: How to Respond to Aggressive/Irate Callers

- Sympathize and offer understanding.
- Agree with the caller if they are right.
- Promise to take corrective action and then do it.
- Advise the caller of your actions and provide them options to choose from (gives them sense of control they probably feel they have not had yet).
- Remain courteous and provide assurance of your genuine wish to help them.

If you cannot meet the demands of your caller:

- Decide if someone else (a colleague, supervisor, other department) can help this caller. Do not transfer the caller without telling them why you think this other person can help them.
- If there is no one else who can help and you have no way to assist the caller, be honest with the caller and ask them what they would like you to do. Sometimes you cannot satisfy callers and they may end the conversation unhappy but if you remain courteous and honest they may vent their anger in a more appropriate direction.

The Passive Caller

Passive callers are usually easy to give service to. Satisfied callers are often passive and therefore a professional goal is to provide the kind of service that encourages callers to work easily with you in the future. They know they will receive the service they need and, therefore, do not need to be assertive or aggressive.

In many telephone contacts a caller may switch from being aggressive or assertive to passive. When this happens it may be a signal that the caller is satisfied with the service they are receiving. Most people want "hassle-free" service. Most people dislike having to be assertive or aggressive.

Summary: How to Respond to the Passive Caller

- Listen carefully to the person's request or complaint.
- Provide choices of various actions to give them a sense of control.
- Add the personal touch to make them feel that their call is welcomed.

Complications: Some Statements to Avoid

"I'm sorry. Mrs. Jones is still at lunch."

The key word is "still" which implies that Mrs. Jones is taking a long lunch.

"I don't know where he is, may I take your number and have him call you?"

You hear this a lot. When there is a call for someone, and you are not sure where the person is, that information should not be shared with the caller. A simple "He is unavailable at the moment, may I have him call you?" will do fine.

"She is in the middle of a big problem right now."

This statement tells your caller that you have "big problems". Why share this type of information? Simply say, "I'm sorry she is unavailable", and offer to take a message or to help the caller.

"She went home early."

Callers get very angry at this one. They need help and discover the person who can help them went home early. The fact that she put in a 60-hour work week does not impress people. Treat this information as personal and do not share it.

"I'm sorry but Mr. Smith has not come in yet."

The word "yet" implies that he's late. Just say, "I'm sorry but Mr. Smith is not available. May I help you?"

"The 'X' Department (or Mr. Brown) takes forever to answer their phone, don't they? Can I help you?"

If you have internal problems it is not a good idea to share the situation with your caller. Don't broadcast problems.

"I'm sorry it took me so long to get back to you."

People are not interested in your problems. Regardless of what you say they probably think you have an easy job and were just moving at a slow pace. Give people direct actions versus excuses for past difficulties. You might try, "You were concerned about..and this is what I suggest we do."

"**Could you please repeat that dear?"**

Never use familiar terms such as dear or honey.

"Mr Smith will send you the TQM media release with the relevant software and documentation."

Avoid using jargon or abbreviations with people who probably don't know that TQM is a quality assurance program, media release is a summary of the new service and that relevant software and documentation means a computer program and its reference manual.

Summary

Effective telephone communication means:

- That you are able to use the telephone to get the information and services you need.
- That other people can use the telephone to receive information and services from you.

You must accept 100% responsibility for clear communications with people if you want to achieve effectiveness as a telephone communicator. You can learn to listen more actively and respond in ways that encourage more direct and clear communications with others.

You will encounter callers who are assertive, aggressive and passive. You will be able to master communications with any of these people if you follow some basic communication techniques suggested in this section. Know what your callers want. Understand how to deal with objections. Be clear in your own messages of what you want. Keep in mind the importance of your body language, your smile, and the tone of your voice.

Your attitude is critical in reflecting your professionalism as an individual and as an organization. Nurture your attitude to reduce your stress and increase your effectiveness as a telephone communicator.

Resources

The following resources are only a few of the many useful resources that you can find in your local libraries, within your own organization, and in your local bookstores. Look for other books but also for journal articles, magazine reports, films, videos and audiocassettes. Also keep in mind how much you can learn from experts in the field, including people in your own organization!

Anderson, K. (1992). *Great client service on the telephone.* New York: AMACOM.

Becker, D., & Becker, P.B. (1994). *Client service and the telephone.* Concord, ON: Irwin.

Career Press's powerful telephone skills: A quick and handy guide for any manager or health care owner. (1993). Franklin Lakes, NJ: Career Press.

Friedman, N.J., & Herould, P. (1995). *Telephone skills from A to Z: The telephone 'doctor' phone book.* Menlo Park, CA: Crisp.

Presentation & Public Speaking

The first thing you need to know is that you are already a successful public speaker. You speak to people everyday in a common language that they easily understand and you speak easily. This is the key to all good public speaking – a common language between speaker and audience.

You probably began speaking in public when you were one or two years old. You have been speaking successfully in public for years ever since. You may be nervous about the more formal speaking events in public but you need to remember that you have already mastered many of the skills to speak comfortably in front of your family, friends, classmates, and colleagues.

Therefore, you already know a lot of the information in this section. The material is designed to build on your speaking strengths.

Many young children learning to speak will talk to anyone, anywhere. However, few of us remain born public speakers. Over time, we learn to worry about people disagreeing with us, laughing at us, or falling asleep when we talk. We lose some of the self-confidence we had as children. **Nonetheless, you have continued to talk in public almost every day of your life**. Concentrate on your successful communication instead of remembering every little mistake you have made as a speaker.

When I was three to five years old I used to climb on a table and entertain adults in the local Dutch cafe across the street from our home. They enjoyed this little boy who tried to make them laugh. We immigrated to Canada when I was five. Other children began to laugh at my strange clothes, my accent and my awkwardness in a new country. I became very shy. I rarely spoke in public except with close friends and family.

When I got to high school I became more involved in extra-curricular activities and found that I needed to speak more in public. I began to watch people who were good at it. I assumed, incorrectly, that they were never nervous. I also watched people I thought were not good speakers to find out what they did that I should not do. I watched the audiences of other speakers to see how they reacted – what they found boring or what they liked and disliked. The information in this material began with that research and has continued for decades since then.

Harry van Bommel

One of the most important things we have learned is that shy, quiet people can become the most dynamic speakers. Many celebrities and movie stars can fill a room with laughter, or dance the dance of a lifetime in a film but are very shy when you meet them personally. Their basic personality does not change when they became better at speaking in public – what changed was their awareness that they knew what they were doing and knew that they could meet their audience's expectations. That is what you need to concentrate on. Your basic personality will not change by learning to be a better public speaker. The only thing that will change is your confidence to make your points in public in a clear, concise and effective way that meets the needs of your audience.

> *I am an extremely shy person. People mistake my* joie de vie *as my being gregarious when it is only my joy at being able to walk. When I get up to speak I am seldom nervous because I have done a lot of relaxation work just to get to that point so my body will stand, speak and move overheads. No one believes me when I say that I am shy but the person who looks so competent is a puppeteer who holds the strings and is the puppet as well. If I can do this with all the extra I must manage, with practice, so can others.*
>
> *Michèle Chaban*

The good news is that there is no artificial "buzz" that can compare with the excitement and joy you feel when you receive sincere applause for a speech or a presentation well given! It becomes addictive and will encourage you to speak more often and become even better prepared for the next speech or presentation.

Definition

We will be using the words *presentation* and *speech* interchangeably throughout this section because most of the points deal directly with both forms of public speaking. There is a difference between the two, however:

Speech A verbal talk with little or no audio-visual support. An after-dinner speech, a toast at a wedding, expressing your point-of-view at a meeting are all forms of speeches.

Presentation A speech using audio visual supports like slides, video, overhead projection, theater and educational tools such as, role playing or computer-based learning. Many aspects of preparing a speech are the same for presentations (e.g., setting your objectives for the talk, finding out about your audience, preparing the material). Presentations are often longer than speeches because there is often more opportunity for the audience to participate during a presentation.

In the resources section there are many books listed that offer excellent advice on public speaking. These books use many stories and examples of how people have prepared, rehearsed and delivered wonderful presentations. We do not have enough space in this section to give many stories or anecdotes. We highly recommend that you go to the library or bookstore and pick up one or two books that appeal to you. Read them for the specific examples they give to encourage you to speak in public more and more. You learn from other people's experiences and these books will tell you what helped, or hurt, other people giving similar presentations to the ones you will be giving.

This material is designed specifically as a how-to guide for public speaking and making presentations. Read those sections that apply to your present needs, go back and read the rest when you have more time. A quick overview of the material will tell you what you need to know to prepare for your next speech or presentation.

One-Time Speech or Presentation

If you need to prepare for only one speech or presentation, then do not read all the information in this material. You will be wasting your time and worrying yourself about nothing. Instead read this section and the ones we mention below.

As we said in the introduction, you have been speaking in public for years. The speech or presentation you are going to make requires a few basics to be highly successful. Forget the fancy memorization tricks, the stand-up comedy routines, the magic act and other things you thought your speech needed to be successful.

The basic rule of any speech or presentation is: Know what your audience needs and wants from the presentation and give it to them as best you can. That's it!

You have probably been asked to speak because you have a particular expertise. Here is what you should do to help prepare for your one-time presentation:

Read the section "The basics: For beginners and experts alike" in this section to help you prepare and rehearse your presentation. Skim through the rest of the material to pick up one or two ideas that may be useful to you. Avoid the rest and concentrate on building on your strengths rather than learning lots of new ways of doing things.

Write an outline of your presentation and show it to a few trusted people to get their comments and suggestions. Speak to people who know what your audience will want so that you can meet their expectations as best as you can. Your outline should:

- Use an attention-getter such as a claim, question, anecdote, very carefully chosen joke (often overdone by speakers) or an exhibit.
- State your topic and narrow it to a small number of points or statements.

- State your objective. Tell them what you are out to accomplish or prove.
- State the benefits that the audience can derive from your message.
- Deliver the body of your message: illustrate and support.
- Summarize your key points and benefits.
- Finish with a strong conclusion – one that is memorable, clear and concise. Tell them how to use your information. Appeal to them to take some form of action, if that is appropriate.

Rehearse the presentation a few times to get the feel for it. Ask a few trusted people to watch you rehearse your presentation to give you encouragement and support. Remember not to memorize or read from your notes. Use them as a cue to say the right things in the right order but, when possible, speak directly to your audience. They are a wonderfully forgiving group of people if you just help meet their needs.

Make your presentation without apologizing for how you present unless you have specific hidden limitations. Bring some food (cookies, fruit, candies) as a gift to your audience (assuming it is small enough). People always feel warmer to a speaker who brings food!

> *I struggle with this all the time. I always begin my lectures with an apology. I apologize for what I cannot do. I confess my limitations, I say I may trip over the microphone wire but not to worry, I will just keep lecturing. I do it with humor and I do it because I am not like others. I, like many of us, have limitations. When I didn't identify these, inevitably, there was someone who shouted out, "Can't hear you" or "Speak louder" which threw me off course and upset me greatly as I then had to admit to my limitations as a deficit rather than my own natural ability.*
> *Michèle Chaban*

After your presentation find out if you met the audience's needs and what they thought of your presentation. Ask a few people individually what they thought. Have one or two trusted people to ask a few others for you.

When you follow these basic five steps you may find out that you actually enjoyed speaking in public. The more people do public speaking the more addicted they become to it. It is so much fun to help an audience meet their needs in an enjoyable and non-threatening way.

The Basics: For Beginners and Experts Alike

Courage *comes from* ***wanting*** *to say it well.*
Security *comes from* ***knowing*** *you can say it well.*
Confidence *comes from* ***having*** *said it well.*
Sharon Bower

It often takes longer to explain the basics of a skill than to actually use or practice those basics. The idea here is to skim those parts you already know from experience and improve your speaking skills with the rest of the information.

Four Parts to Public Speaking

- Preparation
- Rehearsal
- Delivery
- Evaluation of what worked and didn't work.

The Audience

The audience has shown up to learn and perhaps be entertained by your presentation. They want you to be successful so that they can tell other people they made the right decision is coming to hear you. They have their own egos invested in your success so they are there to help you. As an equal to them during this speech, use their desire to make you successful and enjoy their trust and appreciation. If you are prepared and truly want to meet their needs it will be hard to fail no matter how nervous you might be.

Why? (The Purpose)

People need to know why they should listen to you, why they should remember what you say, and why they should use what you have told them. If you know your audience well, then your "why" will fit their needs and you will be successful.

Types of Speeches

You may be asked to speak at different kinds of functions. Later in this section we will look specifically at the location of the presentation, but more important is the reason people have come together. Are they at a breakfast meeting, sales convention, medical rounds or inservice, regular monthly meeting, a social event or a public forum at the local library on a specific topic? The speech should be short (15-20 minutes maximum) so that the audience is left wanting a little bit more.

Breakfast meetings (usually at 7 or 7:30 a.m.) are not good places for in-depth speeches or presentations. Most people are too tired or too pre-occupied with the rest of the day. Leave such times for people to talk among themselves or for giving out awards and leave the speeches for another time.

Morning presentations The advantages of speaking in the morning are that people tend to be more alert than after lunch, they tend to be more willing to get involved in the presentation, and they are fresh to new ideas. The disadvantages are that morning presentations often begin late, the room temperature is too cool or too warm, and the audience expects the speakers to be more dynamic and not waste their valuable energy or time.

Lunch speeches are almost as difficult as breakfast meetings. People want to eat (usually more than they normally eat for lunch), have some drinks (which certainly affects concentration), leave for a stretch before they go off to work or other presentations, talk to people they have not seen for a long time, or just relax after a big lunch. This audience can make you very successful as a speaker if your topic can be energizing and/or change the way your audience can be more successful in their work or personal life. If your topic is rather technical or dull then you will lose your audience quickly (physically or mentally) and have them tell other people that your speech was not worth their time.

> *particularly if there will be wine. My subject (pain control and palliative care) doesn't match very well with wine and liqueur. I remember one very hilarious situation several years ago when one of my after dinner audience had a wee bit too much wine and started to play the piano in the same room while I was presenting. Fortunately, a colleague gently escorted him out. It's funny to look back and remember.*
> *Elizabeth Latimer*

Afternoon presentations have the advantage of low expectations. People come back after lunch full and perhaps tired. If you can get them involved in an activity quickly then you help them get back their energy and enthusiasm. Some speakers even begin by using a videotape of an appropriate stand-up comic to get the audience laughing and feeling good about being together in this particular group with this particular speaker.

After-dinner speaker After a long day at work or at home people want to be entertained as well as educated. They are not interested in a lecture-style presentation on the tragedies of the last economic recession. They are interested in improving themselves without a great deal of effort and thought or examining their present situation in a humorous way. You do not need to be a entertainer as much as provide information in an entertaining way. Unusual facts, real-life human stories that make people laugh or smile with understanding, or a moving anecdote all give people something to think about and discuss with others later on. A good speaker is one that people will want to talk to others about. Remember the speech should be short (15-20 minutes maximum) so that the audience is left wanting a little bit more. Eat a light meal and avoid alcohol (a depressant) even if you are nervous. A little nervous energy is required to present well and a full stomach or a few drinks will not help you present more professionally.

Evening meetings These tend to be more informal meetings at schools, libraries or church halls. Even those held at corporate headquarters or at the evening portion of a convention have less predictability to them about the size of audience, the location, the audio-visual equipment that is available, etc. People tend to arrive late and leave early during your presentation for personal reasons. Your ego must accept these diversions and concentrate on providing your audience (regardless of how small) with the best presentation you can.

We have begun to look at some of the things that lead to a good speech or presentation. To make the alternatives clear, We want to highlight the obvious errors that far too many speakers make that result in poor presentations or speeches. A key to success is to avoid the common errors.

Poor speeches often result if you:

- Come unprepared.
- Waste everyone's time with inaccurate or irrelevant information.
- Talk to yourself (i.e. never look at the audience).
- Talk to your boss.
- Use opinions instead of facts.
- Ramble away from your subject.
- Forget your objective, or your audience.
- Ignore the setting.
- Ignore the clock (i.e. do not start and finish on time).
- Conclude inconclusively.
- Tell inappropriate jokes or stories.
- Make sexist or racist comments.
- Constantly apologize for your speech.

The Audience and Your Preparation

At the heart of every successful presentation is a speaker who knows their audience and genuinely wants to help them leave with their expectations fulfilled.

I always like to check out the layout of the room well before my presentation. Not only things like AV equipment, podium and lighting, but I also like to have a "feel" of the room so I have a flow for my movements. I seldom use a podium anymore. I like to get close to the audience. I also use more overheads than slides because I like to see my audience. It helps me to relax and I think the audience enjoys it more too.
Elizabeth Latimer

Audience Expectations	Audiences Expect That You Will:
Know who they are	Know your specific audience's needs for this specific presentation. Is your talk meant to change the way they do their work? If your audience is composed of both lay and professional people, use theory and anecdotes throughout your presentation.
Assure them	Assure them through your manner and speech that you know your subject and you are well prepared and organized to present it. For example, if you are presenting a part of your work, briefly tell them your experience so they know they can learn something from you; preview your presentation with them so they can hear that it is well thought out.
Respect their valued time	Let them know you understand their time is valuable and that you will not waste it. You do not need to say anything to tell them that. This becomes clear when you preview your presentation so they know what they can expect and you can tell them that you always finish on time.
First things first	Present your most important information near the beginning of your presentation. People are used to getting information fast: many of us watch television advertisements, music videos, the 2-hour movie version of a 1,000 page novel, fast-paced children's programs. People have less patience for speakers who take a long time to get to the point. Recognize this fact in your presentations by making the

main points early on and the audience will wait to hear your supporting information. Do the reverse and build up to a "big finish" and you may have lost half your audience (either physically or mentally).

Clarity Make your main points clearly and memorably. For example, you can help people remember your points with a brief handout, a story to illustrate the main points (people remember stories better than lecture points), an overhead or slide so they can read the points while you are discussing them.

Conclusion Present a strong, logical conclusion. It lets people know you are finished with your presentation but also leaves them with your main points summarized and a conclusion that they can leave with and think about.

Humor Use appropriate humor, stories, and comments. People do not appreciate bad jokes, or efforts at humor that are unnatural to you. You do not have to be a stand-up comic but neither do you have to pretend to be a serious university lecturer on the meaning of life. Be yourself and allow those aspects of your personality that your family and friends appreciate to come out in a natural way. One speaker I know who is very shy uses overheads of a few cartoons to add the humor that she does not feel comfortable adding herself. Another speaker who presents to small groups of 10-30 people brings in home-baked cookies to go along with the morning coffee break. He is uncomfortable with revealing too much of his humor or personality when presenting so uses that wonderful incentive "food!" to be more personable with his audience.

Majority Speak to the whole audience (majority rules): people in smaller groups are less responsive than large audiences because they may be self-conscious. Therefore speak to the whole audience (the majority) rather than trying to get the person who is sleeping or yawning in the back row to enjoy your speech.

Outside influences Recognize any outside influences that are beyond your control. For example, people in the audience may be affected by late-breaking news of a success or disaster (e.g., a favorite home-town sports team has won or lost the championship). A speaker who does not recognize these outside influences will be speaking to an audience who is losing interest. Comment on the event to show that you understand what the outside influence is, and if appropriate, draw that event into your presentation.

Exercise #1
Your Audience: Preparing for the Speech

To prepare for a speech answer the following questions:

1. Do you know, generally, who your audience is and what they expect from you? Do you know if they want to be taught, informed, persuaded or entertained or a combination of these 4? How will you find out?
2. How will you assure them that you know your subject and you are well prepared?
3. How will you tell or show them you understand their time is valuable?
4. How will you make your main points clearly and memorably?
5. What will be your strong conclusion? How will you make it memorable?
6. How will you make sure your humor, stories and comments are appropriate?
7. How will you make sure you speak to the majority audience?
8. How will you recognize any major outside influences that may affect your audience?
9. How will you meet the needs of your audience if they are used to getting information fast?

Preparing and Rehearsing Your Presentations

You now have a basic understanding of your audience's expectations. It's time to look at the specific steps to preparing and rehearsing your presentation. This section has information on:

- Analyzing your audience more specifically than you have done before.
- Preparing technical information and closing remarks.
- Using texts or notes in your presentation.
- Shortening your sentences.
- Rehearsal techniques.
- Developing confidence.

- Visualizations and deep breathing.
- Evaluating your preparation and rehearsals.

Remember there are four main reasons why people go willingly to listen to someone's presentation. They want to be informed, taught, persuaded, and/or entertained. You need to know which of these four reasons fits your overall audience. If they want to be taught something, then it is unlikely that they will want to listen to a 2-hour speech that entertains or asks them for their opinion without any concrete learning material presented.

Once you understand the audience and the overall purpose of the presentation, you need to attract their interest, and then do one or more of the following: inform or teach them something, persuade them, and/or entertain them.

Interest

Capture their attention and maintain it for the rest of the presentation. You can do this by beginning with a dramatic or comical short story, through a strong claim or controversial point, through appropriate humor, or by a direct "this is what I am going to say to you today" approach.

To Inform or Teach

You must make it relevant in terms of what will reach them intellectually, emotionally, and when appropriate, spiritually.

You must make it logical, coherent, and easy to follow.

To Persuade

- The information must have credibility.
- The information must have a benefit.
- It must logically apply to the situation.
- It must be fair and equitable.

Audience Analysis

You have looked at the audience as a whole to find out what you should be presenting and how. Now you need to analyze the audience more specifically to make sure your assumptions are correct.

- Size of group. Some people prefer talking to small groups while others prefer to talk to large groups. Which do you prefer and how will you handle the size expected for your next presentation?
- Age range. Large age differences may not affect your audience if they have a com-

mon interest. However, if your presentation is designed for an audience of people who grew up in the 1950s and 1960s but half your audience was born after the 1969 first landing on the moon, you have to recognize that the personal perspectives of your audience are vastly different.

- What do they want (versus need) to hear?
- What jobs do they have?
- Do they resist change?
- Are they friendly or unfriendly?
- Any corporate or professional politics to consider?
- Do they wish to ask questions?
- Are they motivated or not?
- Do they like information presented in one way more than in other ways?
- What audio-visual aids suit this group?
- Is the topic controversial with this group?
- How much time do they have to hear your presentation?
- Are they bottom-line oriented or detail oriented?
- What social, political, economic or professional prejudices are listeners likely to have?
- What do they know about the subject?
- Can you expect hostility from the group?
- Are you trying to inform or persuade or both?
- Will they respond to humor?
- What possible questions can you expect from the audience?
- Do you have the answers to these questions?
- Do they require a great deal of proof?
- Do you have the proof?
- Are they skeptical of everything?
- Are they pressed for time?
- Are you the only speaker? If not, in what order are you speaking (i.e. first, middle, last)? How will this order affect your audience's ability to listen and learn, if at all?

Interesting Technical Presentation

Statistical, technical, financially detailed or reporting presentations can be long, tedious, dry and dull. Why? Because they contain facts and so often, nothing but the facts. This type of presentation is demanding on the audience in that every word, line, statement is crucial to the understanding of the information. What the presentation needs is material that will make facts interesting and relevant to the audience and will be less demanding on the audience's attention span. In other words, *facts need interpretation.*

Technical presentations can be the most rewarding to give when you add interpretation and variety. People often expect to be bored at such a presentation and anything you do to increase their interest and energy will make the presentation more memorable and enjoyable. You can hardly lose doing such a presentation well since so many other people do it poorly!

Interpretation includes:

- Personal editorials (appropriate to the audience)
- Examples
- Analogies and comparisons
- Anecdotes and experiences
- Humor
- Visual aids
- Listener applications and benefits
- Audience participation
- Testimonials and quotes
- Case studies

Closing Remarks

- Use words like, "In closing" to tell people you are about to conclude.
- Repeat your objective statement (in past tense).
- Remind them what you wanted to accomplish.
- Tell them what you expect or ask of them in terms of: action, behavior, attitude.
- Persuasive: ask for the sales order or call to action.
- Informative: invite questions and/or suggest they read documentation.
- Avoid the introduction of new facts or figures and avoid a long conclusion or producing an anticlimax by mentioning some relatively unimportant point at the last minute.

Text or Notes

There are various ways to write your notes. It is generally not advisable to read your presentation word for word from a podium. The exceptions may be a legal presentation, a press release, or for dramatic effect (e.g., reading a historical, literary or memorable speech, poem or monologue).

1. Use 8.5 x 11 cardboard (file folder). Handles better than paper and doesn't shake as much. Other people use 3 x 5 cards that are less obvious or intrusive. Others

use overheads or slides to show the audience the notes you are speaking from. This may help audience members who learn best visually.

2. Maximum of 6-8 lines per sheet.
3. Typed or printed in big dark letters.
4. Start each sentence on the left.
5. 3-5-7 critical words per idea or sentence.
6. Leave room to add.

   Separate idea per sheet. Avoid having one sentence begin on one page and end on the next.

How to Shorten Sentences

1. Drop the word "and" from your sentences. It usually links 2 or 3 short sentences together, turning them into a paragraph. Replace "and" with a period and start a new sentence.
2. Put the "statement" early in your sentence. Avoid qualifying your remarks before the punch line. In fact, put the qualifiers in separate sentences.
3. Question, then answer. Break up a long sentence by turning the first part into a question followed by the answer which is the second part. For example: "How do you break up long sentences? You ask a question and follow it with a short answer."
4. Springboard. Break a long sentence into 2 or 3 separate ones by using the last word of the first sentence as the first word of the second and so forth. For example, "I have a dream. A dream.."
5. Variations on a theme! If a sentence has 2 or more verbs and/or adjectives or nouns, break them up by writing shorter ones. For example, "Ask not what your country can do for you. Ask what you can do for your country."

Rehearsal

1. Write out in long form, a full draft of your presentation.
2. Edit, revise and shorten your sentences.
3. Prepare "agenda" notes. These will help you remember the order of your presentation and when you may need audio-visual aids during the presentation.
4. Do one rehearsal of your presentation out loud to test the quality of your lesson plan notes.
5. If there are problems with the notes, fix them.
6. Do a second rehearsal and tape it on a cassette player to work on your verbal delivery. Minimize "uhhs" and "ahhs".

7. Do a third rehearsal with visual aids to practice your body language and to become familiar with the room and the visual equipment.
8. Enjoy yourself or no one else will.

Developing Confidence

Lalophobia is the fear of rejection or embarrassment of making mistakes and failing. Every presenter is nervous (if they are any good) and afraid of failing. A certain amount of fear produces adrenaline, which helps all professional speakers. Professionals never lose their fear completely. If they do they probably become over confident, boring and arrogant to their audience. Proper preparation, planning, techniques and rehearsal are important in minimizing fear and nervousness. Positive mental visualization through role-playing is helpful tool.

Visualization and Deep Breathing

A very old technique for dealing with anxiety before a speech is to do some deep breathing and visualize yourself giving the presentation. Ancient Greeks used this technique when preparing for speeches. In modern times, Olympic athletes often spend hours every day after practice going through their activities mentally – over and over again. This helps the mind work best with the body for peak performance.

Deep breathing:

1. Sit, stand or lie down in a comfortable position. You can even do this while walking slowly (e.g., in a park, on a beach, along a quiet street).
2. Breathe in through your nose and try to fill your stomach with air. Your abdomen will expand which means that air is getting deep into your body. If only your chest expands that your breathing is too shallow.
3. Hold the breath for a second or two.
4. Breathe out slowly through your mouth. Breathe out a little more air than you normally would. This helps you take a deeper breath the next time. Breathing out through your mouth helps to relax tight jaw muscles.
5. Wait a second or two before taking your next breath and continue the cycle.
6. As you continue to breathe deeply, concentrate on tensing – then relaxing your major muscle groups: neck, shoulders, arms, chest, abdomen, thighs, calves, hands and feet.
7. Your body should now be somewhat relaxed (this takes practice so do not expect complete relaxation the first few times you do this) Continue to breathe deeply.

Imagine in your mind getting up in front of your audience and giving your presentation. Imagine people smiling, nodding in agreement, laughing and looking thoughtful as you present your material. Imagine yourself full of energy and dedicated to meeting the needs of your audience. Imagine yourself filled with adrenaline that comes from a realistic level of anxiety and turning the adrenaline into the calm, professional air of a confident public speaker.

Imagine this scene several times over several days to get used to feeling successful. If possible, find out where you are speaking and visit the location so that you can see the actual room during your visualizations.

Evaluation

You need to evaluate your rehearsals based on the purpose of your presentation, your audience analysis, your content, your visual presentation techniques, and your verbal delivery during practice sessions. You will probably need the help of a family member, friend or colleague to give you an honest evaluation of how they think you succeeded in meeting the anticipated needs of the audience.

Based on your own evaluation and that of others, you may need to change your presentation. If you do not have time (because of short deadlines) to go through many rehearsals or an evaluation, then you must be sure to get feedback from others after your actual presentation. This feedback will help you make sure the next time you present you will do an even better job. Over time, evaluations will allow you to take less time to prepare and rehearse presentations because you have improved your skills and need less time to "learn as you go".

Presentation Formats

There are different ways to present information depending on your purpose. You have already decided in the previous section what your purpose is: to inform, teach, persuade and/or entertain. Now you must decide whether you want to give an unrehearsed speech (at a meeting perhaps); a well prepared speech that you want to use to influence or convince people about a certain issue or idea, or a presentation that teaches your audience about specific knowledge and skills.

Deciding the purpose of your presentation will help you decide what format the speech should take. Let's examine various types of formats.

If you plan to give a short, unrehearsed speech (at a meeting, social gathering or public forum) you need to concentrate your format on the following.

Short, Unrehearsed Speeches

Short Unrehearsed Speech

1. Discuss only one aspect of the topic.
2. Tell them your main point.

3. Illustrate the point with one example,
4. Support it with one piece of evidence.
5. Restate the point.
6. Tell the audience how your point affects the listener.

All of the above points should take 3-5 minutes maximum if you want to keep the attention of your audience. Remember that this is an unrehearsed speech where you are probably not the main speaker so keeping it short and simple is essential.

Longer Unrehearsed Speech

Same points as above except that you can discuss up to three points of the topic. Each point can be illustrated or supported before you conclude strongly with your own viewpoint. Again, keep it short and simple using common, everyday language. You should not take any more than 10 minutes.

Short Speech-Formats to Influence an Audience

There are three short speech formats that help you to influence or convince your audience about specific issues, ideas or recommendations. One format is designed to have an impact on your audience. You may not influence or convince them to think a certain way but you will give them something to think about. A second format is designed to state a problem to provide background to an audience who must make a decision about what to do next. The third format is designed to provide your audience with recommendations that may help them make decisions. It is different from the second format because you begin with your ideas and recommendations. In the second format you are providing information without putting your own ideas forward.

Impact Speech

State > Comment > Illustrate > Support > Explain > Re-state.

1. State a fact, principle or idea. For example: "Effective client service leads to increased satisfaction and sales."
2. Comment on the fact. For example, what is the organization's stand, policy, philosophy, attitude, and/or comment on your personal likes, dislikes, concerns, interests, worries, etc., and/or comment from a professional point of view.
3. Illustrate the fact or the comments, or both. Use examples, anecdotes, experiences, comparisons, analogies, quotes, testimonials and listener applications.
4. Explain the effect or impact of the fact to listeners. This may include cost, benefits, advantages or disadvantages. They need to know why they should be inter-

ested in this issue.
5. Re-state the fact, principle, idea or comment.

Problem or Opportunity

Establish that there is:

- An urgent need to be addressed.
- A serious problem to be solved.
- A great opportunity to be seized.

Use:

- Cost-benefit analysis.
- Surveys, studies or polls.
- Historical data or documented examples and experiences.
- Expert opinions and third party objective documentation.
- Track record and testimonials.

You leave the possible solutions to the group to decide with, or without, your help. Often this presentation format is used when a person is asked to present a certain issue because of their expertise but it is assumed that people higher up in the organization will make the actual decisions.

Recommendation Format

Submit a recommendation that will satisfy the need, solve the problem or capitalize on the opportunity.

Feature
Application
Benefit

The FAB Method is a short way to tell your audience what the **main feature** of your recommendation is, how it **applies** to their specific situation and what the **benefits** are to the audience and/or organization.

Presentations for Teaching

Teaching an audience specific knowledge and skills requires a "lesson plan". The plan includes:

- What you want them to learn. What they want to learn. Is it the same thing?
- What handouts, audio-visuals, and exercises you will use to help them learn.
- How you, and your participants, will know if they have learned it.

A typical agenda looks like this:

1. You tell your audience what you hope they will learn by the end of the presentation. Check with them to see if that is what they expected or want to learn.
2. Introductions (if group is small enough).
3. Present background information to whatever you are talking about using audio-visual equipment and handout material if necessary. For example, if you are presenting on how to apply a new computer program to the workplace, you might begin with some background information on how this program was selected, what was the purpose for changing programs, etc.
4. Give participants an opportunity to ask questions or comment on material.
5. Provide the audience with an exercise to help them understand knowledge and/or practice a specific skill.
6. Find out how the exercise went. What did they learn? Do they have any questions or comments?
7. Summarize that portion of the presentation and move onto the next part, if any.
8. At the end of the presentation, review the basic knowledge and skills and recommend how participants can begin to use these personally or professionally.

Medical rounds tend to have a set format and the audience may be required to attend. In fact, physicians may have attended similar sessions for years, during their training and professional careers. The quality of such presentations varies greatly. However, those that are memorable in a positive way have been organized, been within the time frame allotted, allowed time for discussion, departed from the "set format", used overheads that are legible and contain highlights only and been presented in a dynamic way. This section on presentations has much useful information for physicians to incorporate in their presentations.
Elizabeth Latimer

Delivering Your Presentation

The following are some tips about delivering your presentation. **Do not try to be the perfect speaker**. Try to be an **effective speaker**. Effective speakers identify their strengths and build on them. They also identify one single delivery skill they would like to do differently the next time they speak. Once they have improved that skill enough to make it automatic, they pick another skill.

When I first began public speaking, I repeatedly used to push my glasses up my nose with my middle finger. When I saw myself on video, I realized that this did not look very

professional (or very polite!). For the next few times I spoke, I forced myself to lift my glasses up by holding one side of by glasses with my thumb and forefinger and gently lifting the glasses up. In this way I never lost sight of my audience and the action was less obvious to them.
Harry van Bommel

In this section on delivery skills you will work on your voice, body language and "stage fright".

Your Voice

Tone

Sound travels on waves so aim your voice at your audience; not at the floor or projection screen.

Volume

Enunciate words clearly, take breaths, alternate between whispers (for attention) and loudness (for drama).

A speech pathologist taught me to imagine great gusts of air being pushed from my diaphragm out through my throat to enhance my voice. She also taught me to deepen my voice while breathing which is no easy feat. The Tibetan monks chant and pray with deep voices. I imagine this before I begin my speeches and I see some results if I stay focused on this image.
Michèle Chaban

Speed

Your audience often breathes at the rate you speak so slow down and speed up to get variety in reactions.

Enunciation

Let people hear the end of each word.

Pitch

Often the faster you speak the higher your pitch. Your pitch also goes higher when your vocal cords are tense. Lowering one's pitch adds authority to your speech, therefore, you must begin by relaxing your vocal cords and practicing speaking lower. A good technique that combines the two is to sing before your presentation (e.g., in your office, in your car, at home) using your abdominal muscles (like opera singers) and sing a key or two lower than normal.

Patterns of Hesitation

When giving information give it in chunks.

Think first, then talk. Too many people begin to talk right away – stopping to think of what to say next – then starting again. This latter way suggests that you are unsure of your topic. It leaves audience hanging and waiting for what comes next (unless that is the effect you want).

I do find some "foibles" and mannerisms of speakers endearing. They demonstrate a vulnerability and personal human connection that tells me that they too, are human like me. Mind you, this is only in the context of a good presentation. Don't worry too much about your personal ways. They are you!
Elizabeth Latimer

Body Language

Gestures

If you watch professional speakers you will find that they use all sorts of gestures. Hand gestures, alone, include their hands in front, in back, in a pocket, waving, pointing, holding the belt, touching the face, etc. All of these gestures are appropriate and none should last a long time. You can basically do whatever you like with your hands if you add a little variety and do nothing objectionable (e.g.,, constantly scratching your ear). It is when people are too disciplined or have taken a public speaking course and write gesture prompts in their speeches that they look fake. The best thing to do is videotape yourself to see if you have any bad habits that you would like to change. Keep in mind that most audiences do not concentrate on your gestures, but on your overall presentation (i.e. words, organization, body language, and voice).

Podium

You may feel more comfortable using a podium at first. You can keep your notes in front of you.

With practice, we strongly encourage you to move away from podiums. It is more personable to speak to people without a hiding behind a prop. You can walk slowly across the front of your audience or even go into the audience occasionally. You can use audio-visual tools to change the pace of the presentation.

Eye Contact

Try to look at your audience throughout your presentation. This gives the audience the sense that they are included and that you are interested in talking to them as individuals.

Stage Fright Versus Nervous Energy

All professional speakers get some form of stage fright: stomach butterflies, feeling chilled, sweaty hands, dry mouth, etc. Stage fright tends to lessen once you have started your presentation. The good news is that all you need to do is deliver some of your presentation well. The audience will concentrate on the good parts and forget any obvious fright you may have had. Remember that the audience will not be able to see sweaty hands or dry mouth. To my own surprise, they cannot even see your knees shake or your hands quiver. Therefore, do not worry that your stage fright will affect your speech or your audience.

Nervous energy, on the other hand, is what the audience can see or hear. For example, some speakers have loose change in their pockets and they keep jangling the coins so that people in the back row can hear it. Others pace up and down away from the podium in a mad pace that distracts from their presentation. Others drum their fingers on a table or they sway back on forth on one spot on the floor. Ed Wohlmuth in his book The Overnight Guide to Public Speaking suggests that people get a rubber ball that fits in their palm. Throughout the day before a presentation they squeeze the ball continually in one hand and then the other. Once you begin the presentation and you feel yourself beginning to do something that shows your nervous energy, just imagine squeezing the ball and you will immediately stop. He swears by this method.

Evaluation

Again, it is important to have people tell you what you did well and what you might do differently the next time you speak. Concentrate on improving your strengths first. Then pick one thing you might do differently for the next few presentations until you have changed that behavior. For example, if you tend to pace to quickly up and down the stage, you might try standing still in one spot for awhile. When your pacing becomes more natural and less like a nervous walk you can concentrate on another thing you would like to do differently.

Exercise #2
Action Planning

You can plan for the preparation, rehearsal, delivery and evaluation of your speech or presentation in as much detail as you like depending on your time, the audience, the expectations about the delivery, the importance of the event, and your own expertise and comfort.

There are key questions for all presentations. Use the sample action plan to help you be as competent and confident a speaker you want to be.

Item	What I Have to Decide or Do	By This Date
Know your audience and their expectations and needs. What is the purpose or objective of this presentation?		
What must I do to prepare- research, audio-visual preparations?		
What format will I use based on my purpose?		
How will I rehearse for this presentation? Who can help me review my content and delivery?		
For longer presentations what will my agenda look like?		
What specific delivery strengths will I concentrate on? What one weakness will I try to improve on during this presentation?		
How will I evaluate the success of this presentation?		

Summary

Natural speakers may be born, but most lose many of their skills by the time they finish elementary school. Public speaking is something that we have done since the age of one or two but we lose some of our confidence as we grow up.

Public speaking is about relearning some of the skills we once had, adding a few new ones and speaking with a confidence that only preparation and rehearsal provide. Concentrating on the following basics will help you develop your skills as you need them and improve your confidence as an effective speaker.

- Come prepared.
- Help people to learn, think and question.
- Talk to your audience to meet their needs.
- Use facts to support your opinions.
- Stick to your subject.
- Concentrate on your objective.
- Make people in the audience think you are talking just to them.

- Establish a comfortable listening setting.
- Finish on time or slightly early.
- Conclude strongly and memorably.
- Tell only appropriate jokes or stories.
- Never use sexist or racist comments.
- Be proud of your efforts.
- Enjoy what you do or no one else will.

Resources

The following resources are only a few of the many useful resources that you can find in your local libraries, within your own organization, and in your local bookstores. Look for other books but also for journal articles, magazine reports, films, videos and audiocassettes. Also keep in mind how much you can learn from experts in the field, including people within your own organization!

When preparing speeches and presentations it may be helpful to use encyclopedias, Canadian, American and World Almanacs and other general resources to have up-to-date information at your fingertips.

Buchan, V. (1997). *Make presentations with confidence.* Monroe, WA: Barrons.

Carnegie, D. (1995). *How to develop self-confidence and influence people by public speaking.* New York: Pocket Books.

Desberg, P. (1996). *No more butterflies: Overcoming stage fright, shyness, interview anxiety and fear of public speaking.* Oakland, CA: New Harbinger.

Engel, P. (1996). *Health care presentations and public speaking.* New York: McGraw-Hill.

Gaulke, S. (1996). *101 ways to captivate a health care audience.* New York: AMACOM.

Hager, P.J., & Scheiber, H.J. (1997). *Designing and delivering scientific, technical, and managerial presentations.* Toronto: Wiley & Sons.

Hendricks, W., Holliday, M., & Mobley, R. (1996). *Secrets of power presentations.* Franklin Lakes, NJ: Career Press.

Maisel, E. (1997). *Fearless presenting: A self-help guide for anyone who speaks, sells, or performs in public.* New York: Watson-Guptill.

Morrisey, G.L., Sechrest, T.L., & Warman, W.B. (1997). *Loud and clear: How to prepare and deliver effective health care and technical presentations.* New York: Addison-Wesley.

Smith, T.C. (1995). *Making successful presentations: A self-teaching guide.* Toronto: Wiley & Sons.

Timm, P.R. (1997). *How to make winning presentations: 30 action tips for getting your ideas across with clarity and impact.* Franklin Lakes, NJ: Career Press.

Urs Bender, P. (1995). *Secrets of power presentations.* Buffalo, NY: Firefly Books.

Wilder, L. (1999). *7 steps to fearless speaking.* Etobicoke, ON: John Wiley & Sons.

Letters, Memos and Reports

Much of this chapter has been on verbal communication. Written communication is equally important in getting your message across. Whether your message was given verbally first and your writing is to reinforce what you said, or your writing is your only communication, the message must be clear, concise and memorable. What you learned in previous sections can help your writing. When your writing improves, so will your verbal messages.

Effective health care writing is not the same as creative writing. Your purpose is to communicate with others in a clear, concise way; not to write a novel or the great screenplay. The people who will read your work are generally not reading for pleasure. They are overloaded with memos, have little time for reading, and they have their own priorities for what they need to do with their time.

Communication comes from the Latin "communis" meaning common. For communication to be effective we must, therefore, use common words and phrases.

It isn't what you write that is important,

It is what people read.

No matter how well you write a letter or memo or e-mail there will be people who read your words differently than you intended. To minimize this you can choose words that are common and easily understood. These words are then put into short sentences (up to 12-20 words) and short paragraphs (2-4 sentences).

Wonderfully developed and crafted memos have vanished in recent years. I can recall a time when it seemed like great fun to send a "memorandum" inviting colleagues together for a meeting. Considerable care was taken to explain the purpose of the meeting, where and when it would be held, and what sort of muffins would be there. Language and style was paramount. All this reflected a gentler time. In the beginning of the 90s, this came to a sad end for many as organizations downsized, managers covered several areas, and E-mail became a significant communication tool. At first, E-mail memos tended to look like hard copy memoranda, but I can remember the day when I received my first E-mail "summoning" me and others to a meeting. ALL PROJECT SPONSORS TO ASSEMBLE AT 0800 IN CONFERENCE ROOM ON MONDAY. Every letter was in upper case and there was no context (and certainly no muffins!). People who opened this terse message late on Friday ruminated over the weekend and were relieved to find the Monday morning meeting was just another check-in and up-date get together.

I think it's a good idea to reflect for a moment on how our E-mail is understood ***before*** *clicking on "send".*
Larry Lewis

There are dozens of books on various techniques to improve letter/memo writing. The main features these books agree on are:
Words and sentences should follow the K.I.S.S. system (Keep it Short and Simple").[3]
Writers must be organized and consistent.
Effective writing takes practice.
Most importantly writers must be persistent and professional.

The only way to accomplish effective letter or memo writing is to learn a few new steps at a time **to enhance the skills you already have** and practice them until you are comfortable.

Your goal is to be a good and effective writer, not a perfect writer.

Most of you write the same type of material over and over again in your work. Once you have carefully worked through your next few pieces of writing you can use them as models for your future works. When you are comfortable with your enhanced style why not pass this section on to someone else?

Writing for Immediate Success

How often have you read something and said: "What's this person trying to prove?" or "Why can't people write like they talk so I can understand what they want?"

The major causes of ineffective writing are:

- The writer trying to impress someone with their language.
- The writer not writing anything that interests or benefits the reader.
- The writer using the passive voice.
- The writer writing like a lecturer, not a communicator.

To improve your writing immediately you can do four things:

- Ask yourself **why** you are writing this? (purpose)
- Ask yourself **who** you are writing to? (audience)
- Write as you normally talk using a friendly and respectful tone.
- Use the active voice.

Let's examine these one by one.

Purpose

There are six main purposes we have in writing: to inform, to apologize, to request information, to sell, to persuade, and to entertain.

When we want to **inform** people in a letter or a memo we are presenting facts, conclusions and perhaps recommendations. There may be elements of persuasion but your primary goal is to inform.

Letters of **apology** to angry readers must answer their complaint and offer a solution. If you have made an error, acknowledge it. A well written apology letter can save organizations from many lawsuits.

Often letters **requesting** information are too lengthy and detailed. Readers need to know immediately what specific information is requested. You can list your request in point form to highlight the exact information you want.

Letters used **to sell** a service, product or idea must clearly describe what the benefits are to the reader. Sales are built on the emotional appeal of the item more often than on the technical merits of a service, product or idea. Readers want to know that what you are selling will at least: make their work easier, enhance their own professional position, reduce costs, increase production, or improve client satisfaction.

Letters that **persuade** are similar to sales letters except in these letters you are trying to persuade someone to do something (other than buy something from you). You may be trying to get donations of money or time. You may be trying to get them to do some work for you or to endorse work that you are doing. You may also be trying to win an argument, negotiate a contract or encourage someone to change their beliefs or behavior. What is similar between these letters and sales letters is that you must clearly describe what the benefits of your letter or memo are for the reader.

Letters that **entertain** your friends, colleagues or clients can include sending a cartoon you have found amusing or a story you think someone would enjoy reading. These letters can be sent solely to entertain someone or as an icebreaker when used carefully.

Outlines

Before you begin to write you must organize your thoughts. Many of us write by beginning at the top of a page and writing until we finish. We don't stop to think about what the end result will look like.

Another technique is to write an outline or draw a "memory map". By using a diagram (beginning in the center of a page and working outward) we will have a one page summary of what our important letters, memos or reports will look like. The memory map can be used to brain storm ideas or summarize reports. At the beginning of each section in this book is the memory map I used to prepare the section.

For an important report you might begin by writing your subject area in the middle of the page. From there branch out to the various points you want to make to your reader. List reasons why your reader can benefit from your report. List your own reasons for writing the report. The finished product will be a single page with every major point written down. You will have a complete summary of what you want to write on this page. You will have the necessary overview you need to help you know what is important to include in your work versus what you may find very interesting but is not directly relevant to the reader.

Once you have your memory map you might make a more detailed outline. A detailed outline can be used for longer reports. The best technique I have found is to number your memory-map points in order of importance. Take these points, in the sequence you think will be most helpful to the reader, and design a shortened version of a Table of Contents. The sequence may follow the standard:

- Introduce your thoughts
- Give people the content
- End with a brief summary

A sequence outlined before you write will help give your overall work a structure to follow for both you and the reader. A good structure helps people remember what you have written and to follow the actions you have requested.

When we do our outlines they end up being the Table of Contents for a report. As you do more work, the Table of Contents becomes more detailed until the work is finished. If you want to change the order of your presentation you can move the Table of Contents around.

Audience

The first thing someone does when they begin to read is to ask themselves: "What's in this for me?" It may be statistics, policy, or a request for action but it must show clearly what the writer wants the reader to know or do.

From the readers' standpoint they likely want to know if your letter or memo can:

- Save them time and money.
- Give them useful information.
- Help them be more effective in their job.
- Make them look good to their staff and boss.

From the writer's standpoint you must answer the following questions carefully:

1. Why should anyone read this?
2. Who is this person to me => boss, colleague, client, general public, or staff?

3. What do they want and how can I help them get it?
4. What else should I be aware of:

Anything that could get in the way of understanding: cultural backgrounds, age, gender, etc.

Anything they are particularly proud of or suspicious of.

Conversational Writing

"Perhaps it would be viable for us to dialogue and interface during our mid-day repast on May 5th in order to share information and data regarding that new technique you communicated to me earlier this day. Please bring your hard copy resource for my subsequent perusal."

The above invitation is a perfect example of ineffective writing. It was written to impress more than to inform. Have you ever sat during a dinner speech, a workshop or presentation where people lectured you versus informing you? What the above invitation really says is:

"Can you meet me for lunch on May 5th to talk about that new technique you mentioned this morning? Please bring the manual so I can read it later.

Writing should be short and simple whenever possible. You do not need to use long words when short ones are clearer. You do not need to fill a page when a few sentences say what you want.

When you write a draft of a letter or memo imagine yourself actually talking to the person. You should read the letter or memo out loud. If your tongue trips over a sentence then it is probably too long and awkward. Remember that you probably only have a few seconds to interest your reader.

Active Voice

"It was decided by the Committee that all future reports must follow the organization's style manual." This sentence is in the passive voice because the action "to decide" precedes the subject "Committee" and makes the decision sound neutral (and boring).

"The Committee decided all future reports must follow the organization's style manual." This sentence is in the active voice and tells you directly who made the decision.

Let's look at some other active versus passive voice sentences.

Passive voice= *The baseball was hit by the Prime Minister.*

Active voice= *The Prime Minister hit the baseball.*

Passive voice= *The new procedure was developed by Susan Telford and it is with great pride that we give her this recognition.*

Active voice= Susan Telford developed this new procedure and we are very proud of her accomplishment."

The second sentences are in the active voice. They show more action and are easier to understand. The passive voice is often used in political speeches or apology letters to seem more neutral to the reader. Who is responsible for an action is less clear in passive voice sentences, e.g., in "it was decided" sentences. This may confuse readers; it will certainly bore them.

Passive voice is easily spotted because the object of the sentence precedes the subject instead of the other way around. In the previous examples: 1) *baseball* = object, *was hit* = passive tense, *Prime Minister* = subject; 2) *new procedure* = object, *was developed* = passive tense, *Susan Telford* = subject. Look at the sentences again to see how you might edit some of your own work.

Exercise #1

Take a letter that you are currently working on. Jot down:

Purpose (Why am I writing this?):

Audience (Who am I writing to: an executive, a colleague, a sales representative?):

Conversational Tone (How would I say this if I was talking directly to them?):

Active Voice (Do I use the passive voice in this letter?):

The First Draft

Once you have your ideas in an ordered memory map or detailed outline you can begin to write. Follow the structure you have designed. If you change the sequence during the draft remember to change your memory map to see how the change will effect the overall work.

Begin writing without stopping for corrections or improving your style. Write the draft of the entire work or a smaller section straight through without interruptions. Let your creative juices flow freely without self-criticism. Get your ideas on paper while you still have them clearly in your mind. Grammar, spelling and stylistic problems will be corrected during the editing and proofreading stages.

A few tips:

- Write on only one side of the paper.
- Double or triple space.
- Have wide margins.
- Use a sharp pencil.

If you follow these tips there will be lots of "white space" on your page so that you can easily make corrections, deletions and additions. If you use a word processor, use the same tips so there is lots of space on your screen.

Note: If you have a detailed outline prepared you can use the idea within each point in the outline to write sections of your work. In general, your outline is the hard work. You should take a long time to prepare a good outline because this is the backbone of your work. Once you know what your work will concentrate on, the first draft is just a method to add content to your basic structure.

Tone

Tone is how your words and style appear to the reader. Do your words indicate your own fear, arrogance and feelings of subservience or snobbery? If your words reflect any of these feelings, you have probably lost your reader. Readers want to learn, be informed or entertained; in health care facility/team writing they do not want to know your personal and subjective negative feelings or thoughts.

Tone is best summarized by showing your respect for your readers, their time and their efforts on your behalf.

Use the word "you" more than you use "I" or "we".

Write positively about things avoiding negative words. Instead of: "You will not get less than 85% commitment from your staff if you follow these plans." write: "You will get more than 85% commitment from your staff if you follow these plans."

Write about people as often as you can. If someone told you something, identify them. If you are apologizing to someone don't fall back on policy or computer problems. Write about what you are doing for them.

Write in clear English by avoiding jargon. Each industry has its own jargon. It may be suitable to include some jargon when writing to other people within your profession but never use too much of it if you want your writing to be smooth and interesting.

Style

Simply put, style is the **you** in your writing. It comes from the way you communicate with people. It is partly your personality and partly the skills you use to express yourself more effectively.

Style is seen by your reader in:

- The format you use.
- The words your choose.
- The punctuation in your work.

If you follow some of the suggestions in this section about *format, word selection and writing as you speak,* your style will become easy to read and easy to remember.

Note: Few people read every word you write so try writing for the "Scanner" who quickly skims over a work to see if there is anything interesting for them. The format suggestions recommended in this section will help you write so that scanners find what they want quickly.

Format

Format is how you visually present your writing. The following suggestions will make your work pleasing to the eye and easier for someone to remember.

- Use wide margins in your letters, memos and reports.
- Use shorter sentences and paragraphs.
- Always have a space between paragraphs in a letter or memo.
- When possible use lists and sub-headings to break up long sections of words.
- Use CAPITAL LETTERS, **boldface**, underlines or different fonts consistently throughout your text to visually emphasize the organization of your content.
- Use photographs, charts, diagrams, graphs and cartoons to add some variety to your work.

By following these format suggestions you help your readers to preview your work. They will see what you consider to be the important points. Once someone has read your work they can use the sub-headings, diagrams, and footnotes to review and summarize what you have written.

Layout of material is so important. I receive newsletters from key senior people that are pages of dense small type with no white space or headlines. The material is no doubt important, but the layout really works against my desire to read and digest it. My heart sinks when they arrive on my desk.

Elizabeth Latimer

Barriers to Effective Communication

What prevents your message from getting across to your reader? Possibly the writer and reader have differences in perspectives or in personal needs. For example:

- The writer and the reader have different vocabularies.
- There are cultural and status differences.
- There are professional differences.
- There are different assumptions between the writer and the reader.
- There are bad feelings between the writer and reader.
- There are age differences.
- There are deadline pressures on the writer and/or the reader.
- The writer or the reader has poor knowledge of the subject or little interest.
- There are outside distractions e.g., family problems.

One contributing factor in a reader missing your point is the length of your sentences. Studies show that sentences between 12-20 words are easily comprehended. In a busy work situation, longer sentences cause the reader to lose interest. Vocabulary differences also prevent a message from being understood.

Exercise #2

What are the definitions for the following words:

biannual	fortuitous	gratuitous
esoteric	prototype	reticent.

- Biannual = twice a year (biennial = every two years)
- Fortuitous = accidental, lucky
- Gratuitous = unearned, unwarranted or given/received free
- Esoteric = intended for or understood by only a small group of people
- Prototype = original model
- Reticent = not inclined to speak, uncommunicative

Name 2 alternatives not described above for each of these words. For example, biannual could be twice yearly or every 6 months.

Whatever your answers to the exercise above, the odds are that other people will define these words differently. These words are often used incorrectly and may mean different things to different people. If you choose to use them, you can expect many people to misunderstand what you mean. Whenever a simpler, more commonly understood word or words will do, use them. Although you want to shorten sentences and paragraphs whenever possible it is often necessary to use several commonly used words rather than one complex one.

How to Write Bias Free

Did you know that "girl" once meant a young person of either sex? Language is constantly changing. People who have difficulty in accepting change forget that the terms they want to use once meant something totally different.

"Man" used to mean a human being or person in Old English. Over time it took on the extra meaning of a male person. Historical events led to its use for both males and the neutral persons.

I think the best way to look at writing bias free is to remember that our writing is meant to communicate with our reader. If, for whatever reason, their choice of words differs from ours we should probably adopt theirs. An obvious exception is refusing to use any racist or sexist language.

We must adapt to the people we are writing to; whether we prefer to write Miss and Mrs. instead of Ms. is unimportant. We must also adapt to societal preferences if we want our message, not our choice of words, to reach the public.

Any reference to a person's gender, heritage, color, age or physical condition is generally unnecessary, therefore don't use it. For example it is not necessary to write: "The powerful woman doctor and confident young surgeon work well together." We can assume the author means that the surgeon is a male because no mention is made of his gender. The use of "woman" adds no useful information to the sentence. If gender was important then the sex of both physicians should be given. Note: no one ever wrote that Walt Whitman was a *male* nurse during the Civil War.

> *The gender language issue is of particular interest to me as a female physician, because I do believe that "language has the power to shape reality". When speaking or writing, I purposely use "she" for the physician to re-frame the thinking of the reader or listener. I will also use "he" for the nurse or social worker. When my male colleagues use "he" for doctor, it drives me crazy. It seems to deny the reality of my existence.*
> *Elizabeth Latimer*

Everyday expressions can also offend some of your readers. There is no need to write:

lily white	white as snow
gay old time	straight as an arrow
thinks/fights like a man	midget brain
yellow peril	

There is a heated debate about the use of he/she or his/her in writing. It is awkward and certainly not a space saver. One recommendation is that "they" or "their" replace these terms. For example: "The individual may need extra support in order to do the job, but they can get support from their co-workers as well." Another option is to alternate the use of he and she throughout your work making sure not to use stereotypical references, e.g., "he" for all mechanics and "she" for all secretaries or clerks.

Did you know that "you" used to be only plural? It began to include the singular form when it replaced "thou". Language changes and we should change along with it when it simplifies and clarifies what we want to say. In fact, most people never notice the use of "they" in the singular unless someone points it out to them. It is also very common when we talk.

The argument against using the plural "they" is that it is grammatically incorrect. Famous authors, including George Eliot, Walt Whitman, William Shakespeare, George Bernard Shaw and Doris Lessing have all used "they" in the singular The important consideration is whether or not your readers find the use of "they" acceptable in this way.

Some people argue that replacing words with "man" in them is taking the issue a bit too far. If we want to be accurate in our writing, however, we should use more specific terms to describe what we want to say. The following is a list of commonly used words and phrases with their more recent adaptations.

Instead of	**Try**
manmade	handmade
manpower	personnel
man-hours	work-hours
cameraman	camera operator
stewardess/steward	flight attendant
draftsman	drafter
office girl	office worker
men	people, inhabitants
salesman	sales representative
Englishmen	The English
to man the machines	operate the machines
to man the booth	to run the booth
to man the operating room	to staff the operating room
spokesman	spokesperson

Perhaps the most argued change has been from chairman to chairperson or chairwoman. Did you know that the term chairwoman has been around since the 17th

Century? Did you know that when people didn't know if the chairperson was male or female that they used the term "chair" back in the 17th Century (Miller and Swift, 1980)?

The term "chair" can be used instead of chairman or chairwomen. This is very similar to using gender neutral words like "Crown" to represent the queen/king or "General" to represent a military rank (regardless of whether the person is a woman or a man).

Editing

Good communication is not written but rewritten.

Write the first draft of a letter or memo. Use your **creative skills** to write everything you want to say, without stopping to correct grammar or spelling. Once everything you want to say is on paper you can use your **editing skills** to improve your style, your content and your grammar. Proofreading corrects typing mistakes, spelling errors and other technical features of your work.

1. Whenever possible put your draft aside for a few hours, days or weeks. In this way you can edit your work more objectively, as if you were the reader.
2. Read the draft **out loud**. This will show you any grammatical errors or when a sentence is too long. If you can read it all the way through evenly and clearly, it is a good sign of effective style.
3. Rework the prose, putting sentences into the active voice.
4. Check to make sure that your sequence of ideas makes sense to you and your readers. If the sequence is disjointed rearrange paragraphs or sections as appropriate. Remember to revise your original outline or memory map as well.
5. Check to make sure that links between paragraphs and sections are correct. If you are reading the work out loud and you find it difficult to move from one paragraph to another, you may need to write a bridging sentence or paragraph. Flow is very important to your work and linking sentences or paragraphs make that possible. It may be something as simple as, "If you agree with the previous points about team effectiveness then.."
6. Rewrite weak sections where a point is not well made or transitions are unclear. Paragraphs usually represent one idea or a series of related points. If paragraphs are long or weak it is probably because a key idea is not clearly present.
7. Re-read the piece over again out loud and begin again with step two until you are satisfied.

Remember that your goal is to write well. You can never be the perfect writer so do not over-edit your work.

Exercise #3

Choose two letters or memos that you have written recently or any two of your form letters. Edit them using the five steps described above. Take the time to do each step well. This will save you a lot of time later on as you master the skills.

Editing for Someone Else

1. If you are asked to edit someone else's work consider the following:
2. Your time equals money so spend the amount of time the work deserves. If the work is a memo about the staff picnic don't spend too much time rewriting it. If the work is a request for funds from a government agency then spend the necessary time to edit the piece well.
3. Act as an advocate for the reader. Are their interests and questions addressed? Is the style an appropriate length or boring? Will the reader spend the time to understand what you have written?
4. Work with the author on simplifying the words and paragraphs, using the appropriate format and answering the questions about purpose and audience.
5. Criticism is best received when the author believes you are trying to make him look good to his boss and colleagues.

Exercise #4

Find a short newspaper article or a memo you received recently. Edit it using the above tips. Remember to look for the purpose, the audience, the tone and style (length of words, clarity, conversational style), and whether the writer used the active voice.

Proofreading

You proofread to check for typing errors, spelling and other technical mistakes. Proofreading requires a special frame of mind. You are looking for specific details and cannot let outside distractions interfere with your work. It is easier to proofread someone else's work; perhaps you can work with a colleague to correct each other's work.

To proofread you must orient yourself to small details. There are too many things to look for at one time so I suggest you go over a piece of work several times looking for different things each time.

Some people find proofreading very tedious work. If you set your mind to the mystery of finding and correcting errors the work can be quite fulfilling. Use a colored pencil or pen for corrections.

1. Scan the work for any obvious errors. Often a typing error will jump out at you when you are scanning.

2. Read the work out loud for obvious grammar and style errors, e.g., do subjects and verbs agree, are the sentences too long, does your tongue trip over parts?
3. Go over the work a second time **reading backwards;** look at each word for spelling. Does the author use American or Canadian spelling? Be consistent in your spelling.
4. Check each title and sub-heading for spelling, location and format.
5. Check each page number to make sure the pages are in sequence and in the correct location.
6. Are margins and indentations consistent? Are there any pages where a paragraph begins at the bottom of the page (move it to the next page if this happens).
7. Are numbers consistently spelled out (e.g., for numbers less than 10)?
8. Are footnotes in sequence and accurate?
9. Are the page references in the Table of Contents, Index, and other tables accurate?
10. Is there enough "white space" on each page to make the page easy to read and pleasant to the eye?
11. Is the work sexually, culturally, racially bias-free?
12. Take an extra minute to get a global look at the work to see if there is anything that you have missed.

Time Management for Writing

Everyone has exactly the same amount of time everyday. It is **taking control** over your time that will distinguish you from your colleagues.

To make any job manageable we must break up our writing into small manageable units so that we don't expect ourselves to write 18 major letters or memos in one day. Take a few each day in order of importance. The same holds true for long reports -- divide them into manageable sections or sections, whenever this is possible.

> *I write for publication and other types of projects. I find that breaking the project into small workable pieces helps me to get down to it psychologically. I can reduce anxiety about completion by seeing that sections are getting done.*
> *Elizabeth Latimer*

The real enemy of time management is our own negative thoughts. This is especially true when it comes to writing, because so many of us feel unable to reach our own writing standards. We, therefore, postpone our writing until the last minute when we have a dozen other things to do and hurriedly dash off something so we have an excuse not to meet our unrealistic standards.

One of my professors had me writing the moment I entered the program. Rather than researching and then writing, he had me writing first and then integrating the research into the thesis over time. Practicing writing and then editing and rewriting is an excellent exercise in learning how to construct your thoughts but give yourself time to develop the skill of expression.
Michèle Chaban

Our negative feelings about our abilities can only be overcome if we have a writing plan to follow.

Some tips on time management for writing:

- Schedule a specific time to prepare an outline and write your draft. Choose a time when you are most energetic and reward yourself when you are finished. (I got a pizza when I finished this section!)
- Take a break every 20-40 minutes to stretch and let your mind wander from your work. You often get your best ideas during a break.
- Always write down an idea or plan as soon as you think of it. Have a pad and pencil by your bed for that 3 a.m. brainstorm!

When I was working and doing my Ph.D., I began to get more requests to lecture. I had too much to do but didn't know what to let go of. Before I went to sleep I would say, "While I am sleeping, I want to think about..." Whether it was an idea for a lecture, my thesis or a situation in my personal life, my mind worked on untaxed as I slept. I often woke at 3 a.m. with a clarity of mind that was not there at 6 or 8 a.m. the next morning. I kept a small dicta phone by my night table for these moments of brilliance, which were few and far between!
Michèle Chaban

Plan for:

- 5-10 minutes for a brief note to a colleague, 1 hour per page for an important, short memo.
- 2 hours per page for a short report on a familiar topic (won't need to do a lot of new research).
- 3-4 hours per page for an important and detailed report to allow for enough research and editing time.

Don't let these times worry you. They include time for research, outlines, drafts, editing, illustrations, proofreading and your final copy. Make your personal deadline one or two weeks before the official deadline to compensate for sick days and delays.

If you have scheduled time to write, avoid phone interruptions or people dropping in for a visit. Writing time should be viewed just as any other important appointment.

- 90% of all things can be done immediately!
- Procrastination is often our way of avoiding evaluation of our work by ourselves or others.
- The fear of evaluation and our own self-doubts or negative thoughts are controlled by us.
- Design your schedule to break tasks into manageable units.

Specific Formats

Letters

Note: The following sections on letters and memos are a review of previous sections. Some beginning points to note:

1. Write to your audience and with a purpose!
2. Read your work out loud. Does it sound like you?
3. Your first and last paragraphs are the most important. Your reader will remember these points best. Get your key point into the first paragraph. Have a strong conclusion or summary in the last paragraph or state clearly what you expect of the reader.
4. K.I.S.S. = Keep It Short and Simple. At times, however, it is more appropriate to replace a less understood word with several simple words for clarity. This will lengthen what you have written but it will be better understood.
5. Make your words sound like a conversation, not a lecture.
6. Use the active voice.
7. Use "you" more than "I".
8. Use the format suggestions listed earlier in this section. Have wide margins, space between paragraphs and use lists and sub-headings when appropriate. You can also use emphatic devices like **bold face**, <u>underlining</u>, or *italics.*
9. Make sure that you have the correct spelling of the person's name, their correct title, degree and address. Correct spelling of someone's name sets the tone for the rest of the letter.
10. Use "Ms." if you are unsure of the woman's preference.
11. If you have no specific name to write to, you could call their department for the information or begin with their title, i.e., " To the Director."

12. The use of Re: comes from memos and is considered by some to be less personal in letters. Re: can be effective, however, in drawing quick attention to the reason for your letter.
13. Delete stock phrases, e.g., at this particular point in time, further to your letter of...

Some Suggested Opening Lines

You're right. We forgot to send you the information you asked for. I hope these charts are what you were looking for.

When we got your letter we called our team together the next day to discuss your request and this is what we decided.

Jack Pollack told me you were the person to talk to. I am looking for someone to help organize our annual fundraiser and your experience last year with the Special Campaign would be invaluable to us.

I have good news for you. You'll be happy to know..

Some Suggested Closing Lines

May we have your reply by June 6?

Please write the answers to my questions in the margin of this letter and return in the enclosed envelope.

If you need any help, please let me know.

Have I given you all the information you need?

Thank you for giving us the opportunity to straighten out this matter.

I will call you on February 12 to arrange an appointment with you.

Follow-up

Sometimes you may want to follow-up a letter to see if the reader has received it and understood what action you expect them to take.

You should follow-up a letter if you think it warrants another 10 minutes of your reader's valuable time.

Follow-up can be a short phone call, a note or even news clipping about the same subject. For someone you know very well, a cartoon may be appropriate.

Always make sure you are adding some extra information that may interest the reader and that your follow-up is courteous and short.

Memos

Letters and memos have a lot in common when it comes to organization, format, and the use of the active voice. I recommend that you read the letter-writing section before reading this memo-writing section.

The main difference between memos and letters is that letters are usually sent outside the workplace and may be more formal in tone. Memos are usually used within the workplace and the tone will depend on who you are sending the memo to.

When you write a memo, you need to have a purpose in writing to a specific audience. Often the audience is one or more of the people you work with and this demands even more respect for their time (other people are always busier than you are (so they think!).

Memos, like many letters:

- Explain or record an action.
- Get your reader to do something.
- Avoid blame for some incident.
- Answer a question.

Memos must be short, clear and to the point. Too many words will bore readers and they won't read it.

As in letters make sure your most important point is in the first paragraph and whatever action you want taken is referred to in the last paragraph.

The first line must clearly tell the reader why they should bother to read your memo instead of filing it into the circular file with everyone else's memos. Memos, even more than letters, are scanned by the reader, so use a format that visibly indicates why this memo is important. Use a lot of white space; emphasize key points by using lists, or use a highlighting marker to underline the most important action you need done by this person.

If you sprinkle your memo with some humor or an appropriate cartoon you may even have your colleagues eagerly awaiting your next effort!

Reports

Who is the report for? Why was I chosen to write it? What restrictions do I have? When is my deadline? Why will anyone read it? What is it trying to accomplish? How will I know if it is successful?

These questions must be answered before you can begin writing a report.

People with different backgrounds will read reports, especially technical ones. Write out a list of the type of people who will be reading it and how you can help them benefit from it, for example:

Executives	Need answers to cost, time involved, organization-wide benefits, community involvement and benefits. They want it short and easy to remember.
Finance	Want costs, accounting procedures, evaluation methods, time frame.
Technicians	Want specifics, statistics, methodology of research, purpose.

Once you know who you are writing to and what the purpose of your report is you can begin your organization with a memory map and outline. Look at other reports that people have praised and see how your report might follow a similar structure. Get other people's ideas about what the report should look like and what it should contain.

Choose a research approach (e.g., reading books and articles, interviewing experts, designing a questionnaire, and/or putting together a workshop) and work on a more detailed outline as you go along. Do the necessary work and break down the task into smaller manageable units.

Draft your report, put it aside for a few days, then edit and revise. Prepare any illustrations and diagrams. Revise your work until you are satisfied.

We recommend the following format if your department does not have a set format for reports.

- Title
- Optional Table of Contents
- Summary and Recommendations
- Description of Work
- Findings and Conclusions
- Appendices

Choosing a Title

A title should tell it all without a long subtitle. It should be straightforward and somewhat interesting, i.e., instead of "1986 Report on Services" try "The Year of Improved Services Within the 'X' Department".

Summary and Recommendations

This section should:

- Give the main idea you want the reader to remember.
- Tell people specifically what you want them to do.

- Set apart paragraphs you want people to use to summarize your work to other people.

This section is specifically designed for scanners who want to see what the report may hold for them.

Description of Work, Findings and Conclusions

This section gives the detail to understand the report more fully and will help supervisors, direct care providers, committee members and others to better understand the key points of your report.

Appendices

Appendices can include statistical charts, engineering diagrams, tables, glossary, index, etc. They are generally used by experts and technicians who want to know how the information was recorded, calculated and used in making the recommendations.

Technical reports often include a lot of jargon to impress colleagues or to save an author the time it takes to write in ordinary English. The findings of any technical subject can be condensed into one or two sentences if some effort is made.

Imagine how long-winded Newton or Einstein could have been with their discoveries. Instead they summed years of work into the following sentences:

"To every action there is always an equal and opposite reaction."

"E = mc2 (Energy equals mass times the speed of light squared.)"

A last point-technical reports of more than 10 pages should have an annotated Table of Contents, glossary, and (if appropriate) an index for easy reference.

Exercise #5

Chose two or three types of written work that you do regularly (e.g., a memo to staff or a monthly report). Use this guide to prepare an outline or Table of Contents for each of these types of writing. Allow yourself to invest extra time in this Exercise so that you can use the outline for all similar writing in the future. Keep the outlines near your desk and use them regularly to save yourself time.

Summary

Some Quotes

- It isn't what you write that is important -it is what people read.
- Your goal is to be a good and effective writer -not <u>the</u> perfect writer.
- 90% of all things can be done IMMEDIATELY.

- Grammar may help you understand techniques but understanding grammar cannot replace PRACTICE, PRACTICE.

Resources

The following resources should be readily available in your personal library:
Canadian Oxford English Dictionary
American Webster's Ninth Collegiate Dictionary
Roget's Thesaurus
World Almanac for general information
Encyclopedia of your trade or profession
Optional: *Bartlett's Familiar Quotations*
A Dictionary of Modern English Usage (grammar text)
A good secretarial handbook for style and format rules.

The following resources are only a few of the many useful resources that you can find in your local libraries, within your own organization, and in your local bookstores. Look for other books but also for journal articles, magazine reports, films, videos and audiocassettes. Also keep in mind how much you can learn from experts in the field, including people within your own organization!

Bailey, E P. Jr. (1996). *Plain English at work: A guide to writing and speaking.* Oxford: Oxford University Press.

Bly, R. W. (1999). *The encyclopedia of business letters, fax memos, and e-mail.* Franklin Lakes, NJ: Career Press.

Bowman, J.,& Branchaw, B P. (1992). *How to write proposals that produce.* Phoenix, AZ: Orzy Press.

Colter, R. (1981). *Grammar to go.* Toronto: Anansi.

Gucker, P. (1966). *Essential English grammar.* New York: Dover Publications.

Hartman, D.B., & Nantz, K.S. (1996). *The 3 R's of e-mail: Risks, rights and responsibilities.* Menlo Park, CA: Crisp Publications.

Heller, B. (1994). *The 100 most difficult health care letters you'll ever have to write, fax or E-mail: Clear guidance on how to write your way out of the toughest health care facility/team situations.* New York: Harper Health care facility/team.

Soden, G. (1995). *Looking good on paper: How to create eye-catching reports, proposals, memos, and other health care documents.* New York: AMACOM.

Strunk, W. Jr., & White, E.B. (1979). *The elements of style.* (3rd ed.). New York: Macmillan.

van Bommel, H. (1985). *Effective health care writing.* North York, ON: Skills Development Publishing.

5.
Team Skills

Group/Team Skills

Effective Meetings

Creative Problem Solving

Group/Team Skills

The prime responsibilities of a team member are:

- To meet the needs of the patients, families or clients.
- To help the team develop into an enjoyable, productive and united group of successful individuals.

Team work, or people working together to reach a common goal, has several benefits. Teams are often better at solving problems and finding opportunities to do things better. They often produce higher quality products and services and at less cost because they combine people with different skills, working styles and interests. In the best version of the old "two heads are better than one" adage, effective teams use the combined similarities, differences and expertise of their members to do the best job possible within given resources and time.

Teams have drawbacks, as well, of course. One example is that some people do not like to work with others. Many people are best at working alone once they are given a specific job to do. Effective teams recognize this fact and incorporate privacy and individualism for their team members who need it. Another drawback is the greater potential for conflict between workers. This requires an organization that recognizes this potential and helps individual team members understand their roles and helps them develop skills to better work within a team. Lastly, teamwork is sometimes hurt when there is insufficient accountability for the work of individual members. People need to accept their own responsibilities and be held accountable for their performance.

Groups or teams in this section means a collection of people who:

Work together to achieve a specific goal in ways that are interdependent. That is, the work of one member affects the work of the other members in either helpful or harmful ways.

Work within an organization such as a company, hospital, department, committee or task force.

Work within an environment that hopefully encourages creativity, enjoyment and successful completion of planned work. This is not required, but it certainly helps.

There are books that define groups as different from teams. For them groups are built of independent people who prefer not to be working together but must for administrative or organizational reasons. These books present teams as defined in the three points above. For our purposes we will use either group or team to represent the three-point definition above. This will allow us to concentrate on what works best for you rather than getting caught up in definitions and theories.

The term team building has many different definitions as well. For the purposes of this material, team building means: helping a team develop their basic skills for working together with a long-term view (if the team stays together) of continually improving their team's performance. Team building can be done intensely as a team forms or over time as the team develops their relationship and work.

There are also many models of team building that different leaders in the field have suggested. This book does not propose a specific model but rather tries to help managers, supervisors and staff understand what knowledge and skills are common to most leaders in any field – for this unit the leaders in the field of team building.

Working Styles

Imagine yourself standing in a very crowded lobby waiting for an elevator. In the crowd there are four people you will be watching who have very different styles of working. As you read the following summary see if you can imagine any of your colleagues or friends who fit the descriptions.

As one of the elevators opens, the first person gets on the elevator quickly, pushing their way through, and presses the button to get to their floor without holding the elevator door for other people to get on.

A second elevator arrives and the second person we are watching gets on, holds the door open and says a hearty "Good morning. How are you today?" to everyone who gets on. To make sure that every possible person can be crowded onto an already full elevator he keeps the door open and says to someone waiting outside, "Come on in. There's always room for one more!"

The third person we have been watching sees the crowd and rather than inconvenience anyone, takes the stairs up four flights to their floor.

The fourth person has waited somewhat impatiently and finally gets on the last elevator to arrive. He gets on the elevator, looks for the elevator license that says how many people can safely be in the elevator and then he asks one person to get off since they have exceeded safety standards.

These fairly extreme examples summarize what many different studies have described as different working styles. Some studies divide people into four categories, as we have done, while others use six, eight and even 16 different categories. The number is less important than what the similarities and differences show us.

We all have different ways of working and communicating. Some of us are shy with some people and assertive with others. Some of us like to lead a group while others like to follow. **There is no right or wrong style**; just different ones. Each of us has a combination of many styles. We use different styles in different situations, with different people and at different times depending on the circumstances.

For example, on a stressful day when you are in a rush you might be like the first person getting on the elevator. On other more typical days you may take the stairs.

When we discuss styles it is important to look at which descriptions fit you **more often than not** rather than on trying to pigeonhole yourself permanently into any one style.

Let's look at our four people one more time. The first person is often seen as the "go-getter" with all the ideas but little time to follow through on the necessary work. They are often seen as military leaders who delegate the work while they concentrate on the next action or idea. Sometimes these people are also called "Type A" personalities because they are driven by their work and have little time for family or socializing. They are the ones that people often say "get the job done". If they have the time and interest they prefer to do the job themselves but often delegate or order other people to do it for them.

The second person is more of a promoter of ideas and actions. These people take an idea or plan and help others to see the benefits. Often these people end up in sales, in teaching or in entertainment. They love to socialize and have less energy to actually get the work done.

The third person is most comfortable when they are not centered out and they prefer to follow the rules to get the work done. They like the way they have been doing things and do not appreciate being told or bullied into doing it a different way. These people (some say about 50% of our population) actually do the work. Family and personal life tends to be more important than work but doing a good job is also very important. The second and third person tend to have family photos prominently displayed while the first and fourth groups tend to display neutral or "powerful" paintings and photos.

The fourth person is the one who evaluates if the ideas, plans and actions are actually done according to the rules. They review lots of information, do studies, enjoy accounting and quality assurance and take great pride in doing things the right way. They are less concerned with their personal lives (like the first person) but take great offence if you disagree with their work.

Keep in mind that none of these four groups is better than another. In fact, you can imagine if everyone fit into only one category and you had a team of all evaluators (group four). You would have little new to do or get little work done. In the same way, if everyone on a team fit into the first group you would have wonderful, dynamic ideas but no one to actually do the work or convince other people that it was a good idea.

When people have been asked about which style they think is the best in a work environment they often answer that their style is most useful to the organization. The first person would say that without ideas and a "go-getter" attitude, nothing would get done. The second person would say that good ideas do not go anywhere unless there are people to educate others about the benefits. She might also suggest that everyone go out for a coffee to discuss the matter in a less formal setting.

The third person, quietly frustrated in the background, knows that without them all the generating of ideas, promotion and evaluation is worthless since no one else will probably do the work. They would prefer that people didn't spend time asking such silly questions and let them get back to work.

The fourth person clearly understands that without her everyone would be doing things without knowing what the results were. They would continue to work in old or new ways without measuring the results and consequences. In fact, she has several hundred studies to prove that exact point and if people would just take the time to read these they would not have to waste company time figuring out whose style is more important.

Exercise #1
Your Work Style

So how does a basic understanding of work styles help you? This exercise will help you understand how you, and others, use your work styles in similar ways, and in different ways. Remember the following groups are just one way of categorizing your work style preferences and that other methods are just as valid. Use this as a self-awareness tool rather than a way to label yourself or others into only one "box".

Look at the following work style categories. Under each group write down the circumstances in which you feel most comfortable using that style. You can use your work, home and social roles to identify similarities and differences.

Style #1: Come up with ideas. Using the force of your personality or your authority to get other people to do the work for you. For example, are you most comfortable generating ideas and energy for a specific action you want to see happen at home or at work or with some friends on a weekend away?

Style #2: Promote ideas. Getting people involved and excited about an idea. Teaching or promoting a new way of doing things. Getting people together to socialize and get away from work for a while. For example, do you prefer to work with lots of other people mixing social chit-chat with work?

Style #3: Do the work. You like to work quietly until the work is done and get home as soon as you can. You prefer to do things the way you have always done them. For example, do you prefer to do the work alone, in a quiet place until it's done? What is your preferred style at home?

Style #4: Evaluate ideas and actions. You like to use numbers and statistics to make sure that the work is being done correctly, accurately and on time. For example, would you rather work late into the night to find a small bookkeeping error than go home and have guests over for supper?

Once you have described when you prefer to do different things, write down which style you tend to use most often at work, at home, with friends.

When you are most under stress which style do you think you tend to use more often and why?

For example, when I am not under much stress I prefer to educate and promote various ways of doing things. This is a useful style for a person who teaches adults for a living. When I am under lots of stress I prefer to isolate myself in my home office and write, stamp envelopes, or do research for a new self-study package. When I am under even more stress I tend to get away from everyone and hide out at a movie theater to escape "real life" for a few hours. Note: None of these styles is better or worse than any other since all serve a purpose that does not harm anyone else.

Contributing factors. We have looked at some of your preferred working styles under different situations. It is important to be clear about various contributing factors that may increase or decrease your likelihood of using a particular style. For example, do you have a high or low need for power and control? Do you enjoy or need a lot, or a little, social interaction? Do you have a high or low need to achieve and/or to be seen as an achiever?

Aside from some of these personal needs and wants there are always outside influences such as: your family and friends, your health, work or personal stresses (e.g., financial, career). Since you cannot always predict these influences it may be helpful to look at your life right now.

What contributing factors affect your work style right now? Do these factors change how you act at work, at home and/or with your friends? What can you do differently, if anything, to allow you to work in a more comfortable style?

Exercise#2
Leadership Roles

Team building assumes that everyone on a team takes on some kind of leadership role at different times. Examine the table below and decide if you do the skills very well, average, or not very well **right now**. Add any notes or ideas you have to different points to remind you of what specifically you would like to continue doing well or what skill you want to improve.

Very well	You do it very well, therefore, there is no need to spend time improving this skill right now.
Average	You have an average amount of this skill but you need to keep up-to-date and/or develop this skill to higher levels.
Not very well	You need to develop this skill within the next few months to reach an average level of competency expected for your job.

Skill Group	**Description**	**Very Well, Average, Not Very Well**
Authoritarian	Sometimes it is necessary for someone to take control to get something done quickly and competently. This includes during a crisis, during a work impasse or when you have legitimate authority over the group to get things done your way.	
Counselor/teacher	At times other team members need someone who can actively listen to what is being said and to help communicate those ideas to others. Teaching skills may also be needed to provide others with advice and skills development.	
Group/team leader	If you are assigned the task of leading a group through a project, you have the skills to keep the team working together to get the job done well, on time and with minimum friction between members.	
Informer	If you witness activities that are unethical or illegal you have the skill to inform the right people about the problem without destroying your working relationship with other members of the team not involved in that specific activity.	

Communicator	You distribute information openly and honestly to everyone who should have it, rather than keeping it to yourself.
Disciplinarian	You have the skill to both praise people when they do things well and the skills to help people see what they are doing poorly without isolating them from the rest of the team or making them resentful of your evaluation. Note: discipline comes from the root meaning – "to follow" rather than the negative meaning we so often give it.
Expert	You keep up-to-date in your work without bragging about your knowledge to others.
Spokesperson	You communicate the position of the team to other people within and outside the organization.
Coordinator	You organize the work between members of a team and any people outside the team affected by the work.
Entrepreneur	You encourage an entrepreneurial environment that helps other members see the short and long term economic benefits of various actions.
Self-promoter	You know when to make others aware of your knowledge and skills. This is different from bragging. Self-promotion is necessary for your valuable contributions to be accepted in a non-threatening way.
Negotiator	You can negotiate between people who have different points in a way that everyone benefits.
Problem solver	You can identify specific problems and use techniques to help your team generate alternative solutions creatively and effectively.
Conflict resolver	You can help others and yourself resolve conflicts as they arise in a mature and respectful manner that brings people closer together, even if they dislike each other personally.
Ambassador	You can play host to people from outside your team and/or organization in ways that enhance the organization's image and the guests' image.

You have identified some of the leadership skills that you do very well, average and not very well. Now you must design a plan of action to reinforce what you do well and learn new knowledge and skills to improve other skills. All of the skills listed above are learned. You do not get them when you are born. All leaders and effective team members need to identify what they are good at and what they need to work on. This type of self-awareness makes it easier for people with different work styles to understand some of the differences between team members and how they can help each other adapt to everyone's strengths and styles.

How Do You Identify What Skills You Need?

Review the table above with special attention to the second column describing specific skills. Which of those skills do you need to strengthen to help you become more effective under the different skill groupings in column 1? For example: to be an effective Ambassador one needs effective communication skills, to be assertive and diplomatic, to present themselves well in public (presentation and public speaking) and to run meetings effectively. They also need some practice in dealing with stress and incorporating appropriate humor. Once you have identified the skills you need to learn, you must think of how you can go about learning them. To help you you may use other sections in this book as well as other literature, your colleagues, and your family and friends.

Use the sample table below to help you plan out what skills you want to improve on and by when. It is also important for you to write down how you will know you have learned the skills and how you can prove it to a colleague or friend who is supportive of you improving your leadership skills. Writing these points out will help ensure you actually improve your skills. Just thinking about improving your skills usually does not lead to changing your behaviors or skills.

Action Plan

Skill	How	By When	Successful? (Check)

Requirements for Success

As well as understanding various working styles and improving your own ability to play various leadership roles in a team, there are some more elements needed to ensure team success.

Attitude

All individual members (or at least a majority) must believe that the team can do the work better together, than any individual can alone.

Team leaders must believe that their role is valuable and that the team (or, again, a majority) is the right mix of people to get the job done.

Organizations must believe that the team approach deserves its support, encouragement and praise when the work is done well.

Above all, there must be an attitude of pride. Pride that this collection of people can achieve something that as individuals would not be done as well, or with as much creativity or with as much enjoyment and excitement. Working together only for the sake of saying that a group works together will fail.

Purpose

The team needs to know its purpose and promote it actively. It needs to return over and over again to its "vision" of what they are doing and why. All decisions must be based on that original or revised vision and goals so that there is consistency in purpose and implementation of the work.

Team is Supported

Individuals are motivated to work together when they receive support.

The organization must support their work through recognition, coaching, support to help the team achieve their goals and objectives, financial and human resources to meet the needs realistically, and structural support to encourage cooperation between teams and to remove any organizational obstacles to getting the job done well.

The organization also encourages the team to be involved in the planning of the work and changing the work based on their ongoing efforts. Since the team is usually closest to the end result (e.g., improved products, patient care services and client satisfaction) organizations should listen to their teams when it comes to making changes.

Ironically some of the most effective teams in history (organizational, sports teams, professional groups) have excelled because they did not receive support. Their individual and group motivation to see a job done was heightened by a lack of organizational or societal support. Like the child who wants to show her parents that she can, in fact, become a scientist, these teams want to prove to themselves and the world that they can be successful. The young team that invented the Macintosh computer is a fine example.

Flexibility

Even though you do not have all the requirements in place for success you should try to complete the work. Organizations and teams have all sorts of constraints (financial, human resources and other resources) that do not always make for ideal work situations. The successful teams understands the compromises it must make, lets those in authority know what those compromises are and does the best job possible under the circumstances. Progress will continue and success will be achieved but they may not happen at the speed or quality originally required.

Team is Knowledgeable and Skilful

Individuals have a range of knowledge and skills that together will get the job done. Recruitment for the team must include looking for people who have knowledge and skill but also people who look at the work world in different ways so that different perspectives can be used to produce the best product and services. Many organizations are now including patients, families or clients in all, or part, of the work of teams to make sure that the work meets the needs of the people using the products and services.

> *The public has increased awareness of their right to give input about care issues. Right now there is a lot of Internet accessibility. We have long-term residents who are 'on line.' In fact, we have a resident on our ethics committee who was able to pull in information and get in touch with an American hospital. This other hospital sought our advice through the Internet connection with a resident. Clearly, the community has so much knowledge. For example, we have a post-polio clinic. Outside people know so much about what we do and what others do at other clinics. When they come in for treatment, they know a lot. They press our staff to be on the leading edge. The new clientele know terrific amounts and they have a right to know. Years ago, for example, people would sign a consent form for surgery. It was just routine. Now it is important to demonstrate that you have communicated in detail, the information the patient needs to consent and that the patient gave feedback that they understood what they were*

consenting to. That is the informed consent. This struck me as part of the new edge that is good for health care receivers and providers. Patients are big players now.
Larry Lewis

If you have little or no control over who is recruited for the team it becomes every team member's responsibility to learn how to adapt their own working style, knowledge and skills to the other team members. It is only through a spirit of cooperation and adapting oneself that a team can effectively achieve its goals.

Recognition of Differences

Individuals recognize that they all have different ways of working and communicating. These differences must be seen as beneficial in order to work together. Equal participation must be required and differences in power between members must be minimized during the work.

Successful teams can exist where individual members do not like each other personally. Although it is sometimes easier to work within a group where people like each other it is not a prerequisite for successfully getting the job done. In fact, sometimes it is better to have a group where there are real differences in personalities because such a group more accurately reflects the society we live in.

Team Identity

Individuals and the organization must recognize the team as a whole as well as its individual members. A set of agreed upon goals, objectives and performance expectations must be the first task the team does. Understanding people's different work styles does not mean that the team as a whole does not have a set of values and expected behaviors that all members must agree to and use. For example, many projects have design, implementation and evaluation stages. Team members will have different ideas about which stage is most important. A team's identity recognizes the importance of all three stages and requires the team to accept this point from the beginning.

Core values take time, mutual experience and reflection to develop but it is essential in terms of arriving at a consensus about what can be expected. For example, if I have a difficulty and I page one of my team members they almost always respond unless they are with a client and cannot be interrupted. I understand that their failure to get back to me is this rather than neglect. If I personalized it, I would waste time and energy. This comes from our commitment to working together as a team and levels of trust on the part of all team members.
Michèle Chaban

Leadership

Teams, even ones without formal leaders, do have one or more individuals who take a leadership role during the work. For example, one week a member experienced in working with certain equipment may take a leadership role when discussing what new equipment to buy. Another week, a different member may be the leader while discussing new personnel policy changes. In an effective team this kind of give-and-take leadership is seen as a benefit. There is often one person who makes sure that the team runs effectively within the time constraints they have even when the leadership role changes from time to time.

Recognize the Ebb and Flow

In most group tasks there are times of real excitement, boredom and fear of failure. These are very normal and when expected, not so intimidating. Whether in producing a community play or designing a new product or service, there will be times when some people, or everyone, may want to quit. A break from the routine tasks of the group can provide new perspective and energy that will bring the process back on track. For example, everyone goes their separate ways for one week to do things they like to do in their own ways without having to consider the other team members. Or the group may decide to go somewhere together (a weekend away, a day at an amusement park, a picnic, etc.) to spend time socializing and getting to know each other better without the pressures of work getting in the way. Anything that encourages laughter, reflection, self-awareness, and relaxation can be very helpful here.

> *We used to have a tradition of getting the team together for discussion and reflection. I found these times enhanced our group process. Then we added a few new members who felt this kind of encounter fractured the boundaries between their professional and personal lives. The team eventually accommodated to these new values but in time this weakened the team and the program. Not having a place to just be with each other and do some team building was a significant loss and ultimately compromised our ability to provide good patient care.*
> *Michèle Chaban*

Informal Climate

The more a team enjoys working together, the greater the level of creativity and productivity. Enjoyment comes from success, from appropriate humor and fun, from recognizing each other's idiosyncrasies and spending some time on non-work related things.

Up-Front Time

Spend the necessary time at the beginning to make sure people are clear about the goals, objectives, behavior and performance expectations. Too often groups begin by too much action and not enough thinking about what the job or task is. Also spend time having the team get to know each other. Each individual's success depends on the success of the other individuals yet many large organizational teams (especially for committee work and task forces) have members who do not even know each other's names. People need to understand the basic ground rules of how they will work together. This is especially true around how decisions will be made during and outside of meetings, understanding what is possible to do and not possible to do given the organization's mission statement and policies, and an understanding that work should be treated seriously without having to be solemn.

> *Doctors sometimes think that team building activities take time away from the "real work" of treating patients. It may take some time before they see that time up-front in team building will actually facilitate their care and make it more effective and efficient. Sometimes the analogy of a football or basketball team can be helpful. They practice as a team many hours a week for a two hour game. We work in teams for many hours with very few hours of practice on how to do it.*
> *Elizabeth Latimer*

Strong beginnings usually lead to strong endings and success. Weak beginnings, with unclear roles, expectations and deadlines often lead to a negative attitude of failure that, more times than not, comes true.

Who is the Boss

As much as we read and practice consensus building within teams there are usually still one or two people who are ultimately responsible for the success or failure of a team's work. It is often the Chair of the Board or President who is fired if their organization is doing poorly. It is the coach of a sport's team that is let go when the team does poorly. Within teams this is also true. Usually there are one or two people whose job it is to make sure that the team's work is done well. You need to know who they are and what expectations they have. You need to help them understand what your role on the team is and what expectations may be unrealistic from the start so there are no surprises at the end of the work.

The Ending

Effective teams know when they have successfully achieved their goals because they have specific criteria for measuring that success. Whether the team is short-term or long-term it is always important to spend some time celebrating that success. It enhances the relationship between team members. It allows the organization to reward excellence. Most importantly it sets the kind of supportive environment that teams hope for when they begin (perhaps with different members) to achieve other goals. Teamwork is a never ending process of beginning, working, accomplishment, learning and beginning again.

Deadlines and Action Plans

People need to know how long they have to complete a task or project. They need to know who will do what, and by when. They need to know how their work will be evaluated for successful completion and what recognition or reward they will receive for their success.

To practice this action planning step examine the list above and select those items that your team wishes to work on in the next few months. Examine who will do what, by when and how you will measure short and long term success.

Use the sample table for each specific goal or project.

Goal or Project Title

Task	By Whom	By When	Achieved? (Check)

Requirements for Failure

Obviously, if you do the opposite of many of the requirements to success you will fail as a team. But there are some other things that organizations and individuals often do that lead to failure. Here are a few.

When a Team is Not a Team

Managers read about the importance of teams and want to encourage their staff to work together so they call their staff "a team". However, they continue to manage the staff as individuals therefore creating a confusing environment of unclear expectations. They may also give the team the illusion that they make decisions as a group while, in fact, it is the manager who makes the final decisions. Management responsibility in decision-making is not wrong. One person should be accountable for the work of a team. What is wrong is giving a team the illusion that they have ultimate authority and accountability when, in fact, they do not.

Another example of when a team is not a team is when an organization tries to create a strong work team in an environment where it is just not possible. This could be because of previous distrust of managers or staff; personnel contracts that discourage it; the size of an organization or outside influences. For example, in hospital health care there has been a real movement toward having doctors work in teams with nurses, pharmacists, social workers and therapists but often with little preparation to do so. Many times doctors are expected to assume leadership roles without the opportunity to acquire the required skills.

> *From an administrative perspective, physicians are generally not staff of the hospital. That's a really complicated piece. The connectedness of physicians to the hospital itself is sometimes very tenuous and other times very tight. The physicians always have some sort of Medical Advisory Council that is important in drafting and ensuring that we have some of the right policies. They play a role in advising administration when they are putting together a report on the direction of the facility. Or if government comes up with some dictum and we want to respond, we need the medical input. They play a crucial role in supporting operational change.*
> *Larry Lewis*

Unskilled Leaders

Whether someone is a manager, supervisor or team/committee leader they must have some of the basic skills required of a leader. They must be able to communicate verbally and in writing. They must be able to run a meeting that gets through a previously distributed agenda with fairness to all participants. They must be able to resolve conflicts, lead people through problem solving strategies, understand differences and similarities among the participants, and understand their own strengths and weaknesses.

The qualities of leadership are not usually given to us at birth so they must be learned. Effective teamwork requires leaders who have learned these skills and who can apply them fairly, firmly and predictably.

Team Member Skills

A team is doomed to failure if it is assumed that the participants have all the knowledge and skills they need to complete the work. They need skills in their own areas of expertise but also skills in working together as a team. Team leaders and the organization must recognize any gaps in members' skills to help them reach their full potential as a team. Whenever new members join the team they must be given time to become a working member of the team while the other members also have time to adjust their working relationship to accommodate the newest member.

> *Whenever a new team member comes, our team takes more time to discuss cases to teach our theories on patient care. We also take time to model team communication, conflict, decision making and play. We teach by example and in turn we find opportunities to share cases with the new member so that we can learn from them. It is a lot of work but if patient care is our goal, we must do it, for a team is greater than the sum of all of its individual disciplines.*
> *Michèle Chaban*

Making All the Decisions Beforehand

Sometimes teams are told what is expected of them without involving them in any of the planning decisions. In essence this team becomes only a workhorse and, therefore, has little invested in seeing the work through to a successful end.

Unclear Objectives

This point cannot be stressed enough. People working with unclear expectations and objectives will never know if they have accomplished the job they have been given or not. A basic cause of many team failures within organizations is when people are uncertain about their own roles (who does what) on a team and are given unclear objectives. It really is that simple.

Time

Sometimes teams are expected to make highly complex decisions without initial time to "team build".

Exercise #3
How Individuals Can Help or Hurt a Team

Most people are aware of the skills required to make a team work. We have been part of teams since we were little children at home and in school. The basics of good team management are similar to the basics of good human relationships. Much of the material in this unit should be a refresher of things you have done well in the past and things you would like to do differently in the future.

We have presented specific points about effective team building and things that can hurt a team. What so often happens in teams, however, is that when things become stressful there are specific individual behaviors than can help or hurt a team. Rather than concentrating on someone's personality (e.g., he's arrogant, lazy, bossy) we can concentrate on specific behaviors that help other team members and, therefore, help the whole team.

Below is a list of specific behaviors that can help a team. Obviously, doing the opposite of these behaviors will not only hurt individual members of the team but will make the team as a whole ineffective over time.

Check off those behaviors you do routinely. Write out how and when you will do those behaviors that you want to do more often. Write yourself a reminder in your calendar or on your "to do" lists.

Behaviors That Help a Team	Check	How & When I Will Do This Behavior More Often
Accept your own responsibility for making the team effective. Take action when needed.		
Help the other members be the best team members they can be. Help them develop their knowledge and skills and ask for their help in return.		
Understand that at different times leadership will shift within a team and promote the success of that leadership and the participation of all members on the team.		
Help establish, maintain and evaluate performance standards.		
Discourage inappropriate humor, gossip and disorder within the team.		
Concentrate on people's behavior, not personalities, when conflicts arise.		

Behaviors That Help a Team	Check	How & When I Will Do This Behavior More Often
Understand the other members' similarities and differences in knowledge, skills and preferred work styles. Adapt as best you can to those differences.		
Accept uncertainty and change to the best of your ability while also helping the team remain focused on the task at hand.		
Speak highly of your team to others even when you disagree with specific actions or behaviors of individual members.		
Follow common courtesies at all times to encourage a spirit of respect, enjoyment and success.		

Exercise #4
Understanding the Needs and Gifts of Others

Often in teams there are people with different work styles, personalities, and ambitions. Rarely do people spend any time trying to understand those differences, nor the similarities within team members. Teams are often so task oriented there is little or no time to understand the individual members.

One technique that can help a team function better is to get each person to write out two lists. On the first are the things they need from other members of the team to work effectively. These things can be anything from acceptance of a different style of working to the need to have privacy to think about a problem rather than coming up with instant answers. Some people also write that they want occasional praise for work well done or time with the team to laugh, get a hug when things get rough or permission to sit on the floor during meetings as this is more comfortable.

On the second list they write down what they have to offer the other team members. This list may include their knowledge and skills, more understanding of others who disagree with them, and/or willingness to express emotion as well as facts. They may also write down that they love to bake and will bring cookies or muffins to meetings. Or they may enjoy music and will offer to bring in a selection of background music that will help the team work in a more comfortable environment.

These lists can be detailed or general and redone every so often if the team stays together for any length of time.

Once the lists are written they are shared with the other members. Sometimes having them up on flip chart paper on the wall makes it easier for everyone to compare their lists. Team members can state which needs they can fulfill on someone else's list of needs and which gifts they are willing to accept from the other members.

Phases of Team Development

There are often different phases that teams go through; recognizing these phases help a team identify possible problem areas. These phases are only one way to break down the progress a team makes to reach a specific goal. There are many different phase or stage theories in team building books but, again, the labels and number of phases is less important than using the material to help your team work as well as possible together.

The Beginning

The beginning of a team finds people unsure of what they are doing, what they should say, why the other members are on the team, and worrying about the future relationship with the other members. People may come with previous good or bad experiences of working with some of the members or they may have heard rumors about how so-and-so works in a team. This can be an uncomfortable, exciting, stressful or relaxing experience depending on each individual's past team experiences and how this new team was brought together and by whom. The first phase is very important and must not be, but often is, underestimated by the people who bring a team together. Time spent deciding on the specific goals to be reached by this group, clear expectations by those who brought it together and time to get to know each other is invaluable and must not be overlooked. The team leader should have a specific plan (over several sessions together) to help people feel comfortable with each other.

> *The team leader should have a specific plan. Our medical director and social work supervisor always begin by asking what I or the group thinks must be done, then we brainstorm ideas, write them down and share those ideas. This type of consensus building and flattened hierarchy has in my experience worked very effectively but it takes trust and creativity to work.*
> *Michèle Chaban*

Conflicts

This phase comes and goes throughout a team process because you have people with different knowledge, skills and expectations working on the same thing. Recognizing that this phase happens reduces its power to destroy the effectiveness of a team. If people can recognize that they are going through a natural phase of disagreement, then they can move forward to areas of agreement. This phase can be frustrating for different members of a team who dislike conflict. Accepting this feeling of discomfort can minimize the amount of personality conflict and can help individual members concentrate on people's behaviors rather than their personalities.

> *As a social worker I am trained in conflict management but if the conflict goes underground in a team or organization, it can be difficult to deal with. A team that can express its thoughts and feelings grows in strength and maturity. Using humor to deal with the conflict and each other's behavior lets us begin a process of reinforcing trust and fortifies our commitment to work together. Through conflict our team has become stronger even though at times it felt threatening.*
> *Michèle Chaban*

We are a Team

At some point, with effective leadership and understanding of teams by the members, the group of people begin to work together as a team. They understand each other better, their goals are clearer and the division of work is agreed upon. Some teams become very close professionally and personally while others maintain a distinct professional air. Neither team is necessarily better. The situation, the membership, the organizational support and the specific goal will help determine how the team develops.

Even when a team begins to work together smoothly, there may still be times of conflict. The better a team works together the more the conflict revolves around specific ideas and actions rather than personality conflicts.

Us versus Them

Some teams experience an "us versus them" attitude of battling other teams or departments within an organization. A competitive edge between teams can be helpful to an organization as a whole but it can be very destructive if the competition becomes territorial and mean-spirited. Organizations must understand this common occurrence and help teams understand that teams working with each other for a common goal can be just as effective as individuals working together on a team.

> *Sometimes distrust occurs between those who provide the service and those who support those who provide the service. You offer an educational program and choose a time that might be favorable to the majority. Those in non-clinical areas can more easily get away for an hour or an hour-and-a-half, where as on the clinical side, where services are being offered to clients 24 hours a day, only a small number may be permitted to attend. So right away there is a gap in accessibility to educational events, or even celebrations. These types of systemic conflicts are not easily resolved. A couple of years ago you just got more money, brought in more staff to cover services. Now the organization does not have the money, in sufficient quantities, to replace the staff.*
> *Larry Lewis*

We are a Successful Team

If a team is given enough support, time and the right mix of members, it transforms itself from a team doing good work to a team that goes beyond good to exceptional. These teams begin to think as a whole. They understand and accept each other's strengths and differences. They work for a common purpose and for a common recognition of their success. When you have participated in such a team you will never want to leave the security and acceptance you find within it. You may experience such a team only once or twice in your career so enjoy it!

A New Team

Over time, teams may change members and the future success of the team will depend on how carefully the older members of the team orient and welcome new members. There are few things as difficult to do at work than to join a team whose membership was so close that new members are subtly, or not so subtly, made to feel unwelcome.

Where Do You Go From Here?

You have just reviewed a lot of information on team building. Where do you go from here?

Once you have reviewed the material carefully and assessed your own strengths and learning needs it is time to look at the team itself. The following steps assume that you are already part of a team. If you are not, then look at the material in this package again to help you begin a new team or become an effective member of a new team.

Assuming you are part of an established team:

1. Make sure you have completed your self-assessment of your own working styles and your ability to take on various leadership roles in a team. This will identify your team building strengths and learning needs.
2. Assess the strengths and learning needs of the team. Ask the team to participate, if possible, in this assessment using some of the material you have just reviewed. Have them look at what makes a team successful and what can cause failure. If your team is not interested in learning more about team building you have several choices:

- Accept the situation as it is.
- If you are the team leader, you can set aside time and have the group either listen to your ideas about team building and/or participate in designing a more effective team together.
- If you are not the team leader, you can ask to speak with them to discuss any concerns you may have about the effectiveness of the team. If the team leader is uninterested and your concerns are serious enough, you may decide:
- To speak to the manager or executive who created the team to discuss your concerns and ideas.
- To speak to someone in the education, training or human resources department and ask them for advice about what to do next.

3. If the team is ready to build its skills together and it has done the assessment in # 2 then they can continue by agreeing on areas to work on as a team. They may decide that they need time to look at each other's gifts and needs for being more effective. They may decide to have you or someone else present the material within this package. They may decide to concentrate on dealing with stress or tensions within the team. They may decide to concentrate on the team strengths before looking at areas of more learning.

   As well as agreeing to areas of team building, it is also necessary for the team to assess how well it has defined its purpose, goals and objectives, the roles and responsibilities of individual members, reasonable deadlines for getting the work done, how to measure success, and what type of external supports they have or need to complete their work.
4. Once the team has agreed to areas to work on they begin to work individually on any personal skills development. They can use the same materials you have to assess their own strengths and learning needs and report back to the team by a certain date on their progress. They can also use other resources, internal or external teachers, friends and colleagues.

5. The team may decide to set aside specific time every week or month for regular progress discussions on where the team is at present, how it has progressed and what still needs to happen. These discussions can be as formal or informal as the team likes depending on the relationship between the members.
6. Team building takes energy and support to truly work. Reward yourselves individually and as a team often to encourage the kind of working environment that allows for **creativity, high productivity and enjoyment**. If you do not have all three of these measurable quantities, review your team again.

Summary

Team building is an acquired skill. The prime responsibilities of a team member are: (1) to meet the needs of the clients, patients, or families and (2) to help the team develop into an enjoyable, productive and united group of successful individuals.

Helping your team members be successful means: making sure that others see them in a good light, that you do nothing to harm their prestige or their abilities, and that you genuinely believe that a successful team means that all members of the team are also successful.

The working styles of the team members will probably differ. Your role as a team member or leader is to understand that you must have diversity on the team to have success. If you have all members with the same style as you, you may have a more enjoyable working relationship but you may not get the work done as effectively.

Self-assessment of your own skills is vital in any skill development. If you do not know what you do well and what you need to learn then progress will always be by coincidence rather than by planning. You do not have to be an expert in every skill required by a team. Knowing what areas you are not expert in allows you to recognize that expertise in someone else and encourage them to use that expertise for the benefit of the team. This self-assessment will also help to clarify those things that you do very well but that you prefer not to do any more. Again, you can see if other team members have that skill or you can help someone else develop that skill so that you do not have to do it as much. For example, you may be tired of taking minutes at meetings but you are very good at it. Over time, you can teach other members to do it almost as well as you do and you will not have to do it alone any more.

As in most skill development, your attitude to the skill will determine how capable you become. Many people can learn team building skills without believing in an attitude of team effectiveness. They can learn communication skills, how to resolve conflicts within a team and the other skills without ever showing a genuine interest in the other members. Technical team building skills can take people only so far. If someone truly dislikes working in a team, that will become evident over time and unless the other team members can help them see the benefits, such a disillusioned person can hurt the effectiveness of the rest of the team.

Many people only get to experience working with a highly successful and enjoyable team once or twice in their careers. I have experienced it several times and there are few experiences that feel as good at the end of a workday. The few teams I was involved with that were enjoyable, highly productive and creative were teams with a great variety of working styles, a true commitment to the success of each individual member and the team as a whole, a shared vision of what they wanted to accomplish and the desire to work through the inevitable conflicts, stresses and different backgrounds of the members. There were times of real frustration, anger and passion. They were recognized and dealt with by effective team leadership. And when the end came, as most teams must end, it was very difficult to leave the other members. In our personal lives we might never have become friends because of our differences. Through our work lives we became friends because of our similarities.

Resources

The following resources are only a few of the many useful resources that you can find in your local libraries, within your own organization, and in your local bookstores. Look for other books but also for journal articles, magazine reports, films, videos and audiocassettes. Also keep in mind how much you can learn from experts in the field, including people within your own organization!

Chang, R.Y. (1994). *Building a dynamic team: A practical guide to maximizing team performance.* Irvine, CA: Chang Associates.

Clemens, J.K., & Mayer, D.F. (1987). *The classic touch: Lessons in leadership from Homer to Hemingway.* Homewood, IL: Dow Jones-Irwin.

Duarte, D.L. & Snyder, N. T. (1999). *Mastering virtual teams: Strategies, tools, and techniques that succeed.* San Francisco: Jossey-Bass.

Dubrin, A.J. (1995). *The breakthrough team player: Becoming the M.V.P. of your workplace team.* New York: AMACOM.

Fisher, K. (1992). *Leading self-directed work teams: A guide to developing new team leadership skills.* New York: McGraw-Hill.

Lipnack, J., & Stamps, J. (1997). *Virtual teams: Reaching across space, time, and organizations with technology.* Etobicoke, ON: Wiley & Sons.

Mears, P. (1994). *Healthcare teams: Building continuous quality improvement-*

Facilitator's guide. Delray Beach, FL: St. Lucie Press.

Schwarz, R.M. (1994). *The skilled facilitator: Practical wisdom for developing effective groups.* San Francisco: Jossey-Bass.

Zander, A. (1994). *Making groups effective.* San Francisco: Jossey-Bass.

Effective Meetings

There are no special secrets to running effective meetings. Meetings are consistently productive and satisfying if they are held for the right reasons, planned, controlled and allow enough time for people to give their ideas and ask questions. An added bonus is when people at a meeting give each other permission (usually informally) to include a bit of appropriate good humor during the slow or tense times of a meeting.

People know they have participated in an effective meeting when they understand why the meeting was called, what the specific goals and objectives are, what the expectations are of all the participants and what actions the group agrees upon.

This section is designed to identify and reinforce good meeting techniques for seasoned participants while providing new participants with some useful guidelines so that they can contribute to making meetings effective.

Often we know the proper thing to do to make meetings more effective, but we tend to fall back on ways we have used in the past to organize or participate in meetings. A quick review may remind people of more productive ways to organize, participate in and utilize meetings.

The Basics

This section is primarily for chairpersons. However, any participant will find it useful to pinpoint trouble spots in meetings they attend.

A review of the following steps will help to ensure that your meetings are effective. The Chairperson of the meeting can improvise on these steps depending on the importance of the meeting, the location and the people attending.

Necessity?

Is the meeting really necessary? Ask yourself:

1. Can all the people who must attend be there?
2. Is there enough time before the meeting for people to plan and prepare for their participation?
3. Are the costs of holding the meeting acceptable?
4. Is the meeting a regular meeting that should be cancelled because there is not enough information or work to do at this time?

   Meetings should only be held for the following reasons:

Decisions

To make decisions, solve problems, examine opportunities:

1. To define problems and/or opportunities.
2. To brainstorm, without judgment, for a wealth of alternatives.
3. To select (through consensus when appropriate) the most suitable alternative(s) and begin an action plan for resolving the problem or working on the opportunity.

Information

To share information:

1. To make sure everyone receives the same information in the same way.
2. To get support for new ideas and plans.
3. To give clear and concise instructions to everyone at the same time.
4. To review accomplishments, difficulties, future ideas or plans.

Morale

To build team morale and acknowledge successes.

Education

To provide in-service education programs.

If your meetings are not held for any of the above reasons, consider replacing the meeting with a memo, a phone call (conference call), a quick informal chat.

> *With a staff of over 800 staff, there are more than 350 computers. We ought to be able to exchange information without having to have a meeting all the time. If much of what we are doing is communicating information or giving data, you don't have to be physically present to make that happen. We are on the edge of making a significant difference in how we meet. That should save enormous amounts of time and give people better information than we have ever had.*
> *Larry Lewis*

Who?

Determine who should attend. Often regular meetings have a pre-determined list of participants. However, a review of who attends should include:

People with the power to make the necessary decisions.

People who can provide information and advice.

People affected by decisions and plans.

People representing groups affected by decisions and plans.
People directly responsible for implementing decisions and plans.
A recorder for minutes.

Facilitate

Who should facilitate the meeting?
Is it the boss?
Is it a rotating responsibility of your colleagues?
Is the person selected by vote at each new meeting?

The facilitator/chair of a meeting is crucial to the smooth running of the meeting. They should understand the rules of running an effective meeting and also understand some of the techniques of managing group dynamics.

Agenda

Ask meeting participants for ideas to be included on the agenda.

Divide the agenda into action/decision oriented topics and discussion topics. Discussion topics often include reviewing the Minutes of past meetings, items arising from the Minutes, and ideas for future meetings.

The agenda should list who will speak on what topics.

Distribute the agenda at least 48 hours before the meeting. Agendas often describe how long a meeting will take. This helps participants understand how much they need to prepare and how much they need to condense their thoughts and ideas. If people know in advance how long a meeting will take and that the Chairperson will stick to those limits, then they will speak briefly and concisely.

Every so often, the agenda of a regularly scheduled meeting should include an evaluation of that meeting similar to one described in this section.

> *One of the things we are trying to streamline is the meeting activity alone. Xerox has come up with an interesting approach. We work with them as a partner in developing an accountability model. We hope this will give us more of a health care focus that will permeate the organization. They have a meeting agenda approach that clearly outlines the purpose of the meeting. Here are the objectives, here is the amount of time we will spend on item 1, item 2, etc. There is a maximum amount of time, with enough space for defining actions that must be taken and who will take the action. It is a very structured agenda that I think is a very clever way of doing things. It has begun to have an impact on how people view meetings and their participation at meetings.*
> *Larry Lewis*

Presenters

People presenting at the meeting should prepare their presentations well in advance of the meeting.

Location

The purpose of the meeting and the number of participants will help determine the type of location. If it is a large group and you are basically presenting information, then a large auditorium is suitable. For small working groups a smaller room with enough tables is better. The room should comfortably fit the number of people attending.

As a chairperson, you may or may not have the power to decide where a meeting will take place. Organizations often have limited funds for renting meeting rooms that meet all of the ventilation and space criteria. People often feel valued and important when they meet away from the regular meeting place. If funds are limited, it is best to save the rental fees for especially important meetings, or as a "perk" to a regularly scheduled meeting.

Ventilation

Check for sufficient ventilation. Also decide in advance if people will be permitted to smoke during the meeting or outside the room during breaks.

Seating

Chairs and tables can be arranged "school style" for presentations and lectures. For working groups you may want the "board room style" with a long table or large circular table, or a set up with several smaller round tables to allow for small group participation. A "U-shape" or semi-circle set up of tables is also effective for group discussions.

Chairs should be comfortable and sturdy. Avoid placing chairs too close together.

A trick that is rarely used but helpful is to hold short meetings with people standing up. This may appear odd but people tend to chat less and focus more when they are standing. Just as some senior executives now raise their desk so they can do some of their work and telephone calls standing up, "standing meetings" encourage people to be concise, alert and committed to finishing on time. Remove all tables so that people must hold their reference materials in their hands. This encourages people to better prepare what they want to say and what they need to bring to meetings.

Harry van Bommel

Before the meeting, check that the lights and climate controls are working, that window shades can be opened and closed, that the room is set up the way you want it and that the A/V equipment is working.

Equipment

Flip charts, overhead projectors, video players, film and slide projectors, etc. are all possible tools to help make a presentation clearer.

When you use A/V equipment make sure, before the meeting, that all your supplies are there and in working order. Place the equipment in suitable locations so that everyone can see without obstruction. Have spare supplies (e.g., light bulbs, magic markers, and paper) in case you run out.

Perks

All meeting participants can take part in making meetings fun, as well as effective. Consider:

Choosing a different location.

When appropriate, circulating cartoons or other humorous materials.

Bringing in muffins or other treats.

Celebrating someone's birthday, anniversary, etc.

Ending the meeting early.

Doing anything that takes little time and puts a smile on people's faces.

Specific Roles

The Chairperson

The chairperson is the pivotal person attending the meeting. Here are some things for the chairperson to keep in mind.

1. Choose a suitable location.
2. Most meetings should have an agenda. Prepare the agenda, with input from participants where appropriate, including the date, place and time of the meeting.
3. The agenda should begin with urgent and important action/decision items first rather than discussion items.
4. Hold routine meetings at the end of the day.
5. Try having your short meetings standing up.
6. Set a time limit at the outset of each meeting.
7. Cancel meetings once in a while to avoid routine.
8. Start and end the meeting on time even though everyone is not there. Punctuality encourages people to be on time.

9. Avoid having any interruptions during a meeting. They are distracting and imply that the meeting is not very important.
10. Assign someone to take minutes.
11. Assign someone to watch the time in every meeting if you do not do this yourself.
12. Follow the sequence of the agenda and tell participants how long you think each item may take to meet the meeting deadline. You might revise the sequence if someone who is presenting has asked for a delay.
13. Prepare minutes of meetings soon after the meeting and follow up on specific actions promptly.

Group Dynamics Ideas for the Chairperson

Get everyone present involved in the discussions and decisions. Encourage creative thought! Draw out the less vocal participants and encourage brevity in people who enjoy talking too much.

Insist that participants suggest solutions for every problem they raise.

Discourage private discussions between participants.

Keep the discussion on the topic by discouraging people from bringing in other issues.

Sum up key points made by the participants to help close the discussion.

As a general rule, do not confront a person directly in a meeting if their behavior is unacceptable. Instead, call a short break and speak to the person privately. If possible to leave it until later, ask to speak with the person after the meeting.

If the group fails to generate discussions or ideas, try the following:

Remain silent. Do not take all the responsibility for maintaining the discussion. People often need this time to arrange their thoughts. This also tends to draw out people who normally allow others to control the meeting –sometimes they just cannot handle the silence!

Ask questions to ensure that the purpose or goal of the discussion is clear.

Address the silence as a problem of process. Ask for alternative ways to generate ideas. This shows your flexibility as a chair and your concern for accomplishing the task in a way that is comfortable to the group. Again, it challenges participants to accept some responsibility for the process.

Chairperson Checklist

_ Location confirmed.

_ Agenda:

Prepared

Sent Out

Time Limit Set

_ Minutes from the last meeting circulated.

_ Minute-taker assigned.

_ Handouts:

Prepared and copied

Distributed beforehand?

_ Audio-visual material prepared.

_ Audio-visual equipment checked.

_ Other specific duties.

Presenters

Prepare in advance, any presentation you will make. Avoid waiting until the day of the meeting in case of unexpected events, illnesses or traffic delays.

Divide your presentation into:

The main point of your presentation.

Supporting information that the participants must know. Break this down into 1-5 easily understood items beginning with the most important.

Supporting information that is interesting but not vital for participants to know. Participants can be given the option to hear the information. Time constraints may prevent presentation of this information.

Any audiovisual aids should be kept to the side until you want to use them, otherwise they may distract the other participants. Keep these aids easy to understand and manipulate. Have spare light bulbs, paper, and markers. Test out the equipment before the meeting.

Give large amounts of written material to the chairperson to distribute along with the agenda. The other participants can use the time before the meeting to read your materials and prepare questions and comments.

Presenter Checklist

_ Prepare your presentation in advance:

Main point

Supporting information

Information for interest

Audio-visual aids prepared.

_ Audio-visual equipment checked.

_ Handouts:

Prepared and copied
Distributed beforehand?

- _ Read agenda, previous minutes, handouts to prepare for rest of meeting.
- _ Other specific duties.

Participants

1. Prior to the meeting ensure that "actions" you were responsible for from the last meeting have been addressed. One good technique is to highlight your responsibilities when you receive your minutes.
2. Prior to the meeting read the agenda and prepare to talk about any items that are important to you. Don't wait till the meeting for inspiration to strike you.
3. Arrive on time. If you know you will be late or absent, tell the chairperson before the meeting.
4. Be an active listener. Give your opinion or ideas only when they are new and relevant to the discussion. Keep any anecdotes and stories for after the meeting.
5. When you speak, be concise and clear. Begin with your main point and any supporting information the other participants must know. Do not give interesting, but unnecessary, information to those who have asked until after the meeting.
6. Show enthusiasm for your ideas and enthusiasm for other people's ideas as well. Help to promote unity within the group whenever possible.
7. Speak first to the chairperson and then draw the other participants into your discussion by looking at all of them.
8. Avoid private discussion with other members at the meeting.
9. Meetings sometimes lead to friction between participants. Be one of those participants who consider the other person's point of view before discounting it or arguing against. Listening and questioning often lead to consensus rather than division. Set an example.

Participant's Checklist

- _ Read Agenda, Previous Minutes, Handouts to prepare for the meeting.
- _ Prepare any personal information, questions or information you need to give the others.
- _ Prepare any information you may be asked for during the meeting based on the previous Minutes or the present agenda.
- _ Other specific duties.

Minute-Taker

- Minutes are critical for several reasons:
- Summarizing the decisions and discussions of a meeting.
- Recording what action was agreed upon and who would follow through.
- Informing those people who were absent when the next meeting will take place (if any) and where.

Role of Minute-Taker

The person who takes the minutes should follow the standard format used for past minutes. However, at times it is important to review how minutes have been taken and whether or not they can be rewritten in a more dynamic way; use the active voice and write more in the way people talk versus the formalized style which is difficult for many people to read.

When meetings are long and involve many decisions, motions and discussions, it is useful to provide a summary of decisions and motions at the beginning of the minutes.

The role of minute-taker is vital but often minimized by other participants. If you are assigned or volunteer to take minutes at all meetings or are responsible for the minutes on a rotating basis it is important for you to request comments from the others. You will need to get the odd perk for doing what has often been a thankless job. Don't wait for the perks; ask for them (nicely!).

Action Plans

Minutes should incorporate any Action Plans that were agreed upon to tell people what is expected, by whom, by what date and how the results will be evaluated.

Easy-To-Read

Minutes should be easy to read. Highlight sections that are for information and sections where decisions were made.

Active Voice

Whenever possible, write in the active voice, for example, "The group decided…" rather than, "It was decided…"

Sent Out

Minutes of the meetings should be sent out to participants within a few days of the meeting instead of waiting to send them out with the agenda for the next meeting.

Minute-Taker Checklist

- _ Read Agenda, Previous Minutes, Handouts to prepare for the meeting.
- _ Prepare any formats, charts or systems used in recording minutes.
- _ Prepare any information you may be asked for during the meeting based on the previous Minutes or the present agenda.
- _ Have extra copies of minutes from the last meeting as well as extra Agendas for this meeting.
- _ Other specific duties.

Evaluating a Meeting

After an important and/or regularly scheduled meeting, do a quick review to help improve future meetings. Have all the participants fill in and return the evaluation to someone assigned to compile the information We seldom evaluate meetings except in a cursory way. This is an important task that can reduce frustration and increase the effectiveness and satisfaction of the participants.

Circle 'Y' or 'N' for the following questions. For any 'No' answers, write suggestions for improving the next meeting you attend with this group.

Y/N 1. Were you informed in advance about the meeting date, place and time?

Y/N 2. Did you understand the reason for the meeting?

___ Share information

___ Make decisions

___ Solve problems

___ Plan

___ Build morale

___ Educate

Y/N 3. Were you given an agenda before the meeting?

Y/N 4. Did the meeting begin and end on time?

Y/N 5. Did the chairperson control the meeting, following the agenda?

Y/N 6. Did the chairperson encourage open and honest communication?

Y/N 7. Was there sufficient time to permit creative thought and active problem solving?

Y/N 8. Did most participants actively listen to each other?

Y/N 9. Was everyone encouraged to participate?

Y/N 10. Were decisions and plans clear and concise? Did people understand what was expected and who would do what by when?

Y/N 11. Did you actively participate and help keep the meeting going according to agenda and expectations?

Y/N 12. Were you satisfied with this meeting: its results, the process followed, the other participants?

What would you do differently next time to make the meeting more effective?

What do you suggest the chairperson do differently next time to make the meeting more effective?

How could other participants help to make the next meeting more effective?

Summary

People know they have participated in an effective meeting when they understand why the meeting is called, what the specific goals and objectives are, what the expectations are of all the participants and what actions the group agrees to do.

You have read about simple techniques for preparing , organizing and evaluating meetings that are easy to follow. There are no special secrets to running effective meetings – just good organizing skills and following the agreed-upon agenda.

It is important to recognize the value of creativity and flexibility within meetings that are called to resolve specific problems or examine new opportunities. Regardless of the reason for the meeting it is also important to encourage appropriate humor in meetings. Humor can acknowledge the importance of the meeting but also the necessity of seeing the broader perspective of any situation.

Resources

The following resources are only a few of the many useful resources that you can find in your local libraries, within your own organization, and in your local bookstores. Look for other books but also for journal articles, magazine reports, films, videos and audiocassettes. Also keep in mind how much you can learn from experts in the field, including people within your own organization!

Doyle, M., & Straus, D. (1993). *How to make meetings work.* New York: Berkley Publishing Group.

Hawkins, C. (1997). *First aid for meetings: Quick fixes and major repairs for running effective meetings.* Clearwater, FL: Career Research Institute.

Haynes, M. (1997). *Effective meeting skills.* Menlo Park, CA: Crisp Publications.

Lord, R.W. (1981). *Running conventions, conferences and meetings.* New York: Amacom.

Perry, H. (1984). *Call to order: Meeting rules and procedures for non-profit organizations.* Burlington, ON: Big Bay Publishing.

Timm, P.R. (1997). *How to hold successful meetings: 30 action tips for managing effective meetings.* Franklin Lakes, NJ: Career Press.

Tropman, J.E. (1995). *Effective meetings: Improving group decision-making.* Thousand Oaks, CA: Sage Publications.

Watson, J. (1992). *The minute taker's handbook: Taking minutes at any meeting with confidence.* Vancouver, BC: Self-Counsel Press.

Creative Problem Solving

We use less than 10% of our thinking capacity. At least that is what many research specialists tell us.

Their argument is based upon thousands of research papers exploring the working of the mind in people who have a genius I.Q. and people who have had severe brain damage and yet can still learn to overcome that damage. The research examines how people learn, what helps and inhibits that learning, and countless other studies to help all of us understand more about the most complex organ in our body.

One of the most interesting concepts to come out of this research is that the mind takes in new information and tries to integrate it with information already stored in memory. The mind sorts and combines information so that when we develop one thinking skill we automatically enhance many other thinking skills. Creative thinking, therefore, is a method of multiplying our thinking processes to get the maximum use of our stored knowledge and abilities.

The human mind is a wonder of technology. It is not surprising that we have not mastered its many uses when we consider that the brain has 100,000 to 1,000,000 different chemical reactions taking place every minute and there are ten billion neurons transferring information continuously.

Our brain controls our bodily movements and the running of our organs (heart, lungs, transfer of blood throughout the system, electrical impulses, systems to combat disease, our speech and hearing and touch, our digestive system, etc.). Our mind is capable of coordinating our thought process when we are working, playing , sleeping and dreaming or studying. Our mind allows us to imagine, to remember, to forecast and to make choices.

Creative problem solving tries to incorporate many of the mind's abilities. In this section, we can present only a simple technique for problem solving. The Resources section at the end of this section can take you on many wonderful journeys into creative problem solving where you use not only your whole mind but also your whole body and spirit.

The word "crisis" is written in the Chinese language as a combination of the words: "danger" and "opportunity". All situations have opportunities. A creative problem solver looks for the opportunity.

Left Brain–Right Brain

In the past decade there has been a great deal written about the left and right sides of our brain. Some people have taken this information literally to mean that the left side of our brain controls certain functions and the right side of our brain other functions. This may be true generally but if the brain has physical abnormalities or has been injured it can often compensate for any irregularities by using other areas of the brain. For any complex thought processes, e.g., listening to music, making decisions and processing language, both sides of the brain are constantly involved and interconnected.

Part of this belief comes from research where surgeons have cut the corpus callosum, the main fiber bridge linking the brain's two halves. Some people who have severe epilepsy have received some relief from seizures by having this fiber bridge cut. A significant side effect of this surgery was that the person could see an object and know what it was (right side) but not be able to speak the words to describe it (left side). As well, people could touch an object while blind folded and draw the object (right side) but not be able to describe it in words (left side).

Since this early research, scientists have found that people who have suffered strokes or other brain damage have been able to bypass portions of their brain thought to control certain functions like body movements, speech, and sight. It appears that the brain is able to develop new control centers when old centers are damaged. Studies in Great Britain have looked at people who were born with damage to large amounts of their brains but who have learned to use other portions of their brains to compensate and be able to function quite normally.

Out of the left/right brain research have come some useful concepts about how we think. I will continue to use the left/right concept of thought but only as a tool to help us understand some of these differences. Always remember that the brain is too complex an organ to assign any one complete function to only one side of the brain. Just as in brain research, our goal in learning about how we think is to learn more about how we can expand our abilities to think and learn more holistically rather than labeling ourselves as right or left brain thinkers.

If we divide how we think into two main categories, we find that:

Left Brain

The left brain is often associated with:

- Sequential thinking.
- Orientation to detail.
- Logical cause and effect.
- Linear thinking (right answer).
- The side that "talks".
- Knows how something is done.

Right Brain

The right brain is often associated with:

- Processing information all at once.
- Global view versus detail.
- Analogic (sees resemblances).
- Lateral thinking (looking for many answers).
- Uses pictures versus words.
- Discovers what is done.

Studies have shown that people who are left handed, for example, can often play certain sports better and can be more creative in the arts. The right side of our brain controls the left hand. The right side is our visual side and can give a slight advantage to athletes who require visual accuracy and coordination such as hockey and baseball players. In fact in the old USSR, athletes and artists were encouraged to be left handed while North Americans have traditionally tried to encourage children to be right handed (logical thinkers, detail oriented).

This information about the left and right sides of our brain allows us to observe our own thinking preferences. Most of us in North American society use the logic of our left brain and largely ignore the creativity and potential of the right brain.

To increase our problem-solving abilities, we can pay closer attention to using our right-brain skills. For example, we can make an effort to back up and look at the whole picture before looking at a specific detail of a problem. We can look for patterns and similarities even if they are not perfect. ("Where have we seen a similar problem? There seems to be a pattern to this situation.") We can produce many answers without judging them. We can draw a picture to stimulate further ideas. We can imagine the problem solved. We can ask a child for their ideas.

If you find that these are the problem solving techniques that you normally use, perhaps you need to pay more attention to your left-brain skills.

The goal is to expand our thinking by using both sides of our brain.

Exercise #1

Take a problem that you are presently experiencing at work, at home or a personal challenge you have set for yourself.

Try using some of the right-brain processes. Write down or draw your solutions. Do not judge them yet. This may feel awkward at first, but persist and try to be aware of the difference in the number and types of solutions you generate. Be daring!

Limitations to Creativity

If it is true that we use only ten percent of our brain potential then we are limiting our ability to learn and to adapt to an ever changing world. What other limits do we set ourselves?

One limitation is that we hear only 20% of what is said. Part of this screening of what we hear is because we are bored. We can hear three times faster than people can speak. If we are listening at less than that maximum speed we can get easily bored if the subject is uninteresting.

We also screen out a lot of information we are listening to because of cultural, sexual, religious and personal biases. We hear so much information in a day that we naturally screen out most information that we disagree with, find uninteresting, or do not have the patience to learn.

These same biases effect how we read. Again we read only about 20% of the words. We may see each individual word as our eye goes by but we do not remember the actual content. How much of the last book you read can you actual retell in great detail; 80% or closer to 10-20%?

Another limitation is our memory. People remember things that interest them or that have terrified them. Nightmares, war experiences, the death of someone close to you are often remembered in great detail. Favorite childhood adventures, your first date, and the time you won first prize in a sport or contest are things you will probably remember.

Most of our days are not filled with these kinds of adventures. We live in the information age where everyday we are given thousands of details: at work, on the car radio, during the nightly television news, when our families and friends tell us details about their day, when we listen to music or watch movies, or when we read novels, a stack of reports, or professional journals.

This wealth of knowledge has forced us to forget much of the details we hear or read everyday. In fact, we forget up to 80% of new information within 24 hours of learning it unless we review what we have learned. In the section on "Improving Your

Memory" you can learn more about how to store important information in your long term memory and how to remember that information when you need to use it.

Stress saps energy from your creative thinking potential as well. This is often tied to time constraints and insufficient time spent setting goals and priorities for yourself.

For the most part, these limitations to creativity can be changed. You can practice being more open to written or spoken information about your problem. There are techniques to improve your memory to help you retain useful information for future reference.

Stress and lack of time can also be addressed in order to approach your problem solving in a more relaxed and more leisurely way. Stress management techniques and relaxation Exercises are useful tools. It is not a coincidence that many of our best ideas come at 2:30 in the morning when our mind and body have had time to relax!

Another limit to creativity is how one defines either the problem or the form the answer is "supposed" to take. A narrow definition of the problem will reduce the quantity as well as the type of solution you come up with. This may be useful for some technical problems, but may hold you back in larger problem-solving situations.

What the solution is supposed to look like will also limit creativity. This particular limit will often take some uncovering. Often the perception of what the solution will look like is so strong that the problem-solving team will not even question the perception. For example, many labor negotiations are limited in their creativity because the options are usually seen as "we get what we want or: a) we will go on strike (union), or b) we will lock you out (management)".

Freeing yourself from a specific type of solution can result in a flood of creative alternatives.

Problem Solving Strategies

Over time, people learn various problem solving strategies that work for them. The strategies you adopt personally often reflect the kind of education you received at school or from your parents. Farmers have different ways of solving problems than lawyers may have or that scientists may have.

The following is a brief list of possible strategies that people can use. Some of you may use different strategies for different situations. At home you may work backwards from a problem while at work you are more likely to use stock solutions. If you are stuck on a problem, try out one of two of the strategies that you do not normally use.

Stock Solutions

May be used by lawyers, engineers or physicians to deal with problems in a similar, predictable way as determined by training.

Constructed Solutions

May be used by such groups as scientists or NASA to break problems into components parts and each then further sub-divide each part until the problem is identified and addressed.

Backwards

Start at the end-point or goal and work backwards to where you are now. In this way you can identify steps needed along the way to reach your goal. This is the opposite of constructed solutions. Also working backwards allows you to look at the possible positive and negative effects of choosing a particular end-point.

Redefine Problem

Redefining problems is used to ask if the problem is really worth solving? What is the real goal? Is the problem real or is the perception of the problem inaccurate?

Cause and Effect

After you identify the problem you examine the major causes are of the problem: procedures, materials, staff, machines, education, outside influences, economic trends, etc.

System Analysis

This problem-solving strategy looks at problems and situations from a very specific system's approach. What are all the inputs to the problem/situation? How is this input processed? What are the specific, measurable outputs? How will the outputs affect further inputs into this circular process?

Provocation

Taking an unreasonable step to see the result (e.g., legislating an industry which pollutes a river to move its outtake pipe upstream so that the industry must use its own polluted water). This provocative solution may encourage people to present more reasonable alternatives.

Force Field Analysis

Force field analysis is useful when examining specific problems and possible alternative solutions. What "forces" will help resolve the problem and make the solution work and what forces will work against the solution. For example which people will help or hinder your solution? What economic arguments will help or hinder it? What systemic forces will help or hinder your solution?

Avoid Problem

By-pass the problem altogether. For example if an engine requires gasoline to power it but there is an energy shortage, perhaps the engine can be redesigned to avoid needing gasoline (e.g., the solar powered or propane gas cars). In this case problems often result in people being forced to create even more effective machinery, procedures or communication techniques.

Exercise #2

Think of three problems or opportunities that you have solved at work recently. What strategies did you use? Put a star beside those strategies listed above. Try to use other strategies to see if your solutions might be different, better, or more/less cost efficient.

Repeat the exercise thinking of three problems you have had at home recently. Try thinking of different strategies and how they might work better or worse than what you chose to do.

Problem Solving Versus Problem Finding

We limit our ability to solve problems if we only deal with situations as they arise. If you read history books and biographies you will discover that the most successful people were able to solve problems as they appeared but also to search out problems to solve and opportunities to test their skills.

People who made large sums of money during the Depression were able to find some opportunities and problems to solve. Inventors actively search out problems in order to get the inspiration to invent something new.

Children are constantly in search of new adventures to test their skills and to learn new skills. Sometimes they fail (and get to hear their parent's lecture) but they do not stop trying until they are older and have "learned their lesson".

People who try to resolve problems only as they arise **react** to roadblocks, while people who actively seek out problems are **proactive.** Proactive people look for challenges and problems to enhance and expand their ideas, programs, and resources.

Creative problem solving incorporates the best of logical problem-solving techniques with the more open, nonrestrictive and creative ideas of people who search out problems.

The key to successful problem solving is using imaginative and creative ideas to develop a lengthy list of possible solutions without judging their usefulness until after the list is complete. Force yourselves to go beyond the standard solutions to problems by using techniques like brainstorming, humor, exaggeration, and silliness to help stretch yourself beyond the normal reactions to a problem.

> *Creative problem solving is called 'out of the box' thinking at our work. We are always faced with the dilemma of wanting to do more, create new services or improve them, but as the budget continues to diminish over time, a lot of time is spent on this 'out of the box' thinking. For example, in offering a service, can it become an ambulatory service and if so, could there be a third-party payer–it puts it on a health care business level. Or is it more efficient, with certain kinds of things, to have a team that will go out of the hospital to do assessments rather than have individuals come to the hospital and stay for a period of time for assessments?*
> *Larry Lewis*

Standard Problem Solving

Sometimes you will use standard problem solving to save time or because it is more comfortable for you to use. This process has helped many individuals and teams find solutions to problems that they thought were unsolvable.

It may help you to understand standard problem solving techniques before expanding your skills to the wider scope of more creative problem solving.

Standard Problem Solving

Define the goal or problem. Is it urgent, like a fire, or is it important, such as designing fire regulations? Be specific in your definition.

Decide on the process for solving the problem. Who will do what and when will you discuss the alternatives or solution?

Decide on how much commitment you will give to this problem. Urgent matters need instant decisions. You cannot sit down and brainstorm during a fire. Someone needs to take command and instruct others what to do. If you are deciding on new fire prevention procedures you can afford to commit more time and energy in developing these procedures.

Develop and examine alternatives. At this point people often depend on previous problem-solving strategies. See the "Problem-Solving Strategies" section of this section for examples.

Expand on selected alternatives and their consequences.

Choose the best alternative.

Act on your decision.

Evaluate the results and the process you used.

In one of my problem solving courses, health care participants were to come up with alternatives for a doctor's strike that was happening at the time. Using the nominal group process described in this chapter, they began with some of the off-the-wall alternatives that no one judged as good or bad. This down-to-earth group used these "goofy" alternatives as a cue to let their imaginations fly. One impossible alternative led the group to a solution that would never have come out naturally during typical problem solving brainstorming. They suggested that the physicians agree to work for free for three days. They were losing income anyway by being on strike but they were getting their patients and community as upset as the medical regulators. By working for free for a period of time, they could pool the income they would normally keep into a special fund through which they could buy some important equipment they were lacking and to get their message across more forcefully through a media campaign–all without inconveniencing their patients.

Harry van Bommel

Creative Alternatives

Creative problem solving does not replace standard problem solving techniques or strategies; it is meant to improve them. Take step 4 ("examining alternatives") in the Standard Problem Solving for example. To change this step into a more creative technique, change that process into the following:

Using the **nominal group process** described here:

Individuals are given specific time to generate a minimum of 5-15 (or more) alternative solutions each. When individuals have generated their ideas they each read out one solution each until all ideas are presented. The group should have at least 30 alternatives to the problem without anyone judging the appropriateness of any alternative. Welcome all ideas, even ones that are "clearly" not going to work.

- You might use yellow stick-it paper or cue cards to write out each alternative. This will make it easier to divide the alternatives into groups later on.
- Each member of the group is given a turn to state an alternative with the group giving that person time to think quietly (this prevents one person from dominat-

ing the session). No one is permitted to criticize or dismiss any alternative. Even "bizarre" alternatives can generate more realistic alternatives later on in the discussions. A person may pass. While one person reads out an idea, others within the group may come up with new ideas. They write these out as well and read them when it is their turn. The group continues generating ideas until everyone has passed a few times.

At a different time or on a different day, group the various ideas into categories. Each participant will then take all the written alternatives and write out their top five alternatives. This will cut down on the number of possible alternatives.

Group everyone's top five alternatives and begin to combine similar ones together. Divide these combinations into areas of similarities, e.g., all ideas for staff changes in one grouping and all ideas for procedural differences in another group.

Choose the alternatives that are most popular plus any alternative that any member of the group feels very strongly about.

- Return to the groupings and examine each alternative separately for:
- Appropriateness as an alternative.
- Whether the alternative (bizarre as it may be) can produce a more appropriate alternative (e.g., shooting someone is inappropriate while expressing honest feelings of anger may be appropriate).
- Whether it can be successful in the present circumstances within your organization.

Prepare a separate list of the chosen alternatives and move on to step number 5 ("expand on selected alternatives") in the Standard Problem Solving techniques described previously.

Creative alternatives may use the standard problem-solving techniques, and expand on one or two of the steps, as described above. Creativity also means:

Taking the left and right brain information into account **before** you start to solve problems.

- Minimizing the limitations of stress and time.
- Recognizing that we only hear or read 20% of the information we are working with and may, therefore, miss something important.
- Taking time to define the problem or search for a problem.
- Making sure the solution is not unnecessarily limited by preconceived notions of what the solution should look like.
- Recognizing that problems give us real opportunities to try something new and exciting.

Exercise #3

Before you sit down to solve your next problem, look over the above list. In what ways will you make your problem solving more creative?

Blocking Creativity

Sometimes people say things in order to block or discourage creativity. They use comments like:

We've tried that before and it didn't work.

It won't work.

That is a stupid idea!

Why do it a new way since we've done it this way for so long.

Do we have this kind of money in our budget?

Is there enough time to do this considering all our other priorities?

We should get more advice from "experts" before we make any decisions.

I don't think senior managers will go for this idea.

We're not ready for that idea as an organization.

Creative problem solving means you have to avoid using statements like this. It also means you have to discourage other people from using these kinds of statements. Creativity requires unrestrained encouragement and trust to try out new ideas without anyone judging their value or usefulness.

If you participate in sessions where people do discourage creative thought, talk to that person privately to help instruct them on the value of creative problem solving to them as individuals and to the organization as a whole.

Summary

We have only sketched over creative problem solving techniques. The world of creativity is so exciting and there are so many alternatives to explore. The Resources section at the end of this section can help you begin to find dozens of alternative ways of being creative in solving your problems and searching out new problems and opportunities.

The principle technique of all problem solving is to identify what you specifically want to examine and what process you will use to do that. When everyone agrees on the process it makes it easier to concentrate on the task rather than on who does what and when.

Generating 30-50 alternatives, or more, forces us to look beyond standard problem solving strategies. In the end the standard strategy may be the one you choose. The difference is that you will know if it really is the best alternative given the set of circumstances you are working with. If you do not generate dozens of alternatives you will never know if there was a more effective, cost efficient way of solving the same problem.

Resources

The following resources are only a few of the many useful resources that you can find in your local libraries, within your own organization, and in your local bookstores. Look for other books but also for journal articles, magazine reports, films, videos and audiocassettes. Also keep in mind how much you can learn from experts in the field, including people within your own organization!

Altier, W. J. (1999). *The thinking manager's toolbox: Effective processes for problem solving and decision making.* Oxford, UK: Oxford University.

Chang, R.Y., & Kelly, P K. (1994). *Step-by-step problem solving: A practical guide to ensure problems get (and stay) solved.* Irvine, CA: Chang Associates.

Claflin, E. (Ed.). (1993). *The experts' book of hints, tips and everyday wisdom: From leading authorities. More than 1,000 problem-solving secrets for easier, healthier living.* Emmaus, PA: Rodale.

Fobes, R. (1993). *The creative problem solver's toolbox: A complete course in the art of creating solutions to problems of any kind.* Corvallis, OR: Solutions Through Innovation.

Higgins, J.M. (1994). *101 creative problem solving techniques: The handbook of new ideas.* Winter Park, FL: New Management.

Noone, D.J. (1993). *Creative problem solving.* Monroe, WA: Barrons.

Prince, G.M. (1970). *The practice of creativity: A manual for dynamic group problem solving.* New York: Harper & Row.

Stevens, M. (1997). *How to be a better problem solver.* Kogan Page.

Stice, J.E. (Ed.) (1987). *Developing critical thinking and problem-solving abilities.* San Francisco: Jossey-Bass.

6. Impassioned Supervision

Impassioned Supervision

Your goal is to be an effective supervisor, not a perfect one.

This section is about supervisory skills, not managerial skills. What is the difference between supervisors and managers?

Supervisors are generally responsible for the work performed by front-line staff. A major portion of their work is, therefore, supervising their staff. Supervisors may also be involved in planning and coordinating work within their area.

Managers are usually involved in planning and coordinating their department and organization's activities. Many managers also supervise the work done by one or more front-line supervisors, therefore, their supervisory skills are important to maintain and improve.

In reviewing your supervisory skills remember that:

- You already have or are developing supervisory skills.
- You need to learn skills and procedures your organization and/or immediate manager requires or encourages you to use with your own staff.

This section examines skills and procedures that you may already have and those skills you may want to develop or enhance. The objective of this section is to prepare new supervisors for the work ahead while also providing a general review for experienced supervisors.

The wide range of skills and abilities a supervisor acquires over time cannot be condensed into a single section. We will touch on many aspects of the supervisor's role but it will be necessary for you to examine those areas you would like to learn more about and use the Resources listed at the end of this, and other sections in this book, to find the information you need.

Sometimes the particular skills or procedures in this section will not be consistent with policies and procedures of your organization, for example, suggestions around performance appraisals or discipline. Each organization has its own policies, for instance, those dealing with legal issues, union concerns, hiring and dismissals. Know what these are in your own organization. Make sure that you review and compare the information in this section with the policies and procedures of your organization. Use only those ideas and skills from this section that will enhance your supervisory skills within your organization's policies and procedures.

Also find out if your organization has internal educational programs to help you understand which policies and procedures affect your work as a supervisor. As well, check to see if your organization recommends any external programs to help you become the best supervisor you can be.

Perhaps one of the best ways to learn supervisory skills is to observe a good supervisor at work. If you find a good role model, you can increase your effectiveness as a supervisor while reducing the amount of mistakes you might make.

Why Do You Want to Be a Supervisor?

It is important to take the time to understand your reasons for wanting to be a supervisor. If you are clear on why you chose this position, and if you find that your job does meet your professional and personal expectations, you may find it easier to deal with the unexpected tasks that accompany your supervisory role. You will know when it is time for another career change if you review your personal goals regularly.

Why did you accept the position? Was it for the increased wages and benefits? Was it because you wanted greater responsibility? Was it because you wanted to learn new skills while improving old ones? Was it because you like to have control and give direction to others? Was it because you saw supervision as a stepping stone to further career moves?

Write out your reasons for choosing to be a supervisor.

Whenever people begin a new position as a supervisor they experience hopes, fears, dreams and anxieties about the change. Write out some of your own hopes, fears, dreams and anxieties about your new job.

Often people's fears and anxieties reflect their lack of supervisory skills, uncertainty with a role, fear of not meeting expectations, fear of not being able to cope with a possible lack of support or fear of failure and success.

When you review your own list consider using some of the following ideas to reduce some of your fears and anxieties:

- Open communication with your managers, peers and/or staff, (ask questions, request feedback, listen to constructive criticisms).
- Use internal and external educational resources and programs to improve or develop your own supervisory skills, including books, articles, speakers, conferences, etc.
- Make sure you get support and constructive feedback from your managers, peers and staff.
- Enjoy the small, positive steps you make each day and week; savor the words of praise and remember how far you have come, as well as how much you still need to learn.
- Keep a list of your achievements and try to use similar strategies in more difficult

situations.

- Allow yourself to be human. Apologize to managers, peers, and staff when you make a mistake while accepting the fact that your own manager and staff will make mistakes too.

Note: The first point above is about open communication with your managers, peers and/or staff. Open communication, in this section, means giving people the information they need to do their jobs well. Ideally you would like to be completely open and honest with everyone you work with but realistically there is information that others do not need to know. In fact, there are times when open communication can be harmful. For example if you share all of your ideas and possible plans with your staff and you or your organization changes your mind, your staff may feel resentful or skeptical of your other ideas and plans.

Pick the right amount of necessary information to give to people. Knowing what to say and when takes practice. Over time you will know who needs what kind of information and who to trust with more sensitive information.

What Makes a Good Supervisor?

Everyone has a different definition of what a good supervisor is. It is a good idea to examine the qualities of a good supervisor to help you identify your strengths and needs in your present supervisory position.

The following is just a brief list of what some people think a good supervisor is. Remember we are looking for good supervisors; not perfect ones. No one can be all things to all people, so use this list as a guide to help you define how you can be a good supervisor.

A good supervisor can have some or most of the following:

Personal Characteristics

A supervisor's character has certain built-in features that can help them achieve excellence. These characteristics are different from skills and knowledge because they reflect a supervisor's attitude toward people and toward their work. These characteristics include:

- A genuine interest in and respect for people -- their staff, their manager, their colleagues and their clients. This includes showing their own integrity and credibility and also:
- Listening to their staff for ideas, criticisms, and opportunities.

- Helping their staff learn as much as they can for their personal and professional growth.
- A willingness to back up their staff when necessary so that staff members are willing to try new things, take calculated risks to improve the overall performance of your area, department and organization.
- A willingness to admit their mistakes. They do not try to appear perfect. They show something of themselves as a person.

Skills and Abilities

Everyone has certain natural skills and abilities. A supervisor needs a wide variety of skills and abilities that can be learned, including:

- A supervision style that is predictable, fair and firm.
- An ability to help set specific goals and objectives with their staff and to help them achieve those goals through constant praise, constructive suggestions and regular performance evaluations.
- The ability to handle stress well and to teach their staff how to manage their own stresses.
- An ability to juggle a wide assortment of demands and requests, along with an ability to make quick, sound judgments on setting priorities.
- An ability to match their own leadership style to the specifics of a situation and to the characteristics of their staff. For example, some supervisors may like to lead by giving specific instructions to their staff while the staff members may want more room to make some decisions on their own. In a situation like this, the supervisor may want to change their leadership style enough to give their staff the support they need to take some risks and learn from their successes and failures.

Knowledge of the Work and Organization

- Give yourself an organizational overview.
- An understanding of the organization's mission statement, and how this statement has everyday meaning to the work done.
- An understanding of the power structures and operational systems in place.
- Knowledge of the specific work done by staff members in their area or department.
- Recognition of the leadership skills of their staff to encourage them to develop professionally and at their own pace.
- Think about other characteristics of a good supervisor.

My favorite boss was a man with unquestionable ethics who had a strong belief in sharing decisions about departmental direction while letting his staff individually determine the methods. Since most people on my team were not interested in writing and I was, he delegated writing projects to me. Although he is an accomplished writer himself, he allowed me to design the finished project and draft the content in my own way. When it came time to edit the draft, he provided excellent feedback without changing my writing style–a very difficult task for one writer to do for another. In this way, Michael brought out my best and helped me to grow in my chosen field. He did the same with the other staff who grew within this protected and challenging environment.

Another gift to us was information. As a director, he was privy to information but always shared as much as he could. Confidential information remained confidential but all the information about the department and organization was shared. We were never in the dark about our future while colleagues in other departments were. When we asked him a question, we always got an honest answer which sometimes included, "I don't know but when I do, I will tell you", or "I can't answer that right now", which meant it was confidential.

When difficulties arose within the team or the organization, Michael encouraged us to go deeper within ourselves to use our leadership and communication skills to our best. We resolved difficulty amongst ourselves and we continued to find humor, interest and energy to get our work done with pride and satisfaction.

Harry van Bommel

Exercise #1

Looking over the previous two lists, what characteristics do you have already? (If you are comfortable with your colleagues or staff, ask them which characteristics they believe you have.)

	Poor 1	Fair 2	Good 3	Excellent 4
Personal characteristics:				
Interest in people				
Listening				
Promote learning				
Support staff with risks				
Able to admit mistakes				
Skills and abilities:				
Predictable, fair, firm				

Able to set clear objectives for self
Able to set clear objectives for staff
Able to manage causes of stress for self
Able to teach stress management to others
Able to balance and set priorities
Able to match leadership style to staff & situation

Knowledge of the work and organization:
Mission statement
Understand power and systems
Understand staff's work
Recognize and encourage staff's leadership skills.

What skills, abilities and knowledge do you want to develop or improve upon in the next 3 months, 6 months, 12 months, 2 years and 3 years?

What is your plan of action to achieve these personal goals?

If you don't know what you can do to achieve these goals, who can you ask? What resources are available?

Exercise #2
What Does a Supervisor Do?

Just as good supervisors have different characteristics, different supervisors have different responsibilities. There are also various levels of supervisors just as there are levels of managers.

You may have some, or all, of the following duties. Look at your job description and check with your manager and other supervisors to see which of the duties apply to you. Put a check mark beside the duties you will have.

___ Reporting to your manager
___ Dividing and scheduling the work
___ Hiring and firing staff with varying degrees of involvement
___ Evaluating your staff's performance
___ Chairing meetings
___ Ensuring the safety of the work environment
___ Teaching or training your staff
___ Checking the quality of the work performed
___ Understanding and applying your organization's policies and procedures
___ Providing information in the budgetary process
___ Resolving conflicts in your area

___ Maintaining good relations with others in the community and in other organizations
___ Contributing to front-line staff duties during times of staff shortages
___ Helping staff solve work problems
___ Acting consistently with union contracts
___ Maintaining records, statistics, files
___ Working with other supervisors when necessary or helpful

Just Beginning

Your Approach

From the beginning, it is important to give a clear message to the staff who will be working with you. From the start:

Tell people what your standards are; for example, you may have personal standards around such things as:

- Punctuality
- Minimal amount of gossip within your area, department and organization
- Creativity
- Honesty
- Independent behavior

Remember that some of your standards may give mixed messages to your staff. For example, you may prefer people to be orderly and conservative in staff meetings but you also want to encourage creative, independent work. Perhaps you will need to change some of your standards to meet the personal and professional needs of your staff.

The secret is to be clear about what you expect and clear when you revise these standards. People want a supervisor who is predictable, fair and firm.

Model your standards. If you expect your staff to do certain things, do them yourself. Do not use the command "Do as I say, not as I do!"

Praise people's behavior and actions when they meet your standards. Be specific in your praise and make an active effort to catch people doing things well so that you can build confidence and rapport. Do not praise routine skills that a person does consistently well as your praise may be seen as insensitive or as patronizing.

Reward people's behavior and actions when they support your standards. Find out what your staff finds rewarding and try to supply those rewards when appropriate. If you value creativity and independent work, reward a staff member during difficult parts of a project or when the work is done. A simple "thank you" is sometimes enough but at other times a tangible expression of respect and thanks is necessary. This can be as simple as a longer lunch, a day-off after lots of overtime, some of your home baking, etc.

What to Do First?

When you accept the position of supervisor you may or may not have a lot of time to prepare. You may be expected to fill in temporarily for a supervisor (an "acting supervisor" position) or you may have been planning this career move for some time.

Regardless of the circumstances there will be certain expectations of what you will need to do in the first few days and weeks as a supervisor. These expectations include what your immediate managers want you to accomplish, what you want to do yourself, and what your staff expect you to do.

It will not be possible to accomplish everything at once. Sometimes you may be given a "breaking-in period" during which you can spend time meeting your staff, going through the previous supervisor's files to determine what is important and what is less important, visiting other supervisors to get their ideas, and more.

At other times you may be thrown into an emergency situation where your front-line expertise is demanded immediately along with skills in directing and supervising other staff (perhaps people you used to work with at the same level).

What do you do first?

Let's look at two possible situations. The first situation allows you time to prepare and organize your new position. The second situation is when you are put in charge with very little time to prepare.

Note: Even if you are already a supervisor, it is useful to review the following pages for knowledge and/or skills you may want, or need, to enhance.

Situation One–A Breaking-In Period

When you join the ranks of supervisors it is important for you to know how decisions are made, who reports to whom, and what you can and cannot do yourself. The following checklist will help you sort out some of the information you will need to collect and understand. The steps are not necessarily in order of importance. Review the items and number them according to what you think should be done first, second, third, etc.:

___ Get a copy of the organization's chart or similar document to know who officially reports to whom in the organization. Find out where you fit in this organization's structure and whom your immediate manager reports to.

___ Get to know the names and positions of people who report directly to you. What do they do? If there are job descriptions and past performance appraisals, where are they?

___ Where is the informal power within that group (the "leader(s)" as determined by the group)?

___ Understand clearly what your own manager expects from you, how they will help you in your work, what you can expect from them, what their position is within your organization, how that affects your work and how often you can expect to meet with them for direction, clarification, etc.

___ Get to know some of the other supervisors to find out more about how your department and organization really works and how they can help you in your position. How do they manage their time? How do they set priorities? Which tasks occur daily, weekly, monthly?

___ Collect copies of minutes of meetings that you will be expected to attend or chair. Who attends? What is the purpose of this meeting? Ask the person who is assisting you in this "breaking-in" period, how well each meeting works.

___ After chairing all required meetings (including one-to-one supervision meetings) 2-3 times, ask the participants to assess the meeting: Do people feel they are productive? Do they meet their needs? Are they well run? Do people have suggestions for change? [Refer to "Effective Meetings" section.]

___ Politics exists in all organizations and that is neither good nor bad. How people use or abuse power is what determines how effective an area, department and/or organization can be in reaching their goals. Understanding and participating in the politics permits people to effect change and to enhance the strength of the whole organization.

From a supervisor's standpoint it is important to understand if the real (informal) power within your area, department and organization is the same, or different, as the formalized power. You need to ask if certain people have more influence than others and how they use that influence? Where do you fit in within this unofficial power structure? Again, using power can be both positive and negative. For example, some secretaries literally control the day-to-day work within an area for which supervisors and managers may be very grateful.

What systems are in place within your area, department and in the whole organization that you need to know more about, and where can you find the information you need, e.g.,:

- Management and supervisory systems for performance appraisals, hiring and firing, discipline, etc.
- The budgetary cycle and your role in collecting important information and in helping to decide priorities for your area.

- The policies and procedures for your area and department.
- Negotiating systems in dealing with union/non-union staff.

Situation Two–No Breaking-In Period

You may not be given the opportunity at the beginning of your supervisory work to collect all of the information suggested in the previous situation. At some time, however, you will need to make the effort to collect this kind of information if you want to be a successful supervisor.

In the meantime you have been given the challenge of supervising within your old area or in a new one. What to do first? Depending on your circumstances you may be able to do some or all of the following. Remember that supervisors often have to adapt what they would like to do with what they are permitted to do.

___ Speak to your own manager and get clear, concise instructions about what they expect from you in the first few days and weeks on the job. Write down the specifics because you will soon be overwhelmed with information and demands on your time. Include how often you will report to her, her standards, her time lines and if they are flexible.

___ Spend some time going through your office or work area to find out what has been done in the past, what is necessary to get done immediately and what can wait. Check to see if there are important phone calls or letters that must be answered within the first day or two. Set them aside until you have met with your staff.

___ If you do not know the staff, set the tone of your future working relationship by meeting with them individually and/or together. Tell them as clearly as you can what you expect in the short-term. Tell them you will need time to sit down and review what has been going on in the past few months before you can be very specific about how you would like things to change or stay the same.

___ Spend some extra time with some of the senior staff members in your area to get an idea of what is going on. Remember that people naturally will try to take the best advantage of a new supervisor to set up new rules and procedures before you understand what was done in the past. Listen to people's ideas and suggestions but do not commit to any firm action until you have had time to settle in.

___ If there are immediate projects or tasks that need to get done, provide leadership by being present with your staff the first few days. Be visible. Let them know your interest in them and their work. Let them learn about your own expertise and what they can expect from you. Find reasons to give specific praise of their work. Do not give general or superficial compliments.

___ During a break in the day, check the phone messages that need answering today. If you have time check the letters and memos that need a response and jot down some quick points you want to include in your answer. Return to this task at the end of the day or delegate the work, if possible, to a secretary, colleague or staff member who knows how to answer the letters and memos on your behalf.

At the end of your staff's work shift, spend some time in your own work area to understand more fully what the previous supervisor did, how they did it, etc. Spend time going through the files, understanding who the main clients/ clients are, what other areas and departments you work most closely with, who works in those areas that you know, etc.

Learn more about time management. For example, begin to write several "to do" lists:

- To do tomorrow and within one week: e.g., get to know the staff, understand what pressing projects and tasks need to be done immediately.
- To do within the first few weeks such as items listed in Situation 1: The Break-in Period.
- To do within the first few months.
- When time permits, review the items listed under "Situation One". Decide the priority in which you will approach each item.

Exercise #3

List the resources that you can go to or use in your organization to help you with your work, e.g., manager, colleague, library, courses, journals, etc.

Coping Strategies

One of the greatest challenges to a supervisor is to cope with the many demands on your time. Being a supervisor involves maintaining a careful balance between:

- Managing last minute crises.
- Reporting information to **your** manager.
- Receiving information from your staff.
- Supporting your staff.
- Preparing administrative work.
- Meeting your manager's priorities.
- Working on your personal goals.

The following suggestions may assist you in achieving this balance.

- Be clear on your own goals and priorities. No matter what, set aside a few minutes to work on these. They provide you with your reasons for coping with the other issues.

- Use **to do** lists.
- If you cannot satisfactorily perform 3 or 4 things at once:
- Delegate one of them to a staff member, secretary, or peer who can handle the challenge.
- Adjust the time line for one of the tasks.
- Cancel a meeting (not too often because people will begin to think meetings are not important).
- Ask your manager for assistance (this is often seen as a conscientious judgment rather than a failure).
- Use a Dictaphone to produce a report.
- Take a good look at your expectations of staff members and the types of performance you are actually rewarding. For example do you expect independence in certain decisions by your staff, yet you make most decisions yourself? Your mixed message really tells people that you value and reward "safe" steps and decisions made by your staff. If you truly value independence, you must reward risk-taking, new ideas, trying and not succeeding the first time.
  Can you make some changes?
- Learn to say "no" more assertively when necessary. Too often, new supervisors try to accomplish too much in too little time. It may be necessary to say "No, I don't have time for that this month" without feeling anger or guilt.
- Lighten up! Change a staff meeting into a luncheon; bring in a cartoon – a few minutes of humor can bring stressful situations into proper focus. A more relaxed staff team will also be more supportive of you.

Exercise #4

Write out your own coping mechanisms based on your present circumstances.

The 1-2-3 Basics of Supervision

Many of the books in the resource section describe the basic concept of supervising people. In all of these books, the basics come down to:

1. Set goals (what you want to get done) and objectives (how you will achieve your goals through an action plan) with the person you are supervising. Working together builds commitment and rapport and makes it clear what is expected of both of you. Also decide on how you will know if the person is achieving their

goals in the time period you have agreed on together.

2. Both the supervisor and their staff should tell each other when they are doing things well. Often it is assumed that only the supervisor should tell a front-line person what they are doing well or what they could do differently. When this becomes a two-way approach the spirit of the team improves dramatically.

   Tell people what they do well must be specific. It is not good enough to say to someone that they are a good worker or that they are a pleasure to work with. Compliments and praise must be specific. Tell the person what they did well specifically and when they did that. This reinforcement will encourage them to repeat that behavior in similar situations.

3. When a supervisor needs to tell their staff that they have done something incorrectly they must also be specific. It is not good enough to tell someone that they have made yet another mistake or that they are incompetent.

   Tell them what they did wrong specifically and when they did it. Never criticize the person, only the behavior or action. Offer constructive suggestions of what they could do differently.

Note: Never begin a criticism with a compliment, e.g., "You know Harry, you are an excellent worker BUT this morning I think you were wrong in how you handled Suzanne's order." If you begin a criticism with a compliment the person will always assume that all of your compliments will end in a criticism.

Instead, tell the person what they did that you found unacceptable or ineffective and how they might do it differently under similar circumstances. If the situation is appropriate you could end your comments with a compliment, e.g., "The way you handled Suzanne's order this morning Harry was unacceptable because you made her feel defensive. Next time you might try asking a few more questions about what is involved in the order before assuming you know the answer. Now I know you were pretty rushed this morning and you certainly don't make this mistake very often but I thought I'd just mention it. Keep up the good work Harry!"

A Supervision Process

Supervision happens in different ways within different organizations. However, in order to achieve the above basics of supervision, the following suggestions are useful.

1. Set specific supervision time with your staff. If possible, this should be a regular time slot that you can both rely on. Do not cancel supervision time without immediately rescheduling. If meetings are postponed or cancelled too often, your staff may think you do not feel supervision is as important as other aspects of your work.

2. Meet in a private room. Discourage all interruptions. Your staff will know how important you think supervision is by where and how you hold the meetings. Your staff should see supervision as their time with you and for that specific time they are the priority on your agenda.
3. Both you and your staff should come with a prepared agenda. The staff person may go through their agenda first, or you may combine agendas and agree on priorities.
4. Avoid saving discipline action for the regularly scheduled supervision time. Discipline is most effective when given immediately and in private. The supervision time should be used as a time of mutual learning. You receive updates on situations and your staff receives direction and feedback.
5. If a supervision time is to be used to complete formal performance appraisal or for any other purpose, let the staff know in advance. There should be no surprises in supervision. A staff person is more able to stretch, grow and adapt during a relaxed, predictable supervision time slot.

Open Communication

Definition

Open communication means:

- Giving your staff enough information for them to do their job well.
- Giving honest feedback (informally and formally) on a person's work performance.
- Requesting and accepting honest and constructive feedback from staff on your own work performance.

Sharing Information

There is a lot of emphasis placed on "open communication" as part of a supervisor's role. The above definition is designed to encourage an honest and respectful sharing of information to ensure quality performance.

Supervisors must learn to Exercise great judgment, however, in deciding which information to share with which staff persons. Open communication does not mean that absolutely all information is made available to staff. At any given time, a supervisor is involved in future planning (as much as five years into the future), assessing current situations and weighing outcomes.

Management teams, in which supervisors may have some input, consider many possible plans, which may or may not work out. Supervisors who share each plan or problem with their staff will find themselves spending a lot of time justifying decisions over which they may not have much control. It is more useful to get ideas and suggestions from staff members when management plans are more clear and certain so that their input encourages them to be involved in real changes.

A few guidelines may provide some guidance until you can develop your own rules:

- Decide what information is necessary for your staff to do a good job. Provide as much detailed information as you can. Answer all questions as clearly as you can. This is where open communication can be most effective.
- Provide information about long range planning in global terms. For example, "The senior management team is developing a five-year plan for the organization. I'll let you know more when their plans become clearer."
- Let your staff know who makes the final decision about how staff input influences planning. For example, "I will pass along your concerns to our department head who sits on the management team. The final decision on the plan, however, is made by the Board of Directors."
- If you feel that additional information is necessary for your staff, try to give any sensitive information so that you:
- Do not state it as a promise of action.
- Give a tentative time line for a more definite answer to specific questions about policies.
- Outline the process of decision-making.
- Allow for further discussion if the plans are not satisfactory.
- Do not give out: a detailed list of alternatives being reviewed by senior managers, information about plans that have little chance of being put into action, or details of conflict between managers/departments over alternatives.
- Strike a balance between openness and friendliness and maintaining your supervisory status. Sharing personal information about yourself with your staff may confuse the lines of authority between you. Sharing of personal information requires a sensitive assessment of benefit and harm and the purpose of doing so.

Performance Appraisals

The real success of performance appraisals is when a supervisor and a staff member work together in establishing personal and professional goals for the staff member and in fact use the performance appraisal system as a learning tool. Although performance appraisals are used for various reasons, they work best when they are used as an opportunity for supervisors and staff members to learn from each other and to plan for a mutually successful future!

Appraising someone's performance is part of a complete appraisal system. It begins with setting specific performance objectives for the person being appraised based on their job description, meeting as often as necessary to review short-term objectives and revising longer-term objectives, providing regular informal feedback and suggestions, and meeting once every 6 or 12 months for a formal performance appraisal.

That said, it is important to recognize that people have had different histories with performance appraisals. In the past did your staff have positive or negative experiences with appraisals? What did they like about appraisals? What did they dislike?

Organizations have different ways of appraising someone's performance. The basic reasons for appraisals are similar however and include most, or all, of the following:
To answer the following questions for supervisors:

- What is the person doing well? What could they do better? What can I do to provide appropriate support? Is this a good time to see about moving the person to another position? What else can I do to help them? What else can they do to help me?
- To answer the following questions for the person being appraised:
- What am I doing well? What could I do better? Is this a good time to see about moving me to another position? Do I need some help to do my job better? Do I need more time, clearer directions, more teamwork with others, new equipment, more training, etc.?
- To evaluate a person's skills and ability in a systematic way and to use this data when it comes time to review salary and benefits, promotion possibilities, training development needs, transfers, demotions or dismissals.
- To ensure that managers, supervisors and staff are qualified to continue in their positions while also giving the person being appraised a set of criteria by which to evaluate their own skills and needs.
- To provide an opportunity for supervisors and their staff to compare notes about their mutual performances and to provide both of them an opportunity to set long and short-term goals and objectives for improving their mutual performances.

The performance that is being appraised should be based on:

- Actual **results** of the person's work.
- Specific **behaviors** that enhance or diminish the work of the individual as well as the work of the group.
- The person's work or behaviors in relation to their job description and performance objectives.

What should not be appraised is a person's personality, gender, age, culture, religion, sexual preference or other discriminatory criteria. Personality is often used as a case for, or against, a person. While personality affects the work of people, it is only their behavior that can be changed or evaluated.

The Performance Cycle

The performance cycle is a systematic approach to helping a staff member to accomplish agreed upon goals and objectives within a certain time period. The cycle begins with defining the specific performance objectives for the staff member. This is followed with regular interim reviews between the supervisor and their staff. At the end of one cycle and the beginning of another one, the staff person's performance is appraised by an agreed upon method and new performance objectives are prepared.

The performance appraisal is only as good as the relationship between the supervisor and their staff. That relationship is dependent on how much a supervisor and their staff members respect and trust each other. This trust and respect takes time to build and is most likely to happen when a supervisor is predictable, honest, fair and firm.

For the actual appraisal to be effective it must be based on clearly defined objectives so that you can evaluate what the person does well and what they can do better. The appraisal includes the opportunity for setting other specific, achievable goals with the person and a method for evaluating the success or failure of achieving those goals.

Effective performance appraisals can be done regularly (monthly to quarterly when necessary) so that both the supervisor and person being evaluated are clear and consistent with each other about expectations and results. There should be no surprises during an appraisal if the supervisor and staff person have been meeting frequently.

Most appraisals fail when the supervisor and staff person are not clear about what they expect from each other. An appraisal is a **two-way discussion** that is built on the premise that the appraisal is a learning tool for both parties with the goal being maintaining or improving results and behavior.

In the extreme situations performance appraisals can be used as supportive evidence for a transfer or dismissal. Regardless of the end result the appraisal should be well organized and well documented to ensure clear and concise communication and a record of decisions made together.

Performance appraisal is an opportunity for clear communication. The supervisor should:

- Encourage the person being appraised to do a self-appraisal of their strengths, accomplishments and needs; the person will only do a self-appraisal in any great detail if they trust the supervisor.
- Encourage the person being appraised to do an appraisal of the supervisor's

strengths and what the person would like the supervisor to continue to do or do differently to make the person more effective in their work. Trust will make this possible or very difficult, therefore, it is important for the supervisor to use the information as constructively.

- Give the person specific feedback on their results and behavior so that the person can use that information to set personal long and short-term goals and objectives for improving their work.
- Encourage the person being appraised to discuss differences of opinion about their results, behavior and goals.
- Work out an objective, measurable method of evaluating the success or failure of achieving the person's goals and objectives. If the evaluation cannot be done through specific measurements, then agree upon the form of "observable" evaluation that is most objective.

A Performance Appraisal Process

Supervisors often do not like to do performance appraisals because they are time consuming and because it involves criticizing someone's work performance. When performance appraisals are part of the everyday working within an area, department and organization then it becomes an ongoing process of effective, efficient teamwork.

The process is generally as follows.

Beginning

The supervisor sets an appointment with the person, chooses a private and comfortable room or location and presents the process as mutually beneficial. The supervisor shows interest in the person they are appraising and has an attitude that says performance appraisals are a two-way street that is very important for the person, for the supervisor and for the organization.

Goal Setting

The supervisor and staff person sit down together (preferably without a desk separating them), evaluate the job description and revise it when necessary, set short and long-term goals and objectives based on work priorities and developmental needs, and how you will measure the success or failure of those objectives. This process may require more than one meeting.

Goal setting is most effective when:

- The performance, based on the goals, is observable and measurable. Both the supervisor and staff will be able to clearly say whether the goal has been met.

- Each goal is given a time frame.
- The goals must be achievable. They fall within the staff person's job description, abilities and time available.
- The goals are limited to the 3-6 most important ones.
- The goals meet long-term plans as well as current priorities. The staff person must understand this relationship.
- The goals carry a high priority for the staff person and the supervisor. The rewards for achievement must be significant: increase in pay, a promotion, able to keep the job, official recognition, a high profile project, etc.

Regular Meetings

The supervisor and staff person meet regularly at first to identify how the process is going and what modifications, if any, need to be made.

Short-Term Reviews

Within a short time (6-8 weeks), the supervisor reviews the short-term performance with the person. They share information and suggestions of how to improve the performances of both of them and how the measurements of these performances need to be maintained or changed.

Continuing

When both are comfortable with the process, they may decide to decrease the number of formal performance appraisals to quarterly, semi-annually or annually with regular supervision sessions in between for less formal goal setting and appraisals.

> *In our setting we have a team or peer appraisal in which everyone is asked to comment on the person's practice, after which the supervisor and employee meet privately to complete the evaluation. It can seem threatening at the time but it is amazingly consistent in its outcome. It isn't acceptable to only comment on what is good about the person's practice. The commentator is also encouraged to share what they would like to see done differently.*
> *Michèle Chaban*

Difficulties with a Staff Member

Regardless of how well people work for you there will be times when you will have difficulties with someone you supervise. Difficulties are caused by poor communications, misunderstandings, differences in beliefs, but also by problems with attendance, punctuality, power struggles, etc. They are not usually just the staff member's problem or fault. You must recognize your own role in the difficulties and the role of other staff members.

An effective supervisor deals with difficulties immediately. Below are some suggestions on how to build upon some of your resolving conflict skills. Also refer to the "Resolving Conflicts" section.

In extreme situations it may be necessary to ask that person to transfer or leave after you have exhausted other ways of dealing with the conflicts. These extreme situations require the assistance of your own manager and/or the Human Resource Department.

Some suggestions:

- Diagnose what is actually going on. Are the difficulties based on lack of knowledge, skills or resources? Is there a personal problem? Has the working environment changed?
- Go to your immediate manager and/or the Human Resources Department for ideas and suggestions. The situation may involve previous history that you do not know about or involve sensitive legal matters. If you are not sure what to do get some advice until you become more confident in your ability to handle similar situations on your own.
- Look at how the working environment, co-workers, your role and other issues affect the person's behavior.
- Restrict yourself to looking at specific behaviors rather than a person's attitude, or personality. Use the job description to help you focus on behavior rather than personality.
- Do not criticize the person or blame them for mistakes but rather look at specific incidents and behaviors and work together on ways to avoid or minimize similar events.
- If the person does not agree that anything is wrong, explain specifically how their work or behavior is affecting you and/or others within your area or department.
- Try to find out why the person changed the way they work or behave. Bring these out in the open with the sole purpose of helping the person understand how their changed behavior may be affecting your work, the other staff members, and overall work performance in your area.
- If the person's behavior has changed because of difficulties outside of work, recommend internal support programs (e.g., Employee Assistance Programs) or external programs (e.g., Alcoholics Anonymous, counseling agencies, etc.). Find out

what your organization recommends before you decide what the person may need.

- Whatever the cause of the changes or behavior, help the person understand the natural consequences of their actions. For example, they may have to be disciplined according to the organization's policies and procedures unless the behavior changes.
- Find out what motivates the person and see if you can incorporate some of that into their work. Nothing changes a person's productivity and behavior as effectively as believing you are helping them achieve their personal and professional goals.
- With the help of the person involved, if possible, try to determine what behaviors are causing the problems.
- Re-state clearly your expectations of work performance, how the person is not meeting this and how this can be changed. Agree on specific changes and a time to re-evaluate. You should take brief, clear notes and give a copy to the staff person of your notes. In this way everyone is using the same information based on mutually agreed upon decisions.

Your Power as a Supervisor

We all use our power and influence to encourage, force, or persuade people to do what we want them to do. As a supervisor, you can use your power and influence to help your staff meet their personal and professional goals. Power can be both positive and negative. How you use your supervisory powers will directly affect how hard people are willing to work with you and how much they trust you.

As a supervisor, you may have several sources of power:

- Power from your supervisory position involves your ability to reward people and your ability to punish people.
- Power from your influence involves your expertise and your staff.

Power from your supervisory position is power used legitimately because of the responsibility you hold in your position of supervisor. People respect this power most when you use it together with clear expectations of what you want your staff to do.

Power based on your ability to reward people is power that you can use to recognize and acknowledge the valuable work done by your staff. Others can see this power as harmful if you only reward staff members you like.

Power based on your ability to punish people is a power that can hurt a supervisor when it is used too often. People prefer to receive constructive criticism over punishment. Punishing people also discourages a team spirit and discourages people from taking initiative and risks that can benefit members of the team. Sometimes, however, "punishing" someone by transferring or firing them can improve the overall team's performance. It is important to speak directly to the rest of the staff to give them accurate information and to reduce the amount of gossip.

Power from your influence is power people give you based on the respect and trust they have in your skills, knowledge, experience and other qualities as a person. This respect and trust is what builds your power as a supervisor over the long term and builds your reputation in the organization at large.

Power based on your expertise is power that comes from people recognizing your expertise in certain situations, with certain information or with certain machinery. Your power is most respected when you also accept responsibility for decisions you make based on your expertise.

Power based on friendship and comradeship is a power that can bind a team together when everyone is included. This power can hurt a team, however, when it excludes certain people. Your purpose is to supervise your staff; not to become their friends.

Exercise #5

This exercise helps you identify what sources of power you use most often and under what circumstances.

1. What sources of power do you use most often?
2. Under what circumstances do you use these sources of powers the most?
3. What sources of power do you use least often and why?
4. How can you use these sources of powers more effectively to encourage your staff to meet their personal and professional goals within your area, department and/or organization?

Decision Making

Different circumstances will allow you, as a supervisor, to help direct decisions made within your area of responsibility. For example, in an emergency you may not spend a lot of time asking people for their ideas and recommendations about what to do. You will probably have to give specific instructions to your staff and expect them to carry them out quickly and without too many questions.

There are several ways to make decisions within your area, and the methods that you choose may depend on the people on your staff and the circumstances.

Here are the main ways that people make decisions.

You Decide

The head of a group usually makes authoritarian decisions. This is true when the leader has a certain unique and acknowledged expertise. The person may also make decisions about minor issues to save the group time

In emergency situations, authoritarian decisions are made to give immediate, non-negotiable directions. In this form of decision making the underlying rule is "Do it my way immediately and without question."

You Ask for Advice

Consulting your staff for their ideas to help you come to a decision is an excellent way to avoid needless errors and to help your staff feel part of the decision making process. It is important that staff understand that they have input into the final decision, but that the decision making rests with you.

You Ask for a Vote

Democratically asking people how they vote on a certain policy, procedure or new idea gives people a way to actively participate in making decisions. Voting can also split people within your staff if the viewpoints are sufficiently different. When you decide to take a decision to a vote, it is essential that you be prepared to go either way. If you are not, simply ask for advice.

Unfortunately, in some areas of health care a "pseudo democracy" has emerged wherein major decisions about downsizing and reorganization are put to a vote. This may result in more personal hurt and systems damage than is necessary. The effect on the systems has yet to be determined.

This form of decision-making is not usually advisable because it often results in more conflicts between staff members and can split groups. It is useful for minor decisions when little is at stake and little commitment to the results is required.

You Work to Get Agreement

Getting consensus amongst your staff may be time consuming but it can encourage people to see several viewpoints to an important issue and also encourages them to work together once the decision has been made. This approach is helpful in assisting staff to accommodate change. You may say that the decision to change is out of their hands, but as a group you all have the power to direct that change.

This form of decision-making is useful when you want active participation and you can live with a decision that may differ from your preferred outcome. As part of the team, however, you must be part of the consensus. Consensus is more positive than a vote in that it does not create a "win-lose" situation.

No One Decides

Some decisions are made by external forces when you and/or your staff do not make decisions. For example, if there are discussions on reallocating resources within your organization and your area or department does not make the necessary decisions, someone else will make them for you. In this situation a group response to the change can be made to diminish hurt feelings.

Exercise #6

Some questions for you to think about:

1. Which style of decision-making is most comfortable for you and why?
2. Under what circumstances in your workplace do you think you would use the different styles listed above?

Delegation

Delegating is an essential supervisory skill. It forms the basis for the overall organization of your work. Delegating work is also an art. You need to match tasks carefully to your staff's job description, abilities and temperament/working style.

People require different degrees of instructions to help them accomplish the task you have set for them. For example:

- Some people need very specific instruction about how to do a task.
- Other people need to know what has to be done but you leave them to decide on how they will do it.

How you delegate work will depend on how comfortable people are with the assignment, how much added responsibility you give them, and how you intend to acknowledge their work when it is successfully accomplished.

If one of your staff members wants to do the task but is hesitant about their abilities, spend a little more time in the beginning stages telling them how they are doing it right or how they might try another approach to make the work easier. Spend time reinforcing their efforts, even if they are making mistakes. Help build their self-esteem so that down the road they will need less and less of your time to accomplish other assignments.

If you are delegating tasks to relatively new staff, begin with tasks that you know will be successful. Build the person's self-confidence through increasing the responsibilities of tasks, as they become more comfortable. Success is a great motivator. Failure can be costly from the organization's perspective as well as for the person's self-confidence.

When you delegate a difficult or risky assignment, give your staff the support they need if they fail. Failure can damage a person's initiative and self-esteem. Failure, with your support, can provide them with a real opportunity to learn and improve their skills. The consequence of their failure rests with your leadership style!

So What's Next?

Learning supervisory skills never stops because supervisors always work with people and we can never learn enough about how to do this well. People are not always predictable. Everyone is different. Situations can be similar, but they cannot be the same. You will always continue to learn new skills and develop old ones whether you stay at your present level or move up to further supervisory roles.

Take a few minutes now to list some of the areas you would like to improve after having read this section. Look at the other sections in this book to see if any of them can help you accomplish some of your learning goals. Also remember your own manager, your colleagues, your staff, your library and friends. They can all help you continue to learn.

Summary

The keys to successful supervision are managing your time effectively, assessing your skills and weaknesses accurately, recognizing and dealing with your own stresses, and learning some of the skills required to direct, co-operate and evaluate your staff.

There is no such thing as a perfect supervisor. However, when you ask yourself who you think was the best supervisor you ever had you will probably agree with most people who answer:

A person who was predictable, fair and firm; you knew where you stood with him or her.

A person who was respectful and trustworthy.

A person who listened to your ideas and allowed you to try new things.

A person who rewarded success with specific praise.

A person who let you take risks and make mistakes and gave you advice and information on how to avoid or minimize similar risks and mistakes.

A person who took the time to find out what your personal and professional goals are and tried to help you accomplish them.

A person who helped you identify specific goals and objectives at work, told you how you would be evaluated and worked with you to ensure success whenever possible.

A person who understood that giving you more and more responsibilities and power was the best way to increase their own power within the organization.

A person who shared the successes and failures with their staff.

There are probably many other things you expect from a good supervisor and you can accomplish all of them!

Resources

The following resources are only a few of the many useful resources that you can find in your local libraries, within your own organization, and in your local bookstores. Look for other books but also for journal articles, magazine reports, films, videos and audiocassettes. Also keep in mind how much you can learn from experts in the field, including people within your own organization!

Bittel, L.R. (1990). *What every supervisor should know: The complete guide to supervising management.* (6th ed.). Toronto: McGraw-Hill.

Burley-Allen, M. (1995). *Listening: The forgotten skill.* Toronto: Wiley and Sons.

Imundo, L.V. (1991). *The effective supervisor's handbook.* (2nd ed.) New York: Amacon.

Lepsinger, R. (1997). *The art and science of 360 degree feedback.* San Francisco: Pfeiffer.

Nelson, B. (1994). *1001 ways to reward employees.* New York: Workman.

Patronis-Jones, R., & Beck, S. (Eds.). (1995). *Decision making in nursing.* Albany, NY: Delmar Publishing.

Russo, J.E. & Schoemaker, P.J.H. (1990). *Decision traps: Ten barriers to brilliant decision-making and how to overcome them.* Saint Louis, MO: Fireside

Schechter, H. (2000). *Conquering chaos at work: Strategies for managing disorganization and the people who cause it.* Saint Louis, MO: Fireside.

Interviewing Skills

Interviewing skills, like all communication skills, depend on understanding who your audience is (the candidates), and what the purpose of the interview is (to inform interviewees about the position and to get enough information from them to help you make a hiring decision).

The interviewing process has historically been the most subjective form of making hiring decisions. The process is easily open to bias and has had little success in predicting the suitability of a candidate for a job. This can change.

When an interview is well planned and consistent for every candidate interviewed, interviewers can compare and analyze the information they collect during the interview with information they have received from application forms, resumes, covering letters and Resources.

Organizations have different policies and procedures for interviewing and hiring people. As a first step, find out what your responsibilities are as a member of your organization's interviewing and hiring process. You have experts (most likely in your Human Resources Department) who are qualified to advise you about proper interviewing techniques. Find out who these people are and ask them to help you improve your skills.

You may find that your area or department also has samples of job fact sheets, a job description model, forms to request a position be filled, series of questions used by "x" department in their interviews, and a reference check form. Do not reinvent the wheel if other people have made the effort to design these forms. Borrow them and modify them to meet your specific hiring needs.

The other role of interviewers is to be the ambassador for your organization and your own department. Whether a candidate is successful or not in getting the job they should leave the interview feeling like they were fairly treated and that the organization would be a good place to work. These candidates will talk to other people about their experience and any positive comments could lead to other people applying to your organization for career opportunities.

Defining an Interview

A job interview is not a conversation, nor an interrogation. It is a methodical process for giving and receiving critical information.

The interviewer needs to be aware of her specific responsibility in the process, as well as the responsibilities of her various colleagues. She has to collect information about the candidate to add to any written information the candidate has presented (e.g., application forms, resumes, covering letters, Resources). The interview provides an opportunity for interviewers to evaluate the suitability of each candidate through standard and consistent interviews of all candidates.

Candidates need to collect information as well. They need to understand what the job description is, the expectations of the organization for the position, the salary and benefits package, and what flexibility there is within the job to allow them to "make the job their own", i.e. take personal initiatives to try new things, improve the area they may work in, and try to achieve personal growth and satisfaction.

The definition, then, of a good interview is when all parties can collect and evaluate the information they need to make a reasonable decision in an environment of mutual respect.

Planning the Interview

There are several steps in the interviewing process: planning, information gathering, the interview, and decision making. Let's begin with planning the interview.

Roles and Responsibilities

Find out what your specific roles and responsibilities are in the interview process and who assumes the other responsibilities. Specifically, find out:

- If your organization has a recruiter and what are their responsibilities?
- Who completes a request to fill a vacant or new position and who is it sent to?
- Who plans and coordinates the process?
- Who gathers and screens the information (e.g., resumes, Resources checks)?
- Who writes or revises the job description?
- Who designs the interview questionnaire?
- Who posts the positions internally and externally?
- Who looks after the mechanics of scheduling the interview, booking a room, etc.?
- Who conducts the interviews (a single person or a selection committee)?
- If there is a selection committee, who determines who sits on this committee?
- Who is permitted to discuss wages and benefits?
- Who presents information about union contracts?
- Who organizes second and third interviews (if applicable)?
- Who makes the final decision (you or are you only allowed to give your opinion)?
- Who else has input into the final decision?

- Who offers the job?
- Who prepares the paper work for adding the successful candidate to your organization's staff?
- Who evaluates the success of the process and recommends modifications if necessary?

The Job Description

If your responsibility includes writing or updating the job description find out if there is a job description, if it needs updating or if you need to write a new one. A job description must define the specific knowledge, skills and other characteristics you want the successful candidate to have. This description should include:

1. Specific competencies, e.g., specific language requirements, education, professional credentials.
2. Specific working conditions that may prevent some candidates from fulfilling your needs (e.g., strength requirements).
3. Major duties.
4. Expected job results.

For each of the above job requirements write out a series of job-related questions that will help you collect specific information about each candidate's competencies, accomplishments, activities, and performance.

Interview Questionnaire

If your responsibilities include designing the interview questionnaire, keep the following tips in mind:

- Write basic questions to clarify the specific knowledge you want the person to have.
- Write situational questions to indicate specific skills and ability to apply knowledge.
- You may want some questions on what motivates a candidate:
- What are they most proud of?
- What successes and failures have they had and what did they learn from that?
- What they like and dislike about past jobs?
- What do they look for in a good supervisor?
- How flexible and adaptable are they to change?
- What are their short and long-term career goals?

Types of Questions

There are several types of questions that lead to different types of answers:

Open-ended questions Questions that often begin with Why, How, Tell me, What, are open-ended because they cannot be answered with a one or two word answer. These are great questions to encourage people to talk openly, and at some length, about things that interest them, e.g., "What has been your greatest professional challenge and why?", "Tell me more about how you would deal with changes in your shift hours?"

Closed-ended questions By definition, these questions are easily answered with a yes or no, or a one or two word answer. For example, many questions beginning with Is, Did, Do, Who are often answered very briefly. These types of questions are excellent to get specific factual answers or to help make someone feel comfortable at the beginning of an interview, e.g., "Did you find our department easy to find?", "Would you like a cup of coffee before we begin?", "How many people do you work with in your present job?"

Presenting choices These questions provide people with alternative answers that they can choose from. These questions can be tricky if candidates can read into your question what they perceive is your bias. They can be very helpful if you are clearing up or summarizing a point made by the candidate, e.g., "So you would prefer a supervisor who gives direction versus one who spends a lot of time trying to build consensus, is that right?"

Case study/hypothetical situations If appropriate, you may want to give actual case studies or hypothetical situations to ask each candidate what they would do under similar circumstances. This will help you understand how the candidates judge situations, solve problems and make decisions.

Non-job related questions Questions that are not specifically job related can lead to muddy legal waters. An opened-ended question about how someone's family, volunteer work, extra-curricular activities at school, has affected their abilities and job satisfaction is permissible. It gives the candidate the opportunity to choose what information they want to give to you. For example, "I see on your resume that you are involved with The Red Cross as a volunteer. What do you find rewarding about volunteer work?"

Will candidate do the job? So often an interview concentrates on a candidate's present knowledge and skills with the assumption that if they are qualified they will actually do the job required of them. In fact, many qualified people are tired of doing the same things they have done in the past. It is important during an interview to make sure that (a) the person is qualified for the job, and (b) they will actually do the job. A clear understanding by a successful candidate of what is expected in the job will help that person fulfill those expectations during their probation period. If they do not meet the expectations you will have clear grounds for ending their employment before the probationary period is over rather than going through a lengthy dismissal procedure after the probation is over.

> *One of my favorite questions to ask in an interview is, "Which of your skills would you prefer not to use in this job?" We sometimes forget that although someone is qualified to perform a certain task, they may not want to do it anymore. For example, a nurse may have extensive experience in providing grief support to families who have just had a loved one die. However, the nurse no longer wants to provide that kind of support given her personal history with loss. Unless we ask people what they no longer want to do, we will continually be surprised that competent people are not performing up to expectations.*
> *Harry van Bommel*

Union and Legal Issues

Understand the union and non-union issues involved for this position and what specific legal guidelines relate to your role in the organization.

The interview process has legal restrictions to ensure equitable treatment of all candidates. An interviewer must be aware of these restrictions when asking for information from the candidates.

Each legal jurisdiction has its own set of regulations. The following list describes areas of discrimination. Each jurisdiction has its own list that may, or may not, include all of the following. An interviewer must understand what areas of discrimination are covered in their jurisdiction to avoid possible lawsuits by unsuccessful candidates.

age
alcohol dependence
ancestry
citizenship
color
creed
drug dependence
ethnic origin
family status
harassment
language
marital status
mental disability
military service
pardoned offence
physical disability
place of origin
place of residence
political belief
pregnancy or childbirth

race
religion
sexual orientation
source of income
record of criminal conviction
sex
social origin

People involved in interviewing candidates may only ask straightforward and job-related questions. In describing the job the interviewer must state any special job conditions to all candidates (e.g., strength requirements, clothing, language requirements, etc.) to avoid possible litigation by unsuccessful candidates on the grounds of discrimination.

Find out what laws and regulations apply to your organization. Speak with the people within your organization that understand the regulations and ask them to review your interviewing questions and procedures to make sure they fall within the required practices set out in law.

Exercise #1
Roles and Responsibilities

Answer the questions below to make sure that you know the interviewing and hiring process in your organization.

- Who completes a request to fill a vacant or new position and whom is it sent to?
- Who plans and coordinates the process?
- Who gathers and screens the information (e.g., resumes, Resources checks)?
- Who writes or revises the job description?
- Who designs the interview questionnaire?
- Who posts the positions?
- Who looks after the mechanics of scheduling the interview, booking a room, etc.?
- Who conducts the interviews (a single person or a selection committee)?
- Who determines who sits on this committee?
- Who is permitted to discuss wages and benefits?
- Who presents information about union contracts?
- Who organizes any second or third interviews?
- Who makes the final decision?
- Who offers the job?
- Who prepares the paper work for adding the successful candidate to your organization's staff?

Exercise #2
The Interview Questionnaire

Develop questions based on points presented under "Planning the Interview" that will allow you to receive the information you need to make a good hiring decision.

- Job related questions (to discover knowledge, specific skills or competencies and if they coincide with the job description).
- Attitude towards their work and whether they will actually do the work they are qualified to do.
- Achievements.
- What is the candidate most proud of.
- What motivates the candidate.
- Which of the candidate's skills do they not want to use in this position? (For example, someone with excellent typing skills may no longer enjoy typing and would prefer not to use this skill in this new position. Usually you do not find out which skills a candidate would prefer not to use until after they have started the job. They do not usually offer this information during an interview.)

Gathering Information

Resume

If your responsibilities include reviewing and screening resumes, check for some of the following points. Keep in mind that all of the following points are not important all the time.

- Appearance: is it neat, organized, complete?
- Cover letter: is it concise, clear and well written?
- Academic achievements: do they match your requirements?
- Experience: is it related to your requirements?
- Specific skills and abilities: do they match your requirements?

Reference Checks

Reference checks should be short and to the point. You must keep in mind any human rights and hiring laws and regulations when you ask specific questions about a candidate. Your purpose is to get information on a candidate's performance; not their personality.

- The types of questions you may generally ask are:
- How long was the candidate employed? (Checks your candidate's reliability and honesty in describing their employment history.)

- What did the candidate do at that position? (Verifies if the candidate's background will meet your needs.)
- What were the candidate's strengths at that position?
- Are there any specific areas that the candidate would benefit from further learning? (You must ask the candidate this question first and use the reference check as a way to verify the candidate's strengths and areas requiring development.)

Telephone Checks

Telephone reference checks are often done at the preliminary screening process or after the first interview to verify a candidate's answers. Often a candidate will not list their Resources until after a first interview. Generally speaking, a reference can only verify a candidate's own information and most organization's are now very hesitant to provide any information beyond that in fear of law suits from past employees.

The types of questions you may ask during a telephone reference check are listed above.

Reference Letters

Reference letters may accompany a resume or may be requested after a first interview.

Note:

- What is the position of the person writing the letter and their relation to the candidate?
- How long did the candidate work for the person writing the letter?
- What specific information is detailed regarding the person's work performance?
- What is not said in the letter, e.g., no mention of the candidate's work performance, their strengths, or their specific abilities and knowledge required for your organization's position?

The Interview

The Environment

Create a relaxed environment so that both you and the candidate are comfortable enough to give and receive the kind of information you need.

Some specific tips:

- Review the candidate's applications, resumes, and other documentation before the interview.
- Ensure that distractions are minimal by forwarding your phone, and make sure that you will not be interrupted.

- Block off enough time for each interview.
- Avoid too formal a presentation of information and questions.
- The room should be well lit, clean and private.
- The environment should reflect the organization.

Managing the Interview

Team Interviewing

If you are part of a selection committee, one person on the committee should act as the meeting Chair and each person's role must be clearly defined before the interview. Each person should be clear about whether or not they will be asking questions, taking notes, etc. Immediately after each interview, the committee should compare notes and exchange impressions.

Note: If you are part of a selection committee the following suggestions about the interview structure need to be modified.

Controlling the Interview

It is very important to recognize that interviewers must control the interview from start to finish. You set the climate and professional mood of the interview and you encourage people to be honest and open by setting that kind of example yourself. Choose your words carefully so that they are clear and inoffensive; courteous and not patronizing. The best questions you can ask are those that lead to clear answers versus questions that reflect the answer you would like to hear. For example, "What characteristics in people do you think lead to developing an effective team?" versus "Would you agree that it is important for people in a team to have high self-esteem while also recognizing the value of other members on that team?" The second question has the preferred answer within it.

Observations

Things to Look For

You may want to record your impressions about some of the following qualities as they relate to a candidate's job performance:

- Communication skills especially ability to listen
- Maturity
- Are they a "go getter" or a methodical "doer" (and which does the position require?)
- Stability (do they move from job to job without apparent reason)
- Aptitude

- Flexibility and adaptability to change
- Loyalty
- Diligence and perseverance
- Leadership skills and potential
- Self-confidence and high self-esteem
- Ability to participate as an equal participant in a team

Body Language

It is important to understand that interviews are intimidating situations for most candidates. To help put people at ease so that you can get the kind of information you need to make good decisions you can move from behind your desk and sit beside the candidate. Keep a comfortable distance from the candidate (about 1-2 yards) just as you would when you have a conversation with a colleague from another department.

Opening Remarks

The Beginning

Greet each candidate as you would like to be greeted in similar circumstances. Put them at ease. Give them an outline of how the interview will proceed. If it is appropriate, give the candidates a list of the questions you will ask them (1/2 hour before the interview). Try to find out what their first impressions are of the workplace, what their needs and expectations are, and why they are interested in the organization.

Humor

Many interviewers and candidates try to use humor to "break the ice". This can be very helpful as long as one does not use humor to ridicule or complain, or use sexist, racist humor.

Note on First Impressions

It is fair to say that most of us make a judgment about a candidate's abilities and personality within the first few minutes of an interview. Rather than pretend that this does not happen, it is more useful to take that first impression and use the questions you have prepared to actively discover whether or not you were right.

Describe the Job

Give the candidates a job description with special emphasis on:

- Duties and responsibilities.
- Expected results.

- How this job relates to the overall organization.
- The benefits to the successful candidate if they accept the job.

Give the candidates whatever literature exists that describes the organization and your department.

Questions

- Ask each candidate the same questions in the same way and in the same order.
- This will permit a fair comparison of the candidates.
- Concentrate on listening and a person's body language.
- Avoid personal bias, hasty conclusions and judgments.
- Get sufficient and specific information.
- Determine a candidate's reasons for their behavior.
- Take notes without fanfare.

Review the types of questions you can ask from the "Planning the Interview" section.

Silence

The proper use of silence is one of the most powerful communication tools available to an interviewer. Most of us are embarrassed by silence and therefore fill the void within seconds of asking a question using the excuse that we want to make the question clearer. Rather, after you have asked a question, keep silent for up to 60 seconds (a very long time when no one is speaking!) to give the candidate:
An opportunity to decide how much they want to say.
How they want to say it in a clear and concise way.

Candidate's Role

Ensure enough time to permit candidates to ask questions about the job. Encourage them to understand the specific details and requirements of this position.

Ending the Interview

At the end of the interview, explain to the candidates how the recruitment process continues from this point, e.g., how long it will take before the candidates will hear from you or Human Resources. If appropriate, let them know how the interview went and your initial reaction.

Decision Making

Choosing

There are few differences between people we might consider winners and losers for specific jobs. Their appearance, personality, ability to communicate, intelligence, education, achievements, ability to succeed in interviews are often very similar. What is different is what motivates people to achieve personal and professional success and satisfaction, as they define it. The duty of an interviewer is to discover if a candidate's personal motivation is compatible with the requirements of the position and compatible with the other members of the working team.

Your Notes

Immediately after the interview, review and add to your notes regarding any observations, impressions and further questions you may want to ask at a follow-up interview.

Use a rating scale (e.g., 1-5 or 1-7) to help you evaluate a candidate's job competencies in key areas. This is especially helpful if you have a large number of candidates to compare or if you have a difficult choice to make.

Input versus Decision

In different situations you may be asked to either: (a) provide your input into a hiring decision without having any decision-making power yourself or (b) make the final hiring decision.

Input

If your role is input, offer the person(s) who are making the decision your written summary notes, your personal opinions of the candidate, any specific observations, and any concerns you may still have.

When you are only permitted to give input into the hiring decision you must recognize that you may disagree with the final decision.

Decision

If your role is to decide who to hire for a position:

1. Listen and evaluate any input you get from other people involved in the hiring process.
2. Compare the job description with the notes and other information you have on each candidate.

3. Reflect on how each candidate might work with other members in your areas.
4. If appropriate, discuss this hiring decision with your supervisor or manager, especially if you are unsure of who to hire. Speaking with your superior will ensure you get support with your final decision.

   A few years ago, I was on the selection committee for a new clinic that was due to open shortly. We were looking for a dynamic experienced nurse who could assess and teach clients dealing with a specific health problem. During the process of reviewing applications, we were amazed to see that the quality of what was submitted ranged from neatly typed and formatted cover letters with resumes to hand-written scrawls on notepaper. Needless to say, the applicants who had made the effort to present professional looking applications were the only ones interviewed for the new position.

   Beverley Powell-Vinden

Exercise #3

Review the questions you designed in Exercise #2. Based on what you have learned in the past few sections add, delete or revise your questions. Once you have customized the questions to your specific needs and the specific job description, have some of your colleagues review your list for recommended changes. If there are union or legal issues involved, have your questions reviewed by the people responsible for these issues within your organization.

Summary

Interviews are a great opportunity to exchange information with candidates and to promote your organization.

Use the expertise within your organization to find out about interviewing policies and procedures.

The key points to remember are that you must plan the interview well in advance with a standard list of questions that you consistently ask in the same way and in the same order. This ensures fairness to all candidates and helps ensure compliance with the human rights legislation related to your organization.

It is very important to keep accurate notes during the interview to allow you to make the best decision you can. Often decisions are made several days or weeks after your interviews and your notes will be invaluable. These notes can also be used to support your decision in cases where an unsuccessful candidate requests specific reasons on how you made your decision.

The types of questions you ask and how you ask them can encourage candidates to answer honestly and openly. The way in which you control the interview environment will reflect on your abilities and on the organization. Make sure that the environment is professional and comfortable.

Most interviewers and candidates are somewhat nervous during an interview. You have the power as the interviewer to make this experience informative and enjoyable. Have some fun!

Resources

The following resources are only a few of the many useful resources that you can find in your local libraries, within your own organization, and in your local bookstores. Look for other books but also for journal articles (in *Personnel, Hospital Quarterly,* and others), magazine reports, films, videos and audiocassettes. Also keep in mind how much you can learn from experts in the field, including people within your own organization!

Cormier, LS. (1997). *Interviewing and helping skills for health professionals.* Sudburt, MA: Jones & Bartlett.

Edenborough, R. (1997). *Effective interviewing: A handbook of skills, techniques and applications.* Kogan Page.

Simon, H. (1999). *Essential managers*: Resumes. London, UK: DK Publishing.

Newell, R. (1994). *Interviewing skills for nurses and other health professionals: A structured approach.* New York: Routledge.

Sayer, J.E., & Hoehn, L.P. (1994). *Interviewing: Skills and applications.* Scottsdale, AZ: Gorsuch Scarisbrick.

Yate, M.J. (1991). *Knock 'em dead with great answers to tough interview questions.* Holbrook, MA: Adams.

7. Change Management

Change in the 21st Century

Change in the 21st Century

We manage change successfully in our lives almost everyday. Some of the change we have experienced have been very positive such as the birth of a child. Other change has left us with deep sorrow or pain such as the death of a loved one. In between such extremes are the daily or yearly changes in work, careers, family dynamics and relationships, seasons, problems with the car, success in our volunteer work and so on.

Our success at work relies, in part, on our ability to manage, accept and grow with the change happening there as well. Change will happen. Some people will resist change or even leave an organization because they disagree or cannot adapt to the change. Some people will accept the change while the change will actually excite others. None of these reactions to change is better than the other. Sometimes resistance to change is a positive reaction to help prevent an organization from making a mistake or creating change for change sake. Sometimes people need to leave an organization when change happens to improve their own careers and to allow the organization to bring in other people more comfortable with the change. Sometimes people get excited by change because they have been waiting a long time for it to happen or because they believe it is the right time and the right way to do something new.

This section will help you deal with change at work and with personal change. The material should help you whether you are a front-line staff, supervisor or a manager in an organization. It aims to build on your change management skills rather than give you a whole new way of doing things. **This material is about large, long-term change in your life. This material is not about dealing with the everyday stresses of life.**

A dictionary definition of change is "to be or cause to be different". Simply put, anything in your life that is different from before can be called change. The birth of a child, a promotion at work, a vacation, sleeping in, calling a friend long distance, a new boss, going back to school, or writing a letter to the editor of your newspaper may all be changes from your normal day. Managing, or even mastering, that change involves individuals directing, controlling or handling that change to the best of their abilities, skills and knowledge.

The new emphasis on change in the last 10-15 years has happened because it feels like we are going through more change more often than before. This feeling is true because technology and our increasing global economy have made change happen faster. When I wrote my first book 10 years ago I did it on a typewriter. My next book was done on a simple computer. My latest computer has 50 times better memory, and is faster, than my first computer (at half the price). Change is happening more quickly but how we manage that change doesn't have to be different one year to the next.

Most of us need a sense of control over our lives. We have developed ways of managing change from ignoring some of it to looking forward to a new change. How we manage the change often depends on how much control we feel we have over the change or how much pressure we feel to accept change. We need to acquire further skills to help us adapt to change more easily and manage change more effectively.

For some people managing change also implies that you always have control over that change. For other people they believe that they have no control over change and must only accept whatever happens to them. The truth, of course, is in between those extremes. We cannot always control change, especially large scale change at work, in our communities and in the world generally. However, **we always have control over how we respond to those changes**.

This material is designed to help you discover what your own strengths in managing change have been throughout your life and to offer you some suggestions on how you can improve on those strengths. We will also look at how supervisors, managers and other leaders can help others manage change most effectively in different situations.

Note: Originally we planned to concentrate on managing change at work. In writing the material, however, we discovered it was impossible to separate professional change from personal ones. The skills are mostly the same and require you to be consistent in dealing with any form of change. For this material to be most helpful to you, we suggest that you think of personal examples after we give professional ways of dealing with change. When we give personal examples, think of ways the material applies to your work place.

Exercise #1
Change You Have Already Managed

Everyone has experienced and managed change in the past. Knowing how you have managed change in the past will be an invaluable aid to managing change now and into the future. Your past change has been both positive and negative. For example a wedding is a wonderful change while the loss of a job can be very traumatic. Both are changes and both require you to manage that change in ways that strengthen you, rather than harm you.

The following is a list of different types of change you may have faced and dealt with before. We have divided them into seven categories of personal development.

The purpose of looking at these seven categories is to help you find a sense of balance. When one part of your life is experiencing a great deal of change you need to consciously find a balance from some of the other six categories. For example, if you are experiencing a great deal of change at work your natural tendency may be to work extra late and spend less time with family and friends, avoid eating well and exercising. It is vitally important to your long-term health and relationships that you minimize this tendency. It is also important to the change happening at work that you maintain your health and relationships. It is your friends, family, and health that will benefit you in long term. This does not mean that you avoid the changes at work but you find a balance between those changes and the other important areas of your life.

In the "Change" column write down some specific changes you want to look at. Once you have reviewed how you managed those changes write your answers in columns two and three.

Write down specific things that you did to help yourself during this change. It could be anything from researching and preparing for the change (e.g., looking for work the first time), to talking with family and friends for support; from working as part of a workplace team implementing the change, to hanging in there during the rough spots until things improved; from putting the whole experience in a lifelong perspective of what truly is important to you, to accepting periods of uncertainty.

Also write out what things you did that did not help you manage the change as effectively as you could today. This could include such things as complaining about lack of control when in fact you were involved in the change, taking a vacation during a change event so you could avoid the change for as long as possible, or abusing food, alcohol or drugs to "help you get through".

Note: Exercise #1 and #2 in this material are lengthy. They take time to complete because you are dealing with major, long-term change in your life. Such change requires time to think, plan and act to help you manage. **You need to write out your answers**. If you read the material, think about your answers and write them down, you are more likely to follow through on managing the change in the ways you want to. If you just think about the answers without writing them down you will not see the patterns of your strengths – you are likely to deal with any present or future change in the same ways that you have in the past. You will continue to do some things naturally that help you and other things that will harm yourself.

Change	What I Did That Helped	What Did Not Help
Relationships: began dating, established committed relationship with partner, birth of children, end of relationship, moved to new home, moved to new town/city, death of a loved one, significant changes in those close to you.		
Physical: improvement or lack of health, disabilities, large weight gain or loss, athletic abilities (+ or -), growing older, change in strength (+ or -), enjoyments, disappointments.		
Emotional: changes to your self-confi-dence and self- esteem (both + and -), improvements in the emotional supports you receive, changes in mood, disappoint-ments in your supports, how you have changed in supporting others.		
Educational: your learning experiences, continuing education, self-study, changes that improved or harmed your ability to learn.		
Economic: changes in your ability to earn the income you need/want, periods when you earned less than you needed, periods when you earned what you needed, lost dreams of winning the lottery, learning about financial planning, achieving financial security.		
Career: your first job, successes and failures at work, career changes, having or not having the job you want, working beneath or above your abilities, the challenges you want at work, experiences with mergers, acquisitions, lay offs, changes in your bosses, multicultural		

aspects of your work, reorganization, expanded demands by clients, technological changes.	
Spiritual: changes in your views of religion, spiritualism, belief in a creator, times when your beliefs strengthened or distressed you, the path you want to see your beliefs and spiritual life take in the next 5-10 years.	
Other: changes that did not come up in the above lists e.g., those you experience with friends, on vacations, doing volunteer work, during periods of inactivity, war experiences, etc. List them below and write about what helped you and did not help you.	

This exercise has taken you some time to complete. Let us make it worth your while!

1. Write out any strategies for dealing with past change that you identified three or more times. These are the skills and strengths that you have already developed naturally to deal with change. Remember to use these for workplace changes and personal changes ahead.
2. Have you identified any successful strategies that you have only used 1 or 2 times? These are skills that you can perhaps use more often in the future to successfully deal with change. Do not forget to use them again.
3. What strategies have you identified to be unsuccessful that you want to avoid in the future? They probably waste your time and drain your energy. They may also be destructive to your physical and emotional health. Choose an alternate method of dealing with this change from the list of successful strategies you wrote in questions 1 and 2.

Helpful hint: If you are in the midst of a lot of change at work, home or with friends right now, post the answers to these questions by your desk, work area, or home refrigerator as constant reminders of what helps, and does not help, in dealing with change. Choose your successful strategies.

Personal Ways to Manage Change

You have already looked at what changes you have managed in the past and what things you did that helped, or did not, help you. This section is the first of three sections on personal, leadership and organizational responses to change. These sections may provide you with other ideas of how to deal with present or future change. Once you have reviewed this material, we suggest you go back to exercise #1 and add any change strategies that you want to try in the near future. Now for some specific suggestions on personal ways to manage change.

Five-Step Process

Change is generally a five-step process from beginning to end:

Expect — 1. You should expect change to happen because it will.

Recognize — 2. You need to recognize when a change happens so that you can begin to deal with it.

Feel — 3. You will experience the feelings of sadness or joy; grief or acceptance that change brings with it. Some change is so forceful and dramatic that you need months or years to accept it (e.g., the death of a loved one). Other changes are less forceful and you need less time to experience those feelings and accept the new situation.

Plan — 4. Plan ahead for change. In learning self-defense, for example, students imagine possible situations and plan how they will defend themselves. It is the same when planning for work change. What will you do if you are promoted, left in the same job for 10 years or laid off? In your personal life, what will you do if you find the partner of your dreams or if you become suddenly ill?

Planning is not about fearing the worst will happen to you every day. Planning is about expecting and preparing for change in your life. Planning does not prevent step 3 (feeling a whole range of emotions) but it may reduce some, or all, of the fear or panic that may accompany those feelings.

Act — 5. When necessary, act on your plans. Do what you have planned to help you manage positive and negative change as best you can under the circumstances.

Life-Long Learning

Recognize that all of your knowledge and skills need continual improvements, revisions and, sometimes, even not using them any more. For example, as much as you enjoy using a slide-rule or manual typewriter, for speed and efficiency sake you may need to use calculators and word processors instead.

Life-long learning also means that you need to develop your learning skills so that you can learn new knowledge and skills quickly and effectively. This may mean, depending on your job and interests, taking notes better, speed reading, better communication and writing skills, study skills, researching skills and presenting or teaching your new knowledge and skills to others.

> *I think if you want to stay competitive in today's market, you must plan for several careers, make yourself diversely skilled while developing several areas of related expertise. I think we lack imagination in how to do this because we think we have to do it in concentrated timeframes and do it brilliantly while working and tending to family and friends. It is possible to do it all if you are careful with yourself and your expectations. I believe that slow and steady wins the race. Balance and pace is essential.*
> *Michèle Chaban*

Balance

Recognize the various elements of your life: family and friends, physical, emotional, educational, economic, career/work and spiritual/faith and see which elements at present are taking more energy and effort than the others. How can you re-balance the other elements in your life to deal with the stressful change you are feeling in one or several parts of your life. For example, if work is demanding a great deal of energy and you feel very stressed, how can your family and friends, other emotional supports and perhaps your spirituality and faith provide you with the balance, loving support and perspective you need to overcome this period of career stress?

Perspective

Since change is a constant in your life, how is the present change relative in importance to others you have faced before (your past experience) and relative in importance to other changes you expect to face in the future (future experience)? Is the situation you presently face likely to remain a vivid memory for you in the years to come or is it more a disturbing, energy-draining nuisance or annoyance that is soon forgotten for more important things? Can the situation you now face, regardless of how important it feels today, be re-worded in your mind to give it a more realistic place in your life's history and, therefore, reduce its perceived power to make you feel physically and/or emotionally hurt? For example, can losing a job you do not particularly enjoy today be re-worded in your mind to an opportunity to find a job you truly enjoy? How long do you reasonably think it will take to turn such a difficult situation into a situation that demands your positive energies and sense of hope for the future? For a quick insight, answer the following questions.

In 5-10 years from now, how would you like to describe a difficult period in your life to other people? If you do not think you will discuss it in 5-10 years, how much energy should you put into it now?	
How would you like to describe it to yourself?	
What do you need to do now to make that future description possible?	

Leave the Situation

Often people remain in work or social positions that cause immense stress because they fear the unknown of leaving, because of economic reasons and because of their belief that they cannot find work or friends elsewhere. As difficult as it is to leave a harmful or stagnant situation, it is sometimes necessary to do so.

Most of us will experience a time in our lives when it is better to leave a situation than to stay. It is always difficult to know when it is better to "stick out" a situation to see if it gets better or to leave. There are several things you can do to prepare yourself for just such a situation:

Personal Limits

Make sure you are clear about your values, beliefs and interests and how you will know if the situation has changed enough for you to leave. If you know where your line of no return is around your values, you will diminish the power of influence that others may have over you during times of intense and personally harmful change. For example, if you have strong views about how people should be treated at work by their bosses and you know that the change being proposed and implemented will dramatically change this and you are not able to influence the change for the better, you may have to leave. You may also have upper limits. These limits tell you the level of challenge and excitement you need. If you remain stagnant in a job for too long, it is also harmful.

Financial Expertise

Begin as early as possible to do financial planning so that the hard-earned money you make is well used and invested. This way, you do not have to stay in a job that is harmful to you. You should have at least three to six months of expenses saved so that you will always have enough money to continue to live as you do now while you look at other options. Read some books at your public library about how you can save on insurance costs, extended warranties, credit cards, purchases, mortgages and more so that you can find more money to save without having to earn more income or give up all the things you enjoy doing.

Network

Keep contacts with people in other organizations who can help you find the type of job or situations you want to move to. Relationships are more important than money so nourish them well and often.

Humor

Perhaps one of the most immediately practical methods of dealing with unwanted change is to find the humor in the situation. This is not always easy but people in the most difficult situations imaginable (e.g., war, prisons, after major emotional traumas such as a death in the family) have used humor to lighten the load if only for a few minutes. Humor provides perspective and an energy release. Good, loud belly laughing for 15 minutes is like meditating for 5-6 hours. After a good belly laugh your blood pressure, heart rate and breathing decrease and produce a calming effect.

Relationships

Many people believe and social sciences research has shown that the most valuable thing you can have in your life is relationships with people who love, respect and support you. These people can be loved ones, friends, colleagues or people you know through volunteer work or socializing. These people can offer you support, guidance and a different perspective. Ask them for help and offer to give it back in return.

Areas of Control

In any change experience there are several areas of control. Discover which area you are in. This will help you choose which strategy for managing the change might be most helpful in this specific situation.

- Area 1: You have total control over the change so you put the most energy into making it work.
- Area 2: You have influence over how the change will happen but the decision is up to someone else.
- Area 3: You are asked to give your input (i.e. ideas, opinions) but you do not have

much real influence and someone else makes the decision.

- Area 4: The decision to change is made without your involvement. You are expected to carry out the change. You have control over how you react to the change but not over the change itself.

Obviously, in Area 1, you have the most control over change while in Area 4 you have none. Your level of control and influence will help you decide how much energy and effort you want to use to affect how the change will be decided on and carried out. Also, the more involved you are in the change the more likely you are to accept the change and even get excited about it.

A hospital merger is beyond your control (Area 4), but the ways in which you work with your colleagues from the new hospital is something over which you can have some control (Area2, 3). Your own reactions to the merger are almost always under your control (Area 1).

Preparing and Helping Others Manage Change

In this section we will focus on managers and supervisors helping other people to deal with change. You can easily adapt the skills and examples to show you how to help loved ones, friends and colleagues deal with personal change as well.

For many years managers and supervisors were expected to lead their staff in the day-to-day operation of a department or organization. They were expected to schedule work time, delegate work fairly among the staff, hire and fire people, and maintain discipline.

In the 1970s and 1980s there were many new theories about effective management including such programs as management by walking around, managing by objectives, and strategic planning models, including total quality management or continuous quality improvement. At the same time, there was also the increased profile of managing change within organizations. The 1980s and the 1990s have seen revolutionary changes in how organizations do their work locally, nationally and internationally. The emphasis on heavy manufacturing (steel, cars and trucks) has been somewhat replaced by an increased emphasis on telecommunications and service industries (computers, telephone, television and satellite developments, health care).

These developments have fundamentally changed how we do our work and with whom. Politically, we have seen Europe unite, the old Soviet Union divide itself into many different countries (and markets) and the movement away from superpower diplomacy to United Nations negotiations.

For people at middle and upper management, these changes have forced dramatic changes in how they manage people. Organizations have changed the way they work because of technology and increased public demands for products and services. Front line staff are being expected to participate more actively in many of their organizations rather than just doing repetitive tasks. Managers and supervisors are expected to do all the things they used to do. They are also expected to prepare their staff for changes in why they do things (their mission or purpose), how they do them (often less staff and more technology), who they do it for (expanding or shrinking markets locally, nationally and internationally), and how they will be evaluated for their results (quality control, client service).

Many people hesitate to accept change because they have experienced change before that has either failed (change for change sake) or harmed them (lay off, friends fired). Managers and supervisors have to deal with such resistance with acknowledgement and support for the healthy expression of emotions, open, honest and concise communication and planning that will prepare their staff for change, help them implement that change and finally help them evaluate the results before moving on to further change.

The following suggestions are some ways you can help others deal with change in the workplace.

Trust

Effective change in any area of an organization or in a whole organization depends, almost completely, on the trust that staff and front-line managers have in each other. Since effective change involves so much support and communication before, during and after the change, if there is no trust then the communication will not be trusted either. If past history within a department includes mistrust between managers and staff, then it is vitally important that a new working relationship begin by the manager taking full responsibility to ensuring a new level of staff trust.

Note: Effective change as defined above does not prevent other types of change from happening. In fact, change is often begun without a lot of effective support and communication. The change happens and may even be a great success. What is different is that people could have been excited or more accepting of the change much earlier on in the process.

Uncertainty

All change, no matter how well planned, involves an amount of uncertainty. No one will have all the facts and not everyone will receive all the information they need to begin making changes at work. Recognizing this fact will allow managers and supervisors to begin changes based on the information they have now. Staff will understand

and accept that there will always be some uncertainty as long as they believe that their supervisor or manager is not holding back information purposefully.

Types of Change

People need their supervisors and managers to be clear about the amount of change they can expect. If the change is a switch over in technology the change can be fairly predictable. If the change is a reorganization of the whole organization the staff will need to know this and will need constant help in adapting to the day-to-day changes that will occur.

Opportunity

Change in the 1990s has often been presented to staff and managers as a wonderful opportunity. In the 1970s and 1980s change was often presented as a learning experience. Both of these terms (opportunity and learning experience) are short forms for "you are probably not going to like this". In fact, these terms have been so over used that they are best not used unless there is real opportunity for positive outcome What people often experience has been the opposite of an opportunity –change has meant more work for less reward or recognition. An honest acknowledgement and support of the losses that come with change is a step that is often missing from the current change process in large organizations Staff need time to grieve and express their feelings in helpful ways.

Change can, in fact, be a wonderful opportunity to do new things, add new knowledge and skills, and develop better products or services to clients and clients. It will be seen as an opportunity if upper and middle management can demonstrate in honest, concrete ways what the benefits of this change opportunity can be. If the change truly does not have many benefits for staff, then telling them so honestly will build trust for the next change in the organization where there may very well be real benefits. Never lose trust for short-term gain. Successful change management involves a long-term approach to satisfying the needs of staff, managers and clients.

When I was a kid my Dad and I would go to the park. We often played catch. Playing ball was fun and in retrospect I learned a lot about psychology from my Dad during those occasions. He was a tall man and no matter how poorly I threw the ball to him, he seemed to catch it by stretching his arms out widely or reaching high over his head. He usually said, "nice throw!" even if it was way off. He took those opportunities to build my confidence and as a result, I became a pretty good ball player or at least an enthusiastic one. Years later, I did the same sort of thing with my own children, praising them for activities that approximated success. Like my Dad, I frequently took the opportunity whenever it arose to reinforce behaviors associated with self-esteem.

Not too long ago, I participated in a performance appraisal where for the first time in many years it was my own performance being reviewed. It was a superb meeting in which discussion of contributions and strengths predominated and I felt more than validated. In two particular areas, it was noted that I could bolster my knowledge by taking the opportunity to attend an upcoming conference. I readily agreed with that observation and recommendation and left the appraisal session feeling great. A few days later, I received the report outlining highlights of the appraisal for my signature. I was taken aback to read that of nine key performance areas, seven were noted as strengths and two identified as opportunities for improvement. I had left that session believing those identified opportunities had referred to attending a conference as a "reward" or "taking time off to do something enriching for myself". I now felt that I had dropped the ball. Ever since, I have occasionally puzzled over the use of the word opportunity and wondered when had its meaning been changed to include a deficit.

Larry Lewis

Consequences

People need their supervisors and managers to be honest about how much the change will disrupt their work, how long before all the difficulties are worked out, what the costs are and what will happen to sort out the inevitable day-to-day problems of going through the change.

Communication

We have stressed the importance of communicating as much as possible about the change before, during and after the change. What is just as important from a middle management and staff perspective is what is not communicated about the change. People will begin with their own assumptions about the change and will gossip about what they believe has not been communicated. Change processes are full of gossip between the participants when they have insufficient information or trust about the change. Only honest, open communication can diminish the negative effects of rumors being spread. You can never stop people spreading rumors based on their fears, limited information or personal perspectives but you can help limit gossip and rumors through constant and consistent communication.

Communication must be two-way so that middle managers and staff can ask questions of those primarily responsible for the change.

Communication must also be sensitive to the cultural and literacy needs and concerns of managers and staff.

Presenting Change at a Meeting

Communication and trust are the primary sources of successful change. Often major change is discussed or presented at meetings. Many of the suggestions listed above and in the section on "Organizational Change" highlight what needs to be done. The most important steps are telling people: where their area, department and/or organization is now, what needs to change for continued success (in detail), and how that change will affect individuals in the organization as well as the clients it serves. Following this presentation of information, ask for comments, questions and concerns from the participants. If the details of the change have not been decided on, ask them for their help in deciding what practical changes must be done, by whom, by when and how. Listen to their feelings as well as to their ideas. If appropriate, tell them how you are feeling (both the enthusiasm for successful change as well as any resistance to change you might feel).

Start Small

If change in the organization has occurred with limited success in the past it is best to begin with small, quick changes that guarantee some success and publicize the success widely. Building on success makes future change that much easier to prepare for and achieve.

Long-Term View

The long-term view of change recognizes those elements of change that you have some control over. Most often, change is necessary because client/client needs have changed, the competition has changed the working environment or because an organization has decided to fundamentally restructure its work. In these cases, middle managers and staff need to examine the following:

1. What aspects of the change are **controlled by others**, e.g., the executive, our competitors, the global marketplace, our clients, or our suppliers?
2. What aspects of the change **can we negotiate** with other people. For example, are there aspects of the change such as deadlines, responsibilities or costs that are negotiable without affecting the final results?
3. What aspects of the change do **I have control** over? For example, do I, as a leader, have control over how we implement the change within the given time deadlines? This question is valid for middle managers, front-line supervisors and staff.

Common Errors

End Users

Failing to take into account the needs of the end users of change often leads to them rejecting or compromising that change to suit themselves. End users may be clients, patients or families other areas within your organization, suppliers, the community or specific people within your own area. For example, health care systems are constantly making radical change to the way care and services are delivered. Despite lip service to the contrary, there is little or no involvement of health care consumers in this change process.

Participants

Failing to identify all the people who should be involved in making the change happen isolates them and makes them more defensive than they might otherwise be. You cannot always include everyone in the decision making process for change but you can always keep them informed. This communication may help reduce resistance to change.

Delegation

Delegating too much of the responsibility without sufficient authority or not delegating enough to keep the expected success for yourself is dangerous. For example, delegating a project that will cause significant change to a department, or to a supervisor, without giving them authority to deal with the inevitable extra costs in their budgets, or their staff overtime needs, will lead to failure and resentment.

Short vs. Long-Term View

Concentrating on only short-term achievements and costs without looking at long-term consequences can be a big mistake. For example, bringing in new technology without recognizing that industry standards are changing to another technology next year is a common, costly mistake.

Costs

Only including technology costs and avoiding human resource costs in overtime, lay offs or increased work force, and/or community public relations costs will lead to unrealistic financial statements.

Evaluating Results

Concentrating on preparation and implementing change without careful and detailed evaluation of the results (both positive and negative) creates a loop of errors that is rarely identified until it is too late or too costly to correct. Much of the change currently under way in health care has little system evaluation in place.

Ignoring Criticism

People who attempt to bring realistic and critical appraisal to the change process are often unfairly labeled as "having a problem", being "negative" or "old fashioned". These judgments are not only hurtful but they also close the door to effective input and make the process of change appear dishonest and closed in nature. It says, "one must speak the party line or not speak at all".

Ignoring genuine criticism has led to enormous financial, human resource, and public relations costs. People at the front-line of any organization have realistic concerns about change that must be addressed. Managers and staff with a long history at an organization can be especially helpful in reminding others about change that happened in the past that failed. Their historical perspective may not be entirely accurate any more but that history needs to be included in the decision-making process to avoid repeat failures and certainly to bring about the commitment of long-service employees.

> *I think a major part of the difficulty in organizational downsizing is that what is "sold" to employees as change, is in reality, loss. The attendant grief, sadness and demoralization of staff is never dealt with. Rather they are labeled as people who cannot deal with change. Change itself can be exciting. Loss, stress and worry wrapped in the all-encompassing label of change can be a source of great concern. Mangers need to deal with the losses that people experience.*
> *Elizabeth Latimer*

Write out some clear, concrete examples of how you as a manager, supervisor or staff person, can put any three of the above suggestions into use. For the suggestion "Consequences", for example, how can you help others understand the real consequences of the change in their everyday work situations? (Some suggestions might be to brainstorm at a staff meeting, write clear, concise memos, discuss staff fears openly and honestly, and clarify your purpose.)

Resistance to Change

People have various reasons for resisting change. Resistance can be both a positive or negative reaction to change. To effectively manage change you must know whether your own resistance, or that of others, include legitimate concerns that need immediate attention. Some change needs to be resisted for legal, ethical, economic or personal reasons. You also need to constructively react to resistance when it is based on an unwillingness to change, a fear of change or lack of sufficient information. The following list is only a few examples of why people may resist change.

Some people naturally hesitate to change their behavior or work methods.

I naturally resist change because I am uncomfortable doing things differently. For example, if it were left up to me, I would never change the position of furniture in my home. I feel real comfort knowing that everything is where it should be! On the first day of school for 12 years in a row I got physically ill at the thought of changing from summer time to school again. By the 13th year I finally figured out how to avoid it. I adapt slowly but when I catch on it works for life. Recognize that change is naturally more difficult for some people than for others and that there is nothing wrong with this.

Harry van Bommel

Some people honestly believe that the present way of doing things is correct and they might be right. You need to listen to people who are convinced that the status quo is better. Find out if they have a good point or if they just dislike change. Listen, without judgment, to make sure you take the opportunity to avoid costly errors in changing something that should not be changed.

Some people believe that change is often done for change sake or because a new manager or boss wants to do things the way they are used to. The end product or service is often not affected. What is affected is the process for doing the work. People may see this kind of change as unnecessary and, therefore, an invalid reason for them to commit to yet another change. This resistance is a common experience for many people who have been in an organization for a long time and who have seen change for change sake. They resist this change in the belief that it will never work or because they believe their new boss will only be around for a few years and they can wait them out. Is their belief correct? If not, communicate more clearly and more often why they are wrong in this case.

Others resist because their cultural, gender or literacy concerns and needs are not addressed in the change. This can come from a lack of communication about change with these sensitivities in mind or because the lack of communication reflects an organizational bias towards a certain group. Other people may have grown up with so much, or so little, change in their lives that this is a new, unfamiliar experience for them. For example, someone brought up in a military family has moved homes and schools every few years. They may actually crave constant change or would prefer some stability in their lives right now. If you recognize this need you can help them manage the change more practically.

Some people fear a loss of identity within their department or organization as a result of change. This fear may be translated into a fear of losing their job, their prestige, their recognized expertise, their power ("turf") or their expectations of future job promotion.

So what can leaders and organizations do to manage change in ways that minimize resistance and effectively deal with any lingering resistance? To minimize resistance one needs to follow many of the suggestions in the previous sections of this material. **You must also discover if the resistance to change is valid and, therefore, you need to adapt your own views and decisions rather than implement the change.** Once you have done your best to identify the validity of the resistance and minimize the rest, you must deal with whatever resistance remains. Some suggestions:

Understand Why

First you must understand why people are still resisting change. Look at some of the examples above for help. Many forms of resistance come from fear, grief or loss and show up as visible anger, anxiety, depression, revenge, not doing their work or doing it badly, trying to hide away in their own areas of expertise, or trying to sabotage the work. If the fears can be accurately identified and discussed then you have an opportunity to change someone's resistance into active support for your plans. Have a genuine negotiation with them to identify, and reduce, the underlying reason for their resistance.

Saving Face

During periods of great change people may say and commit themselves to certain actions. It is important for people not to "lose face" with their colleagues, families and other employees. Downsizing and restructuring in health care is creating role loss in many experienced leaders and a sense that they have been "demoted" although they remain in the organization. Organizations need to articulate and channel the skill set of these people so that their pain and sense of loss is minimized. Diplomacy is the skill required here to allow people to change their views and actions without appearing foolish, defeated or petty. These people, in fact, can become your greatest champions of change if they are given responsibilities to show their strengths and abilities and if their contributions are recognized.

People Need to Leave

In any major change there will be people who will choose to leave, or must be asked to leave, so that the change can go ahead successfully. This most dramatic, and traumatic, method of dealing with resistance will create a storm of rumors and gossip unless prevented by clear communication about what is actually happening. People who must leave must not be seen necessarily as bad employees. An honest difference of strong opinions is not the same thing as people being labeled "trouble makers". It means that under these new circumstances, these employees are not able or willing to change their professional behaviors to make the changes necessary for success. In progressive organizations these people are identified, given an opportunity to change and if unsuccessful, provided the career counseling and support they may need to find employment elsewhere.

Informal Discussions

Another strategy to deal with resistance is to meet in an informal way (e.g., over coffee and a donut, in small groups) to:

1. Talk about old ways of doing things and how they will be missed.
2. Allow people to express their fears, sadness, grief, anger, worries, family concerns with change, etc. Listen actively to what they have to say before you comment or judge their responses and feelings. Allow people to respond to each other, rather than you taking sole responsibility for commenting.
3. Explain how many of the powerful feelings of uncertainty by individuals, their family and friends are natural during change. Give them tips on how to manage some of those feelings (described earlier in this unit) and how their efforts can help make the transition from the old ways to the new ways successful.
4. If possible, end with a positive comment about the coming change and, if appropriate, plan to meet again to review any difficulties and any successes. However, if the change is devastating, for example, downsizing and job loss, do not cloak it in pat phrases with a positive tone.

Exercise #2
Present and Future Change

In exercise #1 you looked at what change you have already managed and what things you did that helped, or did not help, you manage those changes. What present or future change do you think you must manage in your same seven categories of self-development: family, physical, emotional, educational, economic, career, spiritual? What things have you done in the past with success that will help you in the present and future? What things will you avoid doing to minimize any harm that these changes may have on you?

To help you answer some of these questions let's look at the five main steps to change: expect it, recognize it, feel your emotions, plan and act upon your plan. Concentrate on either work or personal changes. This will help you avoid confusion about which strategies will work where. You can also use the following exercise to help you help other people dealing with personal or professional changes.

5-Step Process	What I Can Do To Help	What I Should Not Do
1. **Expecting change** – What kinds of changes do I expect and what resistance do I expect from myself?		
2. **Recognizing change** – How will I recognize change and any personal resistance?		
3. **Feel emotions** – How will I allow myself to feel positive or negative emotion around this change? Who can I talk to for support?		
4. **Plan** – How will I plan for these expected changes and for my expected resistance?		
5. **Act**– How will I act on my plan to benefit myself, those close to me, and others involved in the change?		
6. **Other** – Which of my strengths and weaknesses from exercise #1 should I pay special attention to during this specific change?		

Organizational Change

Organizations have different ways of dealing with change. Change happens whether an organization does it well or not so well. This section highlights several ways of dealing with change with an obvious bias towards the second way. This section is not intended to criticize an organization's methods of changing but to suggest some of the benefits and consequences of doing it in different ways. Managers, supervisors and staff will use the following information best when they apply the most appropriate strategies in those areas where they have some control over the change, or at the very least, significant influence. (Remember the areas of control discussion earlier.)

If you have little or no influence or control, then you can use this information as a tool to understand the process you are going through. This may help you to expect change that is coming, recognize it when it happens, feel the emotions this brings out in you, plan your own response(s), and act accordingly.

Organizations have two basic ways of dealing with change: directed change or planned change. There is a third way when organizations say they are using planned change but actually design and carry out directed change. These organizations pay lip service to techniques of communicating change openly and honestly but are still stuck (often without realizing it) in the directed method of making decisions at the top of the organization without involving middle managers and staff. This third method usually leads to long-term resistance and feelings of mistrust.

Ethics in Organizations

Unfortunately, much of organizational change is not handled in an ethical way. This has created a climate of disillusionment in our society regarding corporate structures. This may be avoidable if organizations could seriously embrace the need to do their work with staff, clients, patients and families in an ethical way.

Therefore, it is of great value for organizations to examine how they do their work and if their policies and practices are ethical. For example,

- The mission statement must match practice. The disgraceful (but all too common) practice of walking staff to the door when their positions are eliminated is not consistent with an organization that says it values people.
- A spirit of openness relies upon mutual trust and respect. This must be the way of doing work and must also be modeled by senior executive and managers. It is unethical to say one thing and do another.
- A code of ethics is not something to develop and have in place. It is something to

guide practice and something in which the organization should take pride.

- Ethical practice depends on ethical people who hold certain beliefs and values and live by them.

The ethics meetings are extraordinary. It is an interdisciplinary group of managers and staff members chaired by a physician. An external participant from a university with a background in ethics/philosophy provides support. We meet on a monthly basis to review policies and research proposals that have already gone through the methodological committee (the scientific group) and to look at any possible ethical impact and required education. A lot of education is needed for the group itself and to raise the level of understanding of everyday ethical issues for the hospital staff.
Larry Lewis

Directed Change

The directed way to change usually divides change into the roles of upper management, middle management and front-line staff. This authoritarian style of managing organizational change often results in people disliking the process of change even if they like the end results. The directed way to change may be necessary when time limits are short or when visionary leaders believe a new way must be tried first before staff will support and understand the benefits.

Upper management (executive) make decisions based on their personal ideas, what they think public demand is asking for, what the competition is doing, on the advice of outside consultants, and the ideas of a selected group of middle managers who are trusted by the upper management. The risk here is that executives may be isolated from the ideas, needs and wants of their middle managers and staff who deal directly with the clients. The executive may also view their middle managers and staff with some contempt because they believe that the managers and staff are resistant to change, defensive about working differently and ungrateful for all the hard decisions and efforts made by the executive. Staff and middle managers may have a similar defensiveness when they talk about the executive.

Middle managers are caught in the middle between their staff (and perhaps front-line supervisors) and their own bosses in the executive. They are told to make changes without, perhaps, having enough information and authority to make it work. They feel cheated out of the decision making process as if their front-line experience is irrelevant. Their own staff may believe that the manager is withholding information and further changes from them and they resent this division.

The front-line staff ends up having to implement the change often without information, supports or a good rationale for why the change was necessary. The veteran staff members have seen change before and either adapt quickly or resist quietly and definitely because they believe that this change will only last a short while before the next one. These veteran staff members have lost faith in their leadership (especially if the leadership changes regularly) and do the minimum in their work to get by. The newer staff members may feel resentful that they were not consulted before the changes were announced. They have learned to expect, through their education and the media, that front-line staff are supposed to have more say in the operation of an organization. They have also been told that organizations are supposed to share in the responsibilities and profits of change with their staff. When they find out that all of their ideas about what changing organizations should be like are false in their own case, they become argumentative, defensive or anxious at their work.

Without visionary and practical leaders, change in such a directed way is often very painful, ineffective and destructive in the short term. In the long-term, though, many organizations end up with effective change because their pattern of change in this directed way is consistent. People dislike the process and some even leave the organization because of it. However, at the end of the process, change is in place and may be accepted as the best solution to the original problem or opportunity.

Planned Change

In planned change there is greater emphasis put on the planning of change rather than the directing of change within an organization. All the people involved with the change from staff, middle managers, the upper management, clients, and the local community is involved in deciding what change is necessary.

The upper management is still ultimately responsible for the overall change within the organization but it does not begin with a pre-conceived idea of what the change must look like before getting other people's ideas.

Successful change in a specific department or area or in the whole organization involves several well thought out steps. These steps follow the old method of who, what, where, when, why and how. In the Action Plan following this section you will use much of the following information to help you identify what is necessary to plan the change effectively. At each step along the way there is a need to allow managers and staff a chance to give their thoughts and even negotiate their strongly held views with others.

Why

People need to know why the change is necessary and necessary now. People have experienced much change in their work lives that had little reason to it or long-term planning involved. They have experienced this change most often when a new manager or President comes to the organization and wants to do things differently.

Organizations must help people to understand where the department or organization is now before accepting that change is necessary. Once people know where they are and where the organization needs to be in future to meet changing needs, the managers and staff can provide useful information and ideas to help make the necessary changes effectively, timely and with minimum disturbance.

Before change is begun the organization must also examine the barriers to the change (demographics, number of people affected and their various backgrounds, communication methods in the organization, policies and procedures, programs and services).

Who is Involved

The People

Get people at all levels within the organization or department involved in deciding what change is necessary. You can get their ideas through meetings, questionnaires and surveys, open forums and one-to-one conversations. Give them enough time to think about alternatives and recommendations rather than giving them all the information in a one-hour meeting and asking for their ideas before they leave the room. **Change led by the executive, without help from others in the organization, may result in long-term change but at a cost of a short-term decrease in staff and management morale and effectiveness.**

The Leader

Whoever leads this change must have the trust and respect of the people involved. If the department or organizational leader lacks that kind of trust, encourage a specially appointed or elected leader to take control over this particular change process. This person may come from within the department or from an earlier task force or team where they showed an ability to get people actively involved in a change project. Note: As I wrote earlier, change can happen (and often does happen) without a trusted leader. For the best short and long-term results, however, a trusted leader is necessary.

Managers and Supervisors

The people who actually achieve the change will be the managers and supervisors working with their staff. Some of them will need support from their own supervisors to help manage this change effectively. They may manage the change by forming teams of managers and supervisors from the different areas or departments involved or act alone within their own area of responsibility. These managers, supervisors and staff will have to implement the change, handle the day-to-day problems that come up, and make sure that the end result is what is wanted.

What

Once you have decided on the change, its purpose and given people an opportunity to get involved in making the overall decisions, you need to give them specific information about what is required before, during and after the change to ensure its success. The "what" can be specific new guidelines, policies, technology change, corporate restructuring, etc.

The "what" is often divided into short and long-term goals (general results expected) and objectives (specific methods for achieving and evaluating goals).

When

People need realistic and achievable deadlines to go through a change process. They need to know who will be responsible for what part of the change and when they have to be ready.

The "when" also represents the time of transition. This is the movement from the understood past (a personal ending for people), to an uncertain future. People, especially in the North American culture, are uncomfortable with periods of transition when things move from one point to another without clear points of reference. While other cultures sometimes embrace uncertainty as times of great creativity, the North American culture often feels the need to get through these transitions as quickly as possible. Recognize which view of transitions your organization, your colleagues and others hold and help them identify their comfort or discomfort.

Where

Knowing where the change must take place encourages managers and staff to go beyond the obvious. A change in one area may affect other areas and departments, other clients and even the local community.

How

The "how" is the coordinated plan. This action plan for change looks at the who, what, where, when and why and puts it together in a step-by-step plan identifying who will do what, where and by when.

Success

When change is successful it is important to thank the people who have made it successful. Too often this last step is forgotten or only the executive and/or a hand-full of token leaders are thanked. Since change is never ending it is important for people to feel appreciated for their efforts so that the next time a major change is presented they understand that their efforts and ideas matter to the organization.

Success needs to be celebrated publicly, often and genuinely. People who have learned new skills, helped solve problems arising from change, and those who unofficially led within their peer groups must be acknowledged for their efforts. This recognition can include letters of praise from the executive to be included in their personnel records, certificates of accomplishment which are prized within an organization, one-time bonuses or special events to which these people's families can be invited to share in their loved ones' successes.

It is important to have an accurate assessment of the overall morale of the staff within the organization before determining how to celebrate the success. Ill-timed celebration will further add to the belief that senior management are out of touch with the needs of the organization.

The Unspoken Third Method

As we mentioned before, there is actually a third method of dealing with organizational change. In this method an organization says it is using the planned method of change but, in fact, is using directed change. In this type of organization, the leadership actually says the rights things and goes through some of the motions of asking for ideas from staff, middle managers, clients and the community but in fact has already decided what to do, how to do it, when it will be done, and how it will be evaluated (if at all). This type of organizational change is the most demoralizing because high expectations are set and not carried through. People may be resistant to change in an organization that traditionally uses directed change but it is predictable and expected and does not pretend to be anything else. When staff and managers expect planned change, participate in meetings and forums to help design that change, and later find out that the upper management never expected to actually use their ideas, they feel like they have wasted their time and misplaced their trust in the organization.

Unfortunately, this third method of change is more common that any of us would like to see. People going through such a process must concentrate on their areas of control described earlier in this material.

Area 1: You have total control over the change so you put the most energy into making it work.

Area 2: You have influence over how the change will happen but the decision is up to someone else.

Area 3: You are asked to give your input (i.e. ideas, opinions) but you do not have much real influence and someone else makes the decision.

Area 4: The decision to make a change is made without your involvement. You are expected to carry out the change. You always have control over how you will react to the change but not over the change itself.

Even when this third method of change management is used, there will be aspects of the change that you may have total control over. Others may decide what change will take place but you may have control over how it is implemented.

Other aspects of the change may allow you an opportunity to influence how the change will be implemented although you will not have control over that process. Your influence or suggestions may, and may not, significantly impact how the change is carried out in your area.

Much of the change in such an organization, however, falls in Area 4 where you have no control. In such a situation you need to examine some of the strategies described earlier in this material. You need to decide how much effort and energy you are going to put into this change process. You might find that you strongly agree with the suggested changes and actively work to make it successful. Again, the third method may result in long-term successful change but certainly at a short-term cost of mistrust and decreased productivity. The long-term effects of the third method have yet to be assessed. It would seem that many employees in large organizations are experiencing dramatic change in their attitudes towards work based largely on what they see as a loss of faith in the way their organization does change.

You might decide that the change is wrong for your own reasons and decide that you will leave that area or job. There are no easy answers in such a situation. You must decide for yourself how these changes that you have no control over fit in with your balanced view of family life, and the physical, emotional, spiritual, career, educational, and economic aspects of your life.

Exercise #3
Action Plan

In the five-step process of change (expect, recognize, feel the emotions, plan and act), steps 4 and 5 are about planning and acting on those plans. Following a plan of action to design, implement and evaluate change is critical to its success. It cannot be done easily on a few sheets of paper, so rather than provide a form to fill in for this exercise, please use separate sheets of paper or a word processor to prepare a sketch of a change event you are presently working on. You will need a lot of time and space to write out your answers to the following list of questions and ideas.

Note: The Action Plan format suggested at the end of this exercise is just one way of writing out an action plan. However, using an action plan format is the **how** stage of planning. You need to, first of all, answer the why, who, what, when and where before you even begin to think of an action plan. The action plan is used after you have identified the **specific** "what" items that need to be done by different people within a certain deadline. When you get that far into your planning you can use whatever variation of the standard action planning form presented in this Exercise you like.

If you are front-line staff and not directly involved in the decision-making process you can still use parts of this exercise to find out the **why** for this change (as best you can). You can ask questions to find out how the decisions will be implemented and how it will affect your work. You can ask your peers, your boss, union leaders, etc. You can also go back to Exercise 2 and use that format to prepare yourself for the coming change.

If you are middle managers and not involved in the decision-making process you can also find out the **why**, **what**, **how** and by **when**. How the change will be implemented will have the most impact on your area so this may be an opportunity to get your staff to feel involved in how to carry out the change even if they (and you) were not involved in making the decisions about change. Again, exercise 2 may help you prepare yourself better for the change ahead.

To repeat, before you can begin to write out a specific action plan you must spend time writing out the answers to the following questions and ideas.

1. Begin by getting the answers to **why** this change is necessary now and what other alternatives can be looked at.

   The organization must then identify the barriers to the change (demographics, number of people affected and their various backgrounds, communication methods in the organization, policies and procedures, programs and services).

   People also need to understand where the department or organization is now, before accepting that change is necessary. Outline where the department or organization is now and where the organization needs to be in future to meet changing needs. Managers and staff can provide useful information and ideas to help make the necessary changes effectively, timely and with the minimum disturbance.
2. Once the "why" is answered you can begin the rest of the research. You need to address the following points to make sure your ideas and plan are possible in the

present organizational climate and circumstances. Remember to get input from all stakeholders (managers, staff, clients, community, service providers, etc.), as much as possible, for each point. **Go back over the more detailed information in the previous section to make sure you do not miss anything.** Once that is complete, answer the following:

Who are the people involved? Which managers, supervisors and staff will be directly involved? Who will be the leader chosen to help make this process as smooth and professional as possible.

What is required before, during and after the change to ensure its success? The "what" can be specific new guidelines, policies, technology change over, corporate restructuring, etc. The "what" is often divided into short and long-term goals (general results expected) and objectives (specific methods for achieving and evaluating goals).

When are the realistic and achievable deadlines for this change process? People need to know who will be responsible for what part of the change and when they have to be ready. How much time have you scheduled for transition?

Where will the change take place? Remember a change in one area may affect other areas and departments, other clients and even the local community.

3. After all of this work, you have finally reached the action planning phase, or the **how**. How you will coordinate the change process is what the actual action plan is designed for. This action plan for change looks at the who, what, where, when and why and puts it all together in a step-by-step plan identifying:

   Who will do what, where and by when.

   The "how" also includes the communication element of change. Decide if you will use newsletters, meetings, memos, special logos, perhaps even a mascot to lighten the solemnness of the change and slogans, T-shirts, etc., to give the change some internal and external public relations that are realistic and meaningful.

   The "how" may be divided into changes in: policies, programs and services, products, personnel practices, communication, education, decision making, community involvement, and changes in performance expectations.

   The following chart is one action plan format that may help you write out some of the details. You may have one general action plan for the whole change process and other action plans within specific areas of the organizations outlining their responsibilities and deadlines. For the purpose of this exercise, just sketch out some specific methods you might use to implement a change you are experiencing at work or at home.

Item	Who	What & Where	By When	How Success?

4. After the action plan has been implemented you must evaluate the results and acknowledge your success. How will you do that? As we said before, this step is too often forgotten or only the executive and/or a hand-full of token leaders are thanked. Since change is never ending it is important for people to feel appreciated for their efforts so that the next time a major change is presented they understand that their efforts and ideas matter to the organization.

Summary

Change is simply moving from a known way of doing things through a transition of uncertainty to a different way of doing things. How people respond to any change depends on their previous experience, their trust of their leaders and organization, how much they believe the change is necessary, if they are involved in designing and making the change, and if they are part of evaluating the success of the change.

Some overall themes in managing change include:

1. You need to keep a sense of balance in your life in the following areas: family and friends, physical and emotional needs, education, economic, career, and spiritual needs.
2. You need to understand the five-step process of: expecting change, recognizing when it happens, feeling the positive and negative emotions that come from the change, planning and acting on that plan.
3. You need to use lifelong learning, perspective, and humor in dealing with change.
4. You need to find out how much control you have in this situation and, therefore, how much energy to put into making it work. The four areas of control are: total control (lots of energy), influence, input and no control except in how you respond (least amount of energy).
5. Leaders within a workplace need to decide if they are going to implement directed change or planned change. They need to know the difference and how to get the most benefits out of either, while minimizing the negative consequences.

Burton Blatt offered the following definition of "optimism" for dealing with change:

> Optimism is not in believing that things will turn out well, objectively; but in believing that we can face things, subjectively, however they turn out.
>
> Optimism is not in feeling good, but in feeling that good has a chance to survive.
>
> Optimism flows not from defeats and bitterness or victories and joys of the past, but in being here now, knowing the past has strengthened you.

Resources

The following resources are only a few of the many useful resources that you can find in your local libraries, within your own organization, and in your local bookstores. Look for other books but also for journal articles, magazine reports, films, videos and audiocassettes. Also keep in mind how much you can learn from experts in the field, including people within your own organization!

Bardwich, J.M. (1991). *Danger in the comfort zone.* New York: .Amacom.

Barger, N.J., & Kirby, L.K. (1995). *The challenge of change in organizations: Helping employees thrive in a new frontier.* Palo Alto, CA: Consulting Psychologists Press.

Bridges, W. (1991). *Managing transitions: Making the most of change.* New York: Addison-Wesley.

Campbell, S. (1995). *From chaos to confidence: Survival strategies for the new workplace.* New York: Simon & Schuster.

Emshoff, J.R. with Denlinger, T.E. (1991). *The new rules of the game: The four key experiences managers must have to thrive in the non-hierarchical 90s and beyond.* New York: Harper.

Haas, E.B. (1990). *When knowledge is power: Three models of change in international organizations.* Berkeley, CA: University of California Press.

Larkin, S., & Larkin, T. J. (1994). *Communicating change: How to win employee support for new directions.* New York: McGraw-Hill.

Peters, T. (1994). *The pursuit of WOW!: Every person's guide to topsy-turvy times.* New York: Vintage Books.

Tushman, M.L., & O'Reilly, C.A. III. (1997). *Winning through innovation: A practical guide to leading organizational change and renewal.* Cambridge, MA: Harvard School Press.

8. Action Oriented Planning

Planning

This section looks at the basic methods of planning. More specifically:
The basic assumptions and values of an organization.
How to write a mission statement.
The long-term and strategic planning of an organization.
The year-to-year operational and budgeting plans (short term planning).

Planning is critical to all organizations. It helps you examine where you are now with your programs and funding while planning for the future. Planning is not a luxury that organizations can spend some time on every 5 years. The systematic planning cycle presented in this section will help save endless difficulties that organizations regularly face because they have no overview of where they are going. Once a system is in place to plan, the process can work much faster and smoother than may be faced by organizations that plan only during a crisis situation.

When plans work out, they should be celebrated. When plans must be adapted to meet unexpected events or needs, they should be celebrated as well because you know what parts of the plan can be postponed to meet the new circumstances. That is the beauty of an effective plan – new circumstances do not destroy your planning; they just revise them and everyone still has a sense of control over what is happening.

I have a wonderful sense of completion and satisfaction when a project is well done or a report is submitted on time as scheduled. This satisfying feeling of completion probably stems from ancient beliefs and rituals surrounding the adage exhorting that we must "plan the work and work the plan". Many of us are probably well used to the experience of planning for three scenarios where financial assumptions include a budget increase of 5%; a reduction of 5%; or no change along with details of how quality services will be maintained or even enhanced. I find that making the planning process even more challenging is the mid-course correction occasioned by shifts in government policy, union pressures and a host of other factors. Despite the external forces that appear to tear your neat plan into tatters, there are the internal factors that suddenly emerge to make you forget about the plan's details altogether or that seriously create a "big" hole. It goes something like this, " I don't know how to tell you but I have accepted a job elsewhere." I think the new planning paradigm is plan/change/plan/change/!

Larry Lewis

When you were a child you planned your life around the school year and summer vacation. Your school year started in September and finished in August (like having a fiscal year end August 31). You knew what major events would happen during the year and had some idea of what your family would do for each one. Here is a brief calendar of what your year might have looked like.

Sept	**Oct**	**Nov**	**Dec**	**Jan**	**Feb**
School starts	Halloween	zoo field trip	report card & winter holidays	New Year's Party	Valentine's Day
Mar	**Apr**	**May**	**Jun**	**Jul**	**Aug**
March break, Patrick's Day	your birthday	Mother's Day	Father's Day, end of school	Summer holidays, odd jobs for neighbors	2-week St. hiking trip

Your long-term plan was to finish school in the next 11 years. Your strategic plan may have been to read your favorite comic books without using a dictionary in the next 2 years. Your plan for this year was to be the best reader in your class and to receive two of your favorite books for your birthday.

As an adult with children your year may also begin in September but it will look a little different. Your long-term plan may be to have a larger home for your family in the next 8 years. Your strategic plan may be to finish your university degree in the next 3 years. Your yearly plan (included in this calendar) is to make your first investment for your retirement.

Sept	**Oct**	**Nov**	**Dec**	**Jan**	**Feb**
school starts, car insurance due	strategic planning at work	operational planning at work	report for shareholders due at work & Christmas	New Year's party at work	program review
Mar	**Apr**	**May**	**Jun**	**Jul**	**Aug**
year end at work, invest for tax deduction	tax return due, AGM at work	staff retreat	semi-annual reports, wedding anniversary	catch up at home and work	2-week hiking trip with family

What you have when you look at your calendar is your yearly events. What is not on the calendar are the unexpected things like weather difficulties, car breaking down, surprise birthday party, winning a prize, your health improving (or not), or your child giving you an expected gift after a particularly difficult day at work.

It is useful to have a yearly calendar of repetitive events, meetings and planning processes. Just as many people plan their year around the school calendar (September to August), organizations have a general rhythm to their meetings, planning processes, budgeting, etc. When this is highlighted on a calendar, people are better able to make short-term plans that fit into the overall calendar.

For example, a department calendar should include:

- Regular department meetings, committee and planning sessions (e.g., spring budget planning for next year, review of strategic/long-term plan, and short-term operational planning).
- Regular review of policies and organization's programs and special projects.
- Annual report schedule.
- Performance reviews for managers and staff and negotiation of labor contracts, if applicable.
- Departmental self-evaluation, training, and new staff orientation.
- Vacation schedule.
- Seeing some different types of yearly plans leads us into long-term, strategic, yearly and daily planning. This section helps you examine each of these areas in the order they should be done. If you only plan on a day-to-day basis, it will be daily crises that decide where you are going and not your organization's well thought out plan.

The Way to Plan

Planning saves you time, energy and a lot of frustration. Planning is something an organization is always doing. Planning is something that parents are always doing. It does not stop after you have written out your first plan, it continues forever and it can be fun! You can also use this format for personal planning. The mission statement in this case will be your overall purpose in life. The way to plan for an organization looks like this:

Six Step Planning Cycle

1. Write out your organization's basic assumptions and values.
2. Write your mission statement (the purpose of your work).

3. Write out your organization's long-term plan (where you plan to be in 5-10 years).
4. Write out your organizations' strategic plan (your top priorities for the next 5 years).
5. Write out your organization's operational (yearly) plan including budget.
6. Review, change and evaluate # 1-5 every year before writing out a new operational plan and budget.

You will see that almost all the points begin with "write out". Planning is a way to think on paper and to make sure that everyone agrees with what you are doing and how you plan to do it. Without written plans, you do things in your head and what you think everyone is doing may be very different from what they think they are doing.

Communication is the most important way to get things done in an organization. Without a written plan, your communication is almost doomed to fail quickly. You may have heard of the saying: "We never seem to have enough time to do it right the first time (planning), but we always seem to find time to do it again." Good planning means you spend less time doing things over again and less time going from one crisis to another.

Different people within an organization do the planning. It is up to the senior management and Board of Directors with help from consumers and staff to do steps # 1-5. Different committees may be involved in steps #4-6. The staff gets most involved, usually, in step 5, but should be involved in giving committees and senior management help with all steps.

If you have difficulty understanding the different steps of this planning cycle, read on. Each step is explained in greater detail. Let's begin with a brief example of what one "make believe" hospital drafted for some of its planning cycle documents.

Everyone's Favorite Hospital

Our basic assumptions and values include:

- All our patients/clients have value and we meet their needs beyond their own expectations.
- When people are upset with our service, we must do what we can to satisfy them – if we cannot meet their needs, we will refer them to someone who may better help them.
- Our hospital will make a contribution to our community so that we are all healthier, safer and happier.

Our mission is to provide a welcoming place for all our patients/clients where they can receive excellent service that meets their health care needs beyond their present expectations.

Our long-term plan (5-10 years) includes:

- To be accessible to our patients/clients 7 days/week, 24 hours a day.
- To be such a welcoming place that our clients prefer to receive the services they need from us, even if it means driving out of their way.
- To have a quality management system that includes the input of our patients/clients.

Our strategic plan (priorities over the next five years) includes:

- To have a dynamic staff with varying backgrounds and abilities to reflect our commitment to our diverse community.
- To nurture ongoing relationships with our most loyal patients/clients so that one day they may actively participate in our quality management system.
- To identify site renovation priorities.

Note: a strategic plan may be divided into one, three and five year plans to further divide the priorities.

Our operational plan includes:

- To communicate more regularly with our patients/clients through a newsletter and open-house meetings starting immediately on the first Thursday night of odd-numbered months with our first newsletter mailed out and distributed within 60 days.
- To identify patients/clients with long-standing interest in our hospital and community.
- To recruit two committee members with renovation experience to the Site Committee by the end of this month; to identify a process for site renovation priorities.

The Basic Assumptions and Values of an Organization

Whenever a group of people come together to begin or continue to plan for an organization, they must begin with their own assumptions and values. They must discuss and find out what beliefs they have in common and which ones are different.

> *With my interest in the behavioral sciences, I sit on a behavior management committee. It's aim is to ensure that staff are well equipped with knowledge, skills and understanding so that if an outburst of aggressive behavior occurs, even in subtle ways, they know how to diffuse it as quickly as possible as opposed to having a group trained to grab the arms and legs of someone in order to immobilize them. That is not how we want to deal with aggressive behavior.*
>
> *Larry Lewis*

For example, imagine that the board has a retreat to do long-term planning. They are the board for a community health center providing services to a specific, identifiable group of people. When they discuss their own assumptions they find that some members of the board believe that the people they serve are hard working, enthusiastic, and active members of their community. Other members of the board believe that their clients are incapable of working hard because of who they are and they need the charity of the board and the health center.

You can imagine that the programs and services proposed by the first group of board members would be seen as unacceptable by the second set. The second group of board members would consider the client population incapable of some of the action-oriented and demanding programs proposed by the first group. You can see from this simple example that assumptions and values do have a fundamental impact on the very work of the board.

You may find this an unrealistic example. However, over and over again in organizations there are people whose basic assumptions about life, about work, and about their clients are completely opposed to those of other people in the organization. They usually do not know that there is a basic difference in their assumptions. Most people would believe that everyone has the same assumptions and beliefs. If they see a difference, they often ignore it.

Have you ever heard staff say something like: "These are really wonderful people we work with, they just can't seem to get up in the morning." Or perhaps your organization has put an ad in the newspaper advertising for a new job. The ad asks for people who are energetic, creative and with relevant job experience. When you hire the person you find that they do not always dress the way you would like them to or arrive on time. Creative people are often not concerned with punctuality since they will work as long as it takes to do the job. You have asked for creativity, but your hidden assumption was that you wanted someone who does things the same way everyone else in the organization does them.

Take a moment and ask yourself what your basic assumptions and values are in the following areas and compare your answers with those of the people you work with to identify similarities and differences:

1. Life in general – Are you an optimist or a pessimist? How do you categorize your clients? Do you enjoy working for your clients?
2. Religion/spirituality – Are your beliefs similar to those of the other people you work with? Do your beliefs help you to understand (versus judge) the people you work with? What other impacts do your beliefs have on your work, decisions and behaviors?

3. Politics – Who do you believe really controls the work of your organization? How does change happen politically in your organization? Who holds power in the world?
4. Your work styles – Do you work in similar ways to the other people in your organization (not likely)? How do you adapt to other people's styles? How do you help them accept your style?
5. Your beliefs about similar organizations – does your competition provide high quality services and products? Do they fill a need your organization does not? Why would someone go to them instead of to you? Why would some of your clients switch to them? Why would some of their clients switch to you?
6. Do your services address: the multicultural diversity in your community, people with physical and other challenges, people with a range of economic backgrounds, older and younger people, people with more or less power, and people with more or less education, because it is the correct thing to do or because it is politically correct?
7. Other questions.

Compare your answers with the people you work with. Where do you agree? Where do you disagree? Why? How can you work better together understanding your similarities and differences?

How to Write a Mission Statement

You should not write or rewrite your mission statement until you understand what your basic assumptions and most important values are. Once you understand your own assumptions and values you need to compare them with those of the other people on the board, senior management and others with whom you work. Without this foundation of common or understood assumptions and values, your mission statement will not work.

A mission statement is a short one or two sentence statement that says what you do as an organization (or service, team, program, clinic), for whom, and why. You describe who will receive the service, why they need the service and what you do (will do) to meet that need.

After you have written a very good mission statement, all board decisions should be compared with your mission statement to make sure that new ideas and plans fit in with your purpose. If something new does not fit in, you either: a) avoid doing it or b) rewrite your mission statement so it includes this new idea or plan.

The second way, rewriting your mission statement, is serious. You must make sure that the people who are receiving services from you want this new idea or plan and that they will support it. New services, no matter how good, will not work if people do not want them, especially if they are not in your original mission statement.

Samples

The following is an example of the mission statement of an Emergency Department:

> To meet the urgent medical needs of all people living or visiting our area using the highest standards of emergency medical practice as defined by the World Health Organization and practiced by compassionate caregivers within a welcoming, efficient *environment.*

The following is an example of a mission statement that will not work.

> To provide our services to whomever wants them. (This mission statement does not state specifically enough who will be the clients, why they would go to this health care organization nor how the organization will uniquely meet their clients' needs.)

Long-Term and Strategic Planning

There is a difference between long-term and strategic planning. Long-term planning gives an organization an idea of where it will be in 5-10 years. It is a broad summary of what people would like to see happen to the organization and the people it serves over the next 5-10 years. For example, suppose your mission is to provide English as a Second Language to staff members who are recent immigrants. This long-term goal must be broken down in the strategic plan into manageable actions that the organization takes over the next 5 years.

Strategic planning, therefore, is more specific and usually concentrates on a few major areas of concern. The plan usually helps an organization come up with ideas of what must be done in the next five years with special attention to three to five service areas.

As another example, an educational organization may have a long-term plan to help unemployed people with less than a grade 12 education finish high school and find work. Ten years from now they hope to have helped 1,000 people get their education and find work. The strategic plan looks at helping three main groups of people who, today, are having particular difficulty finishing school: young mothers, recent immigrants who do not speak or write English very well and young, male drop-out students. The strategic plan looks at helping these three groups particularly for the next 5 years, but will also allow other people who find out about the program to get help.

You can see from the above example why it is so important to have basic assumptions and values and a mission statement before you can begin to do long-term planning and strategic planning. What if many of the board members had difficulty with the idea of helping single mothers, recent immigrants or young, male dropouts? They would have done a lot of planning, but when it came down to the strategic plan for the organization they would probably not say very much about what they felt. At this point it would be difficult for them to lose face in front of other people. They would agree to the plan but would not commit their energy to making it work.

To write strategic plans the board, or a special planning committee, should begin with their assumptions and values, the mission statement and long-term goals of the organization and then:

1. Get as much information about what people in their community, their staff and volunteers and other board members think the organization should do or continue to do. They could use meetings, focus groups, questionnaires or telephone calls to find out what other people think. They could research what similar organizations are doing in other communities. They could find out if their funders (private and public) are satisfied with their plans or their past activities.
2. Review any older strategic plans to make sure what they are now planning is consistent with previous decisions. If new plans are not consistent with previous strategic plans, they must decide which new priorities they will follow and whether they are consistent with their mission statement and long-term goals. Again, if the strategic plans are not consistent with the mission statement and long-term goals, the board must begin a complete organizational review of where they want the organization to go before they accept a shorter-term strategic plan.
3. Review the long-term and strategic plans every year so that an organization does not have to re-invent the wheel every time. If last year's plan still meets the needs of the clients and there are no new services being requested, then stick with a good plan. Do not review the plans too quickly, however, because the organization might miss a wonderful opportunity to improve what they do and how they do it.
4. Once there is enough information, the board needs to examine all the possibilities; determine if there are other ideas that may have been missed; and list the ideas in order of priority. The priorities will depend on the organization's budget, their energy and what the clients think is most important. Some people use the following guidelines to decide on priorities:

Top Priority: What is most important to do now?
2nd Priority: What is important to do in the next year or two?
3rd Priority: What is important to do in the next 3-5 years?
4th Priority: What would be nice to do if we get unexpected money or resources?

5. Draft out the plan and get people inside and outside the organization to give their ideas, criticisms and suggestions.
6. Rewrite the plan, taking into consideration all the comments collected. Note: Some organizations draft a plan knowing that is exactly what they intend to use. They ask for ideas from the staff and clients only to get their support rather than their ideas. This technique works only once or twice before people lose trust in the organization.
7. The board approves the plan and uses it to make all further decisions. Like the mission statement, if new ideas and services do not fit the plan, the new ideas cannot be done or the plan must be changed.

Operational Planning and Budgeting

Operational planning and budgeting are yearly exercises that every organization must go through to stay in control of what they are doing. The operational plan is simply the method an organization decides to use to reach its yearly goals. It operationalizes the strategic plan. The budget planning is the financial side of planning that tells the organization what is, or is not, possible to do in the next year.

Specific committees usually do operational planning. For example, the Community Relations Committee uses the long-term and strategic plans to look at what community information events will take place. The Evaluation Committee decides how to measure overall patient satisfaction.

The steps to take, and who takes them, usually include the following:

1. The board decides on the long-term and strategic plans for the organization. Their report goes to the various standing and ad-hoc committees. The people involved in the committees may include board members, staff, volunteers, and clients.
2. The committees review their activities from the past year to see what went well, what could be done better and what should not continue to happen this year. The committees then review the long-term and strategic plans approved by the board and decide on what is possible for the coming year. They draft specific objectives that will help the organization do what they promised to do in their long-term and strategic plans. They also draft a budget, using last year's information as a

starting point, and send their ideas and recommendations to senior management. (Note: not all new objectives cost more money.)

3. Senior management reviews last year's income and expenses. Based on what money will be available in the coming year, they review each committee's report and budget and make recommendations. They send their comments back to the committees.
4. The committees review and modify their plans and bring them, through the chair, to senior management for approval.

Let's look at a brief example of how one goal may be prepared by a board and its committees.

Long-Term Goal: To be a safe place where young people feel welcomed and able to contribute to their community.

Strategic Plan	**Operational Plan**	**Budget**
1. To have a dynamic, self-directed core of local youth who have designed a successful stay-in-school or career-path program (within 3 years).	*Program Committee:* Begin Friday evening openings within current staff schedules (immediately).	No additional cost
	Work with youth for a Youth Focus weekend meeting to plan future directions of program (by mid-summer).	$5,000
	Personnel Committee: begin specific receptionist instruction on how to respond to, welcome and receive youth callers and drop-ins (within 1 month).	No additional cost
	Public Relations Committee: begin low level media coverage of Friday night openings through popular radio, TV, and local schools (within 3 months). No additional cost	No additional cost
	Fund-Raising Committee: apply to City Council and province for project funding.	No additional cost if added to other grant proposals.

Goals and Objectives

The previous few pages introduced the ideas of goals and objectives. The following information will help you to understand and practice these skills.

The board generally decides on the goals of the organization and what should be done, where and by when. The staff generally change those goals into practical objectives of who, what, where, when, why, and how things will be done. The staff also decides, with management approval, what the standards of success will be so that both staff and management can evaluate the success of achieving any of the goals.

A **goal** is something people want to see happen, such as the goals of improved client satisfaction, better health and safety at work, job satisfaction, or a more loving family. For example:

Board: "One of our organizational goals is to increase the level of client satisfaction with our services."

An **objective** is a statement of the specific results one wants to achieve. After the board has set the goals it is often a work group, with staff suggestions, that writes out the objectives. The staff then decides how to meet the objective.

Objectives describe what the specific result will look like, when it will happen and what is needed to make the objective happen. In writing objectives one also looks at what can cause the objective to not happen. Objectives must be realistic yet challenging. The group of people working on them must agree and commit to making them work.

Committee: "To increase client satisfaction with our services this year we will, by July 1: (a) decrease the time we respond to a patient complaint to within one day, (b) start at least one new program request listed on last year's client satisfaction survey, and (c) invite a loyal customer from the community to sit on the Evaluation committee."

The committee usually writes out the "what, when, where and why" of an objective.

Staff

1. Sue and Jim will get training on our new patient documentation software in May to help them speed up our service by the July 1st deadline.
2. Joan will review medication errors in May and prepare a one-page report for staff.
3. We will decrease the time to wait for an appointment to within 30 minutes of the scheduled appointment."

The staff usually decides on the "who and how" of an objective.

Objectives Checklist

To write objectives that are practical and useful it is important that they meet what some people call the S.M.A.R.T. test:

Specific

Measurable

Achievable

Realistic

Time-lines to complete objective

Objectives must be written so that it is absolutely clear to everyone whether the objective has been met or not met.

The following chart shows examples of unacceptable objectives rewritten to meet the S.M.A.R.T test.

Unacceptable Objectives	Acceptable Objectives
Wastage of unit supplies should be minimized.	To reduce wastage of unit supplies by 25% by next July 1, by forming a work group of staff and management.
To fund a community education program.	To secure 100% funding for a community education program by June of next year by approaching (1) senior management, (2) business and service clubs and (3) pharmaceutical reps.
To provide staff development.	To implement 6 half-hour workshops for staff members over the next year on topics chosen by the staff at the departmental meetings in November.

Exercise #1
Writing Objectives

1. Write down 3 of your organization's annual goals: (or substitute general goals you might have for your committee, department, clinic, team or program).
2. Now write one or more specific objectives (to help you achieve each goal for yourself), your committee, department, clinic, team or your organization, using the S.M.A.R.T. criteria.

Evaluating Success

Internal Evaluations

An internal evaluation is designed to find out whether you did what you said you would, in the time you gave yourself to do it, on budget, and what you learned from the work. The following sample chart may help you evaluate each specific objective.

Objective	Done	Partly Done	Not Done	On Budget	Comments

External Evaluations

When you ask your community to review your services, you may choose to use an evaluation tool. The questions you need to answer may include:

1. Does what we do help or not help you?
2. What do you like about what we do?
3. What do you not like about what we do?
4. What would you suggest we do differently?
5. Can you suggest any ways that other people in the community could help us make our programs and services better?
6. Do you recommend our organization to other people? Why or why not?

Action Plans

One of the easiest ways to plan your work priorities and help schedule that work is to use Action Plans. Have colleagues, supervisors and/or staff participate in dividing the work.

What Is The Task?	Who Will Do It?	By When?	How To Evaluate Success?

Summary

Planning is a constantly changing cycle that pro

vides direction and specific detail about what is to be done, by whom, by when and how. It includes an evaluation step to ensure successes are celebrated, gaps are identified and addressed and that we learn from our mistakes. When plans must be adapted to meet unexpected events or needs, you still have control over the planning process and its resulting actions. That is the beauty of an effective plan–new circumstances do not destroy your planning; you revise them and still maintain a sense of control over what is happening.

Most people either over plan (with not enough time to actually implement the plan), or more likely, do not plan enough. Effective planning saves you time, energy and a lot of frustration.

There is a six-step cascading planning process:

1. Planning is only successful and rewarding when you have a basic set of assumptions and values to use as the cornerstone for all decision making and planning.
2. A mission statement outlines the purpose of your work to provide focus for what it is you will, and will not do. An organization without a mission statement is like a boat without a rudder–you drift aimlessly in whatever direction the current takes you.
3. The long-term plan (looking 5-10 years into the future) provides you with the basic elements of a plan–the core areas in which you want to work.
4. The strategic plan gives you the top priorities for the next five years based on your ten-year plan.
5. The annual operational plan (including the budget) is not about deciding what to do as much as how you will do what is in your strategic plan. An effective operational plan also leaves room for the unexpected events and time-draining day-to-day operational issues of the organization. Whenever you work with people there are human resource opportunities and difficulties. When you work with technology, there are breakdowns, upgrades and whole new systems to add over time. You only have to remember the Y2K problem to know how a strategic and operational plan must be revised because of changing circumstances.
6. Review, change and evaluate steps 1-5 before writing a new operational plan and budget.

This book is about providing practical leadership within your area of responsibility. Planning is the vehicle that provides your leadership with direction and principled focus so that you can enhance your abilities as a fair, firm and predictable role model for others to follow.

Resources

The following resources are only a few of the many useful resources that you can find in your local libraries, within your own organization, and in your local bookstores. Look for other books but also for journal articles, magazine reports, films, videos and audiocassettes. Also keep in mind how much you can learn from experts in the field, including people within your own organization!

Bauer, J.C. (1995). *Statistical analysis for decision makers in healthcare: Understanding and evaluating critical information in a competitive market.* Concord, ON: Richard Irwin.

Bradford, R.W., Duncan, P., & Tarcy, B. (1999). *Simplified strategic planning: A no-nonsense guide for busy people who want results fast*! St. Worcester, MA: Chandler House.

Bryson, J.M. (1995). *Strategic planning for public and nonprofit organizations: A guide to strengthening and sustaining organizational achievement.* San Francisco: Jossey-Bass.

Carver, J. (1990). *Boards that make a difference: A new design for leadership in non-profit and public organizations.* San Francisco: Jossey-Bass.

Drucker, P.F. (1990). *Managing the non-profit organization: Practices and principles.* New York: Harper-Collins.

Fogg, C.D. (1994). *Team-based strategic planning: A complete guide to structuring, facilitating and implementing the process.* New York: AMACOM.

Schwartz, P. (1996). *The art of the long view: Planning for the future in an uncertain world.* New York: Doubleday.

van Bommel, H. (1993). *Learn for yourself: Time management and organizing your work.* Scarborough, ON: Professional Skills Development.

Customer Service

Who Are Your Customers?

This seems to be a simple question but without a written answer everyone in an organization could design their own answer to "who are your clients/customers". For example, you probably have internal and external clients. External clients include those people who buy or use your services and/or products. They may also include your local community (its people and organizations), your suppliers and sometimes even your own competition. Internal clients may include your upper management or executive, other departments, or people in other branches of your organization located in other buildings or even other cities. If you are part of a clinical consultation team in a hospital, your clients will certainly include the patients and families for whom you care. They will also include the services and programs that refer patients to you for your input.

During this section we will use the word client. In your organization, clients could be people coming to buy or use a product or service, for example, health care. They could be students, patients, clients, suppliers, or any other label that fits your specific client group. They could also be people within your organization who use your services. The word client is somewhat incomplete to describe patients and families who are vulnerable in their needs for "service" or care. It does not describe the nature of the relationship between provider of care and receiver of care. This relationship between health professional and patient is one of vulnerability and trust. The professional enters in to a relationship that has features of a covenant or promise to fulfill a role and provide care according to certain principles. This is a higher calling than simply providing service to a client based on a contract. Although the word client is limited in the health care setting, it can provide some insight into the service aspects of the health profession.

What Does "Service Beyond Expectations" Mean?

Quite simply, the sub-title for this unit "Service beyond Expectations" is how effective client service organizations work with their clients. It is based on common sense manners and courtesy, professional attitudes and a genuine willingness to make all people feel welcome to your organization. Treating clients as if they were guests in your home will help gain a greater sense of control. This sense of control will help them deal with any of their fears, anxiety and/or needs.

Client service is not about being someone you are not. You are not expected to be in perfect humor all the time, treat everyone as if they were royalty, be a stand-up comedian or a wise old monk. You are expected to be respectful, kind and considerate of the needs of your clients and of the other people you work with. You are expected to treat other people as you would like to be treated yourself.

Should an organization expect you to behave respectfully and considerately 100% of the time? Is 95% of the time good enough? 85% of the time? Two-thirds of the time?

A few facts:

If 95% of all the phone calls that came to a university teaching hospital were answered professionally, without problems, there would still be 12,500 patients, visitors or other hospital staff (5%) who would not receive the service they want each year.

If services were 99% perfect in North America, clients would still face:

200,000 incorrect drug prescriptions.
No heat or electricity 15 minutes every day.
Drinking water that is unsafe 4 days every year.
2 plane crashes every day at Vancouver International Airport.

Organizations should expect and reward 100% effort from their staff to meet the needs of every client. You may not always get that 100% but settling for anything less could mean serious harm to your reputation.

One last statistic based on research by the Technical Assistance Research Program in Washington, D.C. (1985): 96% of unhappy customers do not report their unhappiness. For every complaint an organization receives there are 26 others (6 serious) that go unreported. Everyone who uses your organization, however, tells at least 10 other people about the service they received if they are unhappy about it, and tell 5 people if they are happy about the service. That is 5 to 10 people who find out how other people think you treat clients, how you orient new staff, how you answer your telephones, how you give directions to others, and how you treat each other. That is 5 to 10 other people who decide whether or not they will come to your organization to receive service or, perhaps, to work. **What would those other people say about you?**

There is a great Hermann cartoon that shows how some people think about service organizations in general. A client is waiting in line for service. There is a sign over the waiting line giving instructions to the client. It says: "Wait here to be tolerated." Ask yourself about the last time you went somewhere to buy a product or service or ask a question at the information desk of a hospital. Did you feel tolerated or welcomed? What do you think people think of the service in your area or department?

Guests Over for the Weekend

Imagine that you receiving a very important guest for the weekend. You do not know the person, but you have agreed to put them up for the weekend as a favor to a close friend. You know very little about the person except that they have come from outside the country and will probably be a little anxious about the new surroundings and the new people.

Exercise #1

Write out the answers to these questions:

1. What do you do to prepare your home before your guest arrives?
2. What do you tell your family or the people you live with, to prepare them for the guest?
3. What do you do if your guest does not speak English?
4. What do you do if your guest cannot eat the food you have prepared (for religious or dietary reasons)?
5. How do you make your guest comfortable in their room?
6. How do you help your company feel at home over the next three days?
7. On the second day of the weekend you find that you cannot spend as much time with your guest as you would like. What do you do so that the guest does not feel lonely?
8. You are now an expert at providing your guest with a comfortable, safe environment. How do you translate those qualities of taking care of a guest into taking care of your clients? What characteristics are similar? What characteristics do not apply and why?
9. Treating someone as a valued houseguest is an ideal form of client service. What do you need to do at work to make your client-service skills similar to how you would treat a houseguest?

   Customer service is not difficult when you do it for yourself first. Helping others usually makes us feel better so when we acknowledge that we do it for ourselves first, we are more likely to continue doing it. One day I was standing by the elevator in our hospital lobby. I have a rule that if someone looks at me, I will say hello. A gentleman in his early 60s was standing by the elevator too. He looked at me and I said, "Good morning, sir. How are you today?" His body language switched from stiff and defensive to slouched and relieved. He put his hand on my shoulder and said, "I have been visiting my wife on the cardiac floor for several weeks now. Aside from the nurses taking care of her, you are the first person to speak to me in all that time. Thank you." I had made his hospital experience less isolating and frightening. He made my hospital experience that day more joyful and energizing. We gave each other a gift and it took no extra time from his day or mine..

Harry van Bommel

Basic Customer Service Rules

The following is a summary of the basic rules of client service.

Your purpose at work is to give your client service beyond their expectations.

Rule #1: Use Common Sense in All Situations. If you are not sure what common sense applies in a specific situation, ask someone who does or read the appropriate policy or procedure in your organization.

Rule #2: Treat Everyone Like a Valued Client. If you supply services to other people in your organization, then they are your clients. Treat them with the same respect and common sense you would treat the people who come to your organization as valued clients.

Rule #3: Put Yourself in The Shoes of Your Clients. Client service is not difficult to provide if you put yourself in the shoes of your clients. Remember what it feels like to go to other organizations and be treated exceptionally well or very poorly. Model those organizations that do it well. There are no other general rules.

Customer Expectations

Now that we have the general rules for service beyond expectations, what are the realistic expectations of our clients? Your role is to meet these needs, and whenever possible, provide service that goes beyond these basic expectations. The following is a general list of reasonable expectations.

To feel welcomed
To receive timely service
To feel comfortable and safe
To get orderly and efficient service
To be understood
To be appreciated
To be recognized and remembered
To be treated with respect
To be treated as a valued individual
To be treated honestly and fairly
To belong
To feel in control

Basic Ingredients of Service

Once you understand general expectations of your clients you need to examine the specifics of your service. Does your service meet these basic ingredients of client satisfaction?

1. Your service is of high quality and available at a reasonable price.
2. You have an added value (e.g., better price than competitor, higher quality, better services, quicker service, etc.) that meets a client need or want.
3. You include methods to measure improvements in client satisfaction.
4. Your training programs or on-the-job apprenticeships help managers and staff improve their client-service skills.
5. You have a long-term goal of keeping clients so satisfied that they continue to refer your services and keep using them themselves.
6. You have an understanding that a client satisfied one day may easily be dissatisfied another day with the same service. Assume that people's satisfaction changes in order to avoid becoming inflexible in what you provide your clients.

What should you do if your services do not have all these ingredients? A few suggestions:

1. Identify what is within **your** power to change to provide service beyond expectations.
2. Identify what you can bring to your colleagues in your own area or other areas as suggested improvements to your service.
3. Identify any problems to your supervisor with at least one (or more) suggested solutions of improving your client service.

First Contact

We have been told for years that you only get one chance to make a good impression. This is especially true in our highly competitive market place. If people do not like the service they get from your organization they can usually find a competitor nearby who may treat them the way they like. This is as true for retail stores as it is for social services, schools, hospitals or professional service organizations. Even if you have a captive audience (e.g., an emergency admission to a hospital), the people you serve will tell other people what they liked about your services and what they did not like. No retail or service organization in the 1990s has completely captive clients.

Within organizations there are departments that serve the needs of people within the organization. For example, education departments, print shops, secretarial pools, cafeteria and human resources all provide service within the organization. Their good reputation depends on providing service beyond expectations and their effectiveness depends on a good working relationship with other departments.

Some tips about what to do when you first meet a client.

Introduce Yourself

Give your name (slowly and clearly) and the department you are from (if it is not obvious).

Know Their Name

Repeat the person's name so they know that you see them as a person rather than another client.

Show Respect

Use Mr./Mrs./Ms, etc. rather than their first name, or "dear", "sweety", or "honey". If they give you permission to use their first name, do so.

Smile

You cannot be expected to smile all the time but a smile when you first meet someone is a wonderful way to say "welcome" or to reassure them of your personal concern for them.

Greet Them

Say "Good Morning", "Hello" etc., to show that they are welcomed to your area or department.

Initiate

People who come to your organization (depending on the service you provide) may often be afraid of what will happen (e.g., in hospitals, service garages, and large stores). They sometimes act rude, inconsiderate or as if your whole purpose in life was to serve them before anyone else. If you anticipate their needs and respond before they ask you for something you will exceed their expectations. In return, they are more likely to treat you with more respect and consideration.

Understand Needs

People have basic needs: physical safety and comfort, a need to belong, and a need to feel worthy. Understanding these needs will help you know what tasks to do first. Obviously someone with great physical problems needs your help before someone who wants a chat to feel like they belong. All needs are important, however, and should be taken care of the best way you can under the limitations of time and resources.

Resolve Complaints

Remain calm. Stop, look and listen to what is going on. Accept that anger is normal when people are afraid or frustrated. You do not need to take verbal or physical abuse but you do need to understand that clients or other staff may be under a great deal of stress (just as you are some days). Accept responsibility to do something: refer to someone else, ask questions, restate problem in other words, agree on solutions.

Communication Tips

Once you have established a working relationship with a new client, new staff member or new departments you need to build on that relationship with effective communication skills. The following are some communication tips designed to help you constantly improve your working relationship with external and internal clients.

Body Language and Courtesy

Hold a door open for someone or hold open an elevator door. Good old-fashioned manners tell clients and other staff a great deal about you and about your organization.

Stand if someone is standing. Sit if they are sitting.

Take things out of your hands to avoid distracting yourself or the other person.

Avoid having a desk, table or other chairs between you and the client.

Look at the other person without staring. For cultural reasons, they may prefer not to have direct eye contact with you. Do not keep looking at passers-by when you are talking with someone. It is very distracting and impolite.

Sit or stand more to one side of someone rather than directly across from the person. It is more comforting and less aggressive.

Be aware that different cultures prefer that you are closer or farther away from the other person. Different cultures also have strict rules about the use of touch. Be cautious until you know what is acceptable. A safe distance is usually slightly more than an arm's length between you and the client.

Use your voice to be encouraging, soothing, clear and welcoming. Avoid being too loud or too soft. If the other person is angry, lower your voice to encourage them to lower their voice too.

If someone appears lost, ask them if they would like directions. If possible, walk a bit of the way with them to make sure that they are all right. Get to know your organization better yourself. Find out where the different departments are, where different offices are, nearby washroom and telephone, parking arrangements, etc.

Avoid talking to others, personally or by phone, with gum or food in your mouth.

Your personal appearance also says a great deal about you. If you look and feel professional, that is the image others will have of you.

Respect a person's privacy. Knock before entering their room or office. This is especially important in hospitals where privacy is often not maintained consistently.

What to Say

Tell the person what you are going to do before you do it. Ask them if they approve of whatever action or procedure you are going to take.

The word communication means "common" language. Speak so that someone understands what you are saying. Do not use big words or jargon to people who don't understand. This could save you hours of work!

Explain to people why there is a delay. Be honest. Accept responsibility for the organization rather than blaming other staff. Try to make the person as comfortable as possible during the delay.

Tell other staff members when you have seen them do something particularly well. If they have anticipated a client's needs before being asked, congratulate them. By recognizing when people do things well, they are more likely to repeat that behavior and also to start telling other people when they do something well.

"Please and "thank you" are still among the most powerful words in the English language. Use them often and genuinely. Like holding a door open for someone, these words tell other people a great deal about yourself and about your organization.

Understanding Time

One of the biggest differences between clients and staff is our understanding of time. Staff often measures time in shifts, by our agenda books or calendars. We are often planning weeks and months in advance. A client who wants to buy a product or a patient who needs a service often thinks more in minutes and hours. Recognizing the difference in time perception will help you reduce people's frustration or anger with delays, policies and procedures.

Referrals

Sometimes you will not know what to say to someone. Perhaps someone else could help them better. Refer them to someone else in your organization out of a genuine interest in helping them. People do not like to be referred because they often feel (rightly so) that they are being "dumped" on someone else. If you become more personally involved in the referral (when possible) you reduce the chances that people will feel unwelcome. For example, you may call the person you are referring the client to, to make an appointment. Then you may walk the person to their appointment (especially in large organizations where places are hard to find) and introduce them to the person they will be meeting or to their receptionist or secretary.

What Not to Say

Do not talk about clients, students, patients or families in hall ways, elevators or in public places. This happens all too often and can be very distressing to others who over hear the conversation.

Do not use phrases like: "It's a policy."

"It's just routine work."

"Don't worry. Trust me."

"This will only take a second."

"I'll be right there."

"It's not my job."

When you were last in a store, garage, hospital or restaurant and someone used these same kinds of comments how did you feel. Did you trust the person? Did you feel comforted by the knowledge that a "second" really meant "when I have time for you"? Were you happier knowing that "policy" meant you had to do it their way without explanation? Did your last blood test feel any better knowing that is was "only routine"? Did you care whose job something was when you were in a hurry, in pain or afraid?

When People Say "X", They Mean..

Whenever we talk about clients and other staff it almost sounds like it is them against us. We are all clients nearly everyday of our lives. What is it we all want? How can we understand what other people want?

Here are some tips.

If Someone Says:	They May Mean:
Listen to me.	Pay attention. Understand me. Please listen to what I have to say. I'm afraid/in a hurry/frustrated, please help.
I want dependable service.	I need to know you will meet your commitments. Do not tell me something will be done by 4 p.m. when you know it will not be done. I would rather wait longer as long as your stated deadline is accurate.
Give me correct information.	Don't guess at the right answer. If you don't know or have to check, okay, but don't give me the wrong information.
Do you know your job?	I depend on your knowledge. Please offer suggestions or practical advice.
I need consistent service.	Be dependable. Treat me like the important client I am.
I expect action.	Don't make me wait unnecessarily. I know you can't always meet my demands, but be as responsive as possible.
I can't hold (on the phone).	I am calling long distance; or don't put me on hold again. Please ask to put me on hold and wait for my answer.
Who is your supervisor?	You are not listening to me. You are not meeting my expectations. (They may also feel more in control if they talk to a supervisor or they may think they more likely to get what they want from someone who has more authority.)

Managing Complaints

There are basic techniques to help manage people's objections. Good techniques will only work if you demonstrate a genuine attitude that says: "This person has a real (legitimate, relevant, serious) objection and I can help." Otherwise your clients will sense that you are only complying with some organizational policy on how to deal with complaints. Even that is usually better than not dealing with the complaint effectively at all.

Dealing with complaints effectively often means that you keep your valuable clients and they refer their family and friends to you as well!

Listen to the specifics of the person's objections. When you are not clear about what the objection is, ask open-ended questions that cannot be answered with a yes or no; questions that begin with who, what, where, when, why, how, versus close-ended questions – did, do, is, will. Do not assume you know their reason for complaining. Ask! They may surprise you with something that is easily resolved.

Who is the person you were talking with?
What can I do to help?
Where were you when this incident happened?
When could you come in to help resolve this problem?

Always provide an immediate response. This is how you can show the person you understand their situation and can empathize with their difficulty. **Many lawsuits against organizations involve the person saying "No one listened to me or cared about my problem."**

State your response in clear and positive terms. Tell them what you can do to help:
Refer her to Ms. Jones who can best help her best because…
Do some research into the matter and call them at 11:15 with some kind of response (always call back even to tell them you need more time).

Do not provide unnecessary information and conversation. Be positive and service oriented by sticking to the details except to make them feel comfortable with you. Ask them for their approval for any action you have suggested.

Dealing with People in Difficult Situations

Every client is different. When you recognize these differences you can provide people with excellent service while also enjoying your work more.

Let's look at four behavior styles clients often demonstrate in difficult situations that require some special attention and understanding. When we know what to do we will deal more effectively with our clients.

The Assertive Person

An assertive person knows what they want and how to get it. When you have contact with an assertive person, it is important to initially be passive and listen closely to what is said. Once you understand what is needed you should become specific and direct. Normally you do not need to ask an assertive person many questions because they make it clear what they want. Closed questions will allow you to manage the conversation. Assertive people are interested in quick and efficient results.

Assertive people are easy to work with if you can meet their immediate needs. Sometimes, however, when dealing with an assertive person you may need to raise your own assertiveness level to simply manage the conversation. Sometimes it is difficult to build rapport with an assertive person because they may not be interested in exchanging pleasantries. It is important not to take this personally. They are simply there to get the job done efficiently.

Summary: How to Respond to Assertive People

- Be passive and listen until you understand the problem or request.
- Be friendly, but specific and direct in your statements.
- Use closed questions to manage the conversation. "Did, do, will, is" are the words that start closed questions which result in yes or no answers and speed the conversation along.
- If your voice is soft, speak slightly louder. Standing up can increase the volume of your voice and your tone of assertiveness.
- Don't get upset if you have difficulty establishing rapport.
- Responsive service will satisfy the assertive person.

The Aggressive or Angry Person

Managing an aggressive or angry person is a great opportunity to show off your skills. If done properly, it can be very rewarding. Your body language can help you handle the person in a professional way. For example, by standing slightly to the side of the person, rather than directly across from them, you give an air of working with the person – not against them.

Diffuse their complaint or request by offering your understanding and sympathy (not by arguing), offering specific help and providing choices.

"I don't blame you for being upset."

"You are right. You were promised and it hasn't happened. Let's get this problem solved now."

"We've made an error. This time we will do it right."

"I'm sorry you are not satisfied. What can I do now to help the situation?"

If you cannot meet the demands of an aggressive or angry person because they are unwilling or unable to listen to you, you may have to advise your supervisor and ask them to deal with the person. Sometimes a person will only respond to someone in a higher position of authority. Don't take their attitude personally! Such people have learned through previous experience that dealing with someone in management or senior management is the fastest way to get results.

Summary: How to Respond to Aggressive or Irate People

- Listen, sympathize and offer understanding.
- Agree with the person if they are right.
- Promise to take corrective action and then do it.
- Advise the person of your actions and provide them options to choose from (gives them sense of control they probably feel they have not had yet).
- Remain courteous and provide assurance of your genuine wish to help them.

  If you cannot meet the demands of the person:
- Decide if someone else (a colleague, supervisor, other department) can help this person. Do not refer the person without telling them why you think this other person can help them.
- If there is no one else who can help and you have no way to assist the person, be honest with the person and ask them what they would like you to do. Sometimes you cannot satisfy people and they may still be unhappy, but if you remain courteous and honest they may vent their anger in a more appropriate direction.

The Violent Person

Violent people typically strike out when they are totally frustrated and feel unable to do anything about that frustration. People may also become violent as a result of illness (physical or psychiatric). Your instincts may be powerful indicators or potential problem behavior. If you feel uneasy with someone, take the following measures:

Do

Get necessary help from other staff first.

Tell the person you understand that they are totally frustrated. Quickly and calmly tell them you will try to help them in any way you can but that you cannot help them if they want to hurt you or destroy any property.

Stay in an open area rather than getting them into a small office. Stay in reach of help and avoid backing yourself into a corner or away from a door. If possible, keep a table, chair or desk between you and the person.

Be honest and clear about what you can do to help them. Keep your voice low and firm. Take charge of the situation.

Use an "open" body position to show that you are not aggressive yourself. Keep your hands open and away from your body. Keep the other person more than an arm's length distance away from you even if that means backing up yourself. Try to move towards an exit without making sudden moves (except in emergency situations where you need to run away). Avoid standing directly across from the person since this is often seen as aggressive. Stand with your body slightly to the side so that you do not need to keep eye contact the whole time. This encourages the other person to also reduce the intensity of their eye contact with you.

Recognize that you cannot prepare for such a situation on the spot. Plan in advance with your colleagues what you will do in such a situation. Practice your plan and get the advice of experienced people in your organization.

Don't

Do not let a situation get out of hand. An ounce of prevention up front can save both the person and you a great deal of effort and energy.

Do not ignore warning signs that the person is about to get out of control. They may begin to yell, swear loudly, clench their fist, move around a lot, or their face may turn red quickly. If they are under the influence of alcohol or drugs be extra cautious. Deal with the situation as calmly and clearly as you can but recognize that your heart will beat faster, your breathing rate will increase and you will feel flushed.

Do not threaten, abuse, touch or "corner" the person. When possible, continue to talk with the person while someone else calls for help. Do not try to be a hero. Ask for help as soon as possible.

Do not see patients alone or offer hours when the clinic or office area is deserted.

The Passive Person

Passive people are usually easy to service. Satisfied people are often passive and, therefore, a professional goal is to provide the kind of service that encourages people to work easily with you in the future. They know they will receive the service they need and, therefore, do not need to be assertive or aggressive.

Over many contacts with the same person, they may switch from being aggressive or assertive to passive. When this happens it may be a signal that the person is satisfied with the service they are receiving. Most people want "hassle-free" service. Most people dislike having to be assertive or aggressive.

On the other hand, it may be very difficult to know if you have met the needs of a truly passive client. It is hard to know what they expect in the way of service. If they are unsatisfied, they just leave and never return. They will not refer other people to your organization. You may never know what went wrong. However, when you identify them correctly and pay them some extra attention, they will shine and may become your strongest allies. They are so used to being "invisible" and ignored that your extra efforts will make them feel like the valued clients we all want to be.

Summary: How to Respond to the Passive Person

- Listen carefully to the person's request or complaint.
- Provide choices of various actions to give them a sense of control.
- Add the personal touch to make them feel that they are welcomed.

Customer Evaluations

You will never know if your organization is providing service beyond expectations if you do not ask the people you serve. There are many different ways to find out what clients and other staff think about your services, for example, client rating scales, focus groups, public meetings, or one-to-one interviews. In health care, patients, families and students may be reluctant to give honest feedback because they are dependent on the group they may be evaluating. "Arms length" evaluation must be utilized, with constant reassurance of anonymity and security of care and service.

The following are a few suggestions you may want to consider for your area or department.

1. Simply ask people what you have done well and not so well within a specific time period.
2. Ask them to fill out a very brief survey at the end of their visit to find out what they think.
3. Interview a random sample for their comments that you publish in your organization's newsletter.
4. Ask them to fill out compliment-complaint forms.
5. Distribute 5 to 10 health care facility/team-size cards to each client who can give one to any staff person who shows excellent service. At the end of each month the people who have "x" number of cards receive a day off with pay or a special prize for them and/or their family.
6. Do a random sample questionnaire with people who have used your services in the past year.
7. Provide a suggestion box on ways to improve and recognize your service.
8. Have a clients' advisory committee meet 2-4 times a year to advise the organization on communication skills and services.

9. Commission an independent audit of your services from a client-centered perspective versus a organizational, financial, or administrative perspective.
10. Use a client rating scale. These scales can be as simple as a five-point scale to a more complicated 100% scale (from 0% to 100% satisfaction) depending on the specific needs of your organization and the time clients will spend helping you evaluate service.

    Often on written surveys with these scales there is also room left for written comments to such questions as:
    What did you like best about our service?
    What did you like least about our service?
    What improvements or changes would you like us to make?
    Any other comments or suggestions?
11. Organize a focus group. Focus groups are a random or pre-selected group of clients who come to a meeting to respond to new ideas around client service. Focus groups concentrate on specific ideas and programs to help an organization understand what its clients truly want in the way of services.
12. Some organizations deal with a large community of clients. Sometimes it may be useful to present new ideas at a public meeting to get immediate feedback from a large cross section of your clients.
13. Counting specific statistics such as number of clients served and number of complaints or compliments is another objective tool for measuring some forms of client satisfaction.

When I was working as the Customer Relations Consultant at a large urban hospital, I had the opportunity to coordinate a number of efforts to measure the satisfaction of patients and families with the care that they received while in the hospital. The interesting part was that regardless of how we measured their satisfaction, information, or the lack of it, had the greatest impact on patient satisfaction. Patients told us that they needed to know what to expect while in the hospital, how to care for themselves at home and the long-term impact of their health problem.
Beverley Powell-Vinden

Action Plan

It is important to take the information from this section and make an action plan for yourself about what things you would like to continue doing and what you want to do differently.

Idea	How to Do It?	Do it When?	How to Know if Successful?
Your ideas (e.g., Find out what clients think of us now.)	Client satisfaction survey of next 100 clients including written and verbal methods.	For the next 2 weeks.	100% responses of satisfaction or better. Repeat survey twice a year.

Providing Staff Service

Earlier in this section we discussed what a client could reasonably expect in the way of service. There is a reverse skill that I highly recommend. Just as clients want to receive service that fulfils their needs, staff also appreciates it when clients return the favor. Try being a "client beyond expectations". In large organizations, many staff are in fact "clients" for/of other staff. Staffs in organizations like to feel the following:

- To feel welcomed
- To feel comfortable and safe
- To be understood
- To feel important
- To be appreciated
- To be recognized and remembered
- To be treated with respect
- To be treated as a valued individual
- To be treated honestly and fairly
- To feel they are in control

To increase your own likelihood of receiving service beyond expectations in your own organization or in other organizations where you pay for products or use a service, try a few of the following things to improve the service you receive.

Learn Names

If you go to the same places often for products or service, learn the people's names and address them by name. People like to be remembered since they meet so many people during a day that do not know them. Also help them remember your name so that they can say "Hello Harry" (or whatever) when they see you in the corridor or on the street.

Understand Job

If you understand the people's job, including their busy times, some of their job stresses, and their interests, then you can build a genuine rapport with them. Recognizing their difficulties and strengths means your long-term relationship will constantly improve. Joining staff of other teams for coffee or lunch occasionally will enhance an atmosphere of mutual exchange.

Try to go to the organization, department or clinic during slower times so you can chat a bit, find out about special sales, upcoming events, etc. You do not have to become a "gossip" but a genuine interest in the other person's work is usually returned with better service. Would not you serve people with an extra bit of energy and enthusiasm if you felt they were interested in what you do?

Special Effort

For people who serve you especially well, make an extra effort to thank them, tell them what you liked about their service, and compare them favorably to other people you deal with.

Summary

There are only a few general rules for providing excellent client service. They are easy to memorize and should be your basis for providing "Service Beyond Expectations".

Your purpose at work is to give your clients service beyond their expectations.

Rule #1: Use common sense in all situations. If you are not sure what common sense applies in a specific situation, ask someone who does or read the appropriate policy or procedure in your organization.

Rule #2: Treat everyone like a valued client. If you supply services to other people in your organization, then they are your clients. Treat them with the same respect and common sense you would treat the people who come to your organization as valued clients.

Rule #3: Put yourself in the shoes of your clients. Client service is not difficult to provide if you put yourself in the shoes of your clients. Remember what it feels like to go to other organizations and be treated exceptionally well or very poorly. Model those organizations that do it well. There are no other general rules.

Now that you know the rules for service beyond expectations you need to know what general expectations your clients realistically have of your organization. Your role is to meet these needs and whenever possible provide service that goes beyond these basic expectations. Your clients reasonably expect:

- To feel welcomed
- To feel comfortable and safe
- To be understood
- To feel important
- To be appreciated
- To be recognized and remembered
- To be treated with respect
- To be treated as a valued individual
- To be treated honestly and fairly
- To feel they are in control

Resources

The following resources are only a few of the many useful resources that you can find in your local libraries, within your own organization, and in your local bookstores. Look for other books but also for journal articles, magazine reports, films, videos and audiocassettes. Also keep in mind how much you can learn from experts in the field, including people within your own organization!

Baker, S. K. (1998). *Managing patient expectations: The art of finding and keeping loyal patients.* San Francisco: Jossey-Bass.

Barlow, J., & Moller, C. (1996). *A complaint is a gift: Using customer feedback as a strategic tool.* San Francisco: Berrett-Koehler.

Blanchard, K., & Bowles, S.M. (1993). *Raving fans: A revolutionary approach to customer service.* New York: William Morrow.

Brown, S.,A., Martenfeld, M.B.,& Gould, A. (1990). *Creating the service culture: Strategies for Canadian health care.* Scarborough, ON: Prentice Hall.

Clemmer, J. with Sheehy, B. (1990). *Firing on all cylinders: The service/quality system for high-powered corporate performance.* Toronto: Macmillan of Canada.

Gale, B.T., & Wood, R.C. (1994). *Managing customer value: Creating quality and service that clients can see.* New York: Free Press.

Gerson, RF. (1993). *Measuring customer satisfaction.* Menlo Park, CA: Crisp Publications.

Katz, J.M., & Green, E. (1996). *Managing quality: A guide to system-wide performance management in health care.* New York: Mosby.

Leebov, W., Scott, G., & Olson, L. (1998). *Achieving impressive customer service: 7 strategies for the health care manager.* San Francisco: Jossey-Bass.

Sherman, S. G., & Sherman, V. C. (1998). *Total customer satisfaction: A comprehensive approach for health care providers.* San Francisco: Jossey-Bass.

Stamatis, D.H. (1996). *Total quality management in healthcare: Implementation strategies for optimum results.* Burr Ridge, IL: Irwin.

9. Life-Long Skills

Stress Management

Time Management

Stress Management

This section is designed to help you understand what causes your stress and how you can deal with it in a productive and positive way.

Stress is inevitable. There are positive and negative stresses. Some of the positive stresses we accept daily are:

- Adventures, holidays
- Self-motivated change
- A new relationship
- Risks for possible personal gains
- Raising children

There are also negative stresses which may, or may not, lead to positive changes:

- Stagnation, powerlessness
- Fear, anger, conflict
- Change forced by others
- Believing we have limited choices

The principle difference between positive and negative stress is our perception of the stress and our personal view about whether or not we have some control over that stress. For some people conflict is always seen as an opportunity for change or improvement while others concentrate only on their perceived powerlessness. For some people adventures in the "great outdoors" are chances to learn new skills while for others, adventures are just another way of describing an outdoor torture perpetuated by the knowledgeable against those of us who enjoy a good movie and popcorn!

The stress cycle for positive and negative stresses is the same. It begins with a specific situation and your thoughts and beliefs about whether or not you think the situation is good or bad for you. These thoughts lead to specific feeling. People often believe that their thoughts and feelings cannot be controlled or changed. This is why people sometimes feel overwhelmed by relatively minor inconveniences. Based on your feelings you are likely to follow an action. If you have faced the situation before, you may respond in the same way (whether healthy or unhealthy). Managing stress is about having control over your thoughts, beliefs, feelings and actions regardless of the situation. This is easier said than done but does work with practice and determination.

People in health care are a stressed group. There are so many requirements of the managers. They have to be clearly prepared to stop on a dime, switch directions, have fabulous planning skills, terrific communication skills, be able to leap tall buildings. If the stress levels on them are too great, it suppresses their positive behaviors and spills out onto their staff. So we constantly monitor this stress through management forums where the president asks the question, "What's cooking?" We have some assertive people who will stand up and say, "Staff is really feeling the pinch, they're stressed out and it's impacting on the clients in some negative ways. It is also impacting on other staff members who may not be dealing with clients but who are supporting the clinical services". The quick response was, "let's collect some information." We did a rough survey and sure enough people were experiencing stress in a wide variety of ways and we are looking at ways to reduce those stresses and it is sort of like the real estate industry–the answer seems to be location, location, location. I think for stress, it is communication, communication, communication. And as much as we communicate, it is still not enough. It seems like a lot of staff are asking for communication sessions where they are not getting information as much as having an opportunity to express how they feel. And that is a tough managerial skill–not to talk; but to listen. Very tough. I see that as an extremely important given the whole atmosphere of rapid change. So the uncertainly levels climb sky high in an organization and that has to be monitored very, very carefully.

Larry Lewis

Recognizing When You Are Under a Lot of Stress

Watch for some of the following signs to warn you about excessive stress (whether positive or negative). Experiencing some of these stresses once or twice is common. However, if you experience some of these stresses regularly, then your stress may be hazardous to your physical, mental and emotional health.

- You are working late more often than not, or harder than you know is really required.
- You are having problems making any decisions, large or small.
- You are constantly making "safe" choices, rather than taking realistic risks.
- You use an increased amount of alcohol, drugs or cigarettes.
- You are over or under eating (a change from your usual).
- Your speech or writing patterns have become vague, disconnected.
- You experience an increased level of anxiety, worry over relatively trivial concerns.

- You constantly repeat the same topic at meetings, in conversations, even though you know the point is not particularly important.
- You experience inappropriate anger, hostility or outbursts of temper.
- You experience feelings of sadness and crying.
- You are constantly putting yourself or others down.
- You become overly concerned about your health.
- You have greater difficulty sleeping.
- You begin to confuse or forget dates, places, times or other details which you remembered easily before.
- You are having difficulty in getting along with people.
- You just know that something is wrong but are not sure what it is.

Exercise #1

Review the previous list of stress signals you may have in your life right now. Put a check mark beside those signs that apply most specifically to you.

Try to identify major stresses in your life now that cause these signs to appear:

Which of these stresses is most dominant in your life right now? You may choose this example for Exercise #3 to identify ways of dealing with this stress.

Ways to Start Dealing with Stress

When I was 23 years old, a drunk driver ran his car into my body. Over the course of the next 8 years, I began to lose functioning in my arms, hands and legs and various other systems in my body became progressively compromised. I lost my ability to continue in graduate studies, to work part time, to walk any distance, to sit, to stand. I lost everything in my life. One day in abject sorrow, I searched for something that was mine alone that had not been taken or diminished since the accident. It occurred to me that I was abundant with suffering. From that day on I studied myself and how I suffered and how those around me suffered.

It was in the years of losing everything that I found an ability to let most things roll off of me. Strong emotions created physical pain for me and I soon learned that I was not allowed freewheeling sorrow. I needed to tend to my emotional and spiritual needs daily. So I began at the end of the day to go to bed early to think over how I had greeted the day and it me. I would take note of what hurt, what helped, what made me laugh and what made me cry. I would balance out each day with music, with time to think, with praying for the day to end, so that tomorrow, if I was lucky and slept well, I might have less pain.

As I learned to walk and negotiate the world again, I kept many of the lessons learned at the center of my being. I fell often. My friends would often walk several steps ahead before they realized that I was "missing in action" and would come back and search for me. I could not change what was but I could change how I responded to such incidents. I asked people not to get upset but to help me laugh as they picked me up and brushed me off. The pain and stress was quite overwhelming but if I let it rule me, it would cause me more harm. To this day one of my colleagues can be heard to say that I always find everything funny. It isn't that I find all things funny but that in the sorrow, there is something profound and sacred about human struggle and integrity. For me humor captures this and allows me to conquer that which threatens to destroy me.

While I still live with pain and a diminished capacity, I am able to accomplish a great deal. I do this through stress and time management. For instance, while working full time, I did a Ph.D. I have trouble sitting after a long day so I found a distance education program that allowed me to study at home. Pacing and balance became the basic stipulations to lead my life. If I pushed myself too far my pain would increase and my body would lose functioning. I wish sometimes that others had the fortune of knowing the limits I know so that they might be more kind to themselves. We are hard on ourselves, others are hard on us and life can be hard. If we do not start with our own self-care, we will eventually pay the price–now or ten years from now when our body gives out.

Michèle Chaban

The following suggestions reflect a wide range of alternatives for dealing with stress. Choose some of the following techniques to add to the stress management skills you already have. Try to practices your choices regularly. Some of these suggestions can help you resolve short-term stresses immediately. Improvise these tips to fit your own situation. These are not golden rules as much as helpful techniques.

Work on developing the capacity to recognize when you are under stress. If you don't recognize the stress you are under, you will never deal with it well.

When you are facing a stressful situation try to isolate what the particular stress is. Can changing your perception reduce the stress? For example, many people think going to the dentist has to be stressful. Can you visit your dentist with a big grin, ask them how they are doing, ask them to educate you about what they are going to do, tell them you are nervous and ask them what other patients do when they are nervous? Use the stressful situation as an opportunity to learn, to laugh and to understand why the situation is stressful.

Laugh! Few stress reduction techniques work as well as laughter. Laughter relaxes you physically (15 minutes of belly laughing equals 5-6 hours of meditation according to Buddhist monks) and laughter relaxes your mind. Laughter is also contagious and your family members or colleagues can join in the laughter and make you feel even better. It is a myth to believe that you must have a reason to laugh. Just start for no reason at all but to feel good.

You cannot control some things. There is a famous prayer that reads: Grant me the serenity to accept the things I cannot change, the courage to change the things that I can, and the wisdom to know the difference. An overbearing boss or subordinate is unlikely to change until you are able to resolve some specific conflicts. In the meantime you do have control over how you react to any situation so use your sense of humor to help you get through.

Ineffective use of your time is a leading cause of stress. Don't procrastinate as much as you usually do. We spend 80% of our time doing only 20% of the things we need to do, e.g., rearranging our desks or going through our mail three times before deciding what to do with it. Learn new time management techniques to use your valuable time wisely.

60-hour work weeks are not productive so cut back. Research shows that productivity drops among people under high stress, but peaks under moderate stress. Long weeks are sometimes necessary but good time management means you should have fewer of these long weeks.

We need friendships to reduce stress. Make an effort to improve a few supportive relationships. Remember friendships take time. People who have supportive relationships suffer less under moderate and severe stress than people who are socially isolated. For example, social isolation is the method we use to punish prisoners.

Schedule short breaks in your day. For example, physicians are wise to leave one or two 15-minute breaks in their office schedule as a safety measure against an increasing backlog as the day progresses.

Not every argument is worth winning. Give in when you have little to gain. Save your energy for what is really important but do not let little irritations build up to a major problem. Talk things out with people before problems escalate. Learn conflict resolution skills to minimize conflicts.

When you are uptight it is important to breath deeply and to stretch your muscle groups. You can also tense and relax your muscles starting with your arms, face and neck, shoulders, abdomen, and finally the legs. These Exercises can be done while you are sitting at your desk, while standing at a bus stop, or relaxing at home.

Don't try to control family members, friends or colleagues. Be supportive instead of judgmental. A supportive environment is much less stressful than one where people play power games.

Take a warm shower or bath to soothe tense muscles and provide a few moments of heavenly privacy.

For immediate relief of stress try to take ten minutes away from the situation for a quick walk. Coffee breaks filled with coffee and sugar treats tend to add to the stress. A quick walk outside, or to another area within a building, will increase your energy, clear your mind, and give you some needed perspective.

If your organization has a library a quick trip to read a magazine article is a wonderful way to hide from reality for a short time.

When things pile up to unmanageable levels, break up major projects into workable units with realistic time frames. You can accomplish all major projects, or combination of projects, if you begin with the priority items and accomplish the other parts of the project as required.

If you are worried about a small problem with a colleague, spend some time talking with that person and telling them how their behavior (and not them personally) is affecting you.

Stop comparing yourself with everyone else. No matter how hard you try you probably cannot paint like Emily Carr, sing like Lena Horne, write like James Michener or win the Nobel Peace prize. You may be able to do some things exceptionally well, but not everything and that's okay! So don't put yourself down if you are not as good as someone else; they can't do everything well either.

When one teaches stress management and similar programs, people routinely send you poems and stories to help you make your points more clearly. I received this anonymous poem recently:
Work as if you didn't need the money.
Love as if you never have been hurt before.
Dance as if no one is watching.
I would add: Help create a loving memory for someone today.
Harry van Bommel

Learn to feel comfortable talking about your problems, hopes and fears. A close friend is a valuable resource, but avoid dumping on the same person all the time. Make sure you also take the time to listen to your friend's concerns.

- Read a good book.
- Watch a good comedy on television or rent a video.
- Get physical. Gardening, walking or dancing are great ways to boost your energy.
- Take a daily music break – with eyes closed sit back and listen to 10 minutes of

soothing music. If you play a musical instrument, take time everyday to play a tune or two.

Avoid doing everything quickly. High stress people often try to do too much within the same 24 hours we all have. Slow down and take time to reflect – North Americans spend too much time doing and not enough time thinking!

Instead of an after-work cocktail, try ice water or juice followed by a 10-minute quiet time, relaxing with your eyes closed. There is great peace when the world is quiet for a short time. This gives you the energy to spend quality time with your family, friends or by yourself later on.

When you arrive home from work and you need to unwind, explain to your spouse and children that you need one half-hour to yourself before being together. If you explain your need your family will probably help. Make sure you give other people in your family the same consideration when they need some quiet time.

Try to make work and living areas as pleasant and comfortable as possible with pictures, plants and ornaments. Personalize your work area.

One of the greatest stress releasers is a big hug from a family member, friend or trusted colleague. Silent empathy is a great healer. Begin by giving other people that kind of support if they feel comfortable with it.

Learn to say no. Ask for time to consider a request. This allows an opportunity to decide if you really want to and can take on an additional task.

These suggestions are not a cure for stress. They are short term coping techniques to help you through some rough spots. At some point you must recognize what your stresses are and develop a whole range of techniques for dealing with them in an ongoing way. Remember your sense of humor. The perspective that you have of stressful situations in your past can provide great background for humorous stories or stories for teaching other people new skills. (Remember that horrible date you once had, the day everything at work went berserk, the vacation trip that failed before you even left!) Ask yourself what will this situation mean in 10 years?

Physicians experience a lot of stress and aren't readily available to see this in themselves or tell other people about it. Our medical education still gives the message that we must be effective and cope all the time and that to do otherwise would mean that we aren't good doctors. Team members working with physicians can help them identify their stress by role modeling stress management and good self-care, and by gently labeling signs of stress they may see in their colleague. Encouraging people to be gentle with themselves can also help a lot.

Elizabeth Latimer

Physically Coping with Stress

Deep Breathing

Deep breathing, taking a brisk walk, doing relaxation exercises, tensing and relaxing our muscles are all ways to immediately relieve the pressure of stress. Deep breathing is one of the easiest techniques to master since it is useful at work, at home, while caught in traffic, and at times when you cannot do any of the other techniques.

Deep breathing can take only 10 seconds or last a half-hour, depending on the circumstances. Regardless of the length, use it to the fullest and enjoy the feelings. Here's one method of deep breathing.

1. Place your hands on your abdomen, right below the navel. The fingertips of each hand should touch one another.
2. Breathe in through your nose; it is healthier than breathing through your mouth.
3. Inhale slowly; as you do, push the abdomen out as though it was a balloon expanding. With your eyes open or closed "feel" the air passing through your nostrils.
4. As the abdomen expands, your diaphragm will move downward, allowing fresh air to enter the bottom of your lungs. Keep your back straight to aid the process of maximizing your breathing. Exhale through your mouth.
5. As you continue to breathe imagine the air filling your lungs, your abdomen and, with each new breath, imagine the air filling your arms, legs and every part of your body. This will help you to concentrate on the various parts of your body and should help you to relax each area.
6. When you feel comfortable, take deeper breaths and hold the breath for a count of 3-5 seconds. Do the same when you exhale your breath, hold for 3-5 seconds before taking your next breath.
7. Picture yourself in a place where you feel particularly comfortable (e.g., on a beach, on a nature walk, in a favorite room, playing a sport, in a childhood memory). Pick just one spot to concentrate on while you continue to deep breathe for as long as you wish.
8. When you are ready, slowly begin to stretch your muscles as if you were yawning. As you feel more relaxed you can begin to return to "the real world".

The definition of stress? Working twelve hour shifts on a general surgery floor on weekends with little medical coverage. Sometimes, it would be all I could do to cope with my own patient assignment, let alone constantly ringing call bells, never ending admissions and discharges and patients in crisis. When my own stress level was high and I felt

like I couldn't handle any more, I would escape to the staff washroom or lounge and take a minute or so to deep breathe. While this didn't leave me 100% refreshed, I was at least able to regain some control of my stress so I could get back to caring for my patients effectively.
Beverley Powell-Vinden

Negative Stress

One of the most effective steps towards managing negative stress is learning to recognize what causes your negative stress. Each person's list is unique and individual. Think of your friend who never gets upset in traffic jams but faints at the sight of blood.

Exercise #2

Pick a day, or a few days, and list the ordinary, day-in, day-out little annoyances that seem inevitable at work or at home. Also list those stresses that are constant in your life (e.g.,, an unhappy working relationship, financial concerns, car problems). Once you have listed some of these stresses, develop some actions that you could try to minimize, prevent or conquer these stresses. Put a star beside techniques or actions that really work for you. Use your imagination!

Stress	What You Can Do

For Particularly Difficult Stresses

Use this sample form to help you resolve some of your really difficult stresses that seem "hopeless". Keep in mind that all stresses are an opportunity to learn about yourself and to discover ways to deal creatively with those stresses. People have gone through concentration camps, wars, the death of a spouse or child, and physical disabilities and many of them have survived and grown stronger. So can you! See the "Resolving Conflicts" section for added suggestions.

Stress

Overcome

How can you overcome this stress?

Avoid

How can you get away from or prevent the stress from happening again?

Accept

How can you live with the stress if it cannot be overcome?
How can you build up a resistance to this stress?
How can you change yourself or your perceptions about this stress?
What is the best option in this case?

I'd Pick More Daisies

The following is a quote attributed to Brother Jeremiah. It has become very popular, however, we were unable to trace its origin. Whenever this was written the words and sentiments are timeless.

If I had my life to live over again, I'd try to make more mistakes next time. I would relax. I would limber up. I would be sillier than I have been this trip. I know of very few things I would take seriously. I would take more trips. I would climb more mountains, swim more rivers and watch more sunsets. I would do more walking and looking. I would eat more ice cream and less beans. I would have more actual troubles and fewer imaginary ones. You see, I am one of those people who lives cautiously and sensibly and sanely hour after hour, day after day. Oh, I've had my moments; and if I had it to do over again, I'd have more of them. In fact, I'd try to have nothing else. Just moments, one after another instead of living so many years ahead of each day. I have been one of those people who never go anywhere without a thermometer, a hot water bottle, a gargle, a raincoat, aspirin and a parachute. If I had it to do over again, I would go places, do things, and travel lighter than I have.

If I had my life to live over, I would start barefooted early in the spring and stay that way later in the fall. I would play hooky more. I wouldn't make such good grades except by accident. I would ride on more merry-go-rounds. I'd pick more daisies.

Brother Jeremiah

Exercise #3

To complete this exercise, imagine yourself nearing the end of your life. Write your own "If I had my life to live over again" in the space below. It is a real gift to be able to write this now and to make those changes you want to make.

If I had my life to live over again I would:

Things I want to do before I die:

Summary

It is difficult to summarize the best ways of dealing with stress. Each of us copes in different ways with the same stresses. The following summary reflects a personal bias. Use those parts of the summary that fit your personal style and use the following page to add your own summary.

Few people can deal with stress alone. We need the support of other people. Therefore we need to have love and friendship in our lives. If you have these things in your life then you must constantly work to maintain and improve them. If you do not have love and friendship in your life right now then you need to develop it by showing how you care about yourself and how you can care for other people.

Make firm commitments to your family and friends and spend time with them to be supportive and to receive support. Encourage honest and open communication between you. Try to be nonjudgmental and accept people as they are while you try to show them alternatives to the way they do things. Accept their ideas and suggestions for modifying your life as well.

People cannot support and encourage you without you caring about yourself. Identify what stresses you have and what strategies you can use to prevent or deal with these stresses. People respect someone who has the self-esteem to try new things to solve old problems.

Have more fun by laughing and being with positive people. Take time to do something by yourself every day. For example, read for a few minutes, meditate or pray, and reflect on the good things in your life for which you can be thankful. Make an effort to think of something special you can do for each day to brighten someone else's day such as bringing in some home made cookies, sharing a new joke, lending them a video of a favorite film, or bringing someone a fresh rose.

Make an effort to reflect daily on the positive qualities you possess and your daily successes, no matter how small they seem. Watch your "self talk", the messages that you say to yourself. Try to reduce the negative, for example, "I could have chosen different words but I handled myself well in a difficult situation", instead of, "What a blunder I made".

We constantly hear about living a better lifestyle. Choose parts of a healthier lifestyle that make you comfortable. Perhaps it is walking a bit each day, having only one ice cream instead of two, or perhaps cutting down on fatty foods. If you choose not to change your lifestyle then try other activities to compensate, e.g., relaxation Exercises, better time management, or resolving conflicts.

You cannot prevent all negative stress, but you can have fun trying to minimize it!

Resources

The following resources are only a few of the many useful resources that you can find in your local libraries, within your own organization, and in your local bookstores. Look for other books but also for journal articles, magazine reports, films, videos and audiocassettes. Also keep in mind how much you can learn from experts in the field, including people within your own organization!

Bernstein, A.J., & Craft Rozen, S. (1994). *Sacred bull: The inner obstacles that hold you back at work and how to overcome them.* Toronto: Wiley & Sons.

Blumenfield, L., & Gawain, S. (Eds.). (1994). *The big book of relaxation: Simple techniques to control the excess stress in your life.* Roslyn, NY: Relaxation Company.

Cherniss, G. (1995). *Beyond burnout: How teachers, nurses, therapists, and lawyers recover from stress and disillusionment.* New York: Routledge.

Davis, M. (1997). *Relaxation & stress reduction workbook.* New York: Fine Communications.

Newman, J.E. (1992). *How to stay cool, calm and collected when the pressure's on: A stress control plan for health care people.* New York: AMACOM.

Noer, D.M. (1995). *Healing the wounds: Overcoming the trauma of layoffs and revitalizing downsized organizations.* San Francisco: Jossey-Bass.

Powell, J.R., & George-Warren, H. (1994). *The working woman's guide to managing stress.* New York: Prentice Hall.

Stearns, A.K., & Lamplugh, R. (1995). *Living through job loss: Coping with the emotional effects of job loss and rebuilding your future.* Saint Loius, MO: Fireside.

Warner, J. (1999). *Creative time management for the new Millennium* Stamford, CT: Hannacroix Creek.

Yeomans, W.N. (1996). *7 survival skills for a reengineered world.* New York: NAL-Dutton

Time Management

This section is not designed to totally change your present methods for managing your time and organizing your work. The following information is not a specific "method" that you must follow to the letter. Instead, the information in this section is to help you to build on your current time management and organizational skills.

Do we need to manage our time? According to a report on CBCs The Journal (July

- 5, 1988) we spend, on average:
- 5 years of our life in line-ups
- 6 months waiting for red lights
- 4 years doing tasks in the kitchen
- 8 months looking at junk mail
- 2 years playing telephone tag trying to speak with others
- Nearly 1/3 of our life sleeping
- Nearly 1/3 of our life working and studying

Compare that to:
4 minutes of each day talking with our spouse
30 seconds per day in meaningful discussion with our children
Little or no time spent doing creative problem solving

In this section we will spend some time understanding how we use our time now and how we can use it better in the future. The key to successful time management and organizing our work is to **take control**. To take control means you need to understand that your day may include work, sleep, eating, family time, listening to music, socializing, exercising, studying, writing letters, personal phone calls, movies, illnesses, vacations, holidays, celebrations (birthdays and anniversaries) and time to do absolutely nothing.

Once you understand your day a bit more you can begin to divide your valuable time based on your personal priorities. Some people find it extremely important to work very hard to achieve financial success. Other people find it more important to spend time at home with children or to do volunteer work or to study.

This section should help you make some of those decisions and give you tips in achieving your own goals.

General Goals and Priorities

To manage your time effectively you must decide what your priorities are. Priorities are where you plan to place most of your time and energy. General areas of priority include:

- Family involvement
- Physical health and appearance
- Emotional concerns
- Educational interests
- Spiritual development
- Economic well-being
- Career enhancement

Within each area of priority you need to set goals. Goals are specific, time-limited actions which can be easily identified and measured. If goals are left vague, you will never know if you have achieved your goal or not. When you set a goal, ask yourself if other people would be able to see that you have achieved it or not. Examples of specific goals within an area include:

- A promotion in your work within the next 18 months.
- An extra one-hour a day with family members.
- An improved grade in your studies to give you an overall average of B+.
- Increased physical fitness to improve your health so that you can walk for an hour comfortably, or decrease your blood pressure to a certain amount, or lose/gain "x" pounds within 12 months.
- Limiting work hours to a reasonable day by leaving the office at a certain time.

Once you have set goals within each area of priority you need to compare the areas and decide what you can reasonably accomplish in the next 1, 3 and 5 years. Perhaps your educational goals will take a lower priority to your family goals, or vice-versa. Perhaps your economic concerns will not be met because you want to accomplish your educational goals. Comparing your areas of priorities will help you to set realistic overall goals.

The goals and priorities you choose are not written in cement. Your personal and professional situation will change over the years but a general sense of your future allows you the flexibility and control to make better decisions rather than let outside influences make those decisions for you.

While working full time with physical pain and reduced limitations, I set out to do a Ph.D. just in case I could not do front line social work. I set out not to succeed, but to try.

T.S. Eliot's saying, "For us, there is only the trying", was my rule of thumb. I worked Tuesday night, Thursday night and Sunday for 6 years. The other nights were for my friends and myself. Doing so much intellectual work, I needed a physical balance so I took up swimming and eventually hiking at a gentle pace. If I became depleted, I retreated and regrouped in my silence and solitude. My disability taught me about my connectedness. My body is connected to my emotions that in turn are connected to my spirituality, which in turn helped me to think critically about what I wanted to write in my thesis. Balance, harmony and small steps, one after another, helped to make my path a successful one.
Michèle Chaban

Negative Thoughts

The real enemy of time management is our own negative thoughts about ourselves. This is true in all aspects of our work and play but is especially true in time management and organizing our work.

Negative thoughts about our abilities to meet a deadline or to achieve our goals drain us of mental and physical energy. There is a story about a man who ran a chip-wagon service along the side of the road. It was a very successful chip wagon. He had signs along the road for miles announcing 'Five miles to Bill's Fresh Fries!" Then the Depression of the 1930s came. Bill's son told him that the Depression was going to ruin their business. The son told Bill not to waste their money on repainting the signs and to expect a decrease in sales. Of course that is exactly what happened since Bill and his son stopped trying to be successful managers of their time and work.

We don't need a depression to know that many of us think in negative ways about our skills. Perhaps a teacher told us that we would never be good at certain things and therefore we stopped trying. Perhaps we failed in some task years ago and now believe that we can never try again. Perhaps we did poorly in school and therefore shudder at the thought of going back to school.

If we speak to anyone over 60 years old and ask them how many of their worries actually came true, I think they will tell you that 80-95% of all their worries were wasted time and energy. The trick is to know what is worth worrying about.

The main reason we have negative thoughts can usually be found in our viewing a large task as a whole instead of its smaller parts. When I began to write this book I thought that the time and effort to research and write it was overwhelming. To break the habit of doubting my abilities, I broke down the task into smaller units that I could manage more easily. I researched these smaller units and tied them together at the end.

Just about any task can be broken down in manageable units! That's the trick.

If someone had told me as I lay looking at ceilings and not being able to cook, clean or tend to myself, that I would one day speak to large audiences of health care professionals, I would have thought them quite daft. If someone told me that one day I'd walk alone on a sidewalk without my cane, I would have smiled and said I hope it will be so. It is true that the journey of a lifetime begins with a single step. I am proof of what is possible if you dream little dreams, one after another, realizing them slowly. They have a way of adding up, of accumulating. Life has surpassed my wildest dreams.
My disability has taught me many important lessons. Perhaps the most important was this-sometimes you need to look to the horizon to see what is up ahead, but sometimes, if you keep your eyes solely on the horizon, you will trip over something and fall. That is why I always watch my feet, one in front of the other, left, right, left, right. Before I know it, I have arrived at my destination.
Michèle Chaban

The Daily Check List

Perhaps no other time management and work organizing tool has been written about so much as the daily check list. Quite simply this list helps you get through busy days.

1. Use a single sheet of paper, a cue card, or, if space is available, your calendar to make a list of the tasks you need to accomplish today.
   Place a number beside each task to give you the order in which you want complete each task. Begin with the most urgent and important tasks e.g., bring children to baby sitters before work; follow with medium sized priorities, e.g., phone calls you need to make that day; and end with low priority items (usually the largest part of our list - e.g., shopping for socks, getting Christmas cards in September, etc.).

   Decide which 20% of your tasks will produce 80% of the day's results and do them. So much of what we normally do (80%) leads to less than 20% of real results. Knowing the difference will help you enjoy your productive work more.
2. Make a separate list of shorter, less important tasks which you may do today or in the following days when you have a few spare minutes, e.g., writing letters to family members living far away, checking the air in your tires, or preparing for a camping trip that is two weeks away.
3. Evaluate, on a daily basis, the success of your time management. Which tasks are you accomplishing? Which tasks never seem to get done? Is there another way to

accomplish these?

Time Management Techniques for Long Term Success

For longer-term success in managing your time, choose from the following list to help improve, or add to, your present skills in time management.

- Keep a daily log of your activities for about a week. This will help you identify where you spend your time, on what, and whether you can find wasted time. Remember, though, wasted time is very different from time spent relaxing!
- Schedule time to be by yourself to think, reflect and plan. We often spend too much time "doing" things and not enough time thinking and reflecting on what we are doing or why.
- Set reasonable deadlines for yourself. Include enough time for unexpected events, illnesses, and car problems.
- Procrastination is both a personality style and a way to avoid evaluation by others. Knowing that you procrastinate is the first step in helping to overcome it! Make plans, appointments and reward yourself for success.
- Take a large project and divide it into manageable units. Schedule work on the smaller units with an ultimate view to the final completion date for the whole project.
- Try to keep your work environment neat. This may help to make you feel more in control of your work and make it easier for you to see your work place first thing in the morning.
- Take time to enhance some of your other skills: improve your reading speed and comprehension; write better memos, letters, reports; delegate your work more efficiently; and communicate more effectively. Pick one or two skills every year and within a relatively short time your overall performance and satisfaction will improve.

Organizing Your Work

In order to complete our work effectively within the time management system you have developed, you need to divide the work by priority, decide on the difficulty involved in completing the work, and schedule the sequence of the work. Let's look at these more closely:

Priorities

Who will receive the finished work (work prepared for the President is usually more urgent than work prepared for a colleague)?

Who needs to be consulted to do the work: clients, supervisors, colleagues, secretarial staff, and external consultants?

Is the deadline for one high priority job approaching faster than work of a similar priority that has a longer deadline?

1st priority Those things that need to be done immediately.

2nd priority Those things that need to be done within the next few days.

3rd priority Those things that can be delayed for more than a few days or until time permits.

Is there competition between co-workers to have certain work done first? If there is, either: plan together to determine the real priorities or have the supervisor make the final decision.

Difficulty

Is the work more difficult than originally thought? If so, change the scheduling to allow more time or give the work a greater priority over other work.

Scheduling

Identify the steps involved in finishing one project and design an Action Plan to divide the work, set deadlines and decide on evaluating the success of the project. (See the sample Action Plan in this section.)

Schedule blocks of uninterrupted time for routine matters; for time to think, plan and evaluate; and for regular meetings. These blocks can be cancelled or postponed but at least it can help you keep track of important tasks that are often left undone because of too many meetings, appointments and phone calls.

Use larger calendars to schedule various major projects at once. Break down these projects into manageable units (use Action Plan) with enough time to deal with unexpected events and illnesses, e.g., set a final deadline date but plan for a deadline weeks or months in advance of that real date.

Use a bring-forward system to help remind people of work needing attention in the future:

Use a file for each month in the year to file correspondence, reports, Minutes, etc. that require attention at a specific date in the future. Organize this material chronologically within the file.

Or when keeping a bring-forward system for several people you can use a cue card system where you have a card for each day of the year, divided by months. Use "Post-it" papers to remind yourself of a file, report, phone call, event, etc. that you need to attend to at a specific date in the future. [Individuals can use their personal calendars to do the same thing.] Begin your day by checking your bring-forward system.

Other Tips

Reward successful completion of major projects. Rewards can be personal or given by the organization. Rewards can be simple or involve extra time-off. Whatever reward is given must be personally satisfying to the people involved.

Handle paper (correspondence, reports, journal articles, etc) only once: either act upon the information, delegate it (with a note of explanation) to someone more appropriate, file it for future action, or throw it away. Do not let it pile up on your desk.

Filing systems are quite personal. Some tips:

The only irreplaceable document is one you create yourself. All other documents are probably copies. Be critical before deciding to keep a document you will probably never look at or refer to.

Keep "thick" files for general types of information. For example one thick file covering all office equipment versus many thinner files for each piece of office equipment, for warranties, for servicing companies, etc. Too many thin files makes it difficult for other people to find things if you are unavailable for help.

Be consistent in filing. Everyone leaves their position within an organization for vacations, transfers, and promotions. It is, therefore, very important to have a logical system for other people to use. Label file drawers, keep files in alphabetical, departmental or chronological order. Inform someone else about any changes you plan to make. Compare notes with other people who are doing filing before changing your system.

Learn to Say "No"

Tell the person requesting the work that you understand it is important but that predetermined priorities have to be done first.

Try to get the person to acknowledge that you cannot do the work now (or perhaps never) by asking, "What else could be done to get this work done for you?"

If someone else is better able to get the work done, or if someone else is actually responsible for that work, tell the person asking you for help.

Always be understanding but firm. Do not be defensive since you cannot be expected to do everything for everyone. Help yourself and others set realistic limits about what is possible. Avoid giving long explanations of why you can't do something.

Once you get into the habit of saying "no" to certain requests, you gain a sense of control over your time and your life. It can feel great. Sometimes you aren't sure if you want or can take on a certain task. I handle this by not answering yes or no at the outset. Rather, I gather information about the time involved, the task itself, deadlines, etc., and then let the person know I will call them back before a stipulated date. This allows me a space to look at the rest of my schedule, my own priorities and to think about the request and whether I can and wish to do it.
Elizabeth Latimer

When using calendars use pencil to write in appointments, phone calls you need to make, tasks you need to do, etc. It is easier and neater to erase.

Beside any appointments write in the person's phone number and the location of the meeting in case you have to call quickly to change the time or location.

If you require special resources for a meeting, write them down in your calendar.

When preparing work for a meeting 2 weeks away, schedule sufficient time over the next few days to complete the work. Many people wait until the night before, which is an ineffective way to prepare, and doesn't allow for any unexpected interruptions.

A Year in the Life of an Expectant Father (1992)
Everyone has years that are busier than others. This was one of mine. The list isn't to impress you with my time management skills. There were clearly days and even weeks when I thought I would go crazy. The list is intended to show you that people survive difficult and/or busy years. The key is to live a balanced life so that when things get overwhelming you can go back to your principles of what is most important to do and what may have to wait.
Personal: Normal day-to-day activities and social life of a married man whose wife is expecting a baby.
Baby: Visiting midwives and doctors regularly including trips to labs and prenatal classes. Reorganizing life with a new person including new clothes, furniture and nursery. Nine-week recuperation for my wife after the birth.
Work: I was self-employed so could juggle work and personal demands with more flexibility than most. My work included: ten-week contract with a teaching hospital to research and write manuals; research, write and edit a book; media interviews promoting the book; teaching 15 courses; public speaking; attending several conferences; moving my business.

House: Moving from an apartment to a house and all that that entails.
Education: Completing my masters' thesis.
Volunteer: Continuing to do volunteer work in palliative care including meetings, reviewing educational materials and assisting two families with a terminally-ill loved one.
Friends: Helping an 86-year-old woman during her last three months of life.
Harry van Bommel

Action Plan

One of the easiest ways to plan your work priorities and help schedule that work is to use Action Plans (see the sample below). Have colleagues, your supervisors and/or staff participate in dividing the work.

What is the Task?	Who Will Do It?	By When?	How to Evaluate Success?

Summary

To practice what we preach, here are a few of the key elements to time management and organizing your work, in timesaving written form!

90% of all things can be done immediately!

Procrastination is often our way of avoiding evaluation of our work by ourselves or others.

The fear of evaluation and our own self-doubts/negative thoughts are of our own making.

Design your schedule to break tasks into manageable units.

Organizing your work involves consistent planning and evaluating your success.

There is no magic formula, just practical tips to help you do better what you have been doing for years.

You have the power to control your time and your abilities. Take that control and enjoy yourself!

Resources

The following resources are only a few of the many useful resources that you can find in your local libraries, within your own organization, and in your local bookstores. Look for other books but also for journal articles, magazine reports, films, videos and audiocassettes. Also keep in mind how much you can learn from experts in the field, including people within your own organization!

Covey, SR. (1989). *7 habits of highly effective people.* New York: Simon and Schuster.

Covey, SR., Merrill, AR., & Merrill, RR. (1994). *First things first.* New York: Simon and Schuster.

Moreau, D., Breuninger, C.C., & Comerford, K.C., (Eds.) (1997). *Tips and timesavers for home health nurses.* Springhouse, PA: Springhouse.

Moskowitz, R. (1993). *How to organize your work and your life: Proven time management techniques for professional and other busy people.* Houston, TX: Main Street Books.

Pollar, O. (1996). *365 ways to simply your work life: Ideas that bring more time, freedom and satisfaction to daily work.* Chicago, IL: Dearborn Trade.

Rechtschaffen, S. (1996). *Time shifting: Creating more time for your life.* New York: Doubleday.

Springhouse's 1,001 nursing tips and timesavers: Quick and easy tips for improving patient care. (1997). Springhouse, PA: Springhouse.

van Bommel, H. (1985). *The busy person's guide to note taking, speed reading, studying and time management.* North York, ON: Skills Development Publishing.

Williams, P.B. (1996). *Getting a project done on time: Managing people, time and results.* New York: AMACOM.

Wright, R.J., & Wright R.A. (1996). *Beyond time management.* Newton, MA: Butterworth-Heinemann.

Conclusion

We will all be patients one day just as all patients can be healers and comforters to us if we give them the chance. This book is about using fundamental skills to enhance your work experience while enhancing the healing experience for your patients.

The chapters are divided by the acronym: PRACTICAL which highlights the type of information provided in this book: Principled Leadership, Resolving Conflicts, Awareness, Communication, Team Skills, Impassioned Supervision, Change Management,

Action Oriented Planning and Life-Long Skills.

It is not important how you divide the knowledge and skills. They are interconnected in unlimited ways to meet the needs of unlimited situations and circumstances. What is important is to apply the skills predictably, consistently and fairly.

What Next?

Each section within the book has specific exercises. Sometimes it will be enough just to review the exercise and mentally answer the questions. If you want to enhance your behavior, however, you will need to reflect, write and implement the behavior changes immediately. All of us have read information and thought, "Oh, I know that". The improvement comes, however, from applying your knowledge and enhancing or developing a new skill.

The next step, then, is to go back to the beginning and chose what specific skills you want to master. Chose only one or two at first until you are satisfied with your improvement in those areas. Only then, go on to other skill areas.

We are often asked by workshop participants and colleagues for advanced skills. "I already know the basics", they say. More often than not, the advanced skills are actually practicing and applying the basic ones. Each of you would make a fortune if you got paid triple your hourly salary for every hour you wasted on meetings that were run ineffectively. Yet the person chairing the meeting and the participants all know the "basics" of running effective meetings. Reflect, write out the answers and implement behavior changes using the exercises in this book to dramatically, and in short order, improve the skills within your own circle of colleagues and customers.

The key exercise is at the beginning of the book. You cannot be an effective leader, communicator and colleague without knowing your own beliefs, assumptions and effective behaviors. You need to understand your morals and basic ethics and how they translate into effective leadership and compassionate care. You need to understand your own story as you continue to learn more about other people's stories–your patients, their families and your colleagues. It is through these stories that we humanize our patients and the bureaucratic healthcare system in which we work. It may often appear that our healthcare system values the bottom line more than the people it serves and the people who provide the service. However, a system is made up of tens of thousands of professionals who have the knowledge and skills to make a difference and to humanize what has always been a very human situation–the healing and caring of sick or dying clients, family members, friends and neighbors.

Index

Acknowledgements

Each co-author brings a lifetime of personal and professional education and experiences to their research and work. We have been fortunate to learn and work with some of the best. We gratefully acknowledge our patients and clients, their families, and our colleagues who helped us to learn to practice and teach the PRACTICAL knowledge and skills presented in this book.

Special thanks to Carol Ann Godard for her helpful ideas early on in the project.

Each chapter has a reference section to acknowledge where the generic, practical skills are further explained. The field of management and staff development is rich in literature and we acknowledge the authors of those works for richly enhancing the information available to help readers.

Lastly, we appreciate the support, encouragement and life lessons of our family and friends. Their invaluable help makes our work possible.

About the Authors

Harry van Bommel, M.Ad.Ed., C.T.D.P. is the author of 20 books, including the fields of management and staff development and health and hospice care. He is co-Executive Director of Legacies: Family and Community Resources, a not-for-profit organization dedicated to providing free or below cost information in the fields of home and hospice care; helping people record their life stories; and community development. He has appeared in over 150 television, radio and print media interviews. Mr. van Bommel has helped educate thousands of people through his workshops and public speaking engagements. Some of his books are available for free reading and printing from his website: www.legacies.ca

Beverley Powell-Vinden, R.N., B.N.Sc., M.Ed. is president of PowerPhrase Communications where she specializes in freelance editing, proofreading and health education consulting. Her clients include not-for-profit organizations, hospitals, community health centres, professional associations, and health care and educational professionals. Ms. Powell-Vinden's experience includes coordinating a provincial professional education program, developing customer service programs for health care organizations, developing educational resources using principles of clear language, consulting on the issue of access to health information and teaching groups how to use the Internet to find health information. She received her undergraduate degree from Queen's University and graduate degree from Brock University. She was a bedside nurse for five years with a specialty in neuroscience.

Michèle Chaban, M.S.W., DPhil. received a Masters degree in Social Work from the University of Toronto, and a Doctorate of Philosophy from the University of Whales. Dr. Chaban is the Director of the Psychosocial-Spiritual Program at the Temmy Latner Centre for Palliative Care. She is a Social Worker and Clinical Thanatologist with the Centre and practices individual, family and group therapy privately. Previously, Dr. Chaban worked in Oncology and Palliative Care with the Department of Social Work at Mount Sinai Hospital. Dr. Chaban is affiliated with the Faculty of Social Work at the Faculty of Family Medicine, and the Centre for Bioethics, University of Toronto. She teaches a course on Spirituality and Ethics in Centennial College's Palliative Care Program. Dr. Chaban lectures on issues related to people who are dying and their families, and how they are cared for by the health care system. Her thesis *An Analysis of the Life Work of Dr. Elisabeth Kubler-Ross and its Impact on the Death Awareness Movement* has recently been published. A second book, *Spiritual Legacies of Suffering* will be published shortly. Dr. Chaban is an active member of the Palliative Care Council of Toronto.

Elizabeth Latimer, M.D., C.C.F.P., F.C.F.P. is a Professor in the Department of Family Medicine, McMaster University specializing in Palliative Care and Pain Management. She is a consultant physician at the Hamilton Health Sciences Corporation, a Fellow of the College of Family Physicians of Canada and a certificant of the American Board of Hospice and Palliative Medicine. Dr. Latimer has published extensively in the fields of palliative care, control of chronic cancer pain, issues in the delivery of health care to the dying, and the ethical basis of practice and decision-making. She has participated as an international scholar at the Hasting's Centre for Biomedical Ethics in Briarcliff Manor, New York and in the Netherlands studying the issue of euthanasia. Dr. Latimer is an international lecturer and consultant and has visited Saudi Arabia and South Africa in this capacity. Before entering medical training, Dr. Latimer nursed for nine years in a hospital and in the community. In 1999, Dr. Latimer received the *Award of Excellence in Palliative Care* from the Canadian Palliative Care Association in recognition of her contribution to the field of Palliative and Hospice Care in Canada.

Most recently, **Larry Lewis, M.A.** was Program Director, Community Living and Director of Education at a Toronto hospital specializing in rehabilitation and complex continuing care. As the former Director of Management Education at the Ontario Hospital Association, Mr. Lewis directed comprehensive management development and leadership training in the hospital industry throughout Ontario for more than ten years. In the private sector, he was a Regional Branch Manager for a large rehabilitation company offering multidisciplinary case management services to the insurance industry. Mr. Lewis was an associate professor of psychology at the University of New Brunswick as well as a registered psychologist. He has an M.A. from the University of Waterloo where he completed extensive doctoral studies and two years of specialized training and research at the Ontario Institute for Studies in Education (University of Toronto). Mr. Lewis maintains a communication and education practice in Toronto, Ontario and Puebla, Mexico. Currently, he is providing educational services to a community care access centre in Toronto.

Notes

1 Humor, laughter, play or jokes based on ridicule, sarcasm, racism or sexism are harmful. They separate people. Appropriate humor and laughter is shared by people and shortens distances between them.

2. The Hutchison Dictionary of Ideas (1994) describes race as follows: "in anthropology, term sometimes applied to a physically distinctive group of people, on the basis of their difference from other groups in skin colour, head shape, hair type, and physique. Formerly anthropologists divided the human race into three hypothetical racial groups: Caucasoid, Mongoloid, and Negroid. However, scientific studies have produced no proof of definite genetic racial divisions. Many anthropologists today, therefore, completely reject the concept of race and social scientists tend to prefer the term ethnic group."

3 This manual stresses clear and effective writing. Sometimes you may choose to write long sentences or use $10 words and the passive voice. You may make this choice to confuse or intimidate the reader or to write in a very neutral style. It may be appropriate to follow this style occasionally but I suggest you avoid it as a personal style.

Using This Book for In-House Training and Development

If your organization, college or university would like to join the many other organizations using the material in this book for its own training programs or courses, you can do this is 3 ways:

1. bulk order discounted copies of the book to give, or sell, to your participants or students.
2. purchase a license to place a master copy of this book in pdf format onto your INTRANET site.
3. have the materials customized by the author for your specific industry and make the revised material available on your INTRANET site.

Note that materials on the INTRANET can be printed off by people who have legitimate access to the materials. They can use it for themselves and, as an added bonus to the organization, to the families of their staff, managers and/or students. This goodwill gesture can improve both the learning and morale of individuals dramatically.

By having the book in-house you have a resource that is available to your managers, staff and/or students 24/7 which is particularly helpful when people work shifts who rarely get the opportunity to attend workshops and courses.

The self-study approach of this material minimizes extra time-off, HR concerns of replacement costs and the actual dollars spent on training and development. This approach further encourages managers, staff and students to work at their own pace, on their own time and using the same ideas and language of their department, colleagues, clients and professors/teachers.

Contact the publisher for more information:

Legacies: Family and Community Resources
11 Miniot Circle
Toronto, ON M1K 2K1 Canada
416.264.4665
harry@legacies.ca

Made in United States
Orlando, FL
05 November 2026

90229829R10223